CROSSING THE NARROW BRIDGE

A practical guide to Rebbe Nachman's teachings

CROSSING THE NARROW BRIDGE

A practical guide to Rebbe Nachman's teachings

by Chaim Kramer

edited by Moshe Mykoff

Published by
Breslov Research Institute
Jerusalem/New York

Copyright © 1989 BRESLOV RESEARCH INSTITUTE

ISBN — 0-930213-40-8

First Edition

For further information:
Breslov Research Institute
POB 5370
Jerusalem, Israel

or:
Breslov Research Institute
POB 587
Monsey, NY 10952-0587

e-mail: info@breslov.org
INTERNET: http//www.breslov.org

Printed in Israel

In loving memory of

Samuel Isaac Toussie
of blessed memory
July 15, 1990

dedicated by

Isaac and **Talia Toussie**

In loving memory

of my dear parents

David and **Dora Steinbigle**

There were never more loving parents.

Seymour

Preface

"Besides being wise, Kohelet also taught the people knowledge; he weighed and sought out, and established many parables."

(Ecclesiastes 12:9)

Our Sages teach: Kohelet (King Solomon) taught the people wisdom — he set forth reasons, illustrations and examples. Until the days of King Solomon, the Torah was likened to a basket without a handle. King Solomon made the handle [for the Torah] (*Eruvin* 21b). Rashi explains: "It is easier to get a grasp on a basket with a handle, than one without."

Moshe Rabeinu received the Torah in the year 2448 of Creation. For almost five hundred years after the Revelation at Mount Sinai, the Torah was studied in its original "raw" form. King Solomon understood that the Torah would not remain accessible forever to all of Israel, unless there were ways to open up its beauty for all the folk. He found a way. "He spoke three thousand parables..." (1 Kings 5:12). "He spoke three thousand parables on *each* item of Torah..." (*Eruvin* 21b). He made a handle for the Torah so that all could grasp it. He refined the art of parable and illustration, applying it to all areas of Judaism, so that the Jews could keep the Torah and mitzvot.

The Prophets followed King Solomon's direction, delivering their prophecies in parables, poetry and song. Our Sages refined this art even further, bequeathing scores of parables and allegories found throughout the Talmud, Midrash and Zohar. The same is true of our leading rabbis and sages of all succeeding generations; they've always made use of the illustrative story and the like to endear the Torah to our people. All appreciated King Solomon's wisdom: that to partake of the inner beauty of Torah, to feel its balance and to taste its sweetness, one must have a "handle" with which to grasp it.

*

For some years now, we at Breslov Research Institute have had numerous requests for a book that would do just that for Rebbe Nachman's teachings. The Rebbe's works comprise many volumes and the topics are dispersed, often even within the volumes themselves. For example, a person might find that Rebbe Nachman emphasizes joy. He wants to be joyous and wishes to read up on it. Very nice. To research all of Rebbe Nachman's teachings on joy and happiness one would have to read some twenty-five volumes, picking out a paragraph here, a sentence there, and so on — all in search of joy. Frustrating in itself, this is not quite the most desirable way to attain happiness.

The books which have separate sections on each topic, such as *Advice* and *The Aleph-Bet Book*, do not, in themselves, clarify how one goes about achieving one's goals. Even those books that were compiled on a single concept, such as *Outpouring of the Soul* (meditation and *hitbodedut*) or *Restore My Soul* (inner strength), lack the single step-by-step instructions for attaining the characteristic or devotion that Rebbe Nachman talks about. And, even if we were able to form a *composite* picture, how would we ever be able to put together a *comprehensive* picture? As Reb Noson writes: "Though the study of musar and ethics is very great and can arouse one to Fear of Heaven, a person still cannot glean all the advice he needs from these teachings. Experience has shown that most advice comes from person to person" (*Likutey Halakhot, Shabbat* 6:18). So, for the full picture and the practical guidance, we need the Breslover Chassidim themselves — those who have *experienced* the fervor and passion of their commitment to Rebbe Nachman and his teachings.

Crossing the Narrow Bridge is an innovation in Rebbe Nachman's works. The book's purpose is to introduce the reader to Rebbe Nachman, the Breslover Chassidim and the Breslov teachings. Focusing on the major topics found in the teachings — from individual devotions to matters of business and home, from moral behavior to the concepts of Tzaddik and the Holy Land — each chapter offers a basic understanding of the subject as seen through the lessons, conversations, anecdotes and parables from and about Rebbe Nachman, Reb Noson and many of the Breslover Chassidim of yesteryear and today. A special effort has been made to illustrate the "how tos" of each topic by offering practical "handles" to grab onto — enabling the reader to translate these teachings into his own life.

The idea for "a practical guide" was presented to us some years ago. At that time, the staff at Breslov Research felt it was first necessary to translate and publish Rebbe Nachman's teachings themselves, before putting together a compilation of his ideas and ideals. The reason was simple. Having the original Breslov works in translation gives the English reader access to the source material itself. In their "purest" form, the teachings — though sometimes difficult to comprehend — remain the most powerful and universal. However, for this essentially popular work, I have, on my own initiative, taken the liberty to present a "non-literal" translation of the material. This was done for clarity's sake, as the problems in presenting Rebbe Nachman's teachings for a twentieth-century, western-oriented readership have a way of creating their own difficult moments.

Rebbe Nachman taught: "The world is a very, very narrow bridge. The main thing is not to be afraid!" (*Likutey Moharan* II,

48). However, it was only with great trepidation that I came to compile and write this book and for a very simple reason. Rebbe Nachman was the Master of Prayer. He appeared to everyone differently (*Rabbi Nachman's Stories* #12). This being so, how could I presume to present an authoritative book on Rebbe Nachman's teachings, laying out guidelines and advice on Breslov ideology and thought? There could be no doubt that to some, what I would say would seem "too much," while others would see it as "not enough"; some would call it "too extreme," and others "too lenient." Each person's approach, his Golden Mean, is different from his neighbor's.

"Many of Rebbe Nachman's teachings, though extremely lofty and abstruse, were understood by his followers. They were men of great learning and stature and felt only limited need for commentary on the Rebbe's writings." So writes Reb Nachman of Tcherin in his introduction to the *Parparaot LeChokhmah,* offering this as the reason why no one had preceded him in writing a commentary on Rebbe Nachman's *Likutey Moharan*. And so, knowing that this book would have to define and clarify points that have been intentionally left vague for many years by the earlier Breslover Chassidim — those who had known the Rebbe, Reb Noson and the other followers of that generation — made the thought of composing this work even more formidable. After all, they had the Oral Tradition, they tasted the "Hungarian Wine" (see *Tzaddik* #260), without leaving us with a detailed handbook on how to explore Breslov ideology.

Even more terrifying than all the above was the simple fact that as the book progressed, I increasingly realized my own distance from every trait and idea ever discussed by Rebbe Nachman, including those presented here. Our Sages taught: "Improve yourself, then improve others" (*Bava Metzia* 107b). Many times I asked myself what right I had even to consider compiling this work, let alone actually doing it. More than once I was ready to give up, for this reason alone.

This book is in no way intended as a "code" of Breslov Chassidut or a standard for Breslover Chassidim. Rather, its aim is to introduce the reader to a logical, systematic approach to Breslov, enabling him to enter the realm of Rebbe Nachman's teachings. The specific presentation of the material has been a personal choice, based on my limited study of Rebbe Nachman's works and workings. In addition, I've drawn from personal experiences and from conversations with the many people I've had the good fortune to meet in the more than thirty years since having been introduced to Breslov. All my knowledge is based upon the teachings as I received them from my rabbi and father-in-law, Rabbi Zvi Aryeh Rosenfeld (1922-1978), and my Rosh Yeshivah, Rabbi Eliyahu Chaim Rosen (1898-1984), may they rest in peace. Short biographies of Rebbe Nachman, his leading disciple Reb Noson, and other leaders of the Breslover Chassidim who appear in this work have been provided in a separate appendix. This, so the reader can familiarize himself somewhat with the movement and its history.

May it be the will of God that we merit to grasp the "handle" of Rebbe Nachman's teachings, so that we may "study, teach, observe and do" (*Avot* 4:6). And in the merit of Rebbe Nachman and all the Tzaddikim, may God grant us the Coming of Mashiach, the Ingathering of the Exiles and the Rebuilding of the Holy Temple, speedily, in our days, Amen.

* * *

Acknowledgements

Reb Noson once said to Rebbe Nachman, "That people in general do not know about you [because of your greatness] — this is not hard to understand. But, how did I merit to know you?" "That," answered the Rebbe, "is also not difficult!" (*Siach Sarfei Kodesh* 1-297). To *HaShem Yisborach*, who provided me with all — "...my whole life until this very day" (Genesis 48:16) — I am totally grateful.

The publication of this book, and indeed all the many works of Rebbe Nachman that God granted us at Breslov Research the privilege to work on, could not have come about without the help and assistance of our many friends. To list them all would be impractical. If we were to list only those who have been with us through "thick and thin," we might inadvertently omit even one name, defeating the very purpose of our attempted thanks. Please let it suffice to all our friends that we appreciate every single thing they've ever done for us. May the merit of Rebbe Nachman be with them, forever.

The suggestion for "A practical guide to Rebbe Nachman's teachings" came from a very close and dear friend, Yitzchok Leib (Trevor) Bell. His insistence, urging and tireless perseverance, prevailed over my obstinacy and stubbornness to begin this book, while his "gentle" suggestions and hints actually brought it to a finish. As one whose reverence of — and interest in — Rebbe Nachman knows no bounds, I am honored to have him as a friend. Many thanks to Yaakov Siegel, whose suggestion that this work be patterned after the *Seder HaYom* gave much direction to the project. And, additional thanks are due to a very special friend, Moshe

Schorr, whose comments, suggestions and review have greatly enhanced the text.

To my colleagues at the Breslov Research Institute, my esteem for them is infinite. The long-standing members have already made their mark, leaving behind a trail of successful Breslov material for the world to savor and delight in.

To Avraham Greenbaum, whose multi-talents, unselfishness and total dedication led to the founding of Breslov Research; to Moshe Mykoff, whose devotion, tenaciousness and commitment have made quality control a Breslov trademark; to Benzion Solomon, whose sincerity and zeal in his musical contributions have brought out the true face of Jewish Chassidic melodies; and to the more recent additions to our staff, Ozer Bergman and Yehoshua Starret, who have given of themselves far and above the call of duty. And to Reb Nachman Burstein, a very special, much appreciated thanks. He has made himself available to us at all times, some very odd ones at that, to assist in whatever difficulties we confronted, guiding us through Rebbe Nachman's teachings as a shepherd would his flock. Additional thanks are due to Reb Moshe Kramer and Reb Yaakov Meir Schechter, for always sharing with us their intimate knowledge of the difficult and obscure.

To my parents and family who nurtured and raised me, and who were always there — even if I wasn't — go my very sincere thanks. Their warmth and great self-sacrifice have instilled all their children with values that help guide us on the straight and narrow through the very stormy waters of today. It would take universes of words to even begin to depict the thanks due them. "The beloved and dear who are still alive, and those whose passing has not broken our bond" (cf. 2 Samuel 1:23).

King Solomon, when constructing the Holy Temple, built two center pillars called *yakhin* and *boaz* (1 Kings 7:21). These two pillars supported the entire building. No acknowledgement could be complete without gratitude to my two pillars: Rabbi Rosenfeld and Rabbi Rosen.

Great is my appreciation for my rabbi and father-in-law, Rabbi Zvi Aryeh Rosenfeld, who brought me "under the wing" of Rebbe Nachman. His genius, foresight and inspiration were responsible for the very first translation of Breslov writings into English — getting Rabbi Aryeh Kaplan to translate *Rabbi Nachman's Wisdom* — thus paving the way for the birth of Breslov Research. Brought to America as a young child, Rabbi Zvi Aryeh turned a "wilderness into water springs" (Psalms 107:35) of Breslov. His selflessness and untiring efforts left an indelible impression upon me in a way that defies description. "Were all the seas ink, all the reeds quills; all the people scribes..." (*Shabbat* 11a), they could not record my thanks.

And to my Rosh Yeshivah, Rabbi Eliyahu Chaim Rosen, whose incredible sagacity, insight and pragmaticism, brought Rebbe's Nachman's teachings to life for me, goes my wholehearted gratitude. With the calmness of an "eye" in the center of the hurricane, he could relate anything to anybody — from serving God to the mundane. His whole being breathed Rebbe Nachman and he was the single most influential cause in the revival of the Breslover Chassidim in the Holy Land after World War Two. When Eliyahu ascended to Heaven, Elisha said (2 Kings 2:12): "My father, my father, chariot of Israel and its horsemen...." Rashi comments: "Because of his prayers, he was more important to the Jews than any amount of chariots and warriors."

Rabbi Akiva was an ignoramus when he married. He left home to study Torah for a period of twenty-four years, returning with a following of twenty-four thousand students! His students saw a poorly dressed woman coming near and tried to block her approach. Rabbi Akiva said, "Let her come. Whatever I have, whatever you have, all is due to her." When they married, Rabbi Akiva said to her, "If I had the money, I would buy you a golden tiara depicting Jerusalem." When he became wealthy, he kept his word (*Nedarim* 50a).

And finally, words cannot express my appreciation to my dear wife, who has sacrificed more for Breslov Research than any mind could conceive. For better or worse, and even for lunch, she has had to put up with many hardships, including my extended absences; with the burden of our household and the raising of our children falling upon her alone. King David prayed (Psalms 90:15): "Grant us joy commensurate with the days we have suffered." May God grant that she and my children be granted a long and healthy life, full of joy and happiness. May they celebrate, together with all Jewry, the Redemption of all Israel, in Jerusalem the Golden, speedily in our time, Amen.

Chaim Kramer
Menachem Av, 5749

Table of Contents

CROSSING THE NARROW BRIDGE

INTRODUCTION

Rabbi Simla'iy taught: Six-hundred-thirteen mitzvot were given to the Jews at Sinai. Two-hundred-forty-eight positive commandments correspond to the two-hundred-forty-eight limbs of the body. Three-hundred-sixty five prohibitions correspond to the three-hundred-sixty-five days of the year (*Makot* 23b,24a).

Judaism in general, and Torah in particular, are more than just a huge body of law and lore. There is a definite, explicit connection between them and ourselves. Rabbi Simla'iy is not just giving us a simple arithmetic lesson. He is telling us that our Jewishness and Torah correspond *directly* to the organs of our bodies; *directly* to the days of our lives. Indeed, they are life itself.

Yet, we only have to look around today to see that Torah and Judaism are more distant from us — or we ourselves are more distant from them and their true values — than ever before. But why? Since Torah constitutes our make-up and that of our daily lives, shouldn't we be very aware of it and its influence? "Each day a Heavenly voice emanates from Sinai, proclaiming: 'Woe to humanity from the humiliation of Torah'" (*Avot* 6:2). Why don't we react automatically to this voice? Do we even *hear* it? Torah is there. It always was, always is and always will be there. But, where are we?

Rebbe Nachman of Breslov (1772-1810) asked the same questions. However, he was not satisfied to leave them unanswered. Instead of lingering with them, he searched for the answers. And, he found them. His life was short, only thirty-eight and a half years; yet, into that short span he managed to squeeze the achievements of many lifetimes — to which even the greatest of men can only aspire.

One of the best known and most often quoted Chassidic masters, Rebbe Nachman was a great-grandson of Rabbi Israel Baal Shem Tov. Growing up in Medzeboz (then the center of the Chassidic movement) and being surrounded by the great leaders of that generation propelled Rebbe Nachman to search for ever greater heights. At a time when the fervor, which Chassidism engendered, was beginning to wane and stagnate, Rebbe Nachman breathed new life and dimensions into the movement. An enigma even in his own time, he foresaw the present generations of Judaism and prepared the foundation for those Jews who would thirst for the waters of their heritage. To some, Rebbe Nachman is best known as a master storyteller, to others, as the great Kabbalist. Still others know Rebbe Nachman through his main teachings: *hitbodedut* — secluded prayer and meditation; hope is never lost; good is found in all; always be happy. To many, he is simply "the Rebbe." No matter what Rebbe Nachman succeeded in accomplishing for himself, he was always careful to share it with his followers. He left a legacy — infinite wellsprings of teachings and advice — for all future generations. Even so, nearly two centuries have come and gone since the Rebbe's passing, and even the most committed Breslover Chassid will sometimes find himself faced with questions regarding Rebbe Nachman's teachings. Did the Rebbe actually mean me? And if so, then how does this translate into my life?

Based on the pamphlet "Seder HaYom" by Reb Yitzchak Breiter of Warsaw (d. 1943 in Treblinka), *Crossing the Narrow Bridge* explores Judaism and Torah in "the two-hundred-forty-eight limbs of the body" and through the "three-hundred-sixty-five days of the year," breaking these down into concepts and ideas, desires and goals, that relate to us all. Presented is a collection of Breslov teachings on the most common topics discussed in Rebbe Nachman's works: Simplicity; Joy; Truth; Faith; Torah; Prayer; the Tzaddik; Peace; Business; Daily Needs; Charity, and so on. It is a composite, and, at the same time, comprehensive picture of Breslov teachings: how they can be applied to one and all — from the raw beginner to the veteran chassid, and all in between.

Rebbe Nachman's teachings are not a body of abstract thought from a bygone era. They are words of wisdom for survival — even good living — in today's fast-paced world. Though these concepts span many generations, what was relevant then remains relevant — and is perhaps even more relevant — now. Rebbe Nachman taught that we can rise above all our difficulties. We *can* attain inner peace. We *can* succeed. All we need is that bit of faith in ourselves that we *are* an important and integral part of God's creation and we *can* realize our ideals.

* * *

1

SIMPLICITY

> Someone once asked Rebbe Nachman, "When I'm praying and I mention HaShem's holy name, what profound thoughts, what deep intentions, should I have in mind?"
> "Isn't the simple meaning — God — enough for you?!" the Rebbe answered (*Tzaddik* #414).

Anyone familiar with Rebbe Nachman's teachings knows that in this exchange, the Rebbe was talking about his favorite topic: serving God. For the Rebbe, serving God encompasses all aspects of life — bar none. This being the case, one would have expected Rebbe Nachman's answer to his follower to have been a long, complex, explanation of God's greatness, His strength, His awesomeness, His omnipotence.... Yet, the Rebbe's answer was anything but that. Actually, his answer was ultimately simple. What should his chassid have in mind? "God!" No more, no less.

Life can be simple. It can be complicated. It depends on what we make of it. Rebbe Nachman's advice: Keep life simple. It's up to us. Whereas the follower assumed that one needs many complex thoughts and intricate intentions, the Rebbe exhorted otherwise: There is just one necessary path — SIMPLICITY!

With simplicity, we have the freedom to accomplish far more than we can imagine. Far more than we would dare to hope.

* * *

WHAT IS SIMPLICITY?

Ironically, simplicity is neither easy to attain nor is it effortless to define. Reb Noson himself tells us: Simplicity, in itself, is a very deep and an extremely difficult concept to understand (*Likutey Halakhot, Birkhot HaPeirot* 5:13). This very inability to find the right words to describe it, as well as the difficulties involved in achieving it, are symptomatic of how far modern man has been distanced from simplicity.

Nevertheless, for even a basic understanding of Breslov Chassidut, it is vital that we understand and appreciate the important role which simplicity plays in the life of a Jew.

Ask most anyone to describe a simple person — a simpleton. You'll probably be given a negative description, a picture of someone dull-witted, foolish or even imbecilic. At best, saying something is *simple* conjures up the image of commonplace and inconsequential. This is very unfortunate and indicative of our own attitudes and prejudices. It is not at all what the Rebbe had in mind when he said: The main goal of a Jew is to serve God with simplicity and without any sophistication (*Likutey Moharan* II, 19).

The Torah, in general, and Rebbe Nachman, in particular, attributes an entirely different meaning to the Hebrew word for a simple person, *tam*. Rather than being simple-minded and lacking in intelligence, the simpleton is someone who is unassuming, sincere, straightforward. He is without guile and shuns twisted reasoning. As for the word simple, it implies wholeness and singularity, and even unity. Simplicity suggests freedom from mixture and convolutions, and denotes something pure and unadulterated. Thus, living life — serving God — simply, means adhering to the essentials, being real, and avoiding all forms of complexity and sophistication.

Accordingly, the paradigm of the simple man is Jacob, whom the Torah explicitly refers to as a *tam* (Genesis 25:27; thus making his outwitting of his brother Esau all the more amazing).

The Jewish people as a whole is called by God: "My dove, My simple one" (Song of Songs 5:2). And God Himself has exhorted us that we should "be simple with God your Lord" (Deuteronomy 18:13).

*

Nowadays, achieving simplicity can be as elusive as defining it. Rebbe Nachman once remarked: People have often said to me that from the way the Holy Land is described in the traditional teachings, as something truly magnificent and extremely holy, they can't imagine how it could possibly be part of this world (Likutey Moharan II, 116). The Rebbe said this because it points to a very valuable and necessary lesson in life. People mistakenly think that because something or someone is holy, it must look or act totally different. A good example of this is the Tzaddik, who though on a much loftier plane than the average person, he appears exactly the same as the rest of us. Outwardly, he eats and sleeps, has a family and may even be gainfully employed, just like everyone else.

The same is true of the Holy Land. Though on an exalted level spiritually, it is still a part of this physical world. Eretz Yisrael, like all the other countries of the world, appears to be governed by the cause and effect factors which produce times of war and times of peace, times of plague and times of plenty. In both cases, people expect to see some outward manifestation of the underlying holiness; some clear-cut sign of how they are different, some proof of how they are special. When, however, it is not forthcoming — when the Tzaddik seems like everyone else and the Holy Land seems to be just another place on earth — people are disappointed. Unfortunately, this disappointment eventually produces doubts. They question that Tzaddik's holiness and wonder if he isn't really *just another simple person* like the rest of us.

The source of this mistaken notion is actually one of man's best friends, his imagination. It just so happens that man's imagination can also be his worst enemy. From the above teaching, we see that we do not have to look for the "extra," for the quality which stands out as obviously different and special, in order to feel that something or someone has merit and worth. Believing otherwise is a trick of the imagination. If we allow it to cloud our thinking, it fools us into rejecting things for their surface and simple value. We become convinced that we need to do more, to be more, and to feel more. Glitz, glitter and the glow of designer products prevent us from appreciating and cherishing that which is unadulterated. As a result, all too often we let our imaginations dominate our perspective of reality; we follow it as it leads us away from the genuine and the sincere, away from the straightforward and the simple truth.

Once, Rebbe Nachman gave a lesson about the greatness of the Holy Land: To be a Jew means to rise time and again, to be forever reaching to ever greater levels. Whoever wants to be a Jew can do so only with the merit of the Holy Land. Getting there is a major battle. But when a person merits arriving in the Holy Land, he is called a "mighty one," for he has won the battle (*Likutey Moharan* I, 20 end).

After the lesson, Reb Noson asked, "What aspect of the Holy Land are you talking about?" He could not imagine that Rebbe Nachman was speaking literally, that he was referring to the land everyone knows as Eretz Yisrael.

"Simply! — I mean this Land of Israel, with these houses and these apartments," the Rebbe answered (*Tzaddik* #141).

Exactly as it is, exactly what you see. That's what Rebbe Nachman wanted Reb Noson to focus on. Simply Eretz Yisrael. And not — as most would have *imagined!* — some extra special feature and some abstract conjecture of the mind.

*

In short, simplicity means not seeking complexities, not reading extra meanings into whatever we encounter. It involves taking things at face value, as the Rebbe advised Reb Noson to do. However, it should be emphasized that this doesn't preclude searching for deeper understanding in one's life. On the contrary, throughout his teachings, Rebbe Nachman praises those who actively seek that inner meaning. In fact, simplicity — in life generally, and in serving God in particular — is the first and foremost tool for ultimately achieving the depth of wisdom which underlies all of existence (see below, "The Sophisticate and the Simpleton").

Nor does simplicity mean we must believe whatever anyone tells us and foolishly fall victim to dishonesty and falsehood. This would be gullibility, not simplicity. Our Sages warned us in this regard: "Respect, yet suspect that which is unfamiliar to you" (cf. *Derekh Eretz Zuta* 5). More than we care to admit, we all have tasted the bitterness which follows having been taken in and charmed by others. In this regard, Rebbe Nachman points out how one must be very careful in financial matters (see *Likutey Moharan* I, 69; cf. *Rabbi Nachman's Wisdom* #281), and how wary we must be of placing our physical well-being and/or emotional welfare in the hands of "reliable" professionals and "tried-and-tested" solutions (*Rabbi Nachman's Wisdom* #50). How much more so need we be cautious when it comes to our spiritual prosperity! (*Aveneha Barzel*, p.43 #64). False leaders and false advice are anything but simple and straightforward. The veil of mystery is very often their sole attraction (cf. *Rabbi Nachman's Wisdom* #6).

What does simplicity demand of us in these cases? The Rebbe explains: It is forbidden to be foolish, even in your simple sincerity. But sophistication is totally unnecessary (*Rabbi Nachman's Wisdom* #51). Thus, while the simple person leaves his mind open, neither forming an immediate opinion nor trying to second-guess the "true" motives of another, he also will not gullibly subscribe to the latest advice, technique, trend or fad that comes his way. And, although by taking things at face value he may well open himself up to dubious and possibly even harmful influences, Reb Noson quotes a proverb of King Solomon (Proverbs 10:9), "He that follows the simple path goes securely." "Surely," Reb Noson insists, "such a person will never stumble. And even if he does err, even if he does inadvertently transgress one of God's commands, he will undoubtedly repent and remain firm in his devotions — secure in the knowledge that there is a process in heaven through which all is set right" (Likutey Halakhot, Devarim Min HaChai 4:49). Or, as King David said (Psalms 116:6), "God protects the foolish."

During one of his conversations, Rebbe Nachman also pointed to a proverb of the wisest of all men: "A fool believes all things" (Proverbs 14:15). "It's good to be such a fool," the Rebbe said. "This is because, while you will believe in that which is false and foolish, you will also believe the truth. In this you are better off than the person who is sophisticated and skeptical of everything. He begins by ridiculing foolishness and falsehood, but eventually ends up ridiculing everything — denying even the truth" (Rabbi Nachman's Wisdom #103).

The rule, therefore, is: accept, but be careful. To paraphrase my Rosh Yeshivah, "It is a pleasure dealing with people. They are trustworthy; they are honest; they are decent people. But remember to count your change!"

*

Another aspect of simplicity is illustrated by the following story:

> "What is the nature of free will?" someone once asked Rebbe Nachman. "Simple!" the Rebbe answered. "If you want, you do. If you don't want, you don't do."

Reb Noson adds: I recorded this, because it makes a very important point. Many people are confused. They see themselves caught up in their habits and helpless to change their ways. They feel that they no longer have the power of free choice. It's just not so! Everyone has free will to do or not to do as he chooses. Understand this! (*Likutey Moharan* II, 110).

Most people think of themselves as creatures of habit. Their response in any given situation is predictable. The Rebbe taught that we need not be slaves to impulse and conditioning. We *can* respond differently. We *can* exercise discipline. This is true of thoughts, speech and deeds. Rebbe Nachman likened this self-control to a rider on a horse that has gone astray. All he has to do is grab hold of the reins to return it to the path (*Likutey Moharan* II, 50). As long as we keep life simple, we can maintain control over many facets of our lives.

Reb Noson expands this idea and shows how it applies in the service of God: A person's mind is constantly moving from thought to thought. Even so, it is impossible for two thoughts to occupy the mind at once. We know that evil thoughts must be rejected. However, there are times when good thoughts must also be rejected. It is well known that people have a tendency to become absorbed in their own train of thought, acknowledging only their own perspective of things. This can prove self-deceptive and misleading. Sometimes a person's goals and desire for holiness are beyond his capabilities. Therefore, he must control himself. He must limit his yearnings and fulfill — *simply* — whatever service to God he is capable of at that moment. Then he must cry out to God for guidance by praying that he be led on the proper path for *his* level and by serving God with simplicity and joy (*Likutey Halakhot, Bet K'neset* 5:24).

* * *

IN TORAH AND MITZVOT

> Rebbe Nachman remarked: "My achievements came mainly through simplicity. I spent much time simply conversing with God and reciting the Psalms"....The Rebbe yearned to serve God like the simple, common people. He often said, "Ay! Ay! SIMPLICITY!" (Rabbi Nachman's Wisdom #154).

The Rebbe wanted us to make every attempt to simplify our lives and our devotions to God. Thus, Reb Noson wrote: The Rebbe's desire was for us to serve God simply, to the very best of our ability, each and every day. He said that our main goal should be to do good and serve Him without any sophistication whatsoever. Every good and holy thing can be done with absolute simplicity. We should study Torah, pray, recite Psalms and other prayers, and perform mitzvot, all with the utmost simplicity and sincerity, and with great joy (Rabbi Nachman's Wisdom #19). The Rebbe loved and praised the simple acts of people: reciting the Psalms, singing zemirot at the Shabbat table, and so on. He would deride those who thought themselves too smart and clever to act simply. Until he became terminally ill, the Rebbe himself would sing a lot at the Shabbat table (Likutey Moharan II, 104).

Every word of Psalms recited is a mitzvah, every word of Torah study is a mitzvah, every song sung at the Shabbat table is a mitzvah. The more we do, the more we accomplish. Simplicity, therefore, is the foundation for all our devotions. With it, we can be constantly occupied doing mitzvot and good deeds. Without it, our deeds are always subject to the philosophical reasoning and equivocations of our minds. If we are always "thinking" and trying to figure out if we are doing the right thing, as opposed to actually doing it, then we cannot accomplish much — we are too busy "thinking." But, if we approach the mitzvot and good deeds with simplicity, we can always find something to do.

Simplicity is also a necessary ingredient in the performance of the mitzvot themselves. Reb Noson, always the careful observer of human nature, once remarked: Often, because a person insists upon performing a mitzvah in the very best way possible, he ends up not performing the mitzvah at all (Siach Sarfei Kodesh 1-571). This can be seen from the following: Ideally, the mitzvah of Sanctifying the New Moon is performed on a clear night. However, even if the sky is cloudy, as long as one can see the moon through the clouds, one should not delay, but recite the blessing (see Mishnah Berurah 426:3). Reb Noson asks: What if, as is often the case in the middle of winter, one has reason to believe that there may not be any more clear nights before the full moon is reached and the time for sanctifying the moon has passed? Should one nonetheless wait for a clear night, as this is the ideal way to perform the mitzvah? Reb Noson rejects this argument. Granted, it would be wonderful if we could perform every mitzvah perfectly and in the precisely prescribed manner. But if we did wait to perform each mitzvah perfectly — with all its fine points, with the specific intentions, and with us in the proper frame of mind — there is good reason to believe that we would end up not performing it at all (Likutey Halakhot, K'riat HaTorah 6:6).

The Jewish people have a "shulchan arukh" (a "set table") upon which all the laws have been laid out for us. More specifically, this set table is a collection of legal rulings from the Talmud and successive Codifiers, all of whom clarified the more obscure sections of the Talmud. Compiled by Rabbi Yosef Caro and annotated by Rabbi Moshe Isserles, each ruling which appears in this work known as the Shulchan Arukh was carefully considered by these two outstanding Torah scholars. They weighed the assessments and opinions offered by the numerous halakhic authorities who preceded them and arrived at the proper balance; their conclusions being the most appropriate solution for those areas where there were differing and/or opposing views. The decisions they recorded stand as law.

Now, when it comes to complying with *Halakhah* (the Codes), we too should adopt balance as our guide. There is no need for us to be overly-stringent, nor overly-lenient, in the observance of the mitzvot. Someone who gravitates to one of these extremes is considered either a fool or wicked (see *Eruvin* 5b). We have to be careful. We have to seek a balance. Even so, this does not mean, for example, that if a person can afford a choice *lulav* and *etrog* that he should not extend himself financially or otherwise when seeking a suitable palm branch and citron for the Sukkot holiday. What it does mean is that when the Four Species which a person has are acceptable halakhically, there is no need for him to spend additional time or money seeking and searching for precisely the one lulav and etrog that might be acceptable to "all views." There is a great difference between "beautifying a mitzvah" and trying to comply with "all the views."

In summary, simplicity in mitzvot means performing the mitzvah because God commanded me to do so. Reading my own special meaning into the mitzvah gives it a specific "shape and form" which is really a constriction or limitation of the mitzvah. In addition, when I think I understand the meaning of the mitzvah and am motivated to fulfill it *because* I understand, this is sophistication. I am actually setting myself up for a fall. There may come a time when things go against my understanding, or a situation arises that contradicts the specific structure I had given to the mitzvah. What happens then? (*Likutey Halakhot, Devarim Min HaChai* 4:49).

Reb Noson's son-in-law, Reb Boruch, once told Reb Noson that he agrees with the Rebbe's system of Torah study (see below, chapter 7). Reb Noson said to him, "If you follow that system because Rebbe Nachman advises so (with faith), then you'll stick to it. But if you study that way because you *understand* that it's right, then there will come a time when you'll reject it. Sure enough, Reb Boruch later returned to his father-in-law and acknowledged that Reb Noson had been correct. He had indeed begun to understand differently (*Rabbi Eliyahu Chaim Rosen*).

Thus, whenever the question arises, "What is the Breslover custom in such and such a case?" the answer is, "Look in the *Shulchan Arukh*. Whatever it says there, that's what Rebbe Nachman did!" Naturally, where the Codes themselves offer differing opinions, each of us should follow his family's customs. Rebbe Nachman's way, his advice and directives, were never intended as a set of halakhically binding rules. The Rebbe was more concerned in teaching his followers to fulfill the *spirit* of the mitzvot. Even where an established Breslov community does have particular customs, adherents who come from different backgrounds will continue to practice the way their families (Sefardic, Ashkenazic) always have.

*

STRINGENCIES?

> Extremism, in any form, is totally unnecessary (*Rabbi Nachman's Wisdom* #51).
>
> Rebbe Nachman teaches: Of those who are overly-strict in serving God it is written (Leviticus 18:5), "You shall live (and not die) by them." Such people have no life. They are constantly depressed, because they never ever feel they've fulfilled their obligations while performing the mitzvot. Because of their stringencies, they don't experience any vitality — any *life* — from their deeds (*Likutey Moharan* II, 44).

One doesn't have to be a rabbi or even a lay scholar to be stringent. An ignoramus can also say, "It is forbidden!" On the contrary, "Just as it is forbidden to permit the forbidden, it is just as forbidden to forbid to permitted" (*Bet Yosef, Tur Yoreh De'ah*, 115, *s.v. Harav Peretz*). The Rebbe's intention was to bring each mitzvah — no matter how exalted — within our reach. With simplicity, we can always feel that we, too, can perform the mitzvah. With straightforwardness, we, too, can fulfill it, and be filled with life by it.

Nevertheless, there are certain instances where keeping the law stringently is valued. In this regard the Talmud teaches: Rabbi Yosef asked Rabbah's son, "In what observance was your father most stringent?" (Shabbat 118b). Each Talmudic sage had a particular mitzvah which he practiced exactingly and according to all of its rigorous details. With this in mind, the Rebbe advised that every person choose one observance and keep it very strictly, with all its fine points (see Sefer Chassidim #529). And even with this observance, you need not be exceedingly strict to the point of foolishness....Keep one commandment strictly, but the others need not be observed with any unnecessary stringencies. If only we would be worthy of keeping all of the Torah's commandments simply, without any excesses (Rabbi Nachman's Wisdom #235).

Reb Dov of Tcherin, one of the Rebbe's followers, wanted to perform one of the more difficult practices in serving God — he wanted to wake up for Chatzot, the Midnight Prayers. The problem was that whenever he did this, the lack of sleep would cause Reb Dov severe headaches. Informed of this, the Rebbe told him, "Sleep and eat. Just heed the time." Afterwards, he advised Reb Dov that his "Chatzot" should not be at midnight, but at three o'clock in the morning (Kokhavey Or p.25).

Then there was another of Rebbe Nachman's chassidim, Reb Naftali, whom the Rebbe counseled to be especially careful in the mitzvah of tzitzit. Once, Reb Naftali climbed a ladder to attend to some repairs and his tzitzit tore. Reb Naftali refused to move until someone had brought him a kosher pair. Afterwards, he never went anywhere without having spare tzitzit with him (Until the Mashiach p.311). (This law is mentioned in the Kitzur Shulchan Arukh 68:6 — One should never travel without spare tzitzit. Thus, if one string should tear, he won't be left unable to perform this mitzvah.)

These two stories show us Rebbe Nachman's approach when advising his disciples concerning stringencies. Reb Dov very much wanted to fulfill the mitzvah of Chatzot by rising at midnight. Even so, the Rebbe warned him that it was not to be at the expense of his health. Yet, when it it came to Reb Naftali's special mitzvah, the Rebbe suggested he be exceedingly careful — and that, he was.

I'm also reminded of what my Rosh Yeshivah would say: "Why is it that people always choose to be stringent in those areas where others can find out about it? Wouldn't it be far better to be strict with oneself in such matters as slander, additional Torah study, greater concentration in prayer...."

*

Shortly before Reb Noson passed away, he gave a very deep sigh. When asked the reason for this, he replied: "It occurs to me that perhaps I have not properly fulfilled what Rebbe Nachman taught."

The people standing around him were amazed. "If not you, then who can honestly say that he has fulfilled the Rebbe's teachings?!"

"As to fulfilling the Rebbe's advice," Reb Noson answered, "I did what I could. The question is, have I fulfilled the teachings with the simplicity that the Rebbe demanded of us?!" (Rabbi Nachman Burstein).

* * *

GOD IS ONE

Simplicity is the highest possible virtue, since God is certainly higher than everything and yet He is ultimately simple (Rabbi Nachman's Wisdom #101).

"The deeds of the Mighty One are simple" (Deuteronomy 32:4).

Rebbe Nachman teaches: Creation has many parts. Yet, all the various parts of Creation emanate from God. He is one. He is simple. Our mission in this world is "to reveal the unity from amongst the many." That is, from all of us — from all our differing thoughts, perspectives, deeds, backgrounds, etc. — we still come to recognize the one God (*Likutey Moharan* II, 2:6).

This is not as complicated as may appear at first glance. Remember that everything emanates from one source — the One Source. Therefore, in our own ways and with our specific differences, each of us reflects that Source. By extension, there is actually no reason to view life in so complicated a manner as most people do. In reality, everything has its root in the unity of the one and simple God. Differences emerge because He manifests Himself to each of us differently. What we have to do is look for God everywhere, in everything. Then we will see that whatever appears complex and diverse is in truth very simple and singular; what appears separate is actually united; what appears fragmented is genuinely whole; what appears to require great sophistication only needs the utmost simplicity.

At the same time, Rebbe Nachman understood that relatively few ever succeed in revealing the unity from amongst the many, and that those who can do so consistently are even rarer. Most of us have a great deal of difficulty just keeping our own lives simple. The Rebbe was able to appreciate our struggles with the diversities of this world and understood the complexities we face. By the same token, he also realized that most people tend to complicate matters far beyond reason. We fret away our days and years, anticipating and contemplating difficulties and problems that we assume are on the way. We set goals — material as well as spiritual — and then tie ourselves in knots over presumed set-backs. We plan having a good time and then fret that this-that-and-the-next-thing will go wrong. We spend time worrying about things that may never happen. Anxiety! Anxiety! Anxiety! Nobody denies that difficult moments can and do come, but we also have no idea how they will affect our lives; whereas, keeping the perspective itself simple solves many of life's most difficult problems. This is why the Rebbe emphasizes simplicity so much. If we took things as they are, one at a time, one day at a time, we could lead a much simpler and happier way of life.

* * *

THE SOPHISTICATE AND THE SIMPLETON

One of Rebbe Nachman's most memorable stories, from his classic work *Rabbi Nachman's Stories*, is "The Sophisticate and the Simpleton" (pp. 160-196). In the story, the Simpleton has very little formal education and is very limited in his abilities. He sews triangular shoes for a living, has nothing but bread and water for sustenance and is so poor that he must share a tattered sheepskin coat with his wife. And yet, for him, this coat serves as "exquisite finery" for every occasion, his daily rations taste like the "finest wines and delicacies." Although with his limited skills the Simpleton earns far less than his fellow shoemakers, his self-confidence and joy are such that he feels absolutely no jealousy or want. "Why must we speak about others," he tells his wife when she criticizes his inability to charge as much as others for his work. "What do I care about that? That is their work, and this is my work!" And when some of the townspeople would engage him in coversation so that they could make fun of him, the Simpleton had but one request: "Just without mockery." If they assured him of their sincerity, he would never probe their motives more deeply. Being a simple person, he never engaged in the sophisticated speculation that would suggest that this in itself might be a means of mocking him.

Indeed, the Simpleton never questions or tries to second-guess anything. He just conducts himself simply and honestly, feeling only a great deal of satisfaction with his lot. No matter what happens, he is always very happy. Because of his simplicity, he never feels any lack, and due to his simplicity, he eventually becomes the Prime Minister of the land, becoming even wiser than his friend, the Sophisticate.

The Sophisticate, on the other hand, has advanced education and training. He is truly a man of the world. He has experience in commerce, craftsmanship, and even medicine, and has broadened his outlook through travel. Despite all this, the Sophisticate is never satisfied with what he has; he is always looking for something better over the horizon. He is also very exacting and very stringent in everything he does. When his work as a master goldsmith is not appreciated by others he feels rejected, yet when minute imperfections in his diamond engraving go unnoticed he chastises himself for what he sees as his flawed skills. In contrast to the Simpleton, the Sophisticate needs public approval, and when his expertise as a physician goes unrecognized, he rejects this profession as well. Furthermore, because his strict standards allow for no flexibility, it is impossible for him to appreciate the work of others. His clothing, his accommodations, his life, have to be just so, or else he is upset and becomes depressed. He is unable to appreciate simplicity or the simple way of life. In fact, he has no life!

The Sophisticate's lack of self-confidence does not allow him to speak with those whom he considers his inferiors, because this would tend to reduce his own status, something he feels he must protect at any cost. As a result, he can unburden himself to no one, and is, therefore, always miserable (*Chokhmah U'Tevunah* 8). His sophistication not only makes him arrogant, but also skeptical and unable to trust anyone. Never satisfied with the obvious meaning of things, he always probes and analyzes for the "true" meaning. This often leads him to wrong conclusions and eventually causes him to lose both his stature and wisdom.

Reb Nachman of Tcherin, one of Reb Noson's students, writes: The Rebbe told this story in order to instill in us the importance of simplicity. Whoever follows this path of simplicity will live a very good life, a joyous and content life (*Rimzey Ma'asiot*).

*

One of the greatest blessings a person can have is the knowledge that in any given situation in life, he did *his* best. God did not create us to be angels (cf. *Avodah Zarah* 3a). Only human, we have our daily ups-and-downs and are subject to variations in mood, feelings and desires. It is irrelevant whether these changes result from internal or external pressures. We *are* subject to them. Because of this, Rebbe Nachman teaches: Keep it simple. Do not expect every day to be the same. Do not expect perfection, even from yourself. Do what you can, when you can. This way you remain flexible enough to adapt to any situation.

This is the Simpleton. He lives in the present, never fretting over past memories or future expectations. He has the confidence to believe that whatever comes his way, he will always do the best he can. This may explain why the same word, *tamim*, is used for simplicity and wholeness. If a person is really whole, then he has enough self-confidence to be simple. He doesn't find it necessary to impress others with his sophistication. In addition, the simple person, like the Simpleton, is always happy because of his simple approach.

The Sophisticate, however, is constantly worried. He frets about the future and despairs over what others think. Will my means of livelihood last forever? Is this fashion and style acceptable in good company? What will others say of me should they discover my work has imperfections? These insecurities demand that he put on an air of sophistication, and occasionally even deception. Due to all this anxiety, his busy and complex life brings him only misery and discomfort.

Rebbe Nachman teaches: Were it true that cleverness and "wisdoms" are required for serving HaShem, how could the simple folk, those who do not have great intellect, be expected to serve God? Use only simplicity in serving Him. Simple fear of heaven. Simple fulfillment of mitzvot and good deeds. Do not complicate matters. This only leads one to deviate from the truth. Above all else, keep it SIMPLE! (cf. *Likutey Moharan* II, 19).

*

Simplicity, especially in these modern, sophisticated times, is a rare and very great blessing. As Rebbe Nachman teaches: There will come a time when a simple religious man will be as rare and unique as the Baal Shem Tov (*Rabbi Nachman's Wisdom* #36).

* * *

2

JOY

"Serve God with Joy!" (Psalms 100:2).

Rebbe Nachman teaches: It is a great mitzvah to be happy always. Strengthen yourself to push aside all depression and sadness. Everyone has lots of problems and the nature of man is to be attracted to sadness. To escape these difficulties, constantly bring joy into your life — even if you have to resort to silliness (Likutey Moharan II, 24).

Joy is the hardest of all levels to attain and maintain (Rabbi Nachman's Wisdom 20). When contemplating our daily pressures and workloads, this is very easy to understand. Happiness is not specified in Torah as a separate mitzvah. Yet, throughout the Talmud, Midrash and Kabbalah, joy is given centrality in all areas of Judaism. The renowned Safed kabbalist, the Ari (Rabbi Yitzchak Luria, 1534-1572), asserted that he attained his exalted spiritual level only because of the great joy with which he performed the mitzvot (Sha'ar HaKavanot, Shemini Atzeret). Indeed, not many of the subjects discussed in Breslov literature receive the detailed attention given to joy and happiness.

Reb Avraham Chazan commented: If Rebbe Nachman taught that it's a great mitzvah to be happy always, then we must believe that there is what to be happy about! (Rabbi Eliyahu Chaim Rosen).

* * *

THE IMPORTANCE OF JOY

One of the reasons we find ourselves distant from God is because we fail to concentrate on our goals. With *yishuv hada'at* (tranquility) a person can think clearly. However, this tranquility cannot be attained without joy. Like exile, depression leads one's mind astray, but joy is freedom. "With joy shall you go out [of the exile]..." (Isaiah 55:12). With joy we can direct our minds — exercise the *freedom* to choose our direction and prevent our thoughts from straying afar. But how do we find joy? We can cultivate joy and happiness by finding good qualities in ourselves. Even if we cannot find anything good in ourselves, we still have what to be happy about: "I am a Jew!" (*Likutey Moharan* II, 10).

*

But is there really something to be happy about? Aren't our daily lives filled with sufficient cause for worry? How are we going to meet the mortgage payment? What did you say happened to the car? Who did you say you're bringing home for dinner?! The list is endless.

Rebbe Nachman teaches: Depression is the bite of the Serpent (*Likutey Moharan* I, 189). Just as a serpent strikes suddenly, so does depression. Suddenly it hits, and you're left wondering how you can ever be happy again. If only you had some room to breathe, you'd be happy. Not necessarily. My Rosh Yeshivah used to say, "People think that difficulties are unexpected in life. They're surprised when sadness comes. But, even if a person were to live for a thousand years, he would still have a long list of problems waiting for him. When one leaves, another is sure to follow on its heels. This is an axiom of life."

Why, then, do we become shocked and upset when something "unexpected" happens to us? It is not unexpected. At least it shouldn't be. It *always* is this way. There is always "something else" — something to bring us down to the depths of depression. Rebbe Nachman also taught that depression and inertia are synonymous. They lead to anger, to a lack of tolerance, and are the main reason why a person fails to succeed (*Likutey Moharan* I, 155). It's a cycle. Something unexpected happens and we get annoyed. The doldrums and depression, still mild, are on the horizon. We're already less tolerant of whatever happens next. Naturally, we anticipate everything going wrong. And it does! At the same time, we get angry, experience greater failure, become more depressed and feel more discouraged and lethargic. The serpent of sadness has struck, without our being aware of what actually happened.

But why is there depression, sadness and suffering? Our Sages teach: Whoever mourns Jerusalem will yet share in its rejoicing (*Ta'anit* 30b). Without experiencing sorrow and mourning, there is no way for us to appreciate its opposite. We have nothing with which to compare our happiness. Therefore, we *must* experience suffering. Only then can we know the true taste of joy. And, because some sadness and suffering are necessary, Rebbe Nachman urges us to strive for joy. We have to use all our strength to attain happiness, since only by being happy will we have the necessary faith, courage and strength to face our sorrows and burdens and overcome them.

Reb Noson once wrote to Reb Ozer of Uman: I heard that you are very, very religious. I heard from Rebbe Nachman that the main thing is joy...and [being] religious too! (*Aveneha Barzel* p.63).

* * *

HOW TO...WITH WHAT...

You'd think that being told to be happy is superfluous. Who doesn't know this? Is it really necessary to coax, urge and encourage people to make sure they're happy? It's a natural desire, not one that has to be worked on. So you'd think. Or would you? Rebbe Nachman certainly didn't. "True joy is the hardest thing of all," he insisted. "You must *force* yourself to be happy all the time" (*Advice, Joy* 35).

Be joyous, always. And serve God with joy. Even if there are times when things look dark and difficult, strengthen yourselves with the "good times" gone by. This can be compared to a blind man who once had the power of sight. Although now he can't see at all, he knows there's light — he's witnessed it. Therefore, strengthen yourself with joy — the joy you once knew. If you do, then eventually the "good days" will return (*Likutey Moharan* I, 222). Elsewhere, Rebbe Nachman teaches that even within a problem, it's possible to find a "reason" to be happy (see *Likutey Moharan* I, 195). Just put yourself outside your situation for a minute or two. You'll realize that with everything crashing down all around you, there are ways in which it could have been even worse.

*

It is easy to be happy when you feel good and things are going smoothly. But what should you do when you do not feel happy, during the times when there's nothing to be joyous about? The Rebbe taught that we should find ways to make ourselves happy. His suggestions include the following:

Forcing ourselves. One of the Rebbe's suggestions for achieving happiness when it's not there, is forcing yourself to be happy. The importance of joy is so great that every effort must be made. It can be compared to a group of people who are dancing in a circle and pulling others in to join them. They join in the happiness while their depression stands off to the side. However, when the newcomers stop dancing, their depression returns. Though the few minutes of joy are valuable, it would be better to bring the depression itself into the circle of happiness and keep it there (*Likutey Moharan* II, 23).

Forcing yourself to be happy will eventually turn the cause of your unhappiness into a real source of joy.

Someone asked Reb Noson how could he become happy when he had so many problems and difficulties. Reb Noson answered, "Borrow the happiness!" (*Siach Sarfei Kodesh* 1-736). When it comes to money, we rarely hesitate to borrow against a future paycheck, dividend, etc. Well, sadness makes a person feel he's missing something. The thing to do, as Reb Noson advises, is to borrow from whatever you can think of that makes you happy. Besides, there's a big difference between owing money and owing happiness. When money is paid back it hurts a bit. However, with happiness, when we pay it back we again have happiness. Thus, forcing joy and happiness actually pays fantastic dividends.

Remembering your good points. Another way you can become joyous when depressed, is by acknowledging that you have at least some good within you. Even if you feel far from God, be happy and praise Him that "He did not make you a heathen." Simply be happy that you can feel proud and joyous about your heritage, which is not even your own doing, but a gift from God (this is explained in detail in the next chapter).

Faking it. Even if you don't feel happy, you can fake it. Pretend to be happy. Who says that if you're feeling down, you can't smile. We fake a smile often enough when trying to be polite, why not now? Try it. A smile, even a put-on smile, is contagious. Not only will it make others happy when they return your smile, but, as studies have shown, smiling relieves tension and really does make your outlook on life a lot brighter (cf. *Rabbi Nachman's Wisdom* #43).

Do something silly. In talking about making every effort to be joyous, Rebbe Nachman said that this even included resorting to acting a bit silly. The price one pays for a little silliness is far less than the price of depression and lethargy. [Unfortunately,] it really doesn't take much for us to act a little silly. Who knows? It might even be a bit of an improvement over many of the "serious" things we do.

Song, music and dance. Music clears the mind and makes us happy. Music has the power to help us pour our heart out before God. It also has the power to sharpen our memories and enable us to concentrate on our goals (*Advice*, Joy 14, 15). Therefore, the Rebbe taught that it's a very good habit to inspire ourselves with a melody. The spiritual roots of music and song are very deep and can arouse our hearts and raise our spirits (*Rabbi Nachman's Wisdom* #273).

Elsewhere, the Rebbe talks about the special power which dancing and clapping have to make us happy and mitigate the negative things affecting us (*Likutey Moharan* I, 169). It is customary in every Breslov synagogue to dance each day after the Morning and Evening prayers. Many Breslover Chassidim dance after learning together, while some even dance daily by themselves. It's a surefire way to arouse a feeling of real joy and happiness.

Reb Noson once said to Reb Moshe Breslover, "I will give you a way to repent. Dance every day!" (*Aveneha Barzel* p.62).

* * *

JOY ON SHABBAT AND FESTIVALS

Rebbe Nachman once said: Even the most average Jew feels great joy and happiness when sitting down at his Shabbat table (*Rabbi Nachman's Wisdom* #155).

Reb Noson once attended the funeral of someone whom he hardly knew. When asked why, he said, "A person should always cry out before God. Whenever an opportunity presents itself, I make the most of it" (*Siach Sarfei Kodesh* 1-635). We must do the same when it comes to happiness: seize every opportunity. Rebbe Nachman's writings are replete with teachings about being joyous, especially on joyous occasions. He encouraged us to take advantage of Shabbat and the festivals by making an even greater effort to be happy and joyous on these days.

Reb Noson writes: Once, when the Rebbe was about to give a lesson about being happy on Shabbat, he asked me, "Are you happy on Shabbat?" "Sometimes I get an arousal of fear and awe on Shabbat," I answered. The Rebbe said, "This is not the way. The main thing is joy!" He then spoke to me a lot about being happy on Shabbat. Afterwards, the Rebbe understood what I was thinking and he said to me, "Now you have what to be depressed about!" He knew that now that I had to be joyous, I would worry about whether I could do it. How would I get myself to be truly happy on Shabbat? This helped me a lot, for it made me realize that I should at least not become depressed over having to be joyous....When the Rebbe told me to be joyous on Shabbat, I told him, "At least I want to be happy." That is, even if I do not feel true joy, at least I *want* to feel it (*Rabbi Nachman's Wisdom* #155).

* * *

OVERCOMING SORROW

Rebbe Nachman teaches: People say that there are two worlds. This world and the World to Come. We all believe that there is a World to Come. This world *may* also exist somewhere. However, with all the suffering that we see in the world and what people must endure, where we are now must be Gehennom! (*Likutey Moharan* II, 119). Reb Noson told one of his followers, "If you were constantly happy, you wouldn't see Gehennom" (*Kokhavey Or*, p.78). The Gehennom that is this world, the suffering which many endure — we will be able to rise above it by forcing ourselves to be happy (see *Garden of the Souls* where this is more fully explained).

*

Once, on an Intermediate Day of Pesach, a young man came to Reb Avraham Sternhartz to speak to him about Rebbe Nachman's teachings. Because the young man had only recently become interested in Breslover Chassidut, Reb Avraham spoke with him at length. At the end of the conversation, Reb Avraham looked at the young chassid and saw how sad and troubled he appeared. The young man sensed this and began to relate all the difficulties and opposition he was encountering since becoming a Breslover chassid.

Reb Avraham said to him, "Nu! Today is Pesach, the time of our redemption," and started speaking to him about the greatness of Pesach, the Exodus and the true meaning of freedom. He gave him much advice and encouragement to help him through these trying times. At the end of the conversation, Reb Avraham said to him, "PeSaCH has the same numerical value as [Rebbe] NaCHMaN (148). How can we connect Rebbe Nachman and the concepts of Pesach? The Haggadah teaches us: This is what Hillel did! He took the Pesach, Matzah and Maror, and ate everything together."

He advised this young man to accept Hillel's teaching. We can partake of the Pesach — the True Tzaddik — only by experiencing bitterness and difficulty! Then we can fully appreciate these teachings. "Now," Reb Avraham said, "go home and have a very joyous Pesach!" (*The Breslov Haggadah* p.54).

*

If only we were joyous, we would not taste the bitterness of suffering and the full measure of life's problems could not weigh us down. This is neither fanciful nor unrealistic. It's simply that we know that sometimes, we can do nothing about our situation except pray. Rather than wallow in sorrow, we can rise above it and make the best of it. Things will eventually work out. Thus, Rebbe Nachman teaches: Joy opens the heart (*The Aleph-Bet Book,* Joy A:2).

* * *

THE REWARDS OF JOY

A person who is always happy, succeeds (*The Aleph-Bet Book,* Joy B:1).

Joy enhances the mind's ability to comprehend (*The Aleph-Bet Book,* Joy A:21).

When happiness comes to a person spontaneously, it is clear that kindness and help are on the way (*The Aleph-Bet Book,* Joy A:26).

*

Rebbe Nachman teaches: The Light of the Infinite shines and descends through all the upper worlds and ultimately reaches this world. The only way to perceive this Light is by performing the mitzvot with joy (*Likutey Moharan* I, 24:2). Conversely, the *Zohar* often asserts that when we are happy, we bring about light and joy to *all* the worlds.

On this topic, Reb Noson has constructed one of his most beautiful discourses (*Likutey Halakhot, Hoda'ah* 6). For some twenty-six pages, he takes the concepts of joy and happiness and relates them to every individual, for every day, in every situation. He opens the discourse as follows: A person should know that the Rebbe's lesson on attaining the loftiest of levels, the Great Light of the Infinite, is applicable to every Jew who performs the mitzvot with joy. The Torah was not given to the angels. It was given to us. To those of flesh and blood. Even we can attain the greatest of all levels — simply by being HAPPY.

*

Always be joyful, for with happiness you can give another person life. Your friend may be in terrible agony and not be able to express what is in his heart. While there is no one to whom he can unburden his heart he remains pained and worried. But, if you come along and greet him with a happy face, you can cheer him up and literally give him life. The Talmud teaches (*Ta'anit* 22a): Two **badchanim** (merrymakers) were declared "dwellers in the World to Come," merely because they made others happy (*Rabbi Nachman's Wisdom* #43).

* * *

SAVED BY JOY

There was a poor man who earned his living by digging clay. Once, while digging, he discovered a huge diamond. Taking it to the local jeweller for appraisal, he was told that there wasn't anyone on the European continent who could afford such a stone. He would have to go to the diamond exchange in London.

The man sold everything he had and made his way from city to city until he finally reached the port. But by then, he had used up all his funds. Approaching the captain, he asked for passage on the ship. He showed him the diamond and explained that at the moment he was short of cash. He would pay the fare upon arrival in London. The captain readily agreed and gave him the best cabin on the ship. He also honored him by visiting him daily in his cabin, where the two men would spend hours talking and passing the time of day.

During his meals, the man would keep the diamond on the table in front of him. He enjoyed looking at it and rejoicing in the glorious future which awaited him. Once, after dinner, he dozed off. Meanwhile, the steward came and cleared the table, shaking the tablecloth with its crumbs and the diamond into the sea. When the man awoke and realized what had happened, he was overcome by worry and sorrow.

"What will I do now?" he asked himself. "What have I left?" He had already sold all his possessions for the sake of the diamond. And if his grief weren't enough, he realized that the captain would soon be joining him for their daily conversation. He knew that the captain was a ruthless man and would not hesitate to kill him for his fare. His world looked like it was about to cave in. It was then that he realized what he had to do. "Come what may," he told himself, "I'm going to put on a happy face."

Having no choice, he continued to act happy, as if nothing had happened. He did this so well that the captain suspected nothing. After talking for a while, the captain said to the man, "I would like a favor from you. I have a full cargo of wheat in the hold. If I bring it in through customs, there will be heavy tariffs to pay. I see that you are a clever and honest person and I trust you. I would like to transfer ownership of the wheat to your name and let you bring it through customs. Afterwards, you can transfer the wheat back to me."

The man agreed. He hoped that this favor would spare him from the captain's wrath when he admitted that he could not pay for his fare. As it happened, as soon as they arrived in London the captain suddenly died. The entire shipload of wheat remained in the man's name, and it was worth far more than the diamond which he had just lost.

*

Rebbe Nachman concludes: The diamond was not his, proof being that he lost it. The wheat, however, was his, since it remained with him. But how did he get what was truly his? Only because he strengthened himself with joy in his darkest moment (*Rabbi Nachman's Stories* #19).

* * *

3

THE GOOD POINTS

Judge everybody favorably! (Avot 1:6). This promotes
peace (Rashi).
One who judges others favorably, is himself judged
favorably (Shabbat 127b).
God's way is to focus on the good. Even if there are
things which are not so good, He only looks for the
good. How much more do we have to avoid focusing on
the faults of our friends. We are obligated to seek only
the good — always! (Likutey Moharan II, 17).

* * *

AZAMRA!

Rebbe Nachman teaches: Know! you must judge all people
favorably. Even in the case of a complete sinner, you must
search until you find some good in him, some small aspect in
which he is not a sinner. By doing this, you actually elevate him
to the side of merit. You can then bring him to return to God.
This can be understood from the verse, "In but *a little bit* the
sinner is not; search carefully his place and he is not there"
(Psalms 37:10). If you find but a little bit of good, then the
sinner is not—he is no longer guilty; search his place and he
is not there—but is now to be found on the side of merit
(Likutey Moharan I, 282).

So begins Rebbe Nachman's lesson *AZAMRA!* Conceivably
the most important lesson in all of *Likutey Moharan*, it is

the only one which carries the Rebbe's exhortation: "Go with this lesson, constantly!" Keep it in mind and practice it, always! (The publication *AZAMRA!* contains the entire lesson and Reb Noson's commentary in translation, explaining these concepts at length.) Why is the message of this lesson so special?

The faculty of judgment is one of man's most powerful tools. If we really knew just how potent, we would certainly be more careful about how we used it. Elsewhere, the Rebbe teaches that judging others can destroy the world. If a person finds fault with another, this judgment can condemn him (*Likutey Moharan* I, 3). Think about it! Your evaluation, your opinion and judgment of others has the power to either elevate or degrade.

The problem is that criticism comes easy. Too easy. We can always find fault in what others do or fail to do. It's not difficult to ascribe ulterior motives even for the worthiest of deeds. This is especially true when we hear slander. Then everyone is quick to jump on the bandwagon condemning the offender for his wrongdoing. We have to realize that every word spoken about another person is, in some way, a form of judgment. If, in our judgment, we find the good points and focus on the positive, we can bring the world — the entire world — to the side of merit and worthiness. However, the reverse is also true. In judging others, if we find fault and focus on the negative, we can bring the world — the entire world — to the side of demerit and unworthiness. This is why we must always try to look for the good in others, even in the worst person we know. Such emphasis on his positive traits affects him, because, as Rebbe Nachman said, our favorable judgment "actually elevates him to the side of merit."

*

After Reb Noson published his *Likutey Tefilot* (the Collected Prayers), his followers suggested that he should be known as the Master of Prayer (after the the main character of the 12th story in *Rabbi Nachman's Stories,* entitled "The Master of Prayer.") Reb Noson replied, "The Master of Prayer is Rebbe Nachman. If I am to be considered as one of the King's men, I am the Bard, the singer of praises. This is because I can even find merit in a person who transgressed the entire Torah 800 times!" (*Siach Sarfei Kodesh* I-591).

* * *

...EVEN ONE'S ENEMIES

Do not judge your friend until you reach his level (*Avot* 2:5).

Judging others favorably applies not only to sinners, but even to our enemies who would harm us. In most cases, enmity between two people stems from petty jealousy. Either I am jealous of my friend, because he has more or has accomplished more than I have, or else he is envious of what I have or of what I have achieved. We are not equals in the area where the jealousy exists. If we were, there would be be no reason for envy. Either I have to raise myself to his position or, if he is on a lower level than I am, I have to elevate him and make him my equal. How? Easily, I judge him favorably. Then, when there are no longer differences between us, there will be no room for jealousies and nothing to fight about (*Likutey Moharan* I, 136).

At first glance, this concept might appear a bit difficult to accept. It cannot be denied that jealousy is a very destructive emotion which can have far-reaching effects. Envy is the mother of strife. Conversely, judging a person favorably can bring about harmony. By always looking for the good points in others, by judging them to be righteous and focusing on their virtues, we can eliminate the cycle of enmity and strife. If, instead of stubbornly clinging to our own comfortable positions and being possessively protective of our things and our achievements, we would give the other guy the benefit of the doubt, we could fashion a much better and more peaceful life, for ourselves and our families.

* * *

...AND ONE'S SELF

"All right," you'll say. "So I'll judge the other guy favorably. Maybe he is okay. Truth is, I don't really know his motives or the things which make him act the way he does. But I can't say the same for myself. I know what makes me tick. And believe me, there's no way — no way! — that I can *honestly* say that I'm okay, too."

Many people adhere to this line of reasoning. Even people who on the outside seem self-confident and generally positive about themselves, when pressed, will admit that they find it hard to judge themselves favorably. They know themselves too well, and basically, their self-evaluation may be accurate. Their good deeds may be motivated by a desire for fame and fortune. Yet the question still remains, is their conclusion — their belief that they are not okay — is that correct? The Rebbe would say, "No!"

AZAMRA! Rebbe Nachman teaches: You must also find this good point within yourself. You must always be happy. When examining yourself, you may find that you do not have any good points — Torah, mitzvot, kind acts, etc. — to be happy about. You must not allow yourself to fall into depression. Instead, search your deeds. There *must* be some good. Even if you find that your deeds are "not clean," that your actions were dictated by ulterior motives and improper thoughts, then at least find the positive aspects within the things you did. Some aspects of your deeds must have been positive. And if not, you can at least be happy that you are a Jew! This good point you cannot fault, because it was God's doing (*Likutey Moharan* I, 282).

*

Reb Meir of Teplik was visiting Reb Noson. When asked about a certain person living in Teplik, Reb Meir replied very matter-of-factly, as if to say that the man wasn't much to talk about. Reb Noson said to him, "If you will look at things negatively and with an unfavorable eye you'll find fault with everyone in the whole world. Think of the people living in Teplik. Start with the person living at the edge of town. If you look at him carefully, you'll certainly find some shortcomings. Now go from house to house until you get to *your* house. Are you the only good Jew in the whole town?" "Me? I'm also not very righteous," Reb Meir quickly replied. "If you're not, then who is?" asked Reb Noson. "But, if you'd look at the world favorably," he continued, "you'd find good in even the worst person; and then certainly in everyone else" (*Kokhavey Or*, p. 75).

*

One of the main reasons people get depressed is failure. A business deal you're working on falls through, a relationship you're trying to develop doesn't work out. "I've failed again," you say to yourself. A family feud upsets you; it's pointless but it leaves you anxious. Sometimes, you wake up on the wrong side of the bed and feel like you have to brace yourself for a day in which everything will go wrong. Be careful, it's not good to allow a feeling of failure, or even a feeling of unaccomplishment, to set in. When you do, you become pessimistic and this invites further failures. What else can you do? You can find a good point. Recharge yourself with optimism and positive thinking. You do have valuable qualities! You can succeed! Adopting this attitude will help you recover from any setbacks. Even in those areas where things were going all wrong, you'll encounter success.

Rebbe Nachman placed much emphasis on this concept. "One must *always* seek the good..." he repeated, again and again. Be forever the optimist. Never despair, never let go!

Whatever good you find, preserve it. Doing this will help you discover your own, unique reservoir of vitality. Like all men, you are in possession of an incredible inner strength — an almost never-ending source of energy inside you, resembling a rechargeable battery that can propel you forward. How do you turn it on? How do you get it going? This is what Rebbe Nachman comes to tell us: Start by seeking the good. Focus only on your good points. Don't despair! You can succeed. You will succeed!

*

Once, fire swept through a part of Breslov. Passing by the site, Reb Noson and his followers spotted one of the distraught homeowners. Although crying bitterly, he was sifting through the rubble of his destroyed house in the hope of finding something, anything that he might use to rebuild his home. Reb Noson said: Do you see what he's doing? Even though his house has been destroyed, he hasn't given up hope. He's collecting whatever might be useful for rebuilding his house. The same is true when it comes to spirituality. The Evil One fights against us, he tries to destroy whatever holiness we've built up by getting us to do something which goes against God's will. Even so, when we are knocked down and all seems hopeless, we must never give up hope. We have to pick up a few good points and collect them together from amidst the sins. This is the way to return to God (*Kokhavey Or* p.78).

*

Rebbe Nachman teaches: A person should interpret the verses of the Psalms as regards himself. He should see the words as applying specifically to him and his situation. In connection with this, someone once asked the Rebbe how it was possible to apply all the verses. "What about where King David praises himself, as when he said, "God, guard my soul for I am a chassid"?" (Psalms 86:2). King David was able to say this about himself, but there was no way this man could honestly say that he could. The Rebbe answered: "A person must judge himself favorably, at all times. Doing this allows the person to be a chassid in at least that *one good point.* We see this in our daily liturgy. At first we say, 'Who are we? What is our life? What is our righteousness?' Then we say, 'But we are the children of Avraham, Yitzchak and Yaakov...' Thus we praise ourselves and find some good points about ourselves. And this brings us to serve God!" (*Likutey Moharan* II, 125).

*

Someone once came to Rebbe Nachman, complaining about how bitter his life was. This man wanted to draw closer to God and mend his ways, but each time he tried, the temptations grew stronger and stronger. Days turned into weeks and years and he had still not managed to better himself in his devotions to God. The Rebbe tried to encourage him, but to no avail. The man just kept bemoaning his fate. The Rebbe then said to him, "Seeing that all is bad, it's clear that I have no one to talk to!" At this the man grew excited and said to Rebbe Nachman, "But I *do* try! I *do* make attempts to change myself. I'm not totally bad." Hearing this, the Rebbe said to him, "Aha! Now make use of the lesson *AZAMRA!* Use your good points to inspire you."

It was Rebbe Nachman's intention that the person *himself* say that all was not lost; that he still had a desire to change his ways. Feeling distant from God, a man begins to think that he might never succeed. By challenging all men in the same way he challenged this man, the Rebbe forces us to acknowledge that we do have good points. Once this is established, we are all capable of going forward (*Tzaddik* #569).

*

Our Sages advised: Every person must say that the world was only created for me (*Sanhedrin* 37a). What does that mean? It means that every person is important and especially you. It's true. You come first. The world was created for you. The only thing is, as Rebbe Nachman explains, this privilege carries responsibility. Because the world was created for me, I must see to its rectification. *I am responsible* for the world (*Likutey Moharan* I, 5:1).

*

Reb Noson not only studied Rebbe Nachman's teachings, he *lived* them. Finding the good points is a theme which appears again and again throughout his discourses in *Likutey Halakhot*. He translates the lesson *AZAMRA!* into practical guidance for better relationships with family, friends and neighbors — and indeed with whomever we come into contact. Imagine, a majority of all arguments in the home—the most common and often the most harmful form of disagreement—would be eliminated instantly if only we could get ourselves to see the good points and focus only on the positive qualities in our spouses and children.

Rebbe Nachman stressed: "Never despair!" (*Likutey Moharan* II, 78). No matter what has happened, no matter how far you've strayed, never despair! Reb Noson adds: You can always find ways to return to God. If you have started, continue. If you haven't yet started to serve God, start now! (*Likutey Halakhot, Masa U'Matan* 4:16).

Reb Noson recognized our need for finding *hitchazkut* (support and encouragement). Yet, whenever he talks about the support we can draw from others, he inevitably shifts over to the support we must draw from ourselves. In the final analysis, no matter how much encouragement we get from others (the Tzaddik, our family, friends, etc.) it comes down to how much we care about ourselves. Therefore, Reb

Noson writes: After all, if you don't take pity on yourself, who will? (*Likutey Halakhot, Netilat Yadayim li'Seudah* 6:37).

In addition, Reb Noson writes: Even a drop of good is never lost! Never! Our Sages teach: "If you've searched and succeeded in finding, believe it" (*Megillah* 6b). Why, *believe* it? If I've found, then I *know* it. What's the point in believing? But, this is the point. No matter how much you seek the good, you may think you haven't yet achieved or attained any. You might feel yourself even more distant from your goal than you were before you started. With this in mind, our Sages specifically taught: *believe it!* Believe that you've found some good, even if you can't see it! (*Likutey Halakhot, Birkhot HaPeirot* 5:1,2).

Reb Noson also illustrates how we can come to see that good, and in the process discover that we have even more good than we think. Whenever we lose something important, something that we need immediately, we'll go looking for it. We'll search high and low, and eventually we'll find it. What often happens in the course of the search is that we come across other "lost" items, things we'd "forgotten" about and didn't remember that we still had. It is the same for the person who is always looking for his really good points in Judaism. In the course of his search, he will inevitably come across other "long lost" tidbits that are his. His alone. Much to his surprise, he will find that he has a lot of "little good qualities" within him (*Likutey Halakhot, Birkhot HaPeirot* 5:4).

* * *

POINT TO POINT

Each of us has some good point which is uniquely our own. With regard to this quality or aspect of your being, you are a "Tzaddik." The same is true of your friend. With regard to his good point, he is a "Tzaddik." Each of you is virtuous and righteous in a different attribute. Make it your business to speak to a friend about serving God every day. This way, you'll be able to receive from his good points while at the same time share your own (*Likutey Moharan* I, 34:4). Thus, Reb Noson writes: The best way to draw knowledge is by illuminating the hearts of our fellow Jews with the faith and knowledge that God is here, waiting for us to turn to Him. This can be accomplished through comradeship and unity, in that we help each other seek the truth (*Likutey Halakhot, Netilat Yadayim li'Seudah* 6:49).

*

Whoever wants to have true pity on himself and think of his ultimate goal, should begin each day anew, as if he were just born. Today is what really counts. Begin anew. Start afresh. Each Jew, as long as he wears his Jewishness proudly, certainly performs at least a few mitzvot every day. We pray, we study some Torah, we give some charity, we do something kind; some of us more, some of us less, but we all do something worthwhile each day. It is essential to realize that the past is gone, the future hasn't happened, and the present is essentially all we have to work with. Today, this day, never existed and will never exist again. As a new creation, it affords us the opportunity to begin anew. If that's the case, then the important thing to remember is: TODAY COUNTS! (*Likutey Halakhot, K'riat HaTorah* 6:17).

*

Rebbe Nachman teaches: The world considers forgetfulness a shortcoming. I consider it a very great advantage. If a person didn't forget, it would be impossible for him to serve God. Remembering all his wrongdoings would prevent him from ever being able to pick his head up [and start again]. With forgetfulness, however, a person can forget the past and face the future [with hope] (*Rabbi Nachman's Wisdom* #26).

Reb Noson illustrates this with the following law: Even before we read the weekly Torah portion in the synagogue on Shabbat morning, a small passage of this reading will have already been read on three occasions during the course of the preceding week: on the previous Shabbat afternoon, then on Monday and Thursday morning. However, this small passage may not be applied to the Shabbat morning reading, when the entire weekly Torah portion must be read from start to finish. [We may not include what was read during the week and begin from where we left off on Thursday morning.] This emphasizes the importance of always making a fresh start. A person should not look back over his past. Whatever happened, good or bad, it has passed. It's now time to face forward, forgetting what has already taken place. Start afresh. Study Torah, pray harder, do mitzvot. The past is gone. Look, with truth, to the future (*Likutey Halakhot, K'riat HaTorah* 6:17).

* * *

I AM A JEW!!!

Once, there was a Tzaddik who fell into a terrible state of depression. No matter what he tried, he could not bring himself to joy. He considered this good point and that good point, yet nothing made any impression on him. Depression and apathy weighed heavy on his mind. To pull himself out, he tried recalling the goodness and kindness that God had bestowed upon him. Still, he did not feel any elation. Every time he found some reason to be happy, an insidious voice inside him pointed to some negative aspect of that thing to be depressed about.

He thought and thought until finally, one thing did occur to him. "God has made me a Jew!" This was not his doing. There was no ulterior motive on his part. It was God's doing alone. "I can be truly happy with this," he told himself. "Truly happy!"

He began to feel very happy. And with this happiness, he started pulling himself out of his depression, lifting himself higher and higher. As a result of his great joy about being Jewish he felt himself soaring many, many thousands of miles. He rose and ascended ever higher, flying through the Upper Worlds, until he came to the level of joy Moshe Rabeinu had reached when he received the Torah at Mount Sinai.

But eventually, the Tzaddik's joy began to ebb. Looking around, he found himself back where he started. Well, not exactly where he started, but no more than a few inches removed from it. The Tzaddik could not get over this. He had flown so far in the Upper Worlds, and yet here, in the lower worlds, he was for all intents and purposes in the very same place!

He then began to understand the importance of finding even a little bit of good, even a drop's worth, within oneself. When a person finds that little bit, that inch of forward movement which a man makes in this lowly physical world, God considers it like thousands upon thousands of miles in the Upper Worlds.

This can be illustrated by drawing a spoke, a circle with a center point from which lines extend. The closer these lines are to the point, the closer they are to one another. The further they extend from the point, the further they are separated from each other. A movement of less than an inch near the center point will be a movement of many, many times that at the circle's outer periphery. Similarly, compared to the supernal universes, this physical world is no more than a dot in a large circle, the center of the spoke. One iota of movement towards good in this world brings a change in position of thousands and even millions of miles in the Upper Worlds (*Rabbi Nachman's Stories* #16).

*

Rebbe Nachman teaches: God takes great pride in each and every Jew (*Likutey Moharan* I, 17:1). He stresses this, because it is not uncommon for a person to doubt his own worth and worthiness. "Now that I've sinned, how can God take pride in me?" As a result, he begins to slacken in his performance of the mitzvot, and even in his desire to serve God. Because of this, Rebbe Nachman emphasized the importance and worth of each and every Jew. "God takes great pride in each and every Jew," no matter what he's done, no matter how far he's fallen. The Rebbe therefore stressed the need for finding the good points in every single person. This will enable him to find the immense amount of good that he has within him. Finding this good, he can then return to God (cf. *Be'Ibey HaNachal* I, 17).

*

In the Ukranian town of Teplik, there was a Breslover Chassid by the name of Feivel. Every night, Feivel would wake up at midnight to recite *Tikkun Chatzot* (the Midnight Lament). Inspired by the great joy which he felt from having performed this mitzvah, he would then dance ecstatically, fervently singing the words *ashreinu, mah tov chelkeinu* (how fortunate we are, how good is our portion) over and over again. Eventually, people started calling him Feivel-Ashreinu.

Whenever Reb Noson happened to visit Teplik, Reb Feivel would joyously come out to greet him. Once, Reb Feivel failed to appear. When Reb Noson asked about him, the people wanted to know which Feivel he was referring to. "Oh! You must mean Feivel-Ashreinu!" they finally said mockingly. "Since you were last here, he passed away." Taking note of the condescending way in which they had referred to the late chassid, Reb Noson took them to task for it. "In the next world, people are punished by being made to repeat the very same acts they performed in this world. I'll tell you this," Reb Noson said. "Reb Feivel's 'punishment' will be to say *Tikkun Chatzot* and dance *Ashreinu* — happy with all the good points he collected in this world!" (*Siach Sarfei Kodesh* 1-786).

* * *

4

TRUTH

The seal of God is truth (*Shabbat* 55a).

There may be many lies, but there is only one truth (*Likutey Moharan* I, 51).

ONLY ONE TRUTH

What is truth? This should be the easiest of questions to answer, yet it is probably one of the most difficult. The truth is one, only one, so the truth should not be at all difficult to locate. All we need is to look for "one." But, what is that one?

"Sh'ma Yisrael... Hear O Israel, God is One" (Deuteronomy 6:4). We know that God is truth, He is One. But there exist other truths too. "*Torat emet*, the Torah of truth..." (Malakhi 2:6). There are also True Tzaddikim. And there is truth within each and every one of us.

However, the truth really is *only* one. This is the concept of simplicity. If we find ourselves in a web of complications, we are distant from the truth. The more simply we approach life, the clearer our perspectives are, the closer we are to truth. And the closer we come to One, to God, the more we can see that all these truths are one.

* * *

REAL TRUTH

The Midrash relates: When God came to create Adam, the ministering angels split into different factions, for and against his creation. Kindness said: "Create man for he will perform acts of kindness." Truth argued: "Do not create man, for he will be full of lies." Righteousness said: "Create man, for he will perform righteous deeds." Peace said: "Do not create man, for he will be full of strife." What did God do? He took Truth and cast it down to the ground. The ministering angels asked: "Is Truth not Your seal? Why did You cast it upon the ground?" God then said: "Let Truth rise up from the ground" (*Bereishit Rabbah* 8:5).

Reb Noson asks: What happened here? Why did God cast Truth down to the ground? Even more puzzling, how was it that of all the Divine qualities, Truth disagreed with God? Seeing that in the end God did make man, then that is the truth, man should be created. How could Truth have argued against that? Also, God Himself is truth! How can Truth argue against the truth?

There are many lies, but only one truth. Where there is *many,* there is a concept of falsehood. Where there is only *one,* there is truth. Man was created. From him came forth the world's population, the "many." We are now faced with a difficult question, where is the truth? Which one of us has the truth, *the real truth,* within us? We are many. How can one discern what is the truth? Who is right? Which is the right path?

God's ways are very deep and hidden from us. Even the angels cannot fathom God or His truth. The angels understood that God wanted to create man to serve Him. How would corporeal man, with his physical body and living in a physical world, be able to understand this truth? Impossible! so they thought, and therefore argued against man's creation. God knew otherwise. He knew that man would have the wisdom, intellect and ability to rise to the challenge — to recognize truth and choose it over falsehood.

*

There is truth and there is the real truth. The angels were correct in stating that man is full of falsehood. He has "many" thoughts, "many" ideas, within himself. He must be constantly occupied in seeking and searching for the truth. If he does, he will find it. But is the truth which man finds the real truth, the ultimate truth? Or is it just a form of truth, a partial and therefore incomplete truth? The answer is that everyone has within himself a measure of truth and the ability to search for truth. At the same time, we must understand that everybody's truth is different — formulated by such factors as disposition, environment, schooling, etc. So much depends on "where you are coming from." Because of this, man's truth, while true, is only partial. And it was this truth, each person's individual truth, which argued against the Creator. It was this truth that God cast down to the ground.

God has a higher understanding. His is an Ultimate Truth which transcends even the most "obvious" truth. The True Tzaddikim have come to this truth, and we, the "many," can also attain this truth. How? By accepting that an ultimate truth — a truth greater than our own — exists, and that we must search for it. Then, the truth, the real truth, will rise from amongst us all (*Likutey Halakhot, Ribit* 5:16-20).

Reb Noson said that a person must always beg and plead with God to lead him on the path of *His* truth. With our own truth we can deceive ourselves, but God's truth is the real, the Ultimate Truth (*Siach Sarfei Kodesh* 1-502). Reb Noson added, "How can you know the real truth when you see it? If you know in your heart that you really desire the truth (only the real truth), and you ask God to let you be worthy of His truth and give all your actions entirely over to Him, then, however He guides you will be the ultimate truth" (*Likutey Halakhot, Beheimah v'Chayah Tehorah* 4:24).

*

There was a time when Reb Noson was being pressured by his father-in-law to take a job as the official rabbi of one of the local districts. He was certainly qualified and such a prominent position would also provide him with the livelihood he so sorely needed. Yet, Reb Noson found himself in a quandary over what to do. He was not sure that this was the true way for him to serve God — that this was what God wanted from him. He turned to Rebbe Nachman for advice.

"Take the position," the Rebbe told him. "Why not? Being an official rabbi would be a good thing."

"But is it the truth? Is it the true thing to do?" Reb Noson questioned.

"Yes," answered the Rebbe. "Who else is as qualified as you are?"

But Reb Noson was not totally convinced. "But is it the *real* truth?" he pressed on.

"You want the *real* truth?!" the Rebbe answered. "The real truth is that you should not take the job." (The Rebbe understood that the responsibility would stunt Reb Noson's spiritual growth.) Reb Noson was always very thankful that he pressed the Rebbe for the *real* truth. Having refused the position, he was able to serve God and spent his life spreading Rebbe Nachman's teachings (*Siach Sarfei Kodesh* 1-175).

*

Rebbe Nachman also teaches: Where there is truth there is peace (*The Aleph-Bet Book,* Truth A:22). When one comprehends the Ultimate Truth — knowing that each of us is different and yet still seeks out the One God — then one can achieve peace (*Likutey Halakhot, Ribit* 5:20). (The publication, *MAYIM,* contains this Midrash together with Reb Noson's commentary explaining these concepts at length).

* * *

RECOGNIZING/ACCEPTING TRUTH

Rebbe Nachman teaches: Truth is performing a mitzvah when alone in the same way you would perform it when among people: with the same care, with the same devotion. Such is the way of a man of truth (*Likutey Moharan* I, 251). A person once spoke to Rebbe Nachman about becoming a *rebbe*. Rebbe Nachman warned against this. "You won't even be able to recite the Grace after Meals properly. All your thoughts will be concerned with acting in a manner acceptable to your followers" (*Rabbi Nachman's Wisdom* #47).

Truth, in this sense, means not needing "assistance" from others. For example, when a person prays, he sometimes needs "help." His intentions and actions are dictated by the fact that others are watching him. He needs the public eye to see how well he is praying. There are others that truly want to pray earnestly, but being in public distracts them, because they may feel they are being watched even when this is not so. Truth is when one does not need "assistance" from anybody else. It doesn't matter who is around, for one is concentrating on serving God (*Likutey Moharan* I, 66:3).

*

With open minds. There's a tendency today to accept truth only when a person "feels like it." This is not enough. There is a great danger in ignoring the truth. Rebbe Nachman teaches: The character trait of *nitzachon* (victory) prevents us from accepting the truth. If, in a conversation or an argument, we recognize the validity of the other person's opinion, we'll twist our own reasoning and opinion, rather than accept — even worse, admit — that the other person may be right (*Likutey Moharan* I, 122). This also applies when we argue with our conscience. We might understand that what we are doing is wrong, but we rationalize; we use "logic," rather than truth, and convince ourselves that what we are doing is right.

Therefore, truth is recognizable if we but approach the things we do with open minds, seeking truth and making ourselves *ready* to accept it. Could the other guy be right? Maybe yes, maybe no. Let's hear him out. Hear what he has to say. *Then* evaluate. Take the good points, the positive points, and accept them for what they are — truth. Because actually, from his viewpoint, they are the truth. Then offer your viewpoint, without looking for "victory." The truth will win out.

*

Recognizing a lie. An even greater danger exists in altering the truth. It is important to recognize this in ourselves and in others. The Prophet bemoans (Isaiah 5:20): "Woe to those who call evil, good; and good, evil. They make darkness [appear as] light, and light [appear as] darkness; the bitter they make sweet, and the sweet they make bitter."

Mathematical equations must be absolute. Even the slightest mistake of a mere fraction, say in engineering, can cause a series of erroneous calculations that can have serious implications. How much more so when a person alters the truth of life and weaves a web of falsehood and lies around himself. Once a lie is told, a second must be created to cover for the first one, and so on. There was a man in Reb Noson's neighborhood who was a sinner and people were misled by him. Yet, he was known as a person with principles who never lied. When asked about him, Reb Noson replied: "Perhaps he doesn't lie. But he lives a lie!" (*Oral Tradition*).

Throughout his writings, Reb Noson exhorts us to search for the truth, and to make our search constant. Of people who publicize their distorted views and call them truth he writes: The word *truth* never leaves their mouths. They say truth. They scream truth. But, woe to them and their truth (*Likutey Halakhot, Shabbat* 7:64).

*

...even when it hurts. Sometimes the truth hurts. Yet, recognition and acceptance of the truth is the very first step in healing. Recognizing illness helps bring about the cure. So too, recognizing the truth of the situation we've been presented with helps us to accept the right path to follow. It is not easy; quite the contrary, it is always very difficult to face up to a problem. But remember: the sooner we accept the problem, the sooner we can get on with life.

It is far healthier to accept the truth as early as possible in life and to make the necessary corrections when we are more adaptable. It hurts less that way. By searching for the truth, and by accepting it, we engage in a constant review of our life. We'll be able to spot the weak points, correct them and build a better future.

*

In others. We also have to recognize the truth in others. Rebbe Nachman once said: People make a mistake when they claim that a Tzaddik cannot commit an error, and if he commits an error, he is no longer a Tzaddik. I say: The Tzaddik remains a Tzaddik and the error remains an error (*Siach Sarfei Kodesh* 1-46).

People have the tendency to criticize. "He's not really religious...he's a faker...he never was...." We find it hard to overlook the mistakes of others. But people are just that — people. And a Tzaddik *is* a Tzaddik. Yet King Solomon taught us: "There is no righteous man that doesn't err" (Ecclesiastes 7:20). Man is human and subject to mistakes. Rebbe Nachman extolls the virtues of truth — real, absolute truth. Where there is error, recognize the error, acknowledge it. This is truth. What is wrong, is wrong. Even so, what is good, remains good. It, too, has to be recognized. (The Tzaddik himself is well aware of his error, yet not defeated by it; cf. *Rabbi Nachman's Wisdom* p.7; #30; #235).

Rebbe Nachman exhorted us to recognize the Tzaddik, and the good points, too. Truth is definitely black and white. Yet, our "humanness" dictates that we also find ourselves faced with gray areas, where the truth — as best we can determine it — could be this way or that.... In such cases, we should judge others favorably. We are free to scrutinize the gray areas of our own truth in black and white, but not the truth in others. The validity of their "gray truth" is not for us to judge with a critical eye.

* * *

TRUTH IS TANGIBLE

The Talmud tells us that falsehood does not last! (*Shabbat* 104a). It has no permanence and offers no true reward. However, this presents a problem. We know that a lust for money is a form of foreign worship, i.e. idolatry, and idolatry itself is the epitome of falsehood (cf. *Sanhedrin* 92a). How, then, can greed and a craving for wealth ever result in gains for one who has them? How can a desire for money ever pay off? The answer can be found in the following talmudic exchange.

The Sixty Wise Men of Athens challenged Rabbi Yehoshua ben Chananya: "Tell us something false!" Rabbi Yehoshua answered: "We had a mule which gave birth. Hanging from the neck of the newborn mule was a note on which was written: My father owes 100,000 coins." They said: "How does a mule give birth?" He answered: "You asked for something false, didn't you?!" (*Bekhorot* 8b).

Rebbe Nachman explains: A mule alludes to idolatry. Birth suggests being fruitful and profitable. When the Sixty Wise Men wondered how a mule could give birth, they were really asking how it was possible for idolatry to yield profits. How could falsehood, the lust for money, give birth? Rabbi Yehoshua answered them that this was the falsehood they had asked for. Such people only think they are profiting. The truth is that they are not. Falsehood yields no benefits, no true reward.... People work hard their entire lives and think that they are actually earning and profiting. In the end, most see that they have nothing from their constant labor. And, even if something does remain of their wealth, it simply means that they have mortgaged *their entire lives* just for money; money which they will in any case not take with them. They run from place to place, job to job, city to city, seeking profit, seeking money. It is as if they were born with an outstanding debt, with a note hanging from their necks that they owe money and have been told to pay it (*Likutey Moharan* I, 23:5).

Reb Noson added: It seems that everyone feels the need to leave something for his children. This itself is a debt. Ask anyone who's ever lived why they work so hard and he'll tell you, "I do it for my children." "You'd think," said Reb Noson, "that since everyone is working for his children, you'd see such wonderful children. I'm still waiting to see that flawless child! [The one that everyone sells their lives for!]" (*Rabbi Eliyahu Chaim Rosen*).

*

Rebbe Nachman once said: The world fools a person. Accept this advice from me: Do not let yourselves be fooled! (*Rabbi Nachman's Wisdom* #51). Rebbe Nachman wanted us to understand that the search for the truth does not begin with the search for worldly needs and possessions. Granted, we have to live: the need for food, shelter and clothing is real. The Torah speaks of the necessity to work in order to survive. But the search for truth is a search for eternity, a "possession" which man can acquire and hold onto forever — the tangible. A person shouldn't have to sacrifice his entire life to "idolatry," to falsehood, just for the ration of bread he needs. Were we to put our energy and resources into searching for the truth, we would have a far more content life even in this world.

Reb Noson once remarked: [The desires of] this world *are not* tangible, and one cannot [ever] attain them. Torah and prayer *are* tangible and one *can* attain them (*Aveneha Barzel* p.86). Some people work their entire lives to reach an objective, perhaps money or some other desire. Sometimes, they even reach their goal. "But," as Rebbe Nachman said, "man and wealth cannot endure together. Either the money is taken from the man, or the man is taken from his money. They cannot remain together forever" (*Rabbi Nachman's Wisdom* #51).

*

Rebbe Nachman emphasized over and over again that truth represents something everlasting, something tangible, something which man can grasp and keep for himself. You have to look out for your family; it is your responsibility. You have to take care of yourself; if not you, then who? But remember your primary responsibility: to strive for the everlasting, the truth — the Ultimate Truth. Look for "births," for futures, for profits — but permanent profits, not the momentary profits that fool and mislead you into running after the transient.

* * *

TRUE LEADERSHIP

The truth will be broken into many groups (*Sanhedrin* 97a).

Someone once said to Reb Moshe Breslover: "We always find in Rebbe Nachman's teachings mention of the True Tzaddik. Who is that True Tzaddik?" Reb Moshe answered: "Yosef interpreted Pharaoh's dream correctly. He informed him of the upcoming Seven Years of Plenty and Seven Years of Famine. Then Yosef advised Pharaoh to appoint a wise minister who would oversee the conserving of the crops during the good years for the famine that was to follow. Pharaoh understood that if Yosef knew the problem and the solution, i.e. he was clear about what had to be done, then Yosef himself must be that wise man. Yosef was the obvious choice for the task. Now," said Reb Moshe, coming to the point, "if Pharaoh could understand that the one who talks about it must be the one who knows about it, then you should also be able to figure it out" (*Rabbi Nachman Burstein*).

*

A true leader is someone who reaches a genuine level of humility, someone who considers himself nothing at all (see *Likutey Moharan* I, 4:7). He devotes himself (finding no sacrifice too great) entirely to the needs of his flock. The perfect example of such a leader is Moshe Rabeinu. When the Golden Calf was made, God wanted to annihilate the entire nation, save Moshe. "Then wipe me out too!" Moshe exclaimed. Throughout our history, our true leaders have put themselves on the block for us, time and again. When a leader recognizes the needs of his flock and acts accordingly, he knows the truth of his position — he is there for the people.

Conversely, we find many people in leadership positions, especially in our age, who see their first and foremost responsibility as getting recognition — for their causes, for their opinions, for themselves. These are false leaders. Rebbe Nachman teaches: There are many people who see themselves as leaders of their communities. However, their aspirations are guided by personal ambition and a desire for prominence. In truth, not only are they incapable of leading others, they are even incapable of leading themselves, because they are victims of their own evil desires (*Likutey Moharan* I, 10:4). Elsewhere he says: Beware of communal leaders and Torah teachers who lack integrity (*Likutey Moharan* I, 28:1).

* * *

Rebbe Nachman once told of a well-known *rebbe* who would pray in his private room adjacent to the synagogue.

Hearing sounds outside his door and thinking it to be his chassidim trying to catch a glimpse of their master's devotions, the *rebbe* prayed with great fervor and enthusiasm. Later, he discovered that the sounds had been caused by a cat scratching at the door. "For nine years he prayed to a cat! God save us!" (*Aveneha Barzel* p. 25).

Especially in the spiritual realm, we must be on guard against falsehood. There are those who misrepresent Torah and Judaism in a manner that diverts people from finding the truth. In the case of the *rebbe* who prayed to the cat, he dressed as a religious person, he acted as a religious leader...yet his devotions were for his own sake: for honor, for wealth, and so on.

*

Rebbe Nachman teaches: The advice given by one person to another creates a union between them; it forms a bond between the giver and the receiver. In a sense, this union is like a marriage. The idea and counsel which one implants in the other grows and develops and is eventually "born" into reality. If the advice comes from a wicked person, if the giver lacks virtue, nothing good can ever come from it. Conversely, the advice one receives from the Tzaddikim is total truth. The end results of their counsel are positive (*Likutey Moharan* I, 7:3).

For this reason, it is very important for us to be associated with true and righteous leaders. The ideas and counsel we receive from them will lead us to the truth and to complete faith, because their advice is pure, ultimate truth. Even if we fail to understand that what they are telling us is true, by accepting it faithfully, we have the truth engraved inside us. Our faith, supported by our desire for the real truth, will ultimately lead us to the correct path.

Of course, it's not always so easy to know who is the true leader and who isn't; whose counsel we should accept and whose we should ignore. Our Sages were aware of this problem and did offer some advice: Come see the difference between the students of Avraham and Bilaam... (Avot 5:23). Why the students? Why not between Avraham and Bilaam themselves? The answer is that many times we find it impossible to differentiate between the True Tzaddik and the false leader. Both are masters, pundits in their own right. Only years later can we clearly see the fruits of their teachings — in those who took them as their leader.

Therefore, Rebbe Nachman teaches: Always seek the truth. The truth of the Tzaddikim. Seek, search, and above all pray to God that we merit seeing it. Throughout the Likutey Halakhot, Reb Noson shows that the truth can be found in Rebbe Nachman's teachings. Yet time and again he exhorts the reader never to cease looking for the truth. If it is to be found in Rebbe Nachman's works and the reader has presumably found it, why the need to keep searching? The answer is that no matter how much truth you think you've found, you must never give up the search. It's a mistake to think that your search is over. Although you may have come to some truth, there is always the Ultimate Truth for which to strive.

*

Reb Noson wrote many discourses on the topic of truth and true leadership (excerpts appear below in the chapter "Tzaddik"). However, you're mistaken if you think that it's easy to find the truth. Reb Noson said of Mashiach, in whose time the Ultimate Truth will be revealed: Mashiach will have more difficulty convincing the chassidim of his identity, than the atheists. He will perform one miracle and all the atheists will believe in him, but the chassidim.... (Siach Sarfei Kodesh 1-525). He implies that we all have so much "truth" and "faith" in our own way of life, that we might never accept the Mashiach if he were to tell us that the truth lay elsewhere.

* * *

5

FAITH

"We have to tremble with fear when considering God's greatness. The whole world is filled with His Glory!" Rebbe Nachman repeated this to us many times. He wanted to instill in us a feeling for God's greatness and a feeling for how much faith we ought to have in Him (*Tzaddik* #414).

Rebbe Nachman said: I believe that God is great. He is very great. He is Omnipotent. I believe He can turn a triangle into a square! (*Tzaddik* #407).

Rebbe Nachman teaches: Faith is like a beautiful palace with many beautiful rooms. One enters and wanders about from room to room, from hallway to hallway...From there one walks on in Trust...then further and further. How fortunate is he who walks in faith! (*Tzaddik* #420).

*

Rebbe Nachman said that "Others consider faith a minor thing. But I consider it an extremely great thing" (*Rabbi Nachman's Wisdom* #33). When the Rebbe told Reb Noson to record his own discourses, he said to him, "In your writings, every word should be measured. But when you come to the topic of faith, let your pen flow!" (*Rabbi Eliyahu Chaim Rosen*). The importance of faith is unparalleled. Without it, we cannot enter the realm of Torah or mitzvot. With it, we can attain the highest of levels.

But, what actually is faith? Why is it so necessary? When is it applicable and where should this faith be placed? How can we attain faith? Questions, questions, questions. We all have them. Aren't we entitled to at least some of the answers?

Since Rebbe Nachman attributes great importance to faith, it stands to reason that there must be a wealth of information in Breslov writings on this topic. And there is. In this chapter, we will attempt to present a composite picture of what faith is: the value of attaining complete, yet simple faith; the power of faith; how we can acquire this faith within ourselves; the parameters of faith (in God, in Torah and mitzvot, in the Tzaddikim and even in ourselves). We will also explore Rebbe Nachman's view of secularism and atheism, while offering advice on how we can remain steadfast in faith despite the currents of today's fast-paced, ever-changing world. Also discussed is faith and trust as they relate to a major area of our daily lives — our financial dealings.

* * *

WHAT IS FAITH?

Faith is the foundation of the world; more specifically it is the fundamental principle of Judaism, Torah, and even of man himself. There is no one alive who doesn't have faith in something or someone. Throughout life, we are forever being asked to corroborate that faith. "Do I have faith in my spouse, my neighbor, my child? Are they deserving of my trust? Do I have to have faith at all?" Well, what choice do we really have? Faith is an attribute without which we cannot survive in this world.

But what is faith? What is this trust that I place in others? First of all, we must "define" faith — see how it is used and expressed in Judaism. Faith applies to that which we don't know or cannot understand. We don't need faith to say that the four-legged piece of wood in front of us is a table, or the four walls surrounding us are a room. We see it. We know it. And we don't need faith to be convinced that if we stick our finger in the fire we're going to get burnt. We feel it. We know it. Faith becomes necessary only when we cannot directly experience the object with our senses or understand the reason for doing something. When told to do something a certain way by his mother, a child will say, "Why do I have to do it this way?" Inevitably his mother's answer is "Because!" This is the celebrated "Because" of faith. "Because I'm the mommy, that's why!" She expects her son to have faith in her; faith that as his mother she knows what is best for him. In essence, she would like him to put his trust in her that she understands what he, as a child, cannot.

However, as we grow older many of us don't know how to believe or what there is to believe in. We shrug off the faith of our childhood, considering it to be no more than the expression of immature thinking and a lack of sophistication. This leaves us wondering where to place our faith and for this we need guidance.

The Revelation at Mount Sinai took place. It is an historical fact. Moshe went up to Heaven and brought down the Torah. He, the True Tzaddik, saw what was available and acceptable, and gave it to us to guide us through our lives in this world. The same is true of all the Tzaddikim. They received the Torah from Moshe (*Avot* 1:1) and transmitted it as a heritage, from generation to generation, until this very day. Rebbe Nachman compares the Tzaddik to a mother: "The Torah is compared to milk and the Tzaddik nurses the Jews with the light of his Torah" (*Likutey Moharan* I, 4:8). Just as a mother knows what is good for her child, the Tzaddikim know what is good for the Jews.

*

For a better understanding of this chapter and these concepts, consider the following quote from Rebbe Nachman and part of a discourse from *Likutey Halakhot* concerning faith and intellect.

The Rebbe teaches: Regarding those things which God granted the human mind the ability to understand, it is a great mitzvah to sharpen one's intellect and comprehension so as to understand them clearly. However, for those things which the human mind cannot comprehend, one must rely totally on faith (*Likutey Moharan* I, 62:2).

Reb Noson writes: The essence of everything in this world can be seen in its "face." Just as man is instantly recognizable by his face, so too, everything in existence can be recognized by its face. This can be understood in business, where we first look to see what's on the "surface" of the deal — is the merchandise good, the price reasonable, etc. Only afterwards, if the thing looks good, do we start to read the fine print. In this sense, the "face" relates to truth, for we can rarely "dress up" the true value of an item. This is why when a merchant is honest and the merchandise he is selling is priced accordingly, he has an "enlightened face." His face discloses his inner truth.

"Shema Yisrael...God is One." The truth is one. There can be countless lies, but the truth can only be one. Anyone who looks for the truth will see God everywhere. This is, in fact, man's mission in this world — to seek out the truth — God — wherever he goes.

But this truth cannot be attained, until we have faith. Faith is the most important prerequisite for achieving truth. The entire world operates on faith. For example: When pricing merchandise you're interested in purchasing, you ask the price. Do you buy it? If you believe that merchant's price is fair, you do. If you suspect there's something wrong and don't trust the merchant, you don't. The same rules of faith apply whether we are talking about purchasing a house, commodities and stocks, or milk and bread from the grocer.

How about accepting someone's check? Do you trust that it will be covered? Wherever you turn, you must have faith in the people you deal with — otherwise, no deal. Unless you have faith and trust in others, you cannot survive in business.

In whom should we have faith? In whom do we put our trust? In someone we consider truthful and honest. No matter how wise and intelligent a person may be, ultimately he must place his faith in someone else. Even chairmen of multi-conglomerate boards must place their faith in their assistants' reports — in the work of people they trust. Thus, all business is ultimately conducted through faith and trust.

Where does this faith come from? As with everything else in this world, it has its roots in a supernal concept above. The faith needed in order to succeed in even the mundane world of business stems from a pure faith in truth, in God. Thus the prophet says of this spiritual faith (Habakkuk 2:4), "The righteous man shall live by his faith." Faith is the foundation of all. With it, we can seek the absolute truth and come to recognize God from and within everything in the world.

Yet, the fact is that not everyone knows which is the best investment, which is the best merchandise to purchase. Actually, very few people do; and even then, we see that only a limited number succeed. Most people do not. The Talmud teaches: "No one knows in which field [of business] he will prosper" (Pesachim 54b). Even with the best intentions, not everyone has the right advisers or devoted truthful friends, who can counsel him how properly to invest and profit. Most people fail to grasp all the intricacies of business, especially when the transactions are conducted in distant lands, and they lack expert advice.

In Torah, however, we were — and still are — very fortunate. Moshe Rabeinu, our True Shepherd, brought us the Torah from Heaven, from God. He visited the "distant land," saw the truth with his own eyes, and brought us the means of success. He was loyal to the Jews: he fought for them, battled for them, and when they sinned before God he stood by them, even offering his own life on behalf of all the Jews. Moshe brought us the means of serving God, the "merchandise" — Torah and mitzvot. By believing in him, by accepting Moshe as a true and loyal friend, we can engage in our search for the absolute truth. Our merchandise is tzitzit, tefilin, Shabbat, Torah, prayer, charity, kindness, etc. With this "merchandise" we can find our prosperity and success.

Furthermore, we do not have to understand it fully. We can rely on Moshe Rabeinu and trust his judgment, that what he gave us is the right advice. Even if we do not fully understand it, it will become clear later on. That is the beauty of having a true and loyal friend upon whom we *can* rely.

Conversely, if we decide we have to understand everything absolutely clearly before jumping into a deal, how will we ever succeed? How will we ever accomplish anything? We'll always wonder if someone isn't pulling the wool over our eyes, always question if the price is right, and so on. Ever notice how quickly successful businessmen move when, after reading the reports and consulting their friends, they feel the deal is right? Imagine what would happen if they tried to ponder every single factor, if they attempted to weigh every detail carefully. They'd never close a deal! By the time they finished making their assessment, the seller would have gone elsewhere or the market would have disappeared.

When it comes to Torah, however, we have the word of our true and loyal friend, Moshe Rabeinu. He brought us the Torah. He gave us the merchandise — i.e. the means to succeed in this world. He knew. He was in Heaven and saw exactly which merchandise is worth investing in. If we have faith — faith in Moshe Rabeinu, faith in the true Tzaddikim — we can — and will — succeed.

Whoever believes in truth is attached to the truth. Truth and faith go together, hand in hand. Each supports and strengthens the other. By believing in the Torah, we draw upon ourselves the truth of the Torah. Though we may not yet understand what we are doing, it will become clear to us as we study and progress in Judaism. But first, we must believe. We must have faith (adapted from *Likutey Halakhot, Giluach* 4:1-3).

* * *

COMPLETE, YET SIMPLE FAITH

Rebbe Nachman often told us how fortunate we were because Moshe showed us the right way. He began the Torah without any philosophical proof, with the simple words (Genesis 1:1): "In the beginning God created...." We are commanded to believe in God through faith alone, and not enter into speculation (*Rabbi Nachman's Wisdom* #5).

God is One. Simple in concept. Therefore, faith in Him should be kept simple, without sophistication. In addition, Rebbe Nachman taught that the main faith is simple faith (*Rabbi Nachman's Wisdom* #32). It is the innocent faith of the ordinary people (*Rabbi Nachman's Wisdom* #33).

When Rebbe Nachman was in Lemberg (1808), he heard someone say, "The old, old, old, God!" Rebbe Nachman found these words very inspiring. He would refer to this time and time again, and on each occasion he would repeat the words "old, old, old" over and over again. The Rebbe's purpose was clear: We should believe in God with full simplicity that He is the Ancient One — older than the oldest. Our faith is very ancient, an inheritance from our earliest ancestors, the holy patriarchs. It has not appeared recently, nor is it the fruits of someone's ideas, but stems from the very beginning of the existence of the world (*Tzaddik* #413).

*

How does faith work? Do I follow someone blindly? Completely? Or will partial faith do? Must I have faith only in a proven path? Or can I choose where to place my faith? Good question. Very good. There is no one single answer.

Who would think of teaching advanced algebra or calculus to a five-year-old? We teach him one, then one plus one, then simple addition and subtraction. As the child develops his understanding of mathematics, we can proceed to multiplication, division and fractions. Then on to algebra, geometry, trigonometry, etc. Instead of starting with calculus, we start with one. With this foundation established, we build the mathematical structure stage by stage, until we have explained the entire picture.

With faith, it is much the same. What do we really understand about God? About Judaism? So we begin with one. One God. He exists. But we have questions. To answer them and the other questions that inevitably arise, we must learn some basics. So we begin to study. Once our knowledge has grown, we are ready to go on to higher levels. However, as in the study of mathematics, all faith ultimately rests upon One. We must strengthen our faith. We now believe in God, in the One. Then we study more. We grow in knowledge. But again we must return to the basic faith of believing in God. And so it goes.

In order to begin, our faith must be blind. What do we know? We accept God. But, we know nothing of Him or how to recognize Him. So, we start to study the Torah, His teachings, His word. The Torah reveals God's will, God's ideals and how we can approach them. As we grow, our faith grows with us. No longer is it blind faith, for we have attained some knowledge of God. But as our knowledge grows, we come to reflect upon a greater level of Godliness — one previously unknown to us. Lacking the means for understanding this new perception, we revert to faith. Our faith helps us transcend all obstacles that, otherwise, may have prevented our comprehension of this level. Then we study more and gain more knowledge. The cycle then repeats itself. Our perceptions grow, we gain greater levels of understanding, but we must again revert to simple faith to carry us even higher.

Rebbe Nachman teaches: It is necessary to have knowledge together with faith. One who has only faith is likely to fall from his level. He *must* [combine his faith] with knowledge (*Likutey Moharan* I, 255). (Though the lesson is about faith in the Tzaddikim, it is equally applicable to all aspects of faith). When combined, faith and knowledge complement each other. We must begin with faith, otherwise we lack the foundation upon which to stand. Yet, knowledge is also a necessity. Without it, we can never be certain that our faith is not, God forbid, misplaced. The only way to determine this is by our constant search for truth. As we become increasingly more knowledgeable, we will be able to discern where the truth is located. This is the knowledge that supports faith.

Complete faith is a must, it has to be immediately nourished with knowledge. Faith and then knowledge, faith and then knowledge; over and over again. Judaism is a proven path. It has outlasted all of its oppressors over many millennia. However, Judaism requires faith, strong faith, solid faith. But aren't there different paths in Judaism? Yes, so choose one and begin to study. Study and study, gain more and more knowledge, but without slackening in faith. Search for the truth. Have patience. There are many paths in Torah. Seek, and go about your search with a combination of faith and knowledge. Eventually, you'll arrive at your right address.

Thus, Rebbe Nachman teaches: Torah study has the power to direct a person with the proper and correct advice in all of his endeavors. It is vitally important to have faith in the Tzaddikim. Then, by studying their words, the Torah will guide him to his proper course in life (*Likutey Moharan* I, 61:1).

* * *

THE POWER OF FAITH

Rebbe Nachman teaches: The Jews are called *IVRim*-עברים because their faith enables them to *oVeR*-עובר (pass over) all the difficulties, all the wisdoms and pseudo-wisdoms which they encounter (*Likutey Moharan* I, 64:2).

The world is a very, very narrow bridge. The main thing is not to be afraid! (*Likutey Moharan* II, 48). Faith keeps us sure-footed on this narrow bridge of life, enabling us to face its challenges and cross over safely to the other side.

With faith, survival is always possible. Even if, God forbid, we are visited with suffering, we can always find consolation in God. This is possible because we believe in Him and trust that whatever He does, He does for our ultimate benefit. On the other hand, a person without faith has no life. As long as things appear to be going okay, his life seems to be in order. But, as usually happens, difficulties and hardships develop, and then he has nowhere to turn. Having no faith to rely upon, his life turns very bitter. The only way to overcome every obstacle is with faith (*Rabbi Nachman's Wisdom* #32).

When one has simple faith in God, one can achieve a very great level of spiritual awareness, a level that is above even great wisdom (*Rabbi Nachman's Wisdom* #32).

Who can say that he has complete faith? Were a person to believe that God listens to every single word his lips utter, he would certainly pray with a tremendous level of concentration and intensity (*Likutey Moharan* I, 62:2). How many of us are on this level? Thus, there is always room for growth in faith.

Rebbe Nachman once said, "Through faith a person can reach such a great state of longing that he goes beyond himself and doesn't know what he is longing for [i.e. he attains a level higher than the one he is on] (*Tzaddik* #425).

"Believe," said Rebbe Nachman, "that if you can spoil, then you can also repair" (*Likutey Moharan* II, 112). This in itself is a most powerful statement. Why do we question ourselves when we think we committed a sin? Because we believe that we made a mistake and this will produce negative results. We are apprehensive. We fret. We may even worry. All because we *believe* it to be wrong. This shows that we already have a degree of faith within us! If so, said the Rebbe, since you already have faith in yourself, then believe that just as you spoiled something, you *can* rectify it (*Likutey Halakhot, Eiruvey Techumin* 5:35).

* * *

BUILDING ONE'S FAITH

Faith is linked to and dependent upon the mouth, as is written, "I will make known Your faith with my mouth" (Psalms 89:2). If a person talks about faith — saying that he wants to believe or speaks words of belief — then his faith is strengthened (*Likutey Moharan* II, 44). By the same token, we must be careful not to utter words contrary to faith, even in jest, for it can bring a person to atheism, God forbid (*Likutey Moharan* II, 44).

Over and over again a person should say to himself: I believe in God! I believe in God! Repeating these words helps instill in us the inherent faith that we all so desperately need. Reb Noson used to say that the more a person repeats something, the more it is embedded in his mind and heart (*Rabbi Eliyahu Chaim Rosen*). Repeat words of *emunah* (faith) to yourself, your family, your friends. Even if it has no effect on them, it *will* have a positive effect on you.

Conversely, we should never utter a word of wickedness. We should never say that we will commit a sin or be wicked, even though we have no intention of carrying out our words. The power of speech is so powerful, it can eventually lead a person to sin. Yeihu was anointed king of the Ten Tribes. He was to replace Achav, a devoted idolator. To convince the Jewish people, who were themselves trapped in idolatry, that they should follow him, Yeihu said: "Achav served [the idols] a little, but Yeihu will serve a lot" (2 Kings 10:18). Though at the time Yeihu was God-fearing, and had absolutely no intention of ever serving idolatry, he did eventually fall victim to his own words. We therefore see the importance of not speaking words of wickedness (*Rabbi Nachman's Wisdom* #237).

A person's faith should be so solid that he sees the thing in which he believes — right there in front of his eyes (*Likutey Moharan* I, 62:4). Believing *is* seeing! Believing in something strongly can bring us to a level of understanding as great as if we saw the thing with our own eyes. Therefore, to attain faith, we should speak it and about it; avoiding its opposite at all costs, even if our true intention is to mock the heretical ideas of the non-believers. We should yearn for faith, and we should constantly pray to attain it.

* * *

THE PARAMETERS OF FAITH

Faith in God. What does it mean to have faith in God? The list is endless. We present here some of the more necessary and basic aspects of faith:

— Faith that God is One. There is no other besides Him.

— Faith that God is King. He is our Ruler.

— Faith that God oversees us with Divine Providence.

— Faith that God listens to and accepts our prayers.

— Faith that God is good. Whatever happens to us is for our good.

Faith in Torah and mitzvot. "All Your mitzvot are faith" (Psalms 119:86). Faith also means faith in the Torah: the Written Law and the Oral Law. The Talmud teaches: Whoever says that he accepts all of Torah, save one single law that he

doesn't accept as coming from God through Moshe — he is
a heretic (Sanhedrin 99a).

*

Regarding the incense of the Holy Temple, if honey were
put into it, no one would be able to take the sweetness
of the fragrance. Why don't we put honey in? Because the
Torah commands us (Leviticus 2:11), "Do not put honey on
the altar" (Daily Liturgy). A Breslover Chassid by the name of
Reb Yisrael Starpachik would recite the daily prayers with
great enthusiasm and intensity. It once happened that Reb
Pinchas of Kublitch, a Sqverer Chassid (then opponents to
the Breslover Chassidim), came upon Reb Yisrael as he was
reciting the liturgical words which relate the laws of the
incense sacrifice. Reb Pinchas was awed as he listened to
Reb Yisrael: "Sweetness of the fragrance...The smell would
be incredibly wonderful. Then why don't we allow ourselves
to put some honey in? Because the Torah commands us...
The Torah commands us... The Torah commands us...." The
fervor and inspiration that flowed from Reb Yisrael's prayers
— prayers which he offered with such simplicity and faith in
the Torah's meaning and message — influenced Reb Pinchas
to become a Breslover Chassid (Rabbi Nachman Burstein).

There are many things that we might do, devotional practices
of all sorts, which would seemingly add to our service to God.
Be careful! If these things appear nowhere in the Torah or in
the teachings of the Rabbis, putting them into practice would
be a mistake. Only the Torah can provide us with the correct
parameters for dealing with and facing life. For this reason,
we must place great emphasis on simply observing Torah
laws. By having faith in Torah and mitzvot we will see the
importance of adhering to the Torah, the positive influence
it has on our lives, as opposed to those who seek new ways
and as a result witness how their ensuing generations fall
away from God, Torah and Judaism.

The Rebbe said, "How can someone who wants to be a Jew study the works built on the tenets of acknowledged atheists? To develop faith one should study only those works written by the Tzaddikim — Talmud, Midrash, Zohar, etc. — for they are all rooted in the Torah that we received at Sinai through Moshe (*Tzaddik* #410).

We must believe that there are very deep secrets connected with performing the mitzvot of the Torah that we received from Moshe, though we do not understand them (*Tzaddik* #411). Have faith, "keep the faith," and eventually the world of Torah will open up for you and you'll begin to understand more of God and Torah.

Faith in the Tzaddikim. "And they believed in God and in His servant Moshe" (Exodus 14:31). The Midrash says: "Whoever believes in God is as if he believes in the the true shepherd, Moshe, and whoever believes in the true shepherd is as if he believes in God, Creator of the world" (*Mekhilta, BeShalakh*).

The Talmud teaches: The Torah is acquired by means of forty-eight qualities. One of these is faith in the Tzaddikim" (*Avot* 6:6). The vast majority of these qualities focus on one's diligence and efforts in pursuing Torah study and rectifying bad character traits. However, innocuously placed in the middle of the forty-eight is faith in Tzaddikim. The Tzaddikim are the ones who transmit the Torah to us, so without faith in their teachings we will never be able to acquire the Torah. That being so, of what value is intellectual pursuit and diligent study?

Thus, an integral part of achieving faith in God is having faith in the Tzaddikim. Given our complex and ever-changing world, how can we ever hope to choose what is right, what is correct — in the mundane and in the sacred? For this, we need the Tzaddikim. These righteous individuals — who have risen above the physical restraints and limitations of the human mind — they know. We can rely on them; much in the same way as a child relies on a parent whom he looks up to as all-knowing.

*

"Most seamen are *chassidim*" (*Kiddushin* 82a). "This is because they are in constant danger and are always turning to God" (*Rashi, ad. loc.*)

A weathered sea captain will not trust a novice to navigate his ship. His training at the helm is something which the beginner cannot hope to match. Yet, occasionally, even seasoned captains need assistance from masters who have even more experience than they. Then again, there are times when even the most experienced of ship-masters encounters waves and turbulence which render him helpless. He then has no choice but to turn to God for help.

Survival in this world is similar to navigating on the sea. Just as it is physically impossible for man to survive in the water and dangerous when sailing upon it, so too, it is impossible to survive in the "sea of knowledge" and dangerous for him to navigate across it without the proper tools. These tools are the advice we receive from the Tzaddikim who guide us on the proper path.

We can relate this to the crossing of the Red Sea. The Jews believed in Moshe, the Tzaddik, and followed him across. The impassable sea was split for them, its waters rising like walls to separate between one tribe and the next. This was symbolic of each being guided through the sea — the "sea of knowledge" — in accordance with his own level of wisdom and understanding. Pharaoh, on the other hand, did not have any belief. Yet he felt that he had the tools with which to cross the sea. He discovered otherwise. Being ill-equipped to handle the turbulent sea, the walls of water came crashing down upon him and his Egyptian army (*Likutey Halakhot, Netilat Yadayim Li'Seudah* 6:39).

Rebbe Nachman said, "From me you can begin to get a glimpse of God's greatness" (*Tzaddik* #284). A Tzaddik is one who has attained Torah and has acquired *Ruach haKodesh* (the holy spirit). Through our faith in the Tzaddikim, their holiness can descend upon us and help us achieve greatness in spirituality. Even the mere mentioning of their names helps us draw from their holiness (*Likutey Halakhot, Netilat Yadayim li'Seudah* 4:6).

...and faith in oneself. When a person's faith is lacking, he must expend a lot of exertion in his devotions to God (*Likutey Moharan* II, 86). Reb Noson writes that when Rebbe Nachman addressed this lesson to him, he was quite shocked. "I always thought of myself as having faith," said Reb Noson, who could not understand the Rebbe's implication. When he mentioned this to the Rebbe, Rebbe Nachman said to him, "You may have faith, but you have no faith in yourself!" (*Rabbi Nachman's Wisdom* #140).

From Rebbe Nachman's remark we learn that a lack of confidence in oneself is also a lack of faith. Said positively: Faith also means self-faith. This manifests in a number of ways.

— To believe that I, as an individual, am very important in God's eyes.

— To believe that no matter how far I may be from God, I have the power to return.

— To believe that no matter how I presently conduct my life, I have the inner strength to change my habits.

— To believe that I, too, have the ability to become a Tzaddik.

— To have the self-confidence necessary in dealing with others.

Reb Noson writes: While it is true that "All beginnings are difficult" (*Mekhilta, Yitro*) — know, one who nears completion of a certain devotion to God encounters even greater difficulties (*Likutey Halakhot, Masa U'Matan* 3:6). However, each of us has tremendous inner strength and we can always finish — provided we really and truly desire to. All it takes is the willpower to complete the devotion. Everyone has this willpower. It just needs to be drawn out of us (*Likutey Halakhot, Masa U'Matan* 3:6).

There are Tzaddikim who face opposition because they lack faith in themselves, or in the original Torah insights which they reveal. Since they do not believe that their insights have worth in God's eyes, they themselves are lackadaisical about their insights. However, the strife which comes their way forces them to study their ways and this reminds them of their true worth (*Likutey Moharan* I, 61:5). Thus, Rebbe Nachman makes it clear that by lacking self-confidence, a person causes his own difficulties.

*

We are often confused about the best way to serve God. Sometimes we feel that one way is best, only later to be convinced that another way would be better. This can make us very confused. About this Rebbe Nachman said, "Why confuse yourself? Whatever you do, you do. As long as you don't do any evil!" (*Rabbi Nachman's Wisdom* #269).

The Rebbe himself served God this way: he would pick a certain path in his devotions and for a number of months never wavered from that path. Even if other possibilities crossed his mind, he would ignore them and follow only the path he had chosen. After having spent some time serving God that way, he would evaluate his objectives and achievements. Only then would he decide whether or not to make a change (*Likutey Moharan* II, 115).

Evaluate a plan, make a decision and stick by it. Don't be wishy-washy every day. "Is it okay?" "Am I doing the right thing?" Have confidence in yourself that you have enough intelligence to choose a path and stick by it for a while. Otherwise you'll never get started. And remember, you can *always* change.

Faith has different levels. Most faith resides in the heart, but the main level is the one in which faith extends throughout one's entire body. This is why, after washing our hands for bread before the meal, we raise our hands opposite our face — to draw holiness (*Sha'ar HaMitzvot, Ekev*). How can we draw this holiness? Only by having the faith that our actions have the power to draw this faith (*Likutey Moharan* I, 91).

Rebbe Nachman teaches: A person must hold three types of "conversations" each day. One with God, one with his rabbi or spiritual mentor and one with a close friend. Each person has to awaken a good point within himself. He "converses with God" on this point. Then he brings it to potential by meditating and speaking about his weaknesses and strengths before God. Next, he must also draw from his friend's good point. This can be accomplished by conversing with him every day. The third point he must receive is the "general point," the good which is presently beyond his capabilities but which is found in people greater than he, i.e., his spiritual mentor (*Likutey Moharan* I, 34:8).

Thus, if we have faith — in God, in the Tzaddikim and in ourselves — we can always find an outlet for our emotions and feelings, always find ways to better ourselves and repair any wrongdoings of the past. We can better face the future, knowing that we stand on a very solid foundation of faith.

* * *

WHAT ABOUT SECULAR WISDOM AND ATHEISM?

Rabbi Yishmael's nephew asked him, "Seeing as I have already studied the entire Torah, am I allowed to study Greek philosophies?" Rabbi Yishmael answered, "Yes, but only during that hour which is neither day nor night!" (Menachot 99b).

On October 9, 1802, Czar Alexander I of Russia issued an *ukase*, to draft a set of regulations against the Jews. These were known as *punkten*, the points decrees, forebearers of the edicts for the forced conscription of Jews into the Czar's army and compulsory secular education. Of these two decrees, Rebbe Nachman particularly feared the secular education law, for, as he declared, it would destroy future generations of Jews (see Until The Mashiach, Historical Overview; Rabbi Nachman's Wisdom #131; Tzaddik #127, #132).

Once, when discussing these decrees, the Rebbe cried, "Woe to us! that we do not even think about the welfare of our children — what will happen to them and their future generations. They will be drowned in the flood of heresies which is spreading so quickly because of our sins!" (Tzaddik #417).

*

Many people have asked: Why does Rebbe Nachman reject outright all forms of philosophy and secular wisdoms, while placing so much emphasis on faith? Especially in this "enlightened" age, can't we assume that we can come up with the right answers?

Let's first make it quite clear that Rebbe Nachman is amongst the foremost exponents of our using our God-given intellectual capacities to the very best of our abilities. Did he not make this quite clear right in the very first lesson of *Likutey Moharan* where the Rebbe says, "A person must use his intellect to the *fullest* in order to find God in all aspects of Creation?" This is something we should do daily, in any situation we face — to find God everywhere. We can do this only if we have a broad enough knowledge to understand how Godliness can exist in everything. Furthermore, if we were to delve deeply into the *Likutey Moharan*, we would find that virtually every lesson talks about the importance of *da'at* (knowledge) and how one must seek to find and develop it.

Secondly, Rebbe Nachman is not rejecting a person's right to seek a livelihood. He, as well as all our talmudic Sages and Codifiers, appreciated the importance of being able to support one's family. However, in the world of secular knowledge there are many, many questions which have no answers; at least no answers which the human mind can comprehend. Man, by definition, is limited: limited in depth of intelligence and limited in length of life. It is, therefore, impossible to answer those questions which pertain to the Source of Creation, for such questions, by definition, relate to the Infinite. These questions and answers are in the realm of *makif* (surrounding) — remaining above human intellect. Many times, when a person asks a question, he also formulates an answer in his mind. This answers the question, but then there emerges another question, one which had previously been a *makif*. It too is given an answer. And so it goes: another question, another answer. One must be very careful in answering these questions, as there exists certain questions which are above human capacity to answer. These questions must remain unanswered, or they will have a negative influence on one's faith (*Likutey Moharan* II, 7:6-8). Elsewhere the Rebbe tells us that a person who has sinned is bound to be constantly bothered by these questions (*Rabbi Nachman's Wisdom* #32).

Rebbe Nachman knew that each word of philosophy not directing us towards God, will automatically propel us away from God. There is no question here of having the "best of both worlds." The two concepts, faith and philosophy, are mutually exclusive. In the study of Torah we are taught to question and to challenge. We just have to observe a single session of talmudic *pilpul* to realize just how much questioning takes place over even a single page of Torah. But there are limitations on what the human mind can conjecture and comprehend. This is the power of faith. Today, we do not understand. Tomorrow? Perhaps. We *accept* in good faith until we are able to understand.

Philosophy, on the other hand, is founded upon the premise that constant questioning is desirable; it teaches that whatever is not understood, need not be accepted. It refuses to acknowledge the limitations of the human mind. But, man is limited. Scientists have spent millions of hours and billions of dollars trying to figure out Creation and all they have are contradictory theories. It is these wasted theories on the nature of life, theories and ideas that challenge the very existence of God — yet lead only to more speculation — to which Rebbe Nachman is vehemently opposed.

*

Thus, Rebbe Nachman warned: I will reveal a secret. A wave of atheism is coming that will engulf the world. I know that my followers will strengthen themselves in faith, even without this revelation. But there might be others who heed this call and will be strengthened by it. It is for their sake that I reveal the future (*Rabbi Nachman's Wisdom* #35). Many times the Rebbe would sigh and groan over the troubles wrought by the spread of atheism. He said that this is how the Jews are going to be tested prior to the coming of Mashiach. One might think that it would be easy to withstand the test of faith, since many, many Tzaddikim also foresaw the forthcoming wave of atheism and warned against it. However the temptations and tests will be so great, that no matter how much a person is aware that he's being confronted with a test, the waves of atheism will still rise against him (*Rabbi Nachman's Wisdom* #220).

Rebbe Nachman teaches: A person's sins bring him to heresy (*The Aleph-Bet Book,* Faith A:22). Elsewhere he says: The heresy in a person destroys his desire to study Torah (*Aleph-Bet Book,* Torah Study A:77). Entering the realm of philosophy places us in a very vicious cycle. If we sin, we bring heresy into ourselves. This heresy destroys our desire for Torah so that we begin to shun, even reject, the all-important influence which Torah should have on our lives. This leads to further sin, which brings us to further heresies, which in turn distance us still further from God.

* * *

REMAINING A JEW

Rebbe Nachman was against philosophy and secular wisdom which teach a person to question God and lead him to atheistic idelogies. These philosophies have been around for thousands of years, yet not one good Jew has resulted from these "wisdoms" (see Rabbi Nachman's Wisdom #5).

The root of man is spiritual, but once he descends into this physical world man tends to lean to the physical "wisdoms." When these thoughts take root in a person's mind, they grow and occupy space. How can we then expect to find God, find spirituality, if we have descended into the depths of atheism? (Likutey Moharan I, 35:1).

The reason we seek "wisdoms" has to do with the fact that Supernal Wisdom is the source of all Creation; as in (Psalms 104:24), "All was created with wisdom." We are actually seeking our source however, we should seek our *proper* source (Likutey Moharan I, 35:1). Wisdom and intellectual achievements should not be seen as a goal unto themselves. Rather, they should be a vehicle for bringing us to the Source of wisdom — God Himself — and not a vehicle that distances us from Him.

As explained earlier, faith applies only when we cannot understand. Through study and prayer we come to understand more of God and His greatness, and can *know* more about Him. However, the key to the gate of understanding is only faith. Without this key, we can never attain true wisdom (Likutey Halakhot, Netilat Yadayim li'Seudah 6:1).

And, even if we have slipped and fallen into atheism and heresy, we must never give up. "I have sunk so far, how will I ever return?" "How will I ever be able to cleanse my mind?" Reb Noson said, "No matter what I hear from a Jew's lips — even things that are not in accordance with our faith — I know that deep in his heart, he will always be a Jew" (*Kokhavey Or,* p. 79 #35). The faith each one of us has in the inner recesses of his soul is forever. We must draw from this inner faith and keep on drawing from it, again and again. Eventually, we will attain pure faith.

*

A person once came to Rebbe Nachman complaining about the problems and questions he had in regard to faith. He felt that he wanted to serve God and have faith in Him, but doubts kept returning. The Rebbe said to him, "All Creation came into being because of people like yourself. God saw that there would be people who will have to struggle, sometimes against all odds, in order to maintain their faith. For these people God created the world (*Rabbi Nachman's Wisdom* #222).

Rabbi Zvi Aryeh Rosenfeld began disseminating Breslover Chassidut in America in the late 1940s. Throughout the many years that he taught, he would always speak of the importance of faith. He succeeded in instilling this faith into hundreds, perhaps thousands, of people. Rabbi Zvi Aryeh would always say that the first step in teaching Judaism is faith. With faith, one can recognize the true beauty of Judaism. He will then understand that he can be a Jew, and how much he can rise and elevate himself in this world. But without faith, a person is nowhere. Thus, Rebbe Nachman teaches, "Whoever has no faith, his life is not a life!" (*Rabbi Nachman's Wisdom* #32). My Rosh Yeshivah would say, "Whoever has faith has no questions; whoever has no faith never has answers" (*Rabbi Eliyahu Chaim Rosen*).

*

"Why does Rebbe Nachman express such resistance to philosophy?" a friend of mine in New York asked. Typically, I answered with a question of my own:

"Do you push your young child to get good grades in elementary school?"
"Yes, of course!"

"For what purpose?" I wanted to know.
"So he can get an education."

"What will he do with it?"
"Go on to college," my friend answered with an air of certainty.

"For what purpose?"
"So he can live his life as well as possible. Earn a living. Pay his bills. Provide a comfortable life for himself and his family."

"Sounds logical," I said, reasoning out loud. "You start the child off from a young age and instill in him educational values during his sixteen or more years in school. Then, from when he's about twenty, he is able to provide for himself, his family and maybe contribute to society for a period of forty or fifty years.

"Only one more question. How long do you want your son to be Jewish?!"

Rebbe Nachman's whole being was Judaism. He thought it and lived it. And therefore, Judaism is what he stressed. Anything that might alienate a person from Judaism, he rejected. Look how much emphasis is placed today on general education. Yet there are people who consider just a few hours of Jewish schooling a week sufficient, expecting that this will be enough for their children to remain true to Judaism and Jewish values for a lifetime.

* * *

FAITHFUL EARNINGS

The Talmud teaches: These are the obligations of a father to a son: "...teach him Torah; teach him a trade..." (*Kiddushin* 29a).

Teaching one's child a trade or profession is an obligatory, not an elective, responsibility. It is incumbent upon a father to teach his child how to earn a living honestly. Included in this obligation is the need for teaching him to have faith. With faith, he will be able to stand up to monetary temptations which promote dishonesty. With faith, he will be able to bear the sometimes incredible pressures and demands that business and work place upon his shoulders. And with faith, he will make sure to keep the Shabbat and Festivals, and make time for Torah study and prayer.

Rebbe Nachman teaches: The lust for money is idolatry. All idolatries in the world are connected to money. The main test of faith is in business (*Likutey Moharan* I, 23:1,4). In the language of the Zohar: She entices them with wealth in this life, then kills them (*Tikkuney Zohar*, Addendum 3). This refers to the Evil One, who tempts people with wealth and the "good life" in this world and then buries them because they have nothing in their lives but the lust for money. Their days have gone by and they are left with only emptiness. They have no faith and so do not spend their time wisely on Torah and mitzvot (*Likutey Moharan* I, 23:end).

Money, or rather the lust for it, devours a person's life and time. Not only that, but the desire for money in itself creates the worst worries. It causes a person to worry at all times (*Likutey Moharan* I, 23:5).

Someone I know lost quite heavily in some property investments, but still had a few million dollars left in the bank. When I approached him for charity, he began complaining about his losses. Seeing the terrible frame of mind he was in, I consoled him and offered the following analogy. "Losing heavily is like having your house burgled. You'll never feel safe again." "That's right!" he exclaimed, relieved that I understood his situation. Actually, I felt great pity for him. His whole security was his money.

Imagine! He was left with enough money to live off the interest for the rest of his life. Yet he's been so shattered by his losses that he'll never again feel safe. Even having more than enough money to last him a few lifetimes cannot provide him with the security he seeks because he lacks faith.

*

"Earning one's livelihood is as difficult as splitting the Red Sea" (*Pesachim* 117a). Just as we cannot hope to split the Red Sea, so too, we cannot hope to control our income. However, just as it is nothing for God to split the Red Sea, so too, it is incredibly simple for Him to provide us with an income. We just need faith (*Likutey Moharan* I, 23:end).

*

When we have faith, then our livelihood is like receiving manna from Heaven — we can rely on Heaven to send it to us. This way, we are content with whatever we receive, and have no desire for more and more. Conversely, when a person does desire more than what he is given, he destroys his whole life with his desire for wealth, for there is no manna in that (*Likutey Halakhot, Netilat Yadayim li'Seudah* 6:85).

* * *

6

TORAH AND PRAYER

"Turn from evil and do good..." (Psalms 34:15).

Reb Gershon of Terhovitza once complained to Rebbe Nachman that it was difficult for him to serve God. The Rebbe answered him: "Just occupy yourself with doing good! The good will remain and the bad will fall away!" (*Tzaddik* #447).

There are very few mitzvot with which we can so totally and consistently occupy ourselves as with Torah study and prayer. Shabbat comes only once a week, the Festivals even less frequently. Giving charity and other acts of kindness are dependent upon having the opportunity and means to perform them. Even most daily mitzvot have specific times and constraints. Not so Torah study and prayer, in which a person can engage just about whenever and wherever he wants. Therefore, we find numerous selections of Rebbe Nachman's teachings dealing specifically with these two mitzvot. In addition, *vis-a-vis* the other mitzvot, both Torah and prayer serve a more comprehensive, encompassing purpose: without Torah study, it is impossible to know what to do, even when one wants to perform the mitzvot and without prayer, it is all but impossible to perform the mitzvot with complete joy and devotion.

"All that God has declared, we will do and we will hear!" (Exodus 24:7). Does this make sense? Who can do before he hears what has to be done? In this verse, the word "hear" means to understand. Thus, the Jews would first fulfill the mitzvot and then come to understand them. "When the Jews said: 'We will do and we will hear!' 600,000 angels descended and adorned each Jew with two crowns, one for *do* and one for *hear*" (*Shabbat* 88a). These two crowns correspond to Torah and prayer. Torah is that which is revealed to us, it is what we can *do*. Prayer corresponds to what we can hope to achieve, as we progress higher and higher in our understanding, in our ability to *hear* (*Likutey Moharan* I, 22:9).

*

Whenever Rabbi Nechunya entered the study hall he would recite a short prayer: "Please God, help me so that I do not err or be the cause of an error; let my colleagues rejoice with me; let me not issue an incorrect decision: ruling neither impure, pure, nor pure, impure; keep my colleagues from error; and let me rejoice with them." When leaving the study hall he would pray: "I thank You God that You cast my lot amongst those who sit in the study hall and haven't cast my lot amongst those who hang around idly chatting. I wake up and they wake up. I wake up to study Torah; they wake up to waste time. I labor and they labor. I labor and receive reward; they labor and receive no reward. I run and they run. I run towards the World to Come; they run towards the Pit of Waste" (*Berakhot* 28b).

Come see the beauty of our holy Torah! Rabbi Nechunya's short prayer contains all the teachings we've discussed in the previous chapters. When entering the study hall, he prayed a *simple* prayer. He asked that he and his friends *rejoice* with each other. In requesting that he not err, he was asking to be guided to the *truth*. He also requested this for his colleagues, because he saw their *good points* and wished them success in their studies as well. Then, when departing, he enforced his *faith* and prayed that he not join those who sit idly chattering

— those that do not have faith in Torah and in the World to Come. His prayers included these teachings, because they are the prerequisites for righteous Torah study and righteous prayer.

*

Reb Noson said that God gave us the Torah — the study of the laws of Torah — through Moshe Rabeinu. However, the Torah — the ways and means to actually feel and fulfill Torah — God gave us through Rebbe Nachman's teachings (*Kokhavey Or,* p. 69 #5). (Torah refers not only to the Bible and Mishnah, but also to all the holy teachings transmitted to us by our righteous teachers throughout the generations.)

Reb Noson also said that Rebbe Nachman's way brought together the virtuous qualities of both the chassidim and the mitnagdim. In general, the chassidim of his day were very steeped in prayer, but were not deeply involved with Torah study. The mitnagdim, on the other hand, were entirely given over to Torah study, but not very devoted to prayer. Rebbe Nachman placed emphasis on both: Torah and prayer (on each individually, and on the inter-connection between the two) (*Aveneha Barzel,* p. 52 #10).

*

Rebbe Nachman teaches: All the Torah that a person studies joins with his prayers to illuminate his words. Torah strengthens and renews prayer; prayer strengthens and renews Torah study (*Likutey Moharan* I, 2:6). The fountain of Torah flows from prayer (*Likutey Moharan* I, 8:7).

There are two types of prayer: praying for one's material needs and praying for one's spiritual needs. When prayer focuses on the material, it is on a far lower level than the study of Torah. However, when prayer focuses on the spiritual, it is on a higher level than Torah. Yaakov symbolizes the Written Law, Rachel the Oral Law and Leah, spiritual prayer. Yaakov

assumed that if he were to obtain a full understanding of
Torah, he would first have to combine the Written Law and
the Oral Law (marry Rachel). Prayer (Leah) would follow.
God knew otherwise and caused Yaakov to marry Leah first.
Achieving the pinnacle of Torah can only be accomplished
through prayer for one's spiritual needs (*Likutey Halakhot, Rosh
Chodesh* 5:29).

Thus, when someone asked the Rebbe how one becomes
a truly religious Jew, Rebbe Nachman indicated that the only
thing to do was to pray, and study, and pray (*Rabbi Nachman's
Wisdom* #287; *Siach Sarfei Kodesh* 1-220).

* * *

A FULL LIFE

There is much for a man to do in life. In order to ensure
survival, he has to prepare himself with a means for acquiring
food, clothing and shelter. After he marries, he has to provide
these necessities for his wife and family. Later, he has to
secure the future of his children, until, and sometimes even
after, they have married. Rebbe Nachman knew all this, yet he
said, "What does a person have to do in this world, but pray,
and study Torah, and pray?!" (*Rabbi Nachman's Wisdom* #287).

We can better understand this after we study the following
talmudic teaching: Eat bread with salt, drink but a measure of
water, sleep on the floor and live a life of suffering. If you do
this, then how fortunate you are, how good it will be for
you. Fortunate: in this world. Good for you: in the World to
Come. (*Avot* 6:4). *Fortunate?!* It's a *good life* when one eats
bread with salt?! You've got to be kidding!

Reb Noson explains this Mishnah with total simplicity. If a
person has as his goal a mansion to live in, choice cuisine at
every meal, the finest clothing, and so on, his life would be
very bitter indeed. How hard he would have to work, how
many long hours he would have to spend, just to have enough

money to pay for all these things. The vast majority of people work most of their lives for nothing more than the bare necessities. Imagine then what kind of workload is required in order to provide oneself with the "good life." And even when a person does devote — "sell" — himself to achieve these goals, will he ever get there? The odds are, he won't.

What's more, when a person does give himself over to such a goal, what time is left for Torah and prayer? How can he ever concentrate on praying in the morning when he has to get to work? How can he ever enjoy a life of Torah when all he has time to think about is money and livelihood?

It's totally different when a person dedicates his life to Torah and prayer. Then he always has time to live, be happy and find comfort. The person whose goal is to live a life of Torah will utilize his time, as best and as much as he can, for developing the spiritual. He limits his needs and is satisfied with his lot (with whatever he does and his achievements in life) and is content to spend any free time on Torah and prayer. By making his goal "bread and salt," he doesn't have to mortgage his life away for greed and lust. *He is indeed fortunate! He does have it good!* (*Rabbi Nachman's Wisdom* #308).

In another review of the above Mishnah, Reb Noson explains that the highest levels to which one can rise in spirituality are achieved by desire — the desire to attain the true goal. Of what use is all the money that a person can earn and save, if he doesn't have a decent relationship with his wife and children; something which unfortunately is only too often the case. Look what sacrifices such a person makes to "attain" his possessions! His desire for wealth leads him nowhere and he is left with strife, worry and depression. There is no pleasure in this world for the one who lusts for it. True pleasure is only felt by the one who is satisfied with his position. His life is considered life. His desires can be fulfilled (*Likutey Halakhot, Netilat Yadayim Li'Seudah* 6:64).

* * *

TIME FOR TORAH

One of Reb Noson's followers owned a small business from which he earned his living. But this man wanted very much to devote all his time and energy to studying Torah, and was ready to give up his means of livelihood in order to do it. Presenting his plan to Reb Noson, he was surprised that it did not meet with his mentor's approval. "Right now, your heart is burning with a desire and yearning for Torah. You're willing to accept the hardships of such a lifestyle. But what happens when this fire cools off? What will you eat then? Will you be able to accept the difficulties and remain happy? Let me suggest another approach. Before you go to your work each day, set aside time for Torah study. Aside from this, I would advise you to keep a collection of different Torah books in your store. Whenever you have a quiet moment make use of the time by studying. If you keep to these hours on a steady basis and still feel a burning desire for Torah, keep your store open an hour less and use that extra time for Torah study. Gradually increase your commitment to Torah and pray to God that He provide you with the freedom to learn full-time. Eventually you will succeed in overcoming the obstacles and be able to devote all your energy to Torah study. On the other hand, if you find that you cannot maintain the schedule, then at least you will have earned a living" (*Aveneha Barzel*, p. 49 #2).

*

When your goals are directed to Torah and spirituality, the work you do at your job is reckoned like the Thirty-Nine Works necessary in the building of the Tabernacle. This means that your every-day work and even the mundane things you do are considered holy. However, if you lack that faith and do not set your sights on holiness, then your work is reckoned like the Thirty-Nine Works of hard work and toil (*Likutey Moharan* I, 11:4).

Set your sights on Torah and prayer. Make them your goals. Everybody goes out to work, but it's your motive that counts. While some work the Thirty-Nine Works and have nothing more to show for it than a life spent acquiring material gratification, others, though apparently engaged in the very same Thirty-Nine Works, have built themselves a holy tabernacle.

Above all, remember: The thing that counts most is your desire. What is it that you *want* to achieve; not what you have or haven't succeeded in achieving. This is true in general, and all the more so when your goals are aimed at spiritual achievements. As Rebbe Nachman said: The main thing is desire — the desire to serve God. There is no one who can say that he serves God according to His greatness and awesomeness. If you have some conception of His greatness, you will not understand how anyone can claim to serve Him. Even the highest angel cannot say that he truly serves Him. Therefore, the main thing is the desire to serve Him (*Rabbi Nachman's Wisdom* #51).

The same holds true when planning your daily agenda. Even though at present you're having difficulty arranging a schedule that gives you more time for Torah and prayers, don't give up your desire to do so. If you want it bad enough, you'll eventually find a way. As the old adage goes: Nothing stands in the way of desire.

*

The Rebbe once remarked: Why do you labor so hard and work your lives away so that nothing will remain? Work less, so that something will remain! (As a person labors for the material things of this world, his days and years pass by and are gone. Even everything he worked for must eventually be left behind. But, by working less for the physical, a person can have time for that which does remain with him — his spiritual accomplishments) (*Siach Sarfei Kodesh* 1-263).

Therefore, Rebbe Nachman teaches that a person has only to pray, and study, and pray. If his desire is for Torah and prayer, then automatically his entire day — even the mundane — is spent in Torah and prayer, in the search for spiritual accomplishments, in Godliness.

* * *

PRAY, AND STUDY, AND PRAY

Reb Avraham Chazan said that every Shabbat morning we fulfill this concept of praying, studying Torah and praying. First we pray *Shacharit* (the Morning Prayer), then we listen to the reading of the Torah. Afterwards, we pray again, this time *Musaf* (the Additional Prayer) (*Rabbi Levi Yitzchak Bender*).

After praying, one should set aside time for Torah study (*Orach Chaim* 155:1). Rebbe Nachman spoke most unequivocally about wearing Rabeinu Tam tefilin, in addition to the Rashi tefilin worn by all men. He also spoke very strongly about the need for studying the Codes every day (see chapter on Torah Study). Reb Ozer of Uman bore witness to a custom implemented by early Breslover Chassidim which combined these two important practices. Every morning, they would study the Codes while still adorned in their Rabeinu Tam tefilin (*Kokhavey Or* p.80). Doing this makes it very simple to "pray, and study Torah, and pray," even during the week. If, after studying the Codes following the Morning Prayers we recite some psalms or some other supplication, the Rebbe's adage has been fulfilled.

*

Just as one should tithe one's earnings — giving ten percent of one's income to charity — so too, one should tithe the hours of one's day for Torah study. Thus, a person whose day is spent working should set aside at least ten percent of the time to study Torah. As for the person who is able to study a whole day, he would be wise to set aside ten percent of his time for studying Rebbe Nachman's teachings (*Rabbi Nachman Burstein*).

* * *

7

TORAH STUDY

THE GREATNESS OF TORAH

Rebbe Nachman teaches: Torah is greater than everything and includes everything. It is greater even than prophesy (*Tzaddik* #421).

Torah study is a prerequisite to attaining fear of sin. However, the fear of sin must itself precede analytical study (*The Aleph-Bet Book, Limud* A:47).

Diligent study rises above the fulfillment of all the mitzvot (*The Aleph-Bet Book, Limud* A:33).

Rebbe Nachman was lecturing someone about Torah study. He said: Why don't you study? What have you to lose? God Himself studies Torah every day. With Torah study, you will merit the World to Come! (*Rabbi Nachman's Wisdom* #17; see (*Avodah Zarah* 3b).

Worldly pity (which people feel for those deprived of worldly things) is obvious. Everyone sees the pity which people have for those who are hungry or thirsty or in serious trouble. They know how people react to a person without clothing or shoes. Yet, pity for the deprived in the World to Come is a much greater pity. If a person lacks clothing in this world, others can take up a collection and buy it for him. Such pity is impossible in the World to Come. There, the only clothing one needs is Torah and mitzvot. Happy is he who is worthy of "eating" many chapters of Mishnah, "drinking" verses of the Psalms and "clothing" himself with some mitzvot (*Rabbi Nachman's Wisdom* #23).

Know! there are chambers of Torah. Whoever is privileged to enter these chambers and discover original Torah insights, will find these chambers to be endless. While there he will be able to accumulate magnificent treasures. Fortunate is he! (*Likutey Moharan* I, 245).

Torah study brings peace (*The Aleph-Bet Book, Limud* A:75).

* * *

HOW TO STUDY

Attempt to go through all the sacred books in the course of your lifetime. You will then have visited every place in the Torah. When reaching the World to Come you will be able to boast about your many "travels" and "journeys," just like all the jet-setters who are always talking about the exotic places they've visited. By studying *all* the books of Torah, you will be able to say, "I was in this book, I spent time in that set of writings" (*Rabbi Nachman's Wisdom* #28).

Don't be frightened or discouraged by how much there is to learn. Even if you forget what you've studied, don't despair. Our Sages taught that in the World to Come a person will remember whatever he studied. Learn to see yourself as the day laborer who is paid to pour water into barrels which have holes. If he is foolish, he says, "Why waste my time?" But the wise man says, "I'm paid by the day. What difference is it to me if the barrels fill up or not? They're paying me to pour water." So too, the person who studies Torah is rewarded for the time he spends studying, not for what he remembers (*Rabbi Nachman's Wisdom* #26; see *VaYikra Rabbah* 19:2).

Torah study is absolutely and unquestionably great. In fact, "It is your life..." (Deuteronomy 30:20). (Were this not so, we wouldn't face so many obstacles while trying to fulfill this most important mitzvah.) It is important to recognize the supreme value of Torah study and to be aware that there are barriers which must be overcome by anyone wishing to enter the wondrous and majestic world of Torah. This chapter will explore Rebbe Nachman's teachings on how to attain Torah study, what to study and from whom to study.

*

Through prayer. As mentioned in the previous chapter, we see the important connection which prayer has to Torah study through Rabbi Nechunya's actions. Someone asked Rebbe Nachman's advice about a certain devotion in serving God. The Rebbe told him to study Torah. When the man objected, "But I do not know how to learn!" the Rebbe answered, "Pray! With prayer, everything becomes possible. The greatest good can be achieved through prayer" (*Likutey Moharan* II, 111).

The first step in Torah study is praying for it. Pray to God, plead with Him, beg Him to allow you the privilege of studying Torah and plead with Him to help you understand what you study. As Rebbe Nachman teaches: One must cry and pray very hard to get to understand Torah (*Likutey Moharan* I, 21:8).

The Rebbe himself did this. When he began to study the Mishnah, he found it impossible to understand. He wept and wept, until he was able to comprehend it by himself. Later, when he studied the Talmud, the same thing happened. Again he cried bitterly until he was worthy of understanding. This was even true of such esoteric studies as the Zohar and the writings of the Ari. Understanding only came after he had prayed, pleaded and cried (*Rabbi Nachman's Wisdom* p.9).

*

Effort and diligence. Rebbe Nachman was once discussing the printing of Torah books, which in his time had become much more prevalent. Everybody was buying books to have in their homes. He said: Our Sages taught that a time will come when the Torah will be forgotten among Jews (Shabbat 138b). Therefore, many books are printed and bought, with people building up their own libraries. Since even the simplest laborer has books, the Torah is not forgotten. But what people don't realize is that these books are of no significance unless they look into them and study their teachings (Rabbi Nachman's Wisdom #18).

Thus, the second step in Torah study is commitment and effort. You have to keep at it. It is not enough to buy the books and display them on bookshelves. Devotion and diligence are absolutely necessary. One of the most important keys to diligence is the setting of realistic goals. It is good to have short-term goals and long-term goals, but above all is the need for them to be feasible. Aiming for what is possible builds enthusiasm; reaching for the impossible destroys it.

Once you've determined the right goals for your Torah study, remember: you've got to stick to them, no matter what. Be determined and make every effort to keep up with your studies daily. If you're delayed and can't manage to finish the amount you intended to cover, or, as sometimes happens to even the most committed person, your day's schedule is upset, then finish at night — that night. No matter how late before you finish, no matter how exhausted you are, do it. It's still better than falling behind and leaving today's learning for tomorrow. Knowing that you're committed to doing this is, in itself, very beneficial. When you know that you're going to have to stay up very late in order to finish your daily studies (especially after a few rough nights), you're going to make sure to be on time, or even early, for your regular studies.

Even with commitment and devotion, there are times when your normal daily goals cannot be met. On certain days, like

Yom Kippur and Purim when everyone is busy with prayer and the mitzvot of the day, it becomes impossible to carry a full load of learning. The same is true of the out-of-the-ordinary days when you've got to travel somewhere, or marry off a child and the like. In such cases, the best thing to do is what Reb Noson himself did. Reb Noson designed different study plans for different days. Thus, for example, the amount of Codes he would undertake to study would depend upon what that day's schedule would allow; so much for a weekday, so much for a Friday, so much for Shabbat, so much for a festival and so on. Each day had different hours available for Torah study: some days more, some days less; the amount was not his main concern. What was most important for Reb Noson — and what is most important for us — was keeping to the goals he himself had established and committed himself to fulfill (*Rabbi Eliyahu Chaim Rosen*).

Reb Noson related: For a long time, I encountered great difficulty in my Torah studies. I would enter the study hall filled with enthusiasm and intending to devote all my energy to my studies. But, no sooner had I begun, when inevitably something would happen to divert me from my intentions, distract my concentration and deflate my determination. And, no matter how determined I was, each day brought a new diversion and a different distraction. It was always something I hadn't anticipated, something I hadn't prepared myself for, and was helpless to avoid. As you can imagine, it did not take long before I was at my wits' end. I was ready to give up. But then I talked to the Rebbe. He told me that when it came to studying Torah, "a little is also good!" Hearing this changed my attitude totally. Afterwards, whenever I couldn't study as much as I desired, I was still satisfied and content with whatever I had managed to accomplish. This way, I was able to counter my difficulties in studying. By grabbing a little bit here, a little bit there, I eventually developed into a serious student (*Aveneha Barzel* p. 78). [It should be realized that Reb

Noson was already a fully accomplished Torah scholar even before he met Rebbe Nachman.]

One of the interpretations of loving God "with all your *effort*," which we say daily as part of the Shema, is "And you shall love God...with all your money" (*Rashi*, Deuteronomy 6:5). This provides us with yet another tool for fostering diligence and determination in studying Torah. Quite simply, wherever and in whatever way possible, try to pay for Torah study. By paying someone to teach or study with you, you will naturally want to get your money's worth. This will guarantee that you won't be lax in your efforts to get as much out of the learning as you possibly can. You'll be loathe to waste any time. Indeed, as a child, the Rebbe would use his allowance to pay his teacher extra money for each additional page of Talmud that his teacher taught him (*Rabbi Nachman's Wisdom* p.6).

Rebbe Nachman once said: "Anyone who fulfills everything I tell them will certainly become a great Tzaddik. Obviously, the more one studies the more successful he will be" (*Tzaddik* #320).

*

Broad knowledge. In conjunction with his desire that his followers "visit" all the sacred books, Rebbe Nachman also strongly emphasized the need for a general and extensive knowledge of the Torah. Accordingly, the Rebbe favored the study-method which produced broad knowledge, rather than the approach which developed analytical prowess. He did not agree that the majority of one's study time should be spent on an in-depth analysis of a few pages of text. Spending months on dissecting a page or two of Talmud may make one a sort of "specialist" and sharpen one's faculty for dialectics, but ultimately it also leaves the majority of students ignorant of most talmudic tractates, not to mention the Torah's other branches, even worse, its Laws.

Thus, another step in studying Torah involves mapping out the areas you intend to learn, focusing on covering as much ground as time will allow. This way you will have little trouble successfully finishing each book you begin, have enough time for reviewing it, and thereby gain a broad knowledge of Torah. Actually, this is the talmudic teaching (*Shabbat* 63a): "Study everything, and then seek to understand!" (That is, first absorb the knowledge. Then sort it out and refine your understanding.)

Rebbe Nachman also pointed out that you need not rush immediately to review your learning. The best way is to continue on in the order of study. For example, when you finish the *Mishnayot* of tractate *Berakhot*, you should go on to the next tractate, *Pe'ah*, rather than review what you just learned. Continue at a steady pace. This way you'll be able to study many of the holy writings completely and then go back to study them again (*Rabbi Nachman's Wisdom* #76).

*

Understanding and enunciating. Rebbe Nachman suggested that we study rapidly — with speed and simplicity — and not spend too much time on each detail. We should try to understand each thing in its own context and enunciate the words of Torah as we study them. There is no need specifically to elucidate the words as we progress down the page; if we just carry on, the meaning will become clear as we proceed (*Rabbi Nachman's Wisdom* #76). It is good, however, for a person to elucidate his studies in the language he understands (*Likutey Moharan* I, 118). Either way, we must work to understand the material we're studying. It's not enough to just repeat the words without knowing what we are saying. Lack of understanding cannot be considered learning (*Sichot V'Sipurim* p.87 #13).

*

Keep on going. What happens when, while just trying to understand the text simply and within its own context, you still don't understand? From Rebbe Nachman's advice it is clear that the thing to do is to keep on going. If, while studying, you come to a sentence or two that you don't understand, or some concept that is beyond your comprehension, don't stop there. Most texts, after all, have difficult passages. Just mark the unclear point and proceed further. This way, your quick study will enable you to absorb a lot. You will be able to review what you have studied for a second and a third time.... And, because you will have studied so much more since you last attempted to comprehend this material, you will succeed in understanding it the next time around. Even if there are some things you never understand, the quantity outweighs all else (*Rabbi Nachman's Wisdom* #76).

This method of study which the Rebbe advises is actually mentioned in the Talmud and in later works (*Avodah Zarah* 19a; *Orchot Tzaddikim* #27; *SheLaH, Shavuot; Maharal MiPrague, Netiv HaTorah* and a good number of other leading Codifiers). Even when he was young, Reb Noson also showed a preference for this more general and direct approach to studying. Unlike his classmates who, whenever they were tested in Talmud, would always try to impress the teacher by searching for difficulties and clever solutions, Reb Noson read and explained the text simply and clearly. When he said that he just didn't have questions like the other boys, his teacher remarked that his simple and accurate recital was far better than the convoluted questions posed by his friends (*Aveneha Barzel* p.3).

When Rebbe Nachman told him to study Kabbalah, Reb Noson complained that there were many points in the *Etz Chaim* (the Ari's main treatise in Kabbalah) that he did not understand. The Rebbe advised him to mark off each part he failed to comprehend. "The next time you study it you will understand it, and then you can erase the mark." Reb

Noson said afterwards that each time he reviewed the *Etz Chaim*, the marks became fewer and fewer (*Rabbi Eliyahu Chaim Rosen*).

*

Guard your tongue. Rebbe Nachman teaches: Every Jew is a letter in the Torah. Thus, there are six hundred thousand letters in the Torah, equivalent to the six hundred thousand Jewish souls in Creation. When you find fault in a fellow Jew, you are, as it were, finding a blemish in Torah and rendering it incomplete. However, by not speaking against or belittling another Jew, and by emphasizing his good points, you will also find the Torah perfectly beautiful. You will then have a deep love for the Torah and this love will lead you to great diligence in your studies (*Rabbi Nachman's Wisdom* #91).

* * *

WHAT TO STUDY

Rebbe Nachman once enumerated how much a person should study every day, a schedule which would fill his entire day. You should study enough each day so that at the end of the year you will have completed 1) the entire Talmud with the commentaries of Rashi, Tosafot, Rif and Rabeinu Asher; 2) the entire *Shulchan Arukh* (Codes of Law); 3) all the *Midrashim*; 4) the *holy Zohar*; 5) the Writings of the Ari (*Rabbi Nachman's Wisdom* #76, some 20,000 pages annually).

*

Wow! Who can imagine going through all of that in one year?! Not to mention, that the Rebbe then went on to say that a person should also set aside some time in the day for studying the Torah in-depth and analytically, reciting the Psalms as well as many additional prayers, and even then his list had not been exhausted. Most people will say, "Impossible!" or, "You've got to be kidding!"

Wait a minute! Before giving up even before you've started, let's look at what Rebbe Nachman has to say. Firstly, there's no point in getting overwhelmed. Obviously, such a schedule is for someone who has already been through the Talmud, *Shulchan Arukh, Midrash, Zohar,* etc. and is familiar with the material. Otherwise, it would take a super-human effort just to recite so many words, let alone understand them. This daily schedule is also predicated on the method of study which the Rebbe advised us to follow. As has been explained, he wanted us to study quickly and eagerly, without confusing ourselves by focusing on intricate details and cross-referencing.

Still, you might ask why Rebbe Nachman set out such a "work-load" if he could hardly expect anyone, but the very learned, to finish it? The answer is really quite simple. We've already seen that the Rebbe understood that no one (not even the greatest scholar and most devout individual) can serve God appropriately as is His due. What then? As Rebbe Nachman has insisted many times, the main thing is desire. We have to desire to serve Him in the way in which His glory warrants. This also applies to the way we serve Him through our study of Torah. Here too, we have to aim for the best — studying the entire Torah in the course of a year. Just as the Rebbe realized that even if we succeed filling his prescription for Torah study we would still not be serving God as is His due, he was also aware that, with the progressive weakening of commitment to Torah study throughout the generations, most of us would never reach the yearly goal he prescribed. However, we can desire the utmost.

It's also worth hearing what the Rebbe said after he listed his *ideal* study schedule. He told us not to be anxious if we found ourselves incapable of completing everything he suggested each day. "One can be a religious Jew even if he can't study that much. Even without being a scholar, he can still be a Tzaddik. Deep perception cannot be attained without talmudic and halakhic scholarship, but even the simplest Jew can be righteous and a Tzaddik." The Rebbe then quoted the Talmudic teaching (*Avot* 2:21): "You are not obligated to finish the work (studying the entire Torah), neither are you free to excuse yourself from it" (*Rabbi Nachman's Wisdom* #76). (See Appendix A for a suggested general study program for beginners and intermediate levels. See Appendix B which covers Rebbe Nachman's works and additional Breslov teachings.)

* * *

Original Torah insights. You may expound on the Torah and originate insights in any area you wish. The only condition is that you do not originate any new laws (*Rabbi Nachman's Wisdom* #267).

Concerning his own work, the *Likutey Moharan*, Rebbe Nachman also said: You can twist my teachings whichever way you wish [to understand them], just as long as you don't depart from so much as a small passage of the *Shulchan Arukh* (*Siach Sarfei Kodesh* I-131).

Developing your own original insights into the Torah is truly a great thing. Firstly, it shows that your thoughts are focused on Torah, as opposed to the many other things that might occupy or distract your mind. This will help clear your mind of all the undesirable data it has collected in the past. Secondly, it is a sign that your Torah study has had an effect on you and that you want to grow in Torah. Original Torah insights also have the power to increase Divine Providence in the world. People will recognize God's rulership of the world that much more because of the ideas you've initiated.

"Just one thing," Rebbe Nachman warned, "be careful not to institute new laws, a new torah that does not align with our Holy Torah." To this end, the Rebbe advised that whenever we attempt to teach one of our insights to others, we should study from the *Shulchan Arukh* beforehand, and then again afterwards. This study of the Law will protect our ideas from being misleading (*The Aleph-Bet Book, Chidushin d'Orayta,* A:7).

One more word about our original Torah insights: We must believe that they count and that they are important in God's eyes and not be slack in thinking of new insights and ideas in Torah that will help bring us, and others, closer to God.

* * *

WHO FROM...

Moshe received the Torah from Sinai and gave it to Joshua; Joshua gave it to the Elders; the Elders to Prophets... (*Avot* 1:1).

Get for yourself a rabbi (*Avot* 1:6).

*

A person cannot successfully learn Torah from everyone. You may have to travel to find the right place for you to study Torah (*The Aleph-Bet Book, Limud* A:92).

As discussed earlier (chapter on Truth), people's perspective of the world differs. This affects all aspects of our lives and is true for Torah study as well. As a result, down through the years several approaches to study have developed: from the deeply analytical approach to the more halachically centered general approach, and everything in-between. Some favor *iyun* (in-depth study), others have stronger memories and select *bekiut* (broad knowledge study)...and so on. This applies not only to the way we study any given subject of Torah — the differences being most prominent in the study of Talmud — but also to the different schools of thought that have developed on what to study in general. Thus, even within the Breslov movement itself, there are those who put more emphasis on a rich diet of Talmud, while others on Rebbe Nachman's teachings.

At first, this may prove confusing. You might find yourself wondering, What's really the right way to study? When it comes to Torah, which one of the methods of study is true? Actually, this question is no question at all, for the answer is that everybody's truth is different. Each person has his own, personal preference. The thing to do is find *your own* level. Find yourself a teacher that suits you and have him guide you according to *your truth*. There's no reason to have to accept someone else's preference. As our Sages said, "A person only studies Torah from a place where his heart desires" (*Avodah Zarah* 19a). This means that you have to seek out the path which is best for you, because only then will your heart be in it — only then will your desire be strong enough so that one day you too will come to fulfill the Torah "work-load" which the Rebbe prescribed.

*

This brings to mind the well-known story of the treasure buried under the bridge in Vienna. This, in short, is how Rebbe Nachman told it:

A Jew once dreamt that under a certain bridge in Vienna he would find a great treasure. He traveled to Vienna and stood near the bridge trying to figure out what to do. A policeman who was passing by became suspicious. Sensing that honesty would be the best policy the Jew explained that he had had a dream that he would find a treasure buried under the bridge. If the policeman were willing to help him dig it up, he would be only too happy to share it with him. The policeman laughed and said: "You Jews are only interested in dreams. I also had a dream, and also saw a treasure." The policeman then went on to describe accurately the man's city and house. "In my dream, that's where the treasure is buried," he concluded. The Jew rushed home, dug under his house and found the treasure. It was then that he realized that the treasure had been his all along, but to find it he had to travel to Vienna.

The same is true in serving God. Each person has the treasure, but in order to find it, he must travel to the Tzaddik (*Rabbi Nachman's Stories* #24).

The treasure is within each individual and he alone has his treasure. Yet, the discovery and development of that treasure only comes about by means of the Tzaddik. The Tzaddik is like a tree with many branches. Issuing from these branches are smaller branches from which leaves grow. All the leaves draw from the roots by means of the tree trunk, each drawing its nourishment via a different path. Similarly, all people draw their Torah through the Tzaddik, the True Tzaddik. But we each have our own path, separate from one another's and each of us has to use the path which is right for us to draw nourishment — the Torah — through the Tzaddik. Thus, Rebbe Nachman teaches: The Tzaddik guides a person to his path (the path of his rectification) (*Likutey Moharan* I, 4:8). To this, Reb Noson added: You must study and receive Torah from your rabbi — a qualified rabbi, who is learned and righteous. By doing this, you will come to understand the numerous hints and ideas which appear on your path to help you draw closer to God (*Likutey Halakhot, Netilat Yadayim li'Seudah* 6:56).

Rebbe Nachman teaches: One's rabbi has to be both a *lamdan* (a scholar) and a *chassid* (pious). He must be learned, because "a boor cannot be pious" (*Avot* 2:6). At the same time, being learned by itself is also insufficient, because one can be very learned and yet wicked at the same time (*Likutey Moharan* I, 31:end).

*

Rebbe Nachman also warned of the dangers in becoming "too learned." He said: a person's erudition can propel him to great spiritual heights. However, when he encounters difficulties and falls in his level [of devotions], he must draw inner strength from his "good points," his righteous deeds, not from his knowledge of Torah. Torah study is very great, but restoring a level of righteousness requires strengthening oneself with one's good deeds. A person's wickedness, however, can lead him to heresy, and all the more so when he is learned (*Likutey Moharan* I, 31:end).

Furthermore, Rebbe Nachman teaches: There are certain teachers of Torah who must be totally avoided. Not only do they drain themselves with their false studies, but they mislead others and make them too weary [and disenchanted] to study Torah enthusiastically (*Likutey Moharan* I, 28:1).

* * *

THE POWER OF TORAH

"They left Me and have forsaken My Torah" (Jeremiah 16:11). Were it that they left Me and kept [studying] Torah. Its light would have brought them back in repentance (*Eichah Rabbah, Pesikha* 2).

More, much more, could be culled from Rebbe Nachman's teachings on the topic of Torah and the power and greatness of Torah study. However, as the scope of this handbook does not allow for an in-depth discussion of any one topic — rather hoping that the reader, after gaining a general perspective of the Rebbe's teachings, will go further on his own — a few choice selections on the awesome power of Torah study will have to suffice.

Torah has the power to elevate a person from the worst impurities, even from the defilement of the Covenant (sexual immorality). When someone questioned this, the Rebbe answered: "Why are you surprised? *Brit* (the sign of the

Covenant) corresponds to *Yesod*. Torah corresponds to *Tiferet*" (*Tzaddik* #573). (Yesod, the ninth of the Ten Divine Emanations (Sefirot), is positioned on a lower level than Tiferet, the sixth Sefirah; see below, "The Seven Candles," where the Covenant and this concept are explained in greater detail.)

An angel is created from every word of Torah studied. This angel has the power to subdue and eliminate the power of the Other Side (*Likutey Moharan* I, 20:7).

Nobody sins unless overcome by a "spirit of folly" (*Sotah* 3a). The sins and spiritual damage a person may have done literally make him mad. This is why the majority of people suffer from all kinds of quirks and idiosyncrasies. The remedy is to study Torah intensively. The Torah consists entirely of the Names of the Holy One, and it has the power to crush the evil inclination and banish all the madness and folly which cling to a person because of his sins (*Advice*, Torah Study 4).

Elsewhere, the Rebbe says that the Torah which you study "forcefully" gives power to the Kingdom of Holiness and helps a person overcome his foolishness (*Likutey Moharan* I, 1). Studying Torah forcefully or intensively can have a few meanings: 1) despite difficult circumstances and in the face of many obstacles: illness, under financial or emotional stress, etc.; 2) when there is no desire to study and one forces oneself; 3) with full concentration or audibly (*Rabbi Eliyahu Chaim Rosen*).

It is often quite obvious that people's personal idiosyncrasies cause them to become eccentric and sometimes even crazy. Yet, they manage (if only barely) to cling to a drop of sanity and not lose their minds completely. This is somewhat surprising, because logically, commensurate with the amount of sins a person has committed, and thus the amount of "folly" he has within him, he should be completely crazy. Still, God has mercy and He leaves each person that "little bit" of clarity he needs to return to a saner way of life— i.e. to God. This can be achieved through the Tzaddikim. They have attained a great level of wisdom and knowledge and can draw that wisdom down to each person's level to help cure him (*Likutey Halakhot, Netilat Yadayim li'Seudah* 6:37). More specifically, this wisdom is the Torah and advice which the Tzaddikim reveal to us.

The Torah that one studies "forcefully" has the power to rectify one's speech. Rectified speech brings modesty and prayer (*Likutey Moharan* I, 38:4-5).

Studying Talmud at night can help a person overcome his impure motives (*Likutey Moharan* I, 3).

Originating Torah insights is a great rectification for all of one's sins (*Likutey Moharan* II, 105).

A person who finds it impossible to study Torah — be it that he never had the opportunity to learn and doesn't know how; or he has no books to study from; or he is travelling — yet his desire to study and serve God is very great: creates a book of Torah in Heaven from this great desire alone (*Likutey Moharan* I, 142).

The Rebbe said that he wanted very much to instill the importance of daily Torah study in people, so that everyone would have a set amount to study every day, without fail. His reason was that the power of Torah is so very great, that even a person who habitually commits the worst sins — can be extricated from the deepest trap! (*Rabbi Nachman's Wisdom* #19).

* * *

8

PRAYER

Mashiach's main weapon is prayer. All the battles he will wage, all the conquests he will achieve — they will come through the power of prayer (*Likutey Moharan* I, 2:1). Reb Noson adds: The essential weapon of each Jew is like that of Mashiach, prayer (*Advice* I, 2:1).

* * *

THE GREATNESS OF PRAYER

Reb Noson was once talking about the greatness of prayer. The Midrash states: After the prayers have been received in Heaven, an angel takes an oath from them and then sends the prayers upward, to the Crown which adorns the Holy One's head (*Shemot Rabbah* 21:4). "Take note," said Reb Noson, "even angels cannot rise to the level which the prayers can reach!" (*Aveneha Barzel* p.88).

Rebbe Nachman teaches: A Jew's main attachment to God is through prayer (*Likutey Moharan* II, 84). Through his prayers, each Jew acquires absolute mastery and control — he can achieve whatever he desires (*Likutey Moharan* I, 97).

The essence of our life-force comes from prayer (*Likutey Moharan* I, 9:1). Prayer brings life to all the worlds (*Likutey Moharan* I, 9:3).

Reb Naftali had a dream in which a soul appeared before him and asked him to teach one of Rebbe Nachman's lessons.

Reb Naftali said, "The essence of our life-force comes from prayer." Hearing this, the soul became very excited. It began to ascend higher and higher. When Reb Naftali related the dream to Rebbe Nachman, the Rebbe replied: "Do you think that in the Upper Worlds they hear my lessons the way you do in this world?!" (*Hishtafkut HaNefesh, Introduction*).

There are three types of prayer: a prayer of David (Psalm 86); a prayer of Moshe (Psalm 90); a prayer of the poor man (Psalm 102). Of the three, the poor man's prayer is by far the most powerful (*Zohar* III:195a).

The poor man's prayers are clearly the most powerful because they come from a broken heart. The pauper stands before God and bemoans his fate: "Why me? Why do I have to suffer?" This prayer is so effective that it breaks all barriers and rises directly before God. How much more so, writes Reb Noson, when the person cries out to God that he is spiritually impoverished, that he is steeped in his physicality and wants to draw closer to God. How much more powerful is such a prayer? It will certainly rise directly before God! (*Likutey Halakhot, Tefilin* 5:43).

Faith, Prayer, Miracles and the Holy Land are all one concept (*Likutey Moharan* I, 7:1). How so? When we pray, it is a sign of our faith. Why else would we be praying? Prayer increases our faith, and, as we pray, we gradually develop a more intimate feeling for our Creator. This in turn can lead to miracles. The more we pray, the more we can attain mastery over the elements. This is because our prayers are directed to God, and He has mastery over all of Creation. Therefore, God can, and will, perform miracles for those whose prayers are filled with a refined level of faith. In addition, these miracles and prayers are conceptually related to the Holy Land, for they reveal holiness and the Kingdom of Heaven.

* * *

THE POWER OF PRAYER

Prayer has the power to change nature (*Likutey Moharan* I, 216). This applies both to the forces of nature and to one's own human nature. Reb Noson once said, "Nothing can help a person break his unwanted desires except prayer. The reason for this is quite simple. Normally, a person who breaks his desires is left with two desires; just as when a person breaks something in half and is left with two pieces." But with prayer, we are able to rid ourselves completely of all our unwanted desires (cf. *Siach Sarfei Kodesh* 1-511).

*

Prayer helps nullify a Heavenly decree before — and even after — it has been issued (*The Aleph-Bet Book, Tefilah* A:14). Once, when Reb Shimon's son was deathly ill, he approached the Rebbe and asked him to pray for the child's recovery. Rebbe Nachman, however, did not respond. Forlorn and without hope, Reb Shimon returned home. His wife understood well the implication of the Rebbe's silence. Yet, instead of despairing, she spent that entire night sitting at the infant's crib and praying for her child. The following morning, when Rebbe Nachman saw Reb Shimon, he ran towards him with great joy, saying, "Look at the great power of prayer! Last night the decree was sealed. The infant's death was imminent. And now, not only has the decree been nullified, but Heaven has granted him long life as well!" Tradition has it that Reb Shimon's son lived close to a hundred years (*Aveneha Barzel*, p. 39 #60).

* * *

THE DAILY PRAYERS

WHEN TO PRAY

Rebbe Nachman exhorted his followers to pray as early in the day as possible. He said: Prayer is so great, who knows if one will have the chance to pray later on in the day (*Rabbi Nachman's Wisdom* 31). Rebbe Nachman wanted his followers to have a head start on the day and he spoke very often of the need to arise for *Tikkun Chatzot* (the Midnight Lament). In most cases, those who did get up stayed awake until after the Morning Prayers. If not, many rose early enough to pray *vatikin*, at daybreak.

Starting your day early has lots of advantages. It gives you a good deal of time for your devotions. You can spend time praying as one should: carefully reciting all the words and concentrating on their meaning. You can also have some quiet time alone in *hitbodedut*, study some Torah, do a mitzvah — all before making your way to your office or place of work to "begin" the day. Getting up late allows for none of this. Even before you've gulped down your prayers and a cup of coffee, it's time to head into the rush-hour traffic that brings you unprepared and still bleary-eyed to face yet another day.

Speaking of a cup of coffee, Rebbe Nachman said that he never drank even so much as a cup of water before reciting the morning prayers. He disagreed with all those who drank coffee and the like before praying (*Rabbi Nachman's Wisdom* #277). Although there are opinions in the Shulchan Arukh which permit this, God says: "After you eat and drink you come to praise Me?!" (*Berakhot* 10b). Quite simply, one's heart is subdued and humble when it wants. Refraining from food or drink before praying gives you a greater desire to feed the spiritual than the physical. Obviously, if you start your day early, this usually presents no problem.

Rebbe Nachman said: Those Tzaddikim that pray after the set time for the Morning Prayers are making a mistake

(*Tzaddik* 487). When asked by Reb Meir of Teplik how people dared to shave their beards and *peyot* with a razor, thereby transgressing five Torah prohibitions daily, Reb Noson remarked, "And how can 'religious' people daily miss out reading the morning Shema in its correct time?" (*Kokhavey Or*, p. 75 #17). It is quite clear from the *Shulchan Arukh* that the correct time for reciting the Shema is up until one quarter of the day. The Morning Service may be prayed up until one third of the day has passed. (This changes according to location and one should check with one's local rabbi.)

*

WHERE TO PRAY

There is no question as to the importance of praying in a synagogue. It is a place of prayer, built especially for prayer. However, if at all possible, one should specifically choose a synagogue that one finds conducive to praying. There are synagogues where praying is timed, not less than "x" amount of minutes, not more than "y" amount of minutes, etc. Furthermore, there are synagogues where talking has become prevalent — even surpassing the prayers. One should use one's discretion. Reb Noson writes that there are those who pray quickly, others who pray slowly, each according to his true feelings (*Likutey Halakhot, Nizkei Shkheinim* 5:2). Still, one should make the effort to put as much *kavanah* (devout concentration) as possible, into one's prayers.

Praying with a *minyan* (quorum) is also of tantamount importance. The Talmud teaches: The prayers of the individual may be rejected, but the prayers of many are never rejected (*Ta'anit* 8a). One should pray there with joy and happiness, even to the point of clapping one's hands and singing the words. As Rebbe Nachman said: I put great value in the Baal Shem Tov's way of praying: with exertion and joy (*Tovot Zikhronot* #5). However, one should not pray in a manner that disturbs others, nor use mannerisms designed to draw attention to oneself. Better to pray simply, with as much *kavanah* as one can muster.

Rebbe Nachman said: You should not say that if you were praying so intensely, you would not hear or feel someone else. People can be annoying, even though it appears that the person is involved totally in his prayers (*Rabbi Nachman's Wisdom* #285). There are some who feel that since they pray differently from others in their synagogue, perhaps it would be better if they were to stay home and pray individually. However, this is incorrect. One should make every effort to pray in a synagogue. If there are disturbances that disrupt his prayers, then he should pray about this too, during his *hitbodedut* (*Oneg Shabbat* p.502).

The Rebbe never asked his followers to give up their "inherited" version of the prayers. Family traditions of *nusach* — Sefardi, Ashkenaz or Sefard (Chassidic) — did not have to be changed. Its makes no difference which version one prays. Rebbe Nachman said: Chassidut has nothing to do with *nusach*. One can be a chassid and still pray the Ashkenaz version (*Siach Sarfei Kodesh* I-90).

*

HOW TO PRAY

Rebbe Nachman teaches: A person should put all his energy into his prayers. This is the deeper meaning of, 'For Your sake are we killed all the day' (Psalms 44:23). By exerting oneself in one's prayers, it is as if one is sanctifying God's Name (*Rabbi Nachman's Wisdom* #12). Similarly, a person should try to concentrate fully when praying. As long as the person praying is aware of another person in his presence, his *kavanah* is not complete. A person should attain a level in prayer where there is only God and himself (*Likutey Moharan* II, 103).

Reb Naftali prayed this way. Once, the Rebbe related: In the Upper Worlds someone was praying very intensely.

I uncovered his face and saw it was my Naftali (*Aveneha Barzel* p.75). As part of the Points Decrees, which began in 1827, the Russian government instituted a compulsory draft, conscripting Jewish children into the Czar's army for as long as twenty-five years. It was quite common for press gangs to enter Jewish homes in search of new conscripts. Even those with deferments were not spared. Corrupt soldiers would ask to be shown the child's identity papers together with the draft deferment and then, after callously destroying the documents, spirit the child away. Once, while such a search was being conducted in Uman, a family whose son did have the necessary documents came running into Reb Naftali's house. Even though Reb Naftali was praying Minchah (the Afternoon Service) at the time, they purposely made a great deal of commotion so as to attract a large crowd. Only then, in the presence of these many witnesses, did they produce their son's papers. Later, when Reb Naftali finished praying, the family members approached him to ask forgiveness for having disturbed his prayers. Surprised by their request, Reb Naftali insisted that he hadn't heard anything at all (*Aveneha Barzel* p.75).

*

Perhaps the most difficult thing to attain in prayer is concentration. The story is told of Rabbi Levi Yitzchak of Berdichov who went to a person in his synagogue one day, right after the prayers, and gave him a very warm *sholom aleichem!* Startled, the man said, "But I've been here the whole time." Rabbi Levi Yitzchak answered, "But during the prayers your mind wandered to Warsaw where you were thinking of your business. Now that your prayers are finished, you have returned here to Berdichov!"

Rebbe Nachman placed great emphasis on concentrating on each and every word, each and every letter. He knew the difficulty involved in this and therefore gave us numerous suggestions on how we can at least attempt to pray with *kavanah*. These are offered in the next few paragraphs.

A person should pray with all his might and strength. If a person were just to concentrate on his prayers, the words themselves would give him the energy to pray with all his might (*Rabbi Nachman's Wisdom* 66).

Furthermore, Rebbe Nachman teaches: Never let shame stop you from praying (*Likutey Moharan* I, 30:end). One should not think that he is not fit to pray, if he has erred or sinned. One should make every effort to strengthen himself during the prayers.

The essence of prayer entails direct, simple understanding of the words (*Likutey Moharan* II, 120). The Rebbe was deathly ill on the final Rosh HaShannah eve of his life (5571/1810). He asked his little grandson, Yisrael, to pray for him. "God! God!" Yisrael called out, "let my grandfather be well!" The people nearby started smiling. The Rebbe said, "This is how to pray. Simply! What other way is there?" (*Tzaddik* #439).

Knowing what you are saying certainly makes the task easier. Rebbe Nachman emphasized *hitbodedut* (secluded prayer) because then you speak to God in your native tongue. It could be this way with our daily prayers, too. Our Sages taught that prayer can be recited in the language one understands (*Orach Chaim* 101:4). Nevertheless, *Lashon Kodesh* (the Holy Tongue) is all encompassing and there are many advantages to praying in the original Hebrew. It therefore seems most advisable to have a Hebrew/English *siddur* (prayer book) so that, wherever you don't fully understand the original, you can look at the translation and appreciate the meaning of what you are saying.

*

On the return voyage from his pilgrimage to the Holy Land, the ship on which Rebbe Nachman was travelling sprung a leak. Everybody rushed to drain the water from the ship. The

Rebbe, who was physically very weak, could not participate in the very strenuous labor. So as not to discourage the others, he made his face red, as if he were exerting himself. Later, when discussing prayer with his followers, the Rebbe said: "You are like I was on the ship. You only pretend to be exerting yourselves in prayer" (*Rabbi Nachman's Wisdom* #121). It takes effort, lots of effort, to pray properly, but Rebbe Nachman teaches that it can be done. Just be careful. Don't fool yourself into thinking that with external motions alone you are praying properly.

We should try to fully concentrate on the words we are saying. It would be wonderful if we could move ourselves to cry and shed tears while praying. "But," Rebbe Nachman taught, "that too is a foreign thought, i.e. to think about crying while praying." If you feel aroused, fine and good. However, the main thing is to concentrate on the words you are saying (*Likutey Moharan* II, 95).

Foreign, distracting thoughts during prayer are like facing the enemy in battle. Like a good soldier, one must get on with the task at hand. Though a person may not be successful in praying the entire prayer with full concentration, he will at least be "wounding" and "maiming" the opposition — the foreign thoughts. Eventually, if he maintains his determination, he will win the battle (*Likutey Moharan* II, 122).

Don't be totally insistent that your prayers be answered. Pray, and pray hard, but don't absolutely insist that God do as you demand. Let your prayers be supplications, entreaties. Otherwise (God will give into your demand, but) it is like stealing from Above (*Likutey Moharan* I, 195).

Once, when Reb Noson was in Uman, he saw a certain Reb Moshe praying very fervently. Some time afterwards, Reb Noson returned to Uman and saw that Reb Moshe was no longer praying with the same intensity and effort. Reb Noson said to him, "Reb Moshe, you've weakened. You're not praying the way you used to. Take my advice and start again. Look at me. My beard is already white, yet I still have intentions of becoming a good Jew!" (*Aveneha Barzel* p.63). We all go through hot and cold periods. The main thing is not to give up.

*

WHAT IF...

Fine. We know that we should pray with *kavanah*. But we also know that it's not so easy. What if we try and do not feel ourselves succeeding, what do we do then?

If you find it hard to maintain your concentration for the entire prayer, then divide the prayers into sections. That is, start off by deciding that you are going to concentrate only on the first few pages. Afterwards, when you reach the next group of pages, make up your mind that you will concentrate only on these pages (*Likutey Moharan* II, 121). The advantage to approaching the prayers in sections at a time is that a person can force himself to concentrate for a short while, without it becoming cumbersome (*Rabbi Nachman's Wisdom* #75).

Also remember: It doesn't pay to look for "quick remedies." They don't work. One has to try again and again. That does work!

Someone suggested to Reb Noson that perhaps it would be better to pray quickly, and in so doing avoid foreign and distracting thoughts. Reb Noson disagreed, maintaining that it was better to pray slowly. By praying quickly, a person can rush through the entire prayer with one foreign thought. But, by praying slowly, there is always a chance that he might concentrate properly on at least a few parts of the prayer (*Aveneha Barzel*, p. 61 #25).

However, on another occasion, a man came complaining to Reb Noson that he had to repeat his prayers over and over again. The man explained that he felt obliged to do this because it was very difficult for him to recite the words with the proper intentions. Reb Noson said, "Is this the only way for you to serve God? With these particular words? If these words come out broken, then go on to some other devotion — recite the Psalms, or some other prayer..." (*Aveneha Barzel*, p. 90). You can't always focus your concentration the way you might like to. When this happens, move on to different prayers. Perhaps these will bring you to an arousal for God.

Reb Noson writes: "Pour out your heart before God..." (Lamentations 2:19). If you can't pray properly, then pour your heart out, even without *kavanah,* just as water might pour out accidently (*Likutey Halakhot, Minchah* 7:44). Eventually, your heart will open in the right way.

* * *

CHATZOT

Whoever feels the awe of God in his heart should rise at midnight and mourn the destruction of the Holy Temple (*Orach Chaim* 1:3). *Tikkun Chatzot* (the Midnight Lament) is the prayer recited to mourn the destruction of the Temple (*Mishnah Berurah* 1:9).

Come hear the words of the Talmud, the Midrash and the *Shulchan Arukh.* Come see the teachings of the Zohar, the Kabbalah and virtually all of the Sacred Writings. They all speak about the importance of *Tikkun Chatzot,* the importance of dragging oneself out of bed in the middle of the night to recite a few specific Psalms, to be moved to feel the bitterness of our national and personal loss by reciting a few selected dirges. *Chatzot* is the breaking of "sleep, which is one-sixtieth of death" (*Berakhot* 57b). It is like a ray of light in the darkest moment of night. In fact, Rebbe Nachman teaches: The main devotion in serving God is getting up for the midnight prayer (*Rabbi Nachman's Wisdom* #301). This section will focus on the Breslov perspective of the great value and importance of rising for *Chatzot* and reciting those prayers.

In the next chapter we will see an additional, even more important, benefit to rising in the middle of the night — for *hitbodedut* (meditation and secluded prayer).

*

IMPORTANCE OF CHATZOT

Conceptually, the Holy Temple corresponds to *da'at* (knowledge). When a person's mind/knowledge is pure, it is as if the Holy Temple were built. However, when man's mind/knowledge/intellect is blemished, then this is indicative of the destruction of the Holy Temple (*Likutey Moharan* II, 67).

The past is gone. God's House was destroyed nearly two millennia ago. Presently, He is waiting to return to us (and for us to return to Him) to rebuild the Holy Temple. Even if we argue that it was not we who caused the destruction of the Temple, the Talmud teaches that we are responsible: If the Temple is not built in one's lifetime then it is as if it was destroyed in one's days (*Yerushalmi, Yoma* 1:1). Or, perhaps in a previous incarnation we actually did cause the destruction of the Temple. Therefore, it is fitting that each of us makes certain that at least we are not responsible for the delay in rebuilding it. Therefore we must make the effort to get up for *Chatzot* and mourn the destruction of the Temple. God has promised to reward all those who mourn by witnessing the rebuilding of the Temple and Jerusalem (*Likutey Moharan* II, 67).

Being distant from God is like being asleep: the deeper the sleep, the harder it is to be aroused to serve God. Furthermore, sleep is compared to "lesser" wisdom, an unconscious existence, while awakening is awareness. Thus, rising for *Tikkun Chatzot* is akin to becoming aware of one's existence and the need for making good use of one's life. It is also analogous to finding the good points in oneself, within the "darkness" that surrounds him. The great value in rising for

Chatzot, is that it "breaks" sleep and eliminates the distance from God (*Likutey Halakhot, Hashkamat HaBoker* 1:12).

*

WHEN AND HOW

The time for *Tikkun Chatzot* is six hours after nightfall, regardless of the season (see *Magen Avraham, Orach Chaim* 1:2; 233:1). For example, in North America, *Chatzot* in the winter would be around 11:30 p.m.; in the summer about 3:30 a.m. In more northerly lands, such as England and Northern Europe, in the winter it might be 10:30 p.m.; in the summer, there may not be any *Chatzot* at all. (In which case a person should try to rise before daybreak; *Rabbi Nachman's Wisdom* #301.)

We've already said that the object of *Tikkun Chatzot* is to mourn our loss of the Holy Temple and all the troubles that have befallen us ever since. It is customary to recite the prayer in the manner of a mourner, hence there are those who remove their shoes and sit on the floor, others who wear sackcloth, and so on. When asked about this, my Rosh Yeshivah said, "It is more important to wake up to recite the *Chatzot* prayer and concentrate on the words, than to concern oneself with the additional customs associated with it."

As for the prayers themselves, their contents are very inspiring. Reb Noson writes: The Rebbe once repeated some of the verses from the *Tikkun Chatzot* and then noted how much these prayers awaken the heart. He greatly praised a certain part of the liturgy, saying that it had the power to inspire a person to serve God (*Rabbi Nachman's Wisdom* #268). Furthermore, the Rebbe said: By saying *Tikkun Chatzot*, a person finds that he can express his feelings freely, as if he were having *hitbodedut* (secluded prayer). Mainly, a person recites *Chatzot* not so much for the past destruction of the Holy Temple, but for what is actually happening to him right now. If a person merits to say *Chatzot* in this manner, he will find that whatever happens to him appears within these words of the *Tikkun Chatzot* (Likutey Moharan II, 101).

Rebbe Nachman teaches: When reciting *Tikkun Chatzot* and other similar prayers, apply the verses to yourself. This is especially true of the Psalms. King David wrote Psalms for all of Israel; for the nation as a whole and for each and every individual. The verses are designed in such a way that a person can find in them all his struggles against the Evil Inclination and all the disturbing thoughts and lusts that dominate a person's life. The enemies that King David seeks to vanquish are the "forces of evil" that surround a person and attempt to deny him the path of life. Prayer is the only weapon that can counter these forces (Likutey Moharan II, 101).

"O God! Nations entered Your *Nachalah* (Inheritance); they have defiled Your *Heichal* (Sanctuary), they have put Jerusalem to waste" (Psalms 79:1). This verse is recited as part of the *Tikkun Chatzot*. From the Kabbalah and the chassidic teachings, we find that *nachalah* is symbolic of the Temple — the Da'at; *heichal* is the mouth; and Jerusalem is the heart. Thus, my Rosh Yeshivah would interpret this verse as follows: "A Jewish mind, the temple, should contain the Talmud: *Bavli* and *Yerushalmi*, Midrash, Zohar, Shulchan Arukh, etc. Instead, we occupy our thoughts with the 'wisdoms' of the nations. A Jewish mouth, the *heichal*, should be uttering praises of God, reciting words of Torah and prayer, and speaking words of kindness and encouragement to our family and friends. Instead, we busy our tongues with slander and mockery. A Jewish heart, Jerusalem (the holy city), should be full of love and fear of God. Instead, we have laid it to waste...." This is an example of how we can "translate" and apply *Chatzot* to our current personal life situation.

Besides, everyone experiences difficult moments in life. There are no exceptions. Because it is a most heartrending expression of suffering and anguish, the *Chatzot* prayer is a perfect vehicle for releasing one's own tormented feelings. After Rebbe Nachman passed away, Reb Noson found it impossible to express his agony over the loss. Only when reciting the *Chatzot* prayer was he able to find consolation (*Rabbi Eliyahu Chaim Rosen*).

*

WHAT IF...

In addition to getting up for the *Chatzot* prayer, it is also important to get all the sleep you need (see Chapter 12, "Daily Needs"). Not everyone can get enough sleep before midnight that will enable him to wake up and function the whole day. There are options: you can break up your sleep, rising at midnight to recite *Tikkun Chatzot* and then sleeping afterwards; or, you can remain awake until after the morning prayers and then get a few more hours sleep. If a person cannot rise at midnight, then at least let him rise before morning (*Orach Chaim* 1:1; *Mishnah Berurah* 1:9).

Reb Dov of Tcherin very much wanted to rise at midnight to recite the *Chatzot* prayer, but found it impossible to wake up. When nothing else worked, he hired a man to wake him and stand over him until he got dressed. But, because he wasn't getting sufficient sleep, Reb Dov began suffering terrible headaches. Finally, Rebbe Nachman told him that his *chatzot* was at three in the morning, thus giving him a few more hours of unbroken sleep. "Sleep and eat, just watch your time," the Rebbe told him. After this, those chassidim who awoke during the wee hours of the morning knew exactly when it was three a.m. by Reb Dov's arrival at the synagogue (*Kokhavey Or*, p. 25 #21).

My Rosh Yeshivah would say, "If a person cannot wake up every night for *Chatzot*, then let him try to get up at least once a week." Perhaps, when someone can't even consistently get up once a week, he could begin with once a month. This would not be so difficult, waking up to recite the Midnight Lament once every thirty days and the best time for this would be Erev Rosh Chodesh, as the Eve of the New Moon is in any case set aside as a day of prayer.

*

THE GREATNESS OF CHATZOT

Rebbe Nachman teaches: *Chatzot* has the power of redemption. It can sweeten harsh decrees (*Likutey Moharan* I, 149).

At the time of *Chatzot*, great Lovingkindness descends from Heaven (*Likutey Halakhot, Hashkamat HaBoker* 1:14).

Just as the Exodus from Egypt began at *chatzot*, so too, the Final Redemption will take place at *chatzot*. This teaches us that the Redemption we await will come due to the merit of those who rise for *Chatzot* (*Likutey Halakhot, Hashkamat HaBoker* 1:15).

Reb Noson said: The reason the song *Adir Hu* (Mighty is He) is sung at the end of the Haggadah on Pesach night is because it corresponds to the *Chatzot* prayer, which bemoans the destruction of the Temple. In "Mighty is He," we ask — in a holiday spirit — that God rebuild the Holy Temple (*The Breslov Haggadah* p. 145).

* * *

PSALMS

THE GREATNESS OF THE PSALMS

Rebbe Nachman teaches: It is a very wonderful thing to recite the Psalms, often (*Likutey Moharan* II, 73).

Whoever wants to repent completely should recite the Psalms (*Likutey Moharan* II, 73).

There are times when we do not feel like repenting. For whatever reason, we aren't motivated to return to God. Then again, there are times we try to repent, but cannot find the right gate. There are twelve gates in Heaven corresponding to the Twelve Tribes of Israel, and each Jew has to direct his prayer to the gate of his tribe, no other tribe will do. Sometimes we begin to repent and successfully find the gate we need; only to discover that, when we get there, the gate is closed. Reciting Psalms has the power to arouse even the unmotivated to repent. The Psalms can also direct our prayers to the exact gate we need or even open the appropriate gate (*Likutey Moharan* II, 73).

Therefore, during times of repentance — Elul, the Ten Days of Repentance, etc. — we find all of Israel reciting the Psalms (*Likutey Moharan* II, 73).

*

There are many protest demonstrations in Jerusalem, for any number of reasons. When he was alive, my Rosh Yeshivah would attend only those demonstrations at which the Psalms were recited. He would say, "The power of reciting Psalms is very great; all the more so, when recited in a large gathering. What difference does the reason make?!"

Reb Isaac Sofer, a resident of Breslov, would recite the entire Book of Psalms twice during the night of Yom Kippur. [There are one hundred and fifty psalms. Twice that is three hundred, equivalent to the Hebrew word to forgive, כפר. It is therefore customary to recite the Psalms twice on Yom Kippur.] Once, Reb Noson passed by the town synagogue early Yom Kippur morning and heard Reb Isaac reciting the Psalms with "a fire" (great yearning and desire). After his followers told him that this was the second time Reb Isaac was completing the entire Book, and with the very same fervor and enthusiasm as when he began, Reb Noson said, "This one belongs with us." Shortly afterwards, Reb Isaac became a Breslover chassid (*Sichot V'Sipurim* p.144 #57).

THE TEN PSALMS

Rebbe Nachman teaches: The Psalms (*Tehilim*) — the Ten Types of Song — have the power to nullify the *kelipah* (the impurity) of the Other Side. The most destructive impurity is "wasted seed" which is caused by the *kelipah* known as Lilit. Psalms has the power to subdue that impurity and rectify it, as indicated by the fact that TeHILiM-תהלים has the same numerical value as LILIT-לילית (adding five for the letters of the name) (*Likutey Moharan* I, 205).

*

THE GENERAL REMEDY

For every sin there is a prescribed rectification. To repair the spiritual damage caused by a particular sin, we must apply the particular remedy appropriate for that sin. Yet the task, when each sin is tackled individually, is more than we can ever hope to handle. Nevertheless, as Rebbe Nachman taught, there is a general rectification. This General Remedy has the power to rectify all sins (*Likutey Moharan* I, 29:4).

The General Remedy consists of the Ten Types of Song. Any ten chapters from the Book of Psalms includes the Ten Types of Song, however, it is the ten chapters specifically prescribed for the rectification of wasted seed that are known as the General Remedy. These are:

16; 32; 41; 42; 59; 77; 90; 105; 137; 150.

By reciting these Ten Psalms, one can rectify all the spiritual damage caused by wasted seed and all one's other sins, and then come to repent (one should first immerse in a *mikvah* if possible) (*Rabbi Nachman's Wisdom* #141; This subject appears in greater detail in chapter 16, The Seven Candles.)

*

In most Breslov synagogues, the Ten Psalms are recited right after the *Musaf* prayer every Shabbat morning. In his *minyan*, Rabbi Zvi Aryeh Rosenfeld instituted the custom of reciting the General Remedy every day after the daily prayers.

Rebbe Nachman said: The revelation of precisely these ten psalms as the General Remedy is a very wonderful and awesome rectification. It is entirely original. From the time of Creation, many Tzaddikim have sought the remedy for this sin. God has been good to me and allowed me to attain this understanding and reveal this remedy to the world...Go out and spread the teaching of the Ten Psalms to all men. Even though it seems quite simple to recite ten chapters of the Psalms, it will still be very hard to fulfill (*Rabbi Nachman's Wisdom* #141).

*

WHERE?

It is advantageous that the Book of Psalms can be recited wherever we are: in a synagogue, at home, at the office, in a hotel, while travelling, etc. Such has been the case for thousands of years. King David's words have accompanied us through thick and thin and you'll find Psalms in all sizes and formats, in everything from the *talit* bag micro to the knapsack mega.

Traditionally, the Book of Psalms has been recited at all holy sites, including the Western Wall, the Tomb of the Patriarchs in Hebron, Rachel's Tomb and the Tomb of Rabbi Shimon bar Yochai, to name a few. It is an ancient custom to pray at the gravesites of Tzaddikim so that in their merit our prayers should be answered. Once, Rebbe Nachman was speaking about the gravesite of the Baal Shem Tov. He said: The graves of the True Tzaddikim have the same holiness as the Land of Israel. It is therefore a very great thing to visit their graves to pray and recite the Psalms there (*Likutey Moharan* II, 109).

In reference to his own grave, Rebbe Nachman said: Whoever comes to my gravesite, recites the Ten Psalms (the General Remedy) and donates something to charity for my sake, I promise that I will intercede on his behalf. No matter how terrible his sins, I will do everything in my power to remove that person from Gehennom! (*Rabbi Nachman's Wisdom* #141). (Rebbe Nachman is buried in the Ukrainian city of Uman, mid-way between Odessa and Kiev.) This is a most incredible promise, one that no other Tzaddik ever issued. Consider the power of this promise. By virtue of his traveling to Rebbe Nachman's gravesite, reciting the General Remedy and giving charity, a person has earned himself the services of a most powerful and eloquent defense lawyer, one who will argue his case before the Heavenly Tribunal on his Day of Judgment.

Reb Noson writes: The General Remedy is a very powerful rectification. In the merit of this rectification, may we be worthy of seeing the coming of Mashiach, the ingathering of the exiles and the rebuilding of Jerusalem. Amen (*Likutey Moharan* II, 92).

* * *

SPECIAL PRAYERS

Aside from *Tikkun Chatzot*, Psalms and the General Remedy, Rebbe Nachman also emphasized the importance of other special and very beneficial prayers. These include the *Yom Kippur Katan* service recited as part of Minchah on the eve of Rosh Chodesh. Because it is the last day of the preceding month, the eve of the New Moon is particularly propitious for aiding anyone who wants to repent for wrongs committed over the course of the entire month. There is also the *Tefilah Zakah*, a prayer written by Rabbi Avraham Danzig of Vilna, author of the *Chayey Adam*, to be recited on Yom Kippur Eve, just prior to *Kol Nidre*. In addition, we find that our Sages composed their own special prayers which they recited daily (*Berakhot* 16bff).

Many times we pray, but do not "feel it." We are distant from the prayers, or perhaps, we don't find the way we feel expressed by the prayers. In this regard, there were many optional prayers written by many of our great scholars who saw a need to originate special prayers for various occassions. These can be found in *Sha'arei Zion, Taktu Tefilot* and other similar works. Rebbe Nachman greatly valued these optional prayers and recited them many times himself (*Rabbi Nachman's Wisdom* p.11).

Rebbe Nachman also teaches: It is also very good when you can make prayers out of your studies. Whenever you hear or study the words of Torah, make a prayer out of it. Ask God to help you be worthy of fulfilling whatever it is you just learned. A wise person will understand how to go about forming these prayers. Although *hitbodedut* is in itself very great, this aspect of *hitbodedut* (turning Torah into prayer) is extremely great. It causes enormous delight Above (*Likutey Moharan* II, 25).

This lesson provided Reb Noson with his major impetus for composing his own book of prayers, the *Likutey Tefilot*. This work contains over two hundred magnificent prayers on all topics and circumstances in life. Focusing on the concepts and advice found in Rebbe Nachman's lessons, Reb Noson wove them into prayers of great longing and holy desire. A two-volume work, the *Likutey Tefilot* is based almost entirely on the Likutey Moharan, with a few prayers centered on some of the Rebbe's conversations in *Rabbi Nachman's Wisdom*. Rabbi Nachman Goldstein of Tcherin, a disciple of Reb Noson and author of many important works in Breslov literature, followed Reb Noson's path and authored *Tefilot v'Tachanunim*, with prayers on *Likutey Moharan, Rabbi Nachman's Wisdom, and Tzaddik*. Reb Naftali's son, Reb Efraim, wrote his own prayers under the title, *Tefilot HaBoker,* and other Breslover Chassidim have also composed various supplications based on the Rebbe's teachings.

As we've said, the idea is to take the Torah subjects we study about and translate them into prayer, beseeching God to help us fulfill our learning to the fullest extent possible. For example, when studying about the sacrifices, though we cannot bring offerings into the Holy Temple today, we can still pray to God that our studies be considered as if we had brought those sacrifices (cf. Menachot 110a). Furthermore, we can say: "God, just as I've studied these laws, let me fulfill them in the Holy Temple, speedily and in our time. Amen."

Similarly, when studying the laws pertaining to tefilin, tzitzit, Shabbat, Pesach, lulav, shofar, matzah, etc. (the mitzvot which do apply today), we should certainly ask God to help us fulfill the mitzvah to the best of our ability and with a wealth of joy and happiness.

When studying the laws pertaining to damages, we can pray that we may never be involved in an accident, neither as the cause nor as the victim (as in the Traveller's Prayer, in which we ask that we come to no harm on the road). There are even ways to formulate prayers for those laws which might not seem applicable, as in the case of the happily married man who studies the laws of divorce. "God, help me so that I never have to get divorced. And, above all, let me never be divorced from You. Always let me come ever closer to You." If we truly desire, we can always find a way to pray for something close to home.

* * *

LIKUTEY TEFILOT

Reb Noson said: Now that the *Likutey Tefilot* has been published, people will have to give an account for each day they failed to recite these prayers (*Kokhavey Or,* p. 77). (An English language translation is currently under way.)

People ask if there is *Ruach haKodesh* (Divine Inspiration) in these prayers. They are even higher than *Ruach haKodesh,* for they emanate from the 50th Gate of Holiness! (*Kokhavey Or*, p. 77).

There are many people who have merited entering Gan Eden by reciting the *Likutey Tefilot* (*Khokhavey Or* p.77).

Reb Noson once said about the *Likutey Tefilot*: The day will yet come when there will emerge a nation that will pray with these prayers (*Khokhavey Or* p.77).

* * *

9

HITBODEDUT

Hitbodedut is on a very high level, indeed, a level above all levels (*Likutey Moharan* II, 25).

One of Rebbe Nachman's major teachings, perhaps his most important and best known, focuses on private, secluded prayer. This practice, known simply as *hitbodedut*, is the ultimate level in our relationship to God. Likewise, *hitbodedut* is the tool with which to seek out and find our place: in the world at large; in our family; among friends and within the community; and, most importantly, within ourselves. It gives us the opportunity to release all our inner feelings — the joys and depressions, the successes and frustrations, that greet us each day. Through *hitbodedut,* we examine ourselves and re-examine ourselves, correcting the flaws and errors of the past, while seeking the proper path for the future. It cannot fail! Reb Noson wrote that Rebbe Nachman attained the level he did primarily through *hitbodedut* (*Rabbi Nachman's Wisdom* p. 7, #10). However, it wasn't only the Rebbe who rose to such great and lofty levels of spirituality because of *hitbodedut*. Rebbe Nachman himself said: All of the Tzaddikim were only able to attain the great levels they did because they practiced *hitbodedut* (*Likutey Moharan* II, 100).

Do your utmost to spend at least an hour every day in private prayer and meditation. Express yourself in your own words in the language you understand best. Talk about all the things you are going through. Admit your sins and transgressions, both intentional and unintentional. Speak to God the way you would to a close friend: tell Him what you're going through — your pain, the various pressures you are under, your personal situation and that of others in your home, and also of the Jewish people as a whole. Talk about everything in full. Argue with God in whatever way you can. Press Him, plead with Him to help you come genuinely closer to Him. Cry out, shout and groan, sigh and weep. Give thanks to God for all the love He has shown you in both spiritual and material matters. Sing to God and praise Him and then ask for whatever you need, spiritually and materially. Have faith that the satisfaction God derives from such conversations with even the lowliest of all people is more precious to Him than all other kinds of devotions, even those devotions of the angels in all the worlds. Even if you can't open your mouth at all, just the fact that you stand there putting your hope in God, lifting your eyes upwards and forcing yourself to speak and even if you say no more than a single word the entire time — all this endures forever (*Likutey Moharan* II, 95-101 etc.).

If you've been practicing *hitbodedut* for years and are convinced there's been no improvement, continue doing it. In the end, you will reach your goal, as King David did. He cried *every* night and continued to do so until he was answered (*Rabbi Nachman's Wisdom* #68).

"Though my enemies encamp against me...I rely on this. One thing I asked of God, that shall I seek — that I dwell in the House of God..." (Psalms 27:3,4). The best protection against the forces of evil is prayer and the desire to serve God. King David knew this. Although he was surrounded by a multitude of enemies — forces that sought to destroy him — King David did not fear. He beseeched God to help him retain his faith and always come before Him: to "dwell in the House of God." His great desire to serve God and his unfaltering faith in prayer were his strength and fortitude against his enemies (*Likutey Halakhot, Netilat Yadayim li'Seudah* 6:55).

Reb Noson also said: We find exceptional advice throughout the Rebbe's teachings on how to serve God and draw closer to Him. But, sometimes the advice itself is extremely difficult to follow. The only advice that has the power consistently to elevate us to all the great levels that we desire to reach and fulfill is *hitbodedut* (*Likutey Moharan* II, 101).

* * *

THE GREATNESS OF HITBODEDUT

A person's prayers before God in *hitbodedut* are a form of *Ruach haKodesh* (Divine Inspiration). This is how King David made up the Book of Psalms. He aroused himself to pray and speak before God. "To You, my heart spoke" (Psalms 27:8), he said. Rashi explains: "To You" — in Your service, as Your messenger — "my heart spoke." His heart served as the messenger of the Holy One, delivering the words which God Himself provided for King David to pray before Him. From these words, words of Divine Inspiration, the Book of Psalms was formed. Each person's level of Divine Inspiration is determined by the extent that he draws upon himself these words — which come from God (*Likutey Moharan* I, 156).

Reb Noson was once describing the greatness of *hitbodedut*. Try to picture the High Priest as he entered the Holy of Holies at the one time of the year that this was permitted, Yom Kippur. In describing his appearance, the liturgy states that the High Priest looked like "one who sits in solitude to pray before God." "Imagine," said Reb Noson, "the High Priest entering the Holy of Holies is likened to the person who sits and pours out his heart before God" (*Hishtafkut HaNefesh, Introduction*). (Through *hitbodedut*, we can, as it were, enter the Holy of Holies each and every day!)

Concerning *hitbodedut*, the Rebbe gave the following analogy: You'll see that thieves generally congregate around the well-known and often-used roads, waiting to set upon innocent passers-by. Someone who wants to outwit them has to find a new road, so that the thieves won't notice him. The same is true when it comes to prayer. The standard, often-used prayers are well-known to the "thieves" — the detractors and forces of the Other Side. *Hitbodedut,* on the other hand, is an entirely new path. Taking this new approach, using new words and original supplications, deceives these spiritual "thieves." Then our prayers are able to ascend without hindrance (*Likutey Moharan* II, 97).

Reb Noson said: Test it out. Practice *hitbodedut* for forty days straight. I guarantee you'll see results (*Aveneha Barzel* p.66).

Reb Noson writes: The Rebbe prescribed different devotions for each of his followers. Some he told to study eighteen chapters of Mishnah a day, while he advised others to fast a certain amount of times a year. Still others were counseled to immerse themselves in a *mikvah* and others were given different devotions to perform. Yet, there were two devotional practices that were universally prescribed for all his followers — in his generation and for all time. They are the daily study of the Codes and the practice of *hitbodedut*. This advice is for everyone, because it is something that every Jew has the ability to perform (*Rabbi Nachman's Wisdom* #185).

*

Every devotion the Rebbe prescribed is helpful as a remedy to rectify both the past and the future. They will help you after your passing, when you'll face the Heavenly Tribunal, stand by you in the Messianic age, assist in the time of the Resurrection, and be of help in the World to Come (*Rabbi Nachman's Wisdom* #185).

* * *

WHEN AND WHERE?

Set aside an hour (or more) each day to meditate in a room or in the fields. While there, speak out whatever is in your heart, with words of grace and supplication. These words should be in the language you normally speak, so that you will be able to express yourself as clearly as possible. When you entreat God in the language you are used to, the words are closer to your heart and will therefore flow more easily (*Likutey Moharan* II, 25).

Concerning the recitation of optional prayers, our Sages say: "If only a person were to pray the entire day" (*Berakhot* 21a). Rebbe Nachman said that it would be very great if we could actually practice *hitbodedut* the entire day. Yet for the majority, this is an impossibility. Most people should therefore set aside at least an hour a day, but those individuals who are very strong in their service to God should spend more time in *hitbodedut* (*Likutey Moharan* II, 96).

The ideal time for *hitbodedut* is at night, when the world around you is asleep. During the day, people are busy rushing after all the material and physical pleasures of this world. This is a distraction and hindrance for anyone wishing to serve God, even if he himself is not occupied with anything other than spiritual pursuits. Thus the best time for *hitbodedut* is in the middle of the night, when the desires and lusts of this world are at rest (*Likutey Moharan* I, 52). Although the night time is the best time, every time is a good time. If you can't get up in the middle of the night for *hitbodedut*, how about trying to find the time to converse with God in the early morning, either before or after the morning prayers — before you get caught up in the rush of yet another busy day? And if that's no good, then really any other time is alright. Whenever...wherever...just remember: the quieter the better.

The main factor is consistency. Rabbi Avraham Chazan used to say: *Hitbodedut* which is consistent (every day) is thousands upon thousands of times greater than *hitbodedut* that is interrupted. On another occasion he remarked: On a day when a person goes without *hitbodedut,* he's taught a "chapter of heresy" by the Evil One (*Rabbi Eliyahu Chaim Rosen*).

Regarding where to practice *hitbodedut,* Rebbe Nachman taught that it's best to find a location which is conducive to meditation and which will allow you to concentrate on your words undisturbed. A private room is good, a park better, out in the fields or forests still better. In short, the quieter and more secluded the place is, the more ideal it is for *hitbodedut.*

In the fields. Rebbe Nachman teaches: Just as the day is less conducive for *hitbodedut* than the night, the city is less conducive than the fields. The city is a place where people chase after "this worldliness," so that even when they are not actually present, the tumult and turmoil they create remains and disturbs one's meditation. This is why the best place for meditation is out in the fields, where the confusing influences of the day and this world are at a minimum (*Likutey Moharan* I, 52).

Know! When a person meditates in the fields, all the vegetation join in his prayer and increase its effectiveness and power (*Likutey Moharan* II, 11). Rebbe Nachman was once walking through a grassy meadow when he said to the person accompanying him, "If only you could hear and understand the language of the grasses. Each blade of grass sings its praise and prayers to God" (*Rabbi Nachman's Wisdom* #163).

In Rebbe Nachman's time, most cities and towns were quite small. Going out to the surrounding fields and forests presented little problem. Today, anyone living in a village or small town can still take advantage of this, however, most people live in a metropolis and find it quite difficult to get away from the city's confines. An alternative might be to use a nearby park. [As for entering fields and parks, Rebbe Nachman taught that one needn't be fearful of the dangers involved in praying in the fields at night, because praying to come closer to God is a great mitzvah and "messengers of mitzvot will not be visited by harm" (*Pesachim* 8b). Also, the dangers of falling into the hands of the "forces of evil" are far greater than those of entering a forest to meditate. It should be made quite clear, though, that this does not include places like New York's Central Park, where one's life is in danger even during the day. Regarding this, the law is most clear: we must not rely upon miracles (*Pesachim* 8b).]

...or at home. But what if you can't go to a park? Or what if you find that whenever you do go, you find yourself concerned for your safety and cannot concentrate on the task at hand? Rebbe Nachman said that it is very good to have a special room set aside for Torah study and prayer. Such a private room, office or study is especially beneficial for secluded meditation and conversation with God. You can also practice *hitbodedut* under your talit. Just drape the talit over your head and converse with Him. This way, you can have your privacy and meditate, even when the room is filled with people. You can also seclude yourself with God while in bed under your covers. King David did this, as he describes (Psalms 6:7), "Each night I converse from my bed...." Or, you can converse with God while sitting in front of an open book. Others will think that you are studying and in this way you will have the privacy to speak your heart out to Him (*Rabbi Nachman's Wisdom* #274-275). Another possibility is to practice *hitbodedut* while walking. The Rebbe himself did this (cf. *Tzaddik* #7). There's no reason to have to wait until you get to your destination in order to begin getting closer to God.

One of Rebbe Nachman's followers was complaining to him about the difficulties he had in serving God properly. The man blamed this on his house being too crowded and not having a private room for his devotions. The Rebbe answered him: "Presumably, if God agreed that the only possibility of your serving Him depended on your having such a room, He would have already given it to you!" (*Tzaddik* # 588). So, we have to make the effort to have *hitbodedut* whenever possible and wherever possible. God will eventually provide us with the right time and place.

* * *

WHAT TO PRAY FOR

Rebbe Nachman teaches: It is good to begin your *hitbodedut* by saying: Today I am *starting* to attach myself to You! Start anew every day. If yesterday was good, I hope that today will be even better. If yesterday wasn't the way it should have been, well today is a new beginning and it will be good (*Tzaddik* #437). The Rebbe himself would start each day by "placing" the day's activities in God's hands, asking that he do everything according to God's will. "This way," he would say, "I have no worries. I rely on God to do as He sees fit" (*Rabbi Nachman's Wisdom* #2).

*

The spiritual. Start your day by having *hitbodedut* that everything go according to God's plan, that you act in accordance with His desire. By doing this, your prayers are automatically focused on God's drawing you closer to Him. The Rebbe said that these prayers can comprise regrets for the past and requests for the future — each person according to his own spiritual level. He stressed that this advice is universal, it is for anyone who wishes to draw closer to God. Whatever you lack, whatever you feel you need in order to serve God, this is the way to attain it (see *Likutey Moharan* II, 25).

The material. Rebbe Nachman was once talking to one of his followers about clothing: One must pray for everything. If your clothes are torn, pray to God to give you new clothes. Although the main thing to pray for is closeness to God, still, you must pray for *all* your needs, large and small. The Rebbe then said: A person who doesn't pray to God for his needs can be compared to an animal. An animal is also fed and sheltered, without asking for it. To be considered a *person*, you have to draw all necessities of life from God through prayer (*Rabbi Nachman's Wisdom* #233).

Reb Noson writes: I was once talking to the Rebbe about something I needed. The Rebbe said, "Pray for it." Having considered it to be an insignificant item, not at all a necessity, I was surprised to learn that one must pray to God even for such trivial things. The Rebbe rebuked me saying, "Is it beneath your dignity to pray to God for something like that?!" (*Rabbi Nachman's Wisdom* #233).

Once, while Reb Nachman Chazan was hammering a nail, the hammer slipped and he hurt his hand. Reb Noson said to him; "Why didn't you practice *hitbodedut* before swinging the hammer? You should have prayed to hit the nail and not your hand..." (*Siach Sarfei Kodesh* I-687).

While standing at the gravesite of Rabbi Shimon bar Yochai in Meron, Reb Avraham Sternhartz was overheard practicing *hitbodedut*: "God, please help me to get up in the morning. Let me say the *modeh ani*, wash my hands thrice, recite the morning blessings, pray...." Whatever we want, we have to ask for it with total simplicity.

*

Hitbodedut encompasses the entire spectrum of life: from the simple, daily affairs of man, to the lofty spiritual heights to which we aspire. When Rebbe Nachman taught that we need to express ourselves in prayer before God for everything we can think of — he meant everything! Whether we need good health (and who doesn't?), success in business and livelihood (and who doesn't?), help with raising our children (and who doesn't?), caring for elderly (or not so elderly) parents, or whatever our hearts' desires, we must raise our eyes, hearts and mouths in supplication before God. We must ask Him to make sure that everything goes alright. If it does, good. If not, pray again. And again. And again. *Hitbodedut* is not something we do once and then stop. *Hitbodedut* is daily.

For example, if your car needs repairs, pray that you get a good mechanic and that he spots the trouble right away. Pray that you won't have to keep going back for repairs. What about your washing machine, sewing machine, refrigerator, etc.? *Hitbodedut* might mean praying that you get the right clothing back from the dry-cleaners, the right products delivered from the supermarket, or even that you don't overpay on an item you purchase. Nothing is too trivial! As long as you even think you need it, pray for it! (The next section will clarify this further.)

Certainly, a person must focus his prayers on the ultimate goal — serving God. Pray, plead, beg, ask and beseech God that He reveal His ways to you, that He show you His mercy, that you merit coming closer to Him. Pray that you will be able to perform His will, each mitzvah in its own time. Pray to feel the beauty in Torah, pray to feel the sweetness in the mitzvot. Reb Nachman Chazan once labored tirelessly to erect Reb Noson's *sukkah*. That evening, while sitting in the sukkah, Reb Nachman remarked, "There is a different feeling of joy and satisfaction when sitting in a sukkah which one has worked very hard to build." Reb Noson replied, "That may be, but this you haven't yet tried. Spend an entire day crying out to God: 'Master of the Universe! Let me taste the true taste of sukkah!' Then see what feelings a person can experience in the sukkah" (*Aveneha Barzel*, p. 52 #12).

Once you grow accustomed to *hitbodedut,* you'll begin to see how it's possible to pray for everything — from the most exalted spiritual desires to the most trivial material needs, and everything between. Don't be put off by the following scenario which sometimes happens. There are those who, as they develop their *hitbodedut,* begin to feel awkward about praying for success in business and the like. "Here I am," this person says, "I'm (finally) praying to God, and all I can think about is money?" If it's not money, it's something else material, and it seems to him that this is not what *hitbodedut* is all about. Feeling guilty, he begins focusing his prayers exclusively on the spiritual. But, because his heart isn't fully in it, his prayers begin to slacken. In time, his *hitbodedut* might even stop altogether. Regarding this, Reb Noson once said: Pray to God for a livelihood. Specifically for livelihood. You'll probably start feeling embarrassed that you're asking and pleading so much for the material and you'll eventually pray for the spiritual, too (*Aveneha Barzel* p.49).

* * *

HOW TO PRACTICE HITBODEDUT

Private conversation with God can be enjoyable or awkward. It depends entirely on you. Keep *hitbodedut* simple and you'll feel such an affinity for it that you'll eagerly await its moments every day. This section offers some advice on, and various examples of, the *how-to's* of *hitbodedut* Often, people will read about conversing and meditating with God, they'll study all the pertinent lessons and teachings on *hitbodedut* and become familiar with all it's details: when and where to practice it, how often, how long and about what. But when it comes to actually going out, or in, and doing it — stagefright! systems crash! Your mind goes blank, your words dry up. What to do? Don't worry, it's not at all uncommon for this to happen, and not only to beginners. The Rebbe once said that when a person is meditating and all he can say is "Master of the World!" this is also very good (*Tzaddik* #440). He also said that just sitting, without being able to say anything, is also valuable (*Likutey Moharan* II, 25); and sometimes, no matter how much we know about *hitbodedut* beforehand, this is all we can do.

In any case, it is helpful to have a practical, nuts-and-bolts notion of how to go about practicing *hitbodedut*. The following suggestions of what one can say while conversing with God, and how one is to say it, are by no means intended as a complete guide. Actually, the possibilities are endless, depending upon the individual person, place and time. These examples are just meant to give the reader an idea of how to go about *hitbodedut*, providing a fair range of subject material applicable to most people. Ultimately, each person should choose the particular words and subjects that are closest to him.

*

Simply and openly. Rebbe Nachman said to Reb Noson: A person should practice *hitbodedut* in a simple, straightforward manner, as if he were conversing with a close friend (*Tzaddik* #439; *Kokhavey Or* p.12 #4). Have you ever had a problem which you spoke about to a friend, a true friend? You start saying something, this leads to something else, and before you know it you're revealing the innermost secrets of your heart. The words just seem to flow. This is because you're close to that friend, and you see no reason to hold back. *Hitbodedut* should be the same way:

"Yankel, you know what happened to me today? I woke up feeling good and went to *shul*. I started praying energetically. But then I saw Avi, with whom I had an argument last week. Next thing I knew, I lost my enthusiasm and felt like dead wood. You know, it's becoming more and more like this every day. Anyway, I went home in a sour mood and ended up fighting with my wife. From there I went to work and had a miserable day. In fact, I wouldn't be surprised if my boss fires me. What am I going to do? I can't seem to get hold of myself. I try to keep things under control and make it through the day on the right foot but it always turns out wrong. What can I do? Maybe you have some ideas?"

Now, instead of addressing your close friend, address your "closest" Friend. Just substitute God for Yankel. You can express and unburden yourself in exactly the same way, with the same frankness and detail. After all, if Yankel can listen and maybe offer help, certainly God can! [It is important to point out that which our Sages state: "There can be no friendly manner towards Heaven" (*Bava Batra* 16a). One may not actually think or talk to God with a familiarity, as if He were a pal. However, this is not meant to exclude direct and personal prayer — *hitbodedut* — in which one addresses the Almighty as one talks to a good friend. The openness and candor with which we "reveal all" to a close friend, and which is desirable when conversing with God, should not be misunderstood as a license for a friendly manner when addressing Him (see also *Gittin* 57a).

Like a child. Rebbe Nachman also drew another analogy concerning *hitbodedut*. In his desire to make it crystal clear how we are to approach this most important practice, he said that it is very good to pour out our thoughts before God, like a child pleading before his father. God calls us His children, as is written (Deuteronomy 14:1), "You are children to God." Therefore, it is good to express your thoughts and troubles to God like a child complaining and pestering his father (*Rabbi Nachman's Wisdom* #7).

*

The following paragraphs offer just a glimpse of some short prayers that can be offered during *hitbodedut*. Remember, any individual thought can be expanded upon, meditated on and prayed for, for hours on end. Combinations of two ideas or two thousand ideas are also possible. Use any approach, any prayers or supplications that you feel, and use your own words. Let it flow freely from the heart.

Coming closer to God. Please, God! I am greatly confused. I hear about Judaism, but have no idea what it's really all about. Help me. Guide me, so that I come to have true faith in You.

Or: God! I am greatly confused. I read about You. I study about You. I hear about You. I hear about Judaism. But I have no idea what it's really all about. Help me! Guide me in Your path that I may learn about You, about Your existence, and come to have true faith in You.

Or: O God! I want to come close to You. I want to experience You, Your goodness, Your kindness, Your boundless mercy. Open Your path to me, the path of Torah, the path of the True Tzaddikim, so that I may be able to learn how to come closer to You. I realize I am very distant from You, I realize that I'm not worthy of any revelation. But I am a Jew! I was created to recognize and serve You. Help me! Guide me in Your path that I may learn about You, about Your existence, and so come to have true faith in You.

Or: O God! I want to come close to You. I want to experience You, Your goodness, Your kindness, Your boundless mercy. Open Your path to me, the path of Torah, the path of the True Tzaddikim, so that I may be able to learn how to come closer to You. I realize I am very distant from You, I realize that I'm not worthy of any revelation. But I am a Jew! I was created to recognize and serve You. You put me on this physical earth. You are the one who placed me where I am, in this situation, exposing me to the daily temptations of a mundane life. I know it is for my good, that I search for and find the truth — You — and rise above the falsehoods that abound. But I am too weak, I can never seem to overcome my desires. Please! Please! Help me come closer to You. Help me to always feel Your presence, so that I may always come closer and closer to You. Help me to be happy always, help me feel joy and happiness in being a Jew and practicing my Judaism proudly.

Torah study. Please God! Help me study Torah, daily. Help me understand what I study, help me remember what I study. Please guide me in a study program, so that I learn what is necessary for me to know. Help me navigate the "sea of Torah" safely, so that whatever I learn brings me closer to You.

Or: Please God! Help me study Torah. Help me study Chumash, TaNaKh, Mishnah, Talmud, the Codes and musar, daily. Whatever I study, please help me understand and remember. Help me navigate the "sea of Torah" safely, so that whatever I learn brings me true knowledge and wisdom to come closer to You.

Or: Please God! Help me study Torah. Help me set aside time every day to study and let me be consistent in this. Whatever I study, help me understand and remember. Guide me to learn only that which is permitted, so that whatever I do learn will bring me knowledge and wisdom to come closer to You. Distance me from the philosophies and false wisdoms that might lead me away from You. Let me find a proper teacher to convey the true meaning of what I learn, so that I am not misguided and am given good advice.

Prayer. Dear God, help me concentrate on my prayers. Please, I am now praying to You, I am now speaking to You, but my heart is very distant from my words. I am not concentrating. My mind wanders. Please let me feel the words. Let me appreciate the beauty of the words of prayer, so that I may find You.

Or: Dear God, help me concentrate on my prayers. Please, I want to pray to You, I want to recite my prayers with joy. Please let me feel the words. Let me appreciate the beauty of the words of prayer, so that I may find You. Open my heart, open my mouth and please let my words pour forth to You with total concentration. Please accept my pleas and guide my prayers directly to You.

Or: Dear God. O God. Please help me. I want to pray, I want to pour forth my heart before You. I want to come closer to You, but I don't know what to say. I am troubled. I am distant from You and I find it difficult to overcome material desires. Yet, I still wish to come closer to You. Please let me practice *hitbodedut* every day, please let me sit before You at least an hour each day, so that I can pray to You and pour out my heart's longing before You. Let me also recite my daily prayers with *kavanah*. And please make sure that I awake in time to attend services in the synagogue, with a minyan.

Truth and faith. O God! Please let me have full faith in You! Full faith in You, in Your Torah, in the True Tzaddikim. Save me from falsehood, from alien philosophies and all sorts of thoughts that can distance me from You. Please God! Lead me on the right path for my soul. Lead me on a path that will bring me ever closer to You. Let me have full faith, unswerving faith, unbending faith, that everything about You is truth. And let me find that truth — You — so that I may come ever closer to You.

Or: I am bothered by many questions. I have too many questions and no answers. I am disturbed by many things that I see, yet do not understand. Please, God, where I am able to understand the answer, please provide it. And where I am as yet unable to understand, please strengthen my faith in You. Strengthen my acceptance of You as King, as Ruler of the universe, and let me truly believe that I, and everything that happens to me, and everything that happens in the whole world, are exclusively in Your hands. Please help me acknowledge this daily and be aware of You at all times. Please bring all Israel and all the nations of the world to recognize Your Sovereignty.

Traits and desires. Please, God. Help me break my bad character traits. I have so many I don't know where to start. I want humbleness, I have arrogance. I want patience, I am full of anger. Okay, so I did lose my temper the other day. All right! It was more than losing my temper, it was a terrible scene. But I'm not all that bad. I still want to come close to You! Maybe I'm undeserving. But, God, I do have good points, I have a measure of good in me that shows I can make progress. Please help me develop that good point, help me overcome my bad qualities. Instill in me good character traits. I don't want to lose my temper any more. Help me to control it. And help me attain other good qualities too.

Or: Please God, help! Today, I really over-did it. No joke. I indulged myself more than ever before. When am I going to learn to curb my appetite? When am I going to learn to say "no!" to food. Help me. Keep me from over-eating, from "stuffing my face." Save me from indulging in excesses. Also save me from slander, from falsehood, from trickery and chicanery, from mockery and from interfering in matters that don't concern me. Help me do what is right. Let me open my mouth for Torah and prayer, for saying a kind word and strengthening a friend. But, save me from wrongdoing!

Children. Today, as You well know, my wife and I were blessed with a beautiful child. Thank You. I ask You, God, please, give this child good health. Help us raise this child easily. Grant us the wisdom and patience needed to deal with children, so that we may raise them to be good Jews.

Or: Today, my four year old told me a lie. I slapped him. I don't know whether I did right or not. Was it to teach my son the severity of the crime, or was the slap only to appease my anger? And did the punishment fit the crime? Perhaps I should have found another means to teach him that lying is wrong? Please, help me control my anger, help me see what really motivates my child to behave the way he does. I ask You, God, please, show me the right way to guide this child. Grant me wisdom and patience, so that I raise him to be a good Jew.

Or: Dear God. Direct me. Guide me. Teach me how to raise my child correctly. This child was entrusted to me by You. I, as parent and guardian, want what is right for her. I want the best for her. But what is the best for her? Only You know, Master of the Universe. Only You can see that she is protected from evil, from the ills of society, from the dangers of the street, etc. Let her develop good character traits, good desires, good intentions, so that she always seeks good. Grant me wisdom and patience so that I raise her to be a fine person and a good Jew.

Livelihood. God! I need help! I have bills to cover. I need money to pay my mortgage, utilities, car expenses, etc. I have tuition bills to pay. They are huge. I have no idea where to come up with such sums. Help me! Either reduce my expenses or raise my income. But help! I am breaking under the load. Please help me climb out from under this crushing yoke.

Or: I found a new business to invest in. It looks good. Should I, or shouldn't I, invest in it? What is the right path for me to take? I need Your guidance. Please show me the correct path, so that I may make the correct decision, with which to benefit myself and my family.

Or: I found a new business to invest in. It looks good. Should I, or shouldn't I, invest in it? What is the right path for me to take? I need Your guidance. Will this business allow me sufficient time to pray, study and spend time with my family? Will it give me sufficient income? Please show me the correct path, so that I may make the correct decision, with which to benefit myself and my family. This way, I'll be able to support the family and have the necessary time to study Torah and serve You.

Or: I found a new business to invest in. It looks good. Should I, or shouldn't I, invest in it? What is the right path for me to take? I need Your guidance. Will this business allow me sufficient time to pray, study and spend time with my family? Will it give me sufficient income to support my family and have enough to donate generously to charity? Or will it be a trap? Will I become enslaved to this business day and night, with very little time left for myself? Will it allow me to be free on Shabbat? Please show me the correct path, so that I may make the correct decision, with which to benefit myself and my family. This way, I'll be able to support the family and have the necessary time to study Torah and serve You.

Vacation time. Boy am I tired! I need a vacation. But where should I go? I want a place where I'll be able to relax and recharge my batteries. Yet, I also want to make sure that I'll remember You even while I'm vacationing. Please let me find a nice resort area, a place where I can find a shul, a mikvah and kosher food. Remind me to take along study books and tapes and my walkman. Most of all, let me make sure not to forget You or my Judaism, while I'm away.

Family and friends. Master of the Universe! Please help me to have peace reign in my house. We have, thank God, a nice family. But there always seems to be some friction between my brothers and this leads to tension in the entire family. Each one by himself is a gem, but together, they are like cats and dogs. Please help us to root out the rivalry and have peace reign in the house. (Naturally, any sibling or even neighbors can be substituted.)

Or: Today I had such and such a conversation which led to a disagreement with my friend (and one can repeat the words of that conversation too!). I think I was right, or at least

I see it so from my point of view. In any case, I had no intention of letting that slip of the tongue happen, but it did. I'm sorry. What can I do to correct it? Help me find a pleasant way with which to set right that which went wrong. At least get my friend to understand that it was not done in malice, God forbid! Help me control my tongue so that I never again say anything that will hurt others. Help me to see another's point of view.

Good health. Please God, in Your great mercy, grant us good health so that we may be able to serve You properly.

Or: My child is not well. He has such and such an illness and is suffering. Please God, send him a *refuah shleimah* (a complete recovery). And, grant us all good health.

Or: My grandparent has to undergo an operation. Please God, send him a *refuah shleimah* so that the operation is not necessary. And if he must have the operation, then please let the diagnosis be correct. Provide the right surgeon, the right nurses and other staff. Please heal my grandparent and all those who are ill. Please God, send him a speedy recovery. And grant us all good health.

*

The thing to remember about *hitbodedut* is this: Choose whatever topic you feel close to *at that time*. Put in whatever feeling you have. Do it daily.

* * *

SIGHING

Rebbe Nachman teaches: One should sigh and groan during *hitbodedut* (*Tzaddik* #441).

The sighing of a Jew is very precious (*Likutey Moharan* I, 8:1).

When you sigh and groan over your unfulfilled yearning for holiness, it causes you to be attached to the *ruach* (the life-force) of holiness. This is because sighing is drawing breath — which is life itself! (*Likutey Moharan* I, 109).

Sighing and groaning are not just for appearances, to impress others or to convince yourself of your sincerity and your desire to repent. Every sigh, every groan, is part of a process through which we draw *ruach* (breath), life. There are quite a few lessons in the *Likutey Moharan* on the concept of *ruach*. Your desires and longing are centered in your heart, the organ used for breathing and desiring. Therefore the Rebbe taught us to groan and sigh when practicing *hitbodedut*. Think about drawing closer to God and think about becoming a better Jew.

Groan away the bad desires. Rebbe Nachman once said: For a quarter-of-an-hour's worth of pleasure, a person can lose both this world and the next! (*Likutey Moharan* II, 108). Rebbe Nachman once took hold of Reb Shmuel Isaac near his heart and said to him: "For the little bit of blood in your heart will you lose this world and the next? Groan it out! Cry and sigh a lot until you get rid of the desires for this world" (*Tzaddik* #441).

The silent scream. You can let out a scream in a room full of people and yet no one will hear it. This is the silent scream known as the "small still voice." Anyone can do this. Just imagine the sound of such a scream in your mind! When you picture this scream and focus your concentration on it, you are actually shouting inside your brain. It is not merely imagination, and it enables you to call out to God even in public (*Rabbi Nachman's Wisdom* #16). Rebbe Nachman placed great emphasis on man's ability to concentrate and direct his thought processes. With regard to the scream, he said that it is possible literally to let out a scream that could be heard round the world. This advanced level of concentration during meditation can also be used to "create" any imaginable set of circumstances to enhance one's *hitbodedut*. For example, one could "relocate" oneself to a snowcapped mountain or near a stream in the forest, or even to the Western Wall in Jerusalem — provided one's ability to picture this in one's mind is strong enough.

* * *

WHAT IF...

Rebbe Nachman teaches: There may be times when a person doesn't feel he can speak to God, doesn't feel the words he is speaking. This can happen and it does happen. Do not be discouraged. Just sitting there before God and wanting to pray to Him is in itself a very great thing (*Likutey Moharan* II, 25).

Reb Yitzchak of Tulchin, Reb Noson's son, would frequently discuss his difficulties in spiritual development with his father. He once expressed his frustration, saying that his devotions had weakened and he could not meditate properly. Reb Noson told his son that King David's greatness manifested itself in precisely this area. Many times King David would want to pray, but could not find the words to speak to God. Yet he knew that one should never despair. Instead of giving up, he would groan and cry out to God that his mouth was closed, that he could not find the appropriate words with which to pray. *This* became his prayer. God would then accept his entreaties and provide King David with the inspiration to find the right words with which to pour out his heart. Indeed, God wants us to pray to Him for guidance in praying properly (*Aveneha Barzel*, p. 70 #53). You need never despair of *hitbodedut*. If you can't speak before God, just keep trying. Come back day after day, to your place in the forest, to your special

room, or wherever, and keep trying. Eventually the words
will come.

*

Rebbe Nachman also teaches: You can also make a prayer
of this itself. The very fact that you have come to pray and
cannot, can itself be something to pray about (*Likutey Moharan* II,
25). Even when you cannot speak, even when all you can get
out of your mouth is one word — only one word! — it is
still worth all the efforts you put into *hitbodedut*. Repeat
this one word again and again. Even if this continues for
a few days, constantly strengthen yourself with this word.
Ultimately, God will open your mouth and send you the
necessary words to be able to pray and meditate properly
(*Likutey Moharan* II, 96).

For example, you might want to say: O God. It just isn't
working. I don't feel like talking. I just don't feel like anything.
Please open my mouth. Please! Please! Please!....

As mentioned earlier, the Rebbe also said: Even if one
can only repeat the words, "Master of the World!" this is
also very good (*Tzaddik* #440). Someone once came to Reb
Noson praising a certain student who knew 1,000 pages of
Talmud by heart. Reb Noson said: "But my student, Reb
Ozer, can say 1,000 times 'Master of the World!'" (*Aveneha
Barzel* p. 49).

*

Rebbe Nachman teaches: You need to be extremely
stubborn in your devotions and service to God (*Likutey
Moharan* II, 48). At the same time, Rebbe Nachman himself
was known to be very easygoing and tolerant. He was
never stubborn (see *Tzaddik* #430). This might seem to be
contradictory, but it's not. When it came to everything else,
the Rebbe preached against being obstinate, and this is what

he practiced. However, regarding one's prayers to God, one's *hitbodedut* and supplications to be a worthy Jew —the Rebbe admired obstinacy (*Rabbi Eliyahu Chaim Rosen*).

And even here, a distinction has to be made. Our obstinacy should be in the *practicing* of *hitbodedut*, not in our willingness to accept God's will. We must never cease praying, pleading and begging. The Rebbe taught us that everything we need, is obtainable from God through *hitbodedut*. As he himself said, "Had I known when I was younger the great power of prayer, I would never have performed the self-abnegations that had such a devastating effect on my body" (*Hishtafkut HaNefesh, Introduction*). This determination and tenacity in prayer is part of what the Rebbe calls "holy stubbornness." However, when it comes to accepting God's answer to our requests, obstinacy has no place. The decision must be left to Him, we must trust that God will provide what *He* knows is necessary, what *He* knows is best.

*

In short, the *how-to*'s of *hitbodedut* are really unlimited. There are many, many different ways and techniques to meditate and pour out your heart and soul before God; just as there is a seemingly endless list of what to pray for. It takes stubbornness, great stubbornness, to sit day after day, week after week, year after year. But, if you persevere, if you practice your *hitbodedut* persistently, you will certainly see results — far greater than you've ever imagined.

Perhaps, the most important point to remember about your *hitbodedut* is that every word counts. Every word spoken, even if not from a broken heart or flowing with feeling, makes a difference. Shortly before he passed away, Reb Avraham Chazan was overheard saying during his *hitbodedut*: "God! Please help me to believe that no word ever gets lost! No good thought is ever forgotten from You!" (*Rabbi Eliyahu Chaim Rosen*).

* * *

THE POWER OF HITBODEDUT

Rebbe Nachman once said: How is it that we allow God to bring evil to the world?! We must call God away from all His other tasks. We must draw Him away from issuing these decrees (this was at the time of the Czar's *Ukase*). We must tell Him to put everything else aside and listen to us. Whenever a Jew wants to talk to God, to pour out his heart before Him in prayer, God ceases whatever He is doing at that moment, as it were. Instead, He turns to listen to that individual who wants to draw closer to Him (*Rabbi Nachman's Wisdom* #70).

*

"God is good for all" (Psalms 145:9). God is good for everything. Everything a person needs he can pray for — and God can supply it. Whether it's health, sustenance, children, other necessities of life or especially spiritual needs — God can provide everything (*Likutey Moharan* I, 14:11).

*

"How does one arouse one's heart to serve God?" Reb Yudel once asked the Rebbe. "Through the power of speech," the Rebbe answered. "Articulate the words with your lips, recite the Psalms and other prayers, say them constantly, and your heart will become aroused" (*Tzaddik* #441). Elsewhere, Rebbe Nachman teaches: speech has a tremendous power to arouse a person to serve God. Therefore, even if you feel your words lack heart, keep saying them. Say them in whatever way you can. After a while, these "heartless" words will arouse you to serve God (*Likutey Moharan* II, 98).

*

"Your bodies are so gross and attached to physicality," Rebbe Nachman once said to his followers. "You must wear it down with words of holiness!" (*Tzaddik* #443). The Rebbe told the following parable about the greatness of persistent prayer: A king asked his son to transfer an extremely large stone to the tower of the palace. No matter what the prince tried, he could not figure out a way to lift such a huge stone, let alone get it up to the tower. Finally, the king said, "Do you really think I expect you to carry it in one piece? Chip away at the stone with a chisel and hammer, and each day bring up the pieces. Eventually, the entire stone will have been brought up to the tower." Similarly, in serving God, persistent, daily prayer — *hitbodedut* — chips away at the heart of stone and elevates a person to God (*Tzaddik* #441).

*

Rebbe Nachman teaches: The wise person will pray his entire life to speak just one totally truthful word to God (*Likutey Moharan* I, 112). There are different levels of truth. There are those whose speech transmits a little bit of truth. They have truth within themselves, but it cannot radiate out to enlighten others. Then, there are those special individuals who have such a high level of truth within themselves, that each and every word they say has the power to enlighten others with truth (*Likutey Moharan* I, 9:3).

You might ask yourself, "how much truth do my words transmit?" If you're truthful with yourself, you'll probably want to raise your level. After all, if the Rebbe says that it's worth spending an entire lifetime to speak just one totally truthful word.... The key to achieving this is *hitbodedut*. Praying in your own words, with your own truth, and with the deepest feelings of you heart, will bring you to ever higher levels of truth. Then, to whatever degree you have achieved this, your words will transmit that truth and may even enlighten others.

* * *

HITBODEDUT ANECDOTES

When Rebbe Nachman mentioned the importance of *hitbodedut* to Reb Noson, the latter asked: But surely man has free will?! The Rebbe did not answer explicitly, yet indicated that even though he might not be able to explain this to him completely, it was still necessary to follow this practice. Reb Noson understood that the same question might be asked about the formal prayers compiled by our Sages (*Tzaddik* #436). Reb Noson's question was this: Why should we pray to God to draw us closer to Him? Doesn't this defeat the purpose of free will? By asking Him to determine what we do, aren't we essentially asking Him to remove our free choice? The Rebbe answered him: although this may be hard to understand, the best way to exercise our free will is to ask God that we submit to His will. As the Mishnah teaches: "Make your will His will" (*Avot* 2:4).

When Reb Noson first became a follower of Rebbe Nachman, he would spend an occasional Shabbat in Breslov. On Friday night, after everyone had gone to sleep, he would descend to the bank of the Bug River and spend the night crying out to God. He would say, "God! There is a fire burning in Breslov. Enflame my heart with that fire!" (*Siach Sarfei Kodesh* 1-689).

After Rebbe Nachman's passing, Reb Noson moved (from his birthplace, Nemirov) to Breslov. At first, he rented a one-room apartment in someone else's house. However this soon proved inconvenient, and he prayed to God for better accommodations. His prayers were answered and he was able to move into his own quarters. Yet even this new apartment had no private room where Reb Noson could practice *hitbodedut* and study Torah. Having no better alternative, he erected a room divider in the corner of the kitchen. It wasn't perfect, and he was often interrupted by his children, but at least it was "his own four ells." Things stayed this way until many years — and many prayers — later, when Reb Noson was finally able to add on an attic to his house. He praised and thanked God for having found him worthy to have his own room after all those years (*Aveneha Barzel*, p. 62 #30).

Reb Noson once stopped at an inn together with a friend. While eating, a small bone became lodged in Reb Noson's throat. Opening his mouth wide, as though he were choking, the bone became unstuck. "Did you see," said Reb Noson to his friend, "when the bone was stuck I opened my mouth and looked upward? There is nothing else we can do but look to Heaven for all our needs — even when we cannot speak, but only moan" (*Kokhavey Or*, p. 71 #8).

Before departing Europe for the Holy Land, Reb Elchonon Specter went to visit the man responsible for almost singlehandedly introducing Breslover Chassidut to Poland, Reb Yitzchak Breiter. When Reb Elchonon arrived, Reb Yitzchak was engaged in *hitbodedut*. Reb Elchonon waited for six hours. After Reb Yitzchak emerged from his room, Reb Elchonon said to him, "You must have really felt an arousal!" Reb Yitzchak replied, "I haven't even begun to speak my heart!"

When Kalev went to Hebron to pray at the graves of the Patriarchs, he was in considerable danger of being caught by the inhabitants of the land (Numbers 13:22, *Rashi*). He went anyway, because a person under pressure and in desperate need of something doesn't take danger into account. He knows only that he must act (*Zohar* III:158b). Reb Noson taught the same is true in serving God, especially in practicing *hitbodedut* in the fields. We should feel the pressure from the Evil Inclination, and not make an accounting of all the so-called dangers involved in serving God (*Kokhavey Or*, p. 71 #9).

When discussing this point and the practice of going out to the fields at night, Reb Noson told of the time the Haidemacks [a band of Cossacks] fell upon a town and forced its inhabitants to flee. Among those running away was a man known to be afraid of literally everything. While fleeing, this man found himself alone in the town's cemetery and having no choice, he spent the entire night there. The next day, when the inhabitants returned to the town, they asked him, "How were you able to stay alone in the cemetery?" "I was too afraid to be afraid!" he replied (*Siach Sarfei Kodesh* 1-555).

One of the six questions put to a person by the Heavenly Court is: "Did you hope for the Redemption?" (*Shabbat* 31a). Rabbi Nachman Chazan said that this refers not only to the redemption of the Jewish Nation, but also to each individual's personal redemption. Did you lose hope and give up? or, did you hope and pray for God's salvation to bring you out of all your troubles? (*Aveneha Barzel* p. 80).

* * *

10

PEACE

God found no suitable vessel to contain His blessings other than peace (*Uktzin* 3:12).

Rabbi Yehudah the Prince taught: The power of peace is very great. God even overlooks the sins of Jewish idolators when there is peace between them. But if there is strife, they are made to account for every sin. See therefore how beloved is peace and how strife is abhorred (*Breishit Rabbah* 38:6).

*

Peace: mankind's most sought after, yet elusive, blessing. Peace: with it, everything is good; without it, what good is everything else? We all need blessings. Some of us need a blessing for health or *nachat,* others a blessing for livelihood or wisdom or something else. The list is endless. Yet even when we have the blessing, if it is not accompanied by peace, what we have is of little value. Of what use is it to be blessed with all the money you need, if getting it or keeping it has filled you with turmoil and anxiety? It's not much different with our spiritual endeavors. No matter how much we may have worked at praying or acquiring Torah knowledge, no matter how many mitzvot we've performed in order to bring ourselves closer to God, there is no completeness without peace. Ultimately, peace is the clearest proof that our efforts have proven worthwhile and successful.

* * *

SOME OBSTACLES TO PEACE

Yet, if peace is so desirable, so vital to everything else, why is it so hard to acieve? Why has man rarely succeeded at being at peace with himself? Why has mankind never really succeeded at bringing peace to the world? Obviously, peace is not all that easy to come by. If it were, we would have had it long ago.

As Rebbe Nachman said, "Many of the foolish and misguided notions which people in previous eras believed in have disappeared. This includes such practices as sacrificing one's children, worshiping idols and so on. But the foolishness involved in the pursuit of war has not been abolished." The Rebbe openly expressed his contempt for the scientists who develop new weapons: "What great sages they must be! Look how they make wonderful new weapons that can kill thousands of people at once!" (*Tzaddik* #546).

What makes peace so elusive? Surely, there is no one answer. The list is actually quite formidable. Dominant are the character traits which form such powerful barriers to truth that peace becomes an impossibility — for man as well as for all mankind. We shall discuss some of these traits — victory, jealousy, slander, conceit and anger — with the hope that recognizing them and understanding how they keep us from attaining peace will help us fulfill our desire to eliminate them once and for all.

*

Nitzachon! Victory. Of course you want it! Who doesn't? But at what price?! Rebbe Nachman teaches: Our desire to be victorious — *nitzachon* — prevents us from accepting the truth. If, in a conversation or an argument we recognize the validity of the other person's opinion, we'll pursue our own reasoning, rather than accept — even worse, admit — that the other person may be right (*Likutey Moharan* I, 122).

The character trait of *nitzachon* is a frequently-discussed topic in *Likutey Halakhot*. Reb Noson writes: In the Torah, the word for eternal — *NeTZaCH* — also means victory — *NiTZaCHon*. These two meanings are really one. Which victory can be called a true victory? Only that which is eternal. History has proven time and again that a conquered nation or an oppressed people will not remain silent forever. It may take years, a new generation may arise, but sooner or later the cycle of time turns round and the victor — because his victory was not eternal (permanent or final) — finds himself suffering at the hands of the victim. Likewise, this is true on the personal level. "Conquering" one's competitor in business also creates feelings of hostility and a desire for retribution in the loser. Ultimately, such victories are empty and worthless. For the moment, one may have achieved one's desired goal, but this contributes nothing to one's Eternal Life.

Conversely, as Reb Noson tells us, everything you do for your Eternal Life remains with you forever. A mitzvah performed is a mitzvah credited. No one can ever take it away from you. If you perform a second mitzvah, that too is credited to your account. The real *nitzachon* is when you conquer your evil traits, your bad characteristics and desires. Then you are the true victor, with every good thought, yearning or deed credited to your eternal account. Seek the truth, the eternal truth, then you will always be victorious and always at peace (*Likutey Halakhot, Birkhot P'ratiyot* 5:2).

Learning to focus on the eternal worth of something is a very valuable asset. While trying to decide whether to do something or not, look at its eternal benefits, not at its temporary gains. This is especially true when you're faced with a difficult decision on a controversial issue. Let's say you feel you must take an unpopular stand on some issue. Fine. Take that stand. Be firm about it. You're entitled. But, warns Reb Noson, before you debate the point with those who disagree with you, be certain that you've looked at it from the eternal perspective. If your position yields eternal gains, then you know you've made the right decision. If, however, all you're going to accrue is some short-lived satisfaction and some temporary self-congratulations that you made your point, then you're really the loser, and a big one at that.

Seeking honor at someone else's expense is also a form of *nitzachon* and is considered detestable and despicable. The Talmud teaches: The person who gains from another's embarrassment loses his share in the World to Come (*Yerushalmi, Chagigah* 2:1). This may be blatantly obvious when the "victor" gleefully gloats over the other guy's misfortune, or it may be much more subtle. Who can say that he's never promoted his own cause by saying something like, "Oh no, I would never do what so and so did. That's not for me at all!" Again, it's an example of the victor and the vanquished, where *nitzachon* has created strife and destroyed peace.

The way to overcome *nitzachon* is through prayer. One must repeatedly make this the focus of his *hitbodedut*. Plead with God to help you. Whenever you're faced with a possibility of *nitzachon*, ask Him to help you overcome your desire for a victory which is false, or temporary at best. Strive only for *nitzachon* that is eternal. Remember, it is better to lose face (and even more) while saving the eternal soul, than to resort to conquering others and forcing your way upon them.

Even in a situation which demands an immediate decision, you can utter a short prayer: "God! Help me choose Your way. Help me make the right move and not allow *nitzachon* to play a part in my decision." If you always try to find God's will, then you'll certainly not seek to win a temporary, meaningless victory at the expense of the entire war. You'll ultimately find the right balance needed to live a life that will bring you eternal victory.

Another way to defeat the desire for victory is to make a point of engaging in dialogue with the one who disagrees with you. Dialogue can lead to compromise and truth (see below, "Truth and Dialogue"). Regarding litigation, our Sages teach: "An equitable compromise is the best solution" (Choshen Mishpat 12:2). Compromise is an art that requires all one's skills in dealing with people. There isn't anyone walking the face of the earth who doesn't need to practice compromise, just as there is no one who lives a peaceful life without compromise.

*

Jealousy. Rebbe Nachman teaches: The Evil Inclination hates man [and seeks to harm him] physically and spiritually (Rabbi Eliyahu Chaim Rosen). We can understand that the Evil Inclination seeks man's spiritual harm, but why his physical harm also? Just look at how much effort it puts into undermining man's physical and material well-being. The Zohar points out: "Come see the power of the Evil Inclination. An animal is born with a natural instinct for survival. It senses predators and avoids danger right from birth. Not so the human child. He runs straight towards danger. He seeks out any perilous situation and jumps right in! This is because he is born with the yetzer hara (Zohar I:179a).

Another way the Evil Inclination succeeds in endangering or destroying our physical and emotional well-being is through the trait of jealousy. One of the most ingrained of human attributes, jealousy emerges at an early age. Even as infants, we desire what someone else has. And as we all know, it doesn't stop there. Jealousy is arguably the most destructive of traits, because it leaves us without satisfaction, comfort, or peace, ever.

Our Sages taught: "Whoever has jealousy in his heart, his bones will rot" (Shabbat 152b). We generally think of the body's decay as a natural consequence of death. What we don't realize is that jealousy eats away at a person's body well before the soul leaves it and the corpse is placed in the ground. How can he rest, if Joe has a Mercedes-Benz and all he has is a BMW? Or Harry and his family took three vacations last year! Or his best friend just landed a top job...a great *shidduch*...a prestigious award. Jealousies such as these have the power to destroy a person. They eat away at his peace of mind, his heart, his health. They wear away his emotions and what's worse, leave an imprint on his soul. What peace can he have in his life when his entire being is consumed by burning desires — for things not rightfully his?

Rebbe Nachman taught that jealousy is rooted in the Evil Eye. Often misunderstood as some abstract mystical power, the Evil Eye referred to by the Rebbe is also the very commonplace quality of looking at our friends and neighbors with a negative or critical eye. The Talmud describes it as "someone who is always looking into another's house" (see *Bava Batra* 2b). Rather than thinking positively about our neighbors and friends and wishing them the best, we tend to covet their possessions and their good fortune. This Evil Eye leads to slander and many other terrible destructive forces that, once let loose, shatter one's peaceful life.

This is also true in spiritual matters. Rebbe Nachman once taught: If people only held on to *this* [trait]...that too would be very great. Even if you cannot attain a high level yourself, you can still be supportive of others and desire that they attain what you cannot reach. "Even if I cannot be a good, religious Jew, at least my friend should be one" (*Rabbi Nachman's Wisdom* #119).

Reb Noson comments: I thought that it was obvious. Of course, if I cannot be a good Jew at least my friend should be one. Of course, I wish him success. But as I grew older, I began to realize that this is a major cause of strife and derision among Jews. We see many people who have tried to become truly religious. They exert great effort, make serious attempts, but do not fully succeed and eventually drift away. Instead of encouraging others, they become intolerant and jealous of those who do pray intensely and who do study Torah. "If I can't make it, they also can't (or won't or shouldn't)," they tell themselves, and will do whatever they can to prevent others from succeeding. However, a true Jew must do the exact opposite, he should want others to serve God, even when he himself is unable to do so. This is true Jewish love! (Ibid.).

Elsewhere, Reb Noson writes: The verse states: "Those who honor Me will be honored. Those who despise Me will be denigrated" (1 Samuel 2:30). Of Aharon it is written, "Those who honor Me," for he honored God by drawing close those who were distant from God. However, there are those who denigrate people, as if they themselves were perfect and without blemish. They are always finding fault in others, especially those who attempt to come closer to God. Such people despise God and by denigrating others they cast aspersion on God. Of them it is written, they "will be denigrated" (Likutey Halakhot, Netilat Yadayim li'Seudah 6:59).

Look at what jealousy has caused: Cain was jealous of his brother Abel so he killed one quarter of mankind. Joseph's brothers were jealous of him and because of their actions, our forefathers went into bondage in Egypt (Shabbat 10b). Korach's jealousy of Moshe and Aharon (Numbers 16), brought about not only the first rebellion in the history of the nation, but also the deaths of over fourteen thousand people (Numbers 17:14). King Saul nearly killed David, because of his jealousy towards him. The list is endless, and, if such outstanding individuals can fall prey to jealousy and *nitzachon*, what chance do we have? (See Likutey Moharan II, 1:1; Parparaot LeChokhmah, loc. cit.).

Reb Noson writes: Strife and arguments have become so prevalent among Jews, that truth is extremely difficult to find. This lack of peace is the main reason for the long delay in the rebuilding of our Holy Temple. It, more than anything else, is responsible for our having had to wait so long for Mashiach to come (Likutey Halakhot, Netilat Yadayim li'Seudah 6:74).

Is there a remedy? There sure is. First, we have to recognize that the problem exists. Most people don't see themselves as being jealous. "Who me? I'm not jealous of my friends — not of their possessions or of their achievements in Torah." Look again! Recognition is the very first step in correcting any situation, especially the subtleties of personality. Rebbe Nachman was aware of this. He understood how the cancer of jealousy is capable of spreading, eventually destroying a person both physically and spiritually, even before he realizes what's happening. Luckily, the Rebbe offered a solution so that we do stand a chance. Not surprisingly, that answer is prayer — hitbodedut. Again and again, we have to turn to God to save us: "Help us see ourselves as we really are. Please, keep us from the snare of jealousy." Sounds too simple for such a difficult problem? Maybe it does, but it works! If we truly turn to God with this request daily, and then some, we can, and will, overcome it.

Another way to subdue jealousy is by finding the good points in others and judging them favorably. The Rebbe teaches us that by focusing on the good, we are looking at them not with an Evil Eye, but with a Good Eye. Finding good brings merit and worthiness to the world, and helps dissipate and cool off the burning flames of jealousy.

Rebbe Nachman said, "It is difficult for two prominent individuals to live [peacefully] in the same city." Reb Noson said, "I and Rabbi Aharon can live together in the same place" (Siach Sarfei Kodesh I-612). Rabbi Aharon was the Rav, the halakhic authority in Breslov. Rebbe Nachman, himself, afforded Rabbi Aharon great honor and respect. As for Reb Noson, his greatness and brilliance are made obvious by his unparalleled writings. Yet these two prominent people could live together in the same city. Why? Because they were both modest. Neither was jealous of the other, there was no competition between them. Rather, their intent was to serve God, and in this they helped and complemented each other.

Slander. Another serious obstacle to peace is slander. The Talmud calls this the most severe of all sins (see *Erkhin* 15b), and there is little doubt that slander has destroyed more lives than any war since the beginning of time. Casting aspersions on something or someone good has the power to dissuade and discourage anybody, no matter how dedicated. Defamation of character can lead to the best of friends becoming the most bitter enemies. Rebbe Nachman, in accord with the above-mentioned passage of the Talmud, teaches: When a person slanders others, the Holy One says to the ministering angel of Hell, "I will judge him from above, and you from below" (*The Aleph-Bet Book*, Slander A:1). Surely, such a person will have no peace, neither in his body nor in his spirit.

In general, slander can be divided into two categories: slandering God and all that is connected with coming closer to Him, and slandering one's fellow man.

Slandering God. People can be greater deterrents to serving God than even the Evil One himself (*Rabbi Nachman's Wisdom* #80). Some people spread slander against God. They cast aspersions on the Torah and the mitzvot, and conceal the light of God and Judaism. If you were alone, without the influence of others, you might be confronted with every type of worry, confusion and frustration, but eventually, everything would work out. It becomes much more difficult when others are the cause of your confusion or frustration. Their ridicule of and sarcasm towards everything sacred can be contagious. The confusing doubts which their ideas foment can quite easily dissuade you from serving God (*Rabbi Nachman's Wisdom* #81).

Sometimes, the problem is compounded because the person slandering God and the Torah is someone who gives the appearance of being a God-fearing person. Such a person, who dresses and talks like a devoutly religious Jew, but whose opinions and advice discourage people from the right path, can be an even greater deterrent to one who truly wants to serve God. We take him more seriously and we trust that he knows what he's talking about. In truth, he is the worst slanderer of God and the Torah, for he has the power to entirely dislodge those who trust in him from holiness (*Rabbi Nachman's Wisdom* #81).

The perpetrator of this type of slander is one who gives false interpretations of our holy Torah. Such false interpretations give the impression that they are rooted in Torah, that they are God's will, and therefore, the views they express represent true Judaism. God forbid! These views are slander against the Torah. Based on philosophies and ideologies that are alien to Torah, or at least not rooted in Torah, they often defame the great Sages of Talmud and cast aspersions on anyone who continues to remain true to their teachings. These specious interpretations are espoused by those ignorant of the Talmud and the rabbinic posture regarding the Oral Law. They prevent people from discovering what God and Torah truly mean. (One can and should think of original Torah expositions, as explained above in the chapter on Torah. However, these insights have to be rooted in traditional sources.) Such slander causes a very wide rift between God and the Jews.

The worst misfortune to befall the Jewish people was the destruction of the Holy Temple. Although there were immediate reasons for God's House being taken from the Jewish people, the Temple's destruction had been etched into history nearly a thousand years earlier. The cause: slander spoken by the messengers sent to spy out the Holy Land. When they returned from their mission, the report they issued caused all the Jews to cry and bemoan their fate. Instead of rejoicing in the good fortune which God was about to bestow on them, they were dissuaded from entering the land. God said: "You cried for no reason at all. There will yet come a time [on this day of Tisha B'Av] when you will have good reason to cry" (*Ta'anit* 29a). Had the spies not spoken against the Holy Land, the Jews would have entered their inheritance right away. As it was, slander and strife led them away from it (*Likutey Halakhot, Netilat Yadayim li'Seudah* 6:74).

How do you avoid either accepting or spreading slander? Rebbe Nachman teaches: Truth saves one from slander (*The Aleph-Bet Book,* Slander A:9). You have honestly to search for the truth. Study Torah and find out what our holy Torah does teach. Find out what the mitzvot really mean. Discover the nature and depth of our true relationship with God. This knowledge will bring you peace — peace with God and with yourself. The Rebbe also teaches: Seeking the truth promotes peace (*The Aleph-Bet Book,* Peace A:6).

Slandering People. The second type of slander is speaking against one's fellow man. One utters a word: it only takes a minute, sometimes less. Before you know it, the remark is out and can *never* be retrieved. If something is said about someone else, even unintentionally, the damage has been done — and sometimes that damage is fatal. The slanderer has succeeded in separating two people who would otherwise have been at peace with each other. He has ruined their accord and tranquility. He has also destroyed his own peacefulness — perhaps forever.

Well, almost forever. The Zohar (III:47a) states: "The sin of slander is so severe, there is no repentance for it." Though this opinion is later reversed in the Zohar, it does give us an inkling of how seriously we should take the prohibition against slander. The Talmud takes this further: "Slander separates man from man, husband from wife. It is as if the slanderer sunders the Jews from God; akin to idolatry" (*Erkhin* 15ff). Rebbe Nachman relates all this to the fact that the person who slanders and spreads gossip destroys the chances for peace — both individual peace and universal peace (*Likutey Moharan* I, 14:12).

Rebbe Nachman teaches: Slander actually derives from imagination, the ability to fantasize. Both humans and animals have this faculty (albeit in different manifestations). But man was created to rise above imagination — to attain knowledge and intelligence. And the more one slanders, the more he descends into fantasy (*Likutey Moharan* I, 54:5).

People readily judge others according to their actions, rather than by their actual motives. The slanderer only surmises the reason for the other person having behaved in a specific way. He doesn't *know* for certain. He judges with presumption, with his power of imagination, and not according to reality. He slanders to satisfy his imagination! The slanderer is thus compared to an animal. He reads into a person's actions something that may never have been there.

The first step in guarding your tongue would be to study the laws of *lashon hara* (slander). Undoubtedly the most thorough work on this topic is *Chofetz Chaim*, by Rabbi Yisrael Meir Kagan (1840-1933); translated into English as *Guard Your Tongue* by Rabbi Zelig Pliskin.

A second step involves working to acquire the quality of humility (*Likutey Moharan* I, 197). When you think of yourself as insignificant, you will not be so quick to criticize and slander others. When teaching about slander, my Rosh Yeshivah would say, "A person busy thinking about himself has no time to think of others." Quite simply, what he meant was that when a person thinks about himself — how distant he is from perfecting his personality, improving himself and acquiring good qualities — he won't spend his time and efforts attempting to belittle and bring dishonor to others.

A third step, naturally, is prayer. Practice a lot of *hitbodedut,* asking God to spare you from situations where slander may be spoken. If you find yourself in a group of people or with a person who speaks slander, quickly say, "God! Please save me from slander!" and try, quickly, to find a way out of the situation. If you can't, make a determined effort to disbelieve the slander you are being told.

"A person's mouth is like a millstone," said Reb Avraham Chazan. "As long as one keeps a millstone grinding it produces what to eat. Keep your mouth grinding, keep speaking words of Torah and *hitbodedut*. Move your lips! Move your lips!" (*Rabbi Eliyahu Chaim Rosen*). The power of speech is a gift which God gave exclusively to man. We must use it positively. Be determined never to misuse it. Flee from slander. Don't say it. Don't repeat it. Don't even listen to it. Don't have anything to do with it.

Conceit and anger. When things are not going according to plan, this is a sign of conceit and arrogance (*Likutey Moharan* II, 82).

It's natural for us to make plans. We make schedules for today, map out our tomorrows, design entire blueprints for the future. But, as we all know only too well, things don't always work out the way we planned, scheduled, mapped out or designed. True, sometimes pumpkins do turn into fancy carriages. Sometimes our plans do work out the way we want them to, the way we expect they should. But more often, it seems that Life doesn't bother to read the script we have written for it. Our ideas are upset, our dreams become nightmares, our hopes are shattered. What of our plans then?

When things do work out the way we want them to, it's called *k'seider*. When they don't work out, it's called *shelo k'seider*. Literally, the word *seder* means order. Are things ordered and going according to my will? Or are they out of order and going against my will? But, wait one minute. Who is it that makes things happen, anyway? Who is it that determines how things will or won't go?

There is God's will. There is my will. They should coincide, but don't always. What happens then? When I desire something and God desires something else, there can be no doubt that God's will is going to prevail. He is the one that makes things happen and His will determines how they will happen. Then the logical question is: How do I accept this? Or, at least: Am I willing to accept it? Can I accept that God created me and knows the paths and directions — the plans, schedules, blueprints — that my life must follow. Can I say this is from God, it's His will, and I will do my best with the present situation? Or, do I reject the situation? Do I say this is not what I want and look for ways to change what has happened against my will?

The way I ultimately choose to deal with what happens when my will and God's are not in perfect agreement is going to influence how I get along in life. It will have a lot to do with whether I'm at peace with myself and the world, or not. Rebbe Nachman explains that our choosing to accept or not accept God's will has to do with the concept of *"ana emlokh"* (I rule). If I always accept God's will, then whatever happens, positive and negative — is according to my will. By looking for the Godliness in whatever occurs, I believe everything that happens to me is God's will and therefore *k'seider.* God rules! But if I do not accept everything as God's will, if I do not look for the Godliness in everything, then there will always be things happening which are against my will. I will see things as *shelo k'seider* and try to change them. I rule! (*Likutey Moharan* II, 82).

The desire of those who do not accept God's will, but seek to change things, is the epitome of arrogance and conceit, which constitute our fourth major deterrent to peace. When a person is arrogant, God departs from him. As our Sages teach: God says of the arrogant, "He and I cannot dwell together in the same world" (*Sotah* 5a). In other words, God abandons him to his own machinations and lets him solve his problems on his own. What happens? Simple: his arrogance leads to frustration; his frustration leads to anger; his anger destroys his peace.

Everything is okay until an "I rule" person encounters a hitch in his plans. It's a *shelo k'seider,* and his arrogance won't allow him to accept that it's coming from God. Now he really does have to come up with a solution, because God has left him to solve his troubles on his own. He'll come up with a solution and map out a plan of action, no doubt still believing he controls his own destiny. But, as has happened to every man since the First Man tried to solve life's problems without God, he soon discovers that no matter how many plans, schedules and blueprints he comes up with, things continue to go against his will — *shelo k'seider*. Sooner, rather than later, this leads to his becoming frustrated. He wonders why he can't succeed, why he can't get things right. Inevitably, this frustration causes him to lose patience and become angry with what he sees as his own ineptitude. Question: Can such a man know peace? Can he ever be at peace with himself?

This gives us an idea of how conceit — and its partner, anger — are obstacles to peace. If you truly believed that everything comes from God, you'd never get upset. You'd accept any situation, any unexpected disruption of your daily routine or long-term plans, and make the best of it. At the very least, you would try to control your emotions; never become frustrated with yourself or lash out at anyone else. Not the arrogant person. He thinks he's in charge, in control. Then, when something occurs against his will, it upsets him. He gets angry. The *shelo k'seider* shows him that he's not really in control of his life, and this upsets him. Each *shelo k'seider* is yet another reminder of his lack of control, yet another proof of his defeat. How does he compensate for this? What does he do? He takes his frustrations out on others. They suffer. He screams at his wife, his children or he shouts at his partner, his friends and neighbors — all because things did not go his way. Question: Can such a man know peace? Can he ever be at peace with others?

Obviously, humility is the key to banishing one's arrogance. It is also a solution to anger. If I consider myself lowly and distant from God what is there to get angry about? About a *shelo k'seider*? About not having succeeded? Because others don't listen to me? Who am I, anyway?

At the same time, it is important to understand what humility is and, more precisely, what it isn't. Rebbe Nachman teaches: Look how hard we work and pray to attain *mochin d'gadlut* (an expanded awareness of God). Then, because we think that humility requires our seeing ourselves as nothing, we submit to *katnut* (a constricted awareness of God) and insignificance (*Likutey Moharan* II, 22). Humility does not mean walking around with your head down, feeling depressed and dejected. It does not mean thinking of yourself as small and of no value. The only way to attain true humility is to pray to God for His guidance in discerning what true humbleness is (*Likutey Moharan* II, 72). Basically, humility is recognizing our insignificance *vis-a-vis* God. This produces modesty which then filters down to our relationships with people. Much more can be said and yet nothing more can be said, because the particulars and situations which govern the true nature of humility are endless. As the Rebbe says, only prayer will take us there.

And, of course, prayer helps. We must ask God to grant us proper control over our arrogance and anger. We have to plead with Him for the ability always to be conscious that "He rules!" Actually, praying in itself is a sign of our acceptance. When we pray, we acknowledge *His* control over all *our* plans, schedules and blueprints. It is proof that, to whatever degree, we recognize that He is in control of the *seder* and that we reject our own arrogance. Why else would we be praying to Him?!

* * *

TWO TYPES OF PEACE

Rebbe Nachman teaches: There are two types of peace. There is an inner peace, the peace in one's bones. And there is universal peace, the peace which prevails when the world is illuminated with God's glory (*Likutey Moharan* I, 14:2,8).

Now that we've encountered the personality traits which are major obstacles to harmony and considered some suggestions for overcoming them, it's time to find out what Rebbe Nachman sees as the nature of the goal itself: the precise nature of peace.

Rebbe Nachman teaches: The entire world is full of conflict. There are wars between nations; battles between states and regions. There are quarrels between families; conflicts between neighbors. There are arguments between husband and wife; strife between father and child; discord within the home. No one pays attention to life's goals. A person dies a little each day. For that day, once it passes, will be no more. Once lost, it is gone forever and will never return. Thus each new day brings us a little closer to death....

Know! All is one. Man is a microcosm, a miniature world. His personality, with its complex structure of traits, encompasses all the different nations, all the variant factions. Because of this, all the wars, conflicts and arguments that take place in the macrocosm are mirrored in his daily life — and indeed, in his very being....Just as there are nations who desire neutrality but are anyway drawn into the conflict, there are times when man tries to still the conflict within himself but to no avail (*Rabbi Nachman's Wisdom* #77).

We can understand the positive from the negative. From the Rebbe's analysis of the absence of peace, we can understand the nature of peace when it does exist — the nature of peace we are to strive for. Rebbe Nachman tells us, the nature of peace is one. Peace in the world — universal peace — is inextricably bound up with the individual's peace — inner peace. A man without peace is a world at war; a world in harmony is a man with peace.

Inner peace. Rebbe Nachman tells us that inner peace is the peace you know in your bones. "Bones," on the literal level, refers to the body. Inner peace implies health, a proper balance between the building blocks of corporeality known as the Four Elements (fire, air, water, earth). Illness, on the other hand, is a symptom of internal conflict and imbalance. The body's "ingredients" are at war and disease prevails. "Body" also applies to the health of the mind. Lack of inner peace indicates an absence of peace of mind. Thoughts and counsel are forever split, decisions are uncertain and divided. The mind is at war. Dis-ease prevails (see *Likutey Moharan* I, 4:8, 14:8).

Another meaning of "bones" is essence: inner peace is the peace you know in your essence. It is the peace between your soul's desire to serve God and your body's desire to serve itself. If the body rules the soul, there can be no peace, for the body always wants, it always desires; be it a desire for money, immorality, food, honor, etc. The soul, on the other hand, is spiritual. It desires only the spiritual. A person steeped in earthly wants and lusts is not at peace and never can be. He is forever looking to satiate that which cannot be satisfied. If there is to be inner peace — peace in the "bones" of one's essence — the soul must rule the body (*Likutey Moharan* I, 14:9).

Inner peace is a quiet sense of confidence within the self. No anxiety, no excess worries, rather a self-assurance in being able to face whatever comes. This stems from a peace between the soul and the body. The body is in tune with the soul and obeys it (*Parparaot LeChokhmah, Likutey Moharan* I, 14).

Universal peace. Every person must say, "The world was created for me!" (*Sanhedrin* 37a). And since the world was created for me, as Rebbe Nachman tells us, I am responsible for the world. I must always look for ways to improve the world and make it a better place in which to live (*Likutey*

Moharan I, 5:1). What better way is there to rectify the world than to fill it with the blessing which brings blessing: peace. That is, Universal Peace, the peace which prevails when the world is illuminated with God's glory.

Rebbe Nachman teaches: As peace spreads in the world, the whole world can be drawn to serve God with one accord. When men are at peace with each other they can freely engage in an open and honest dialogue. Together they can think about the purpose of the world and all its vanities. In talking to each other about the realities of life...they will abandon their illusions and their idols of silver, and aspire only to God and His Torah. Their only aim will be to serve God and seek out the truth (see *Likutey Moharan* I, 27:1; *Advice,* Peace 4).

Reb Noson writes: The essential reason for all of creation was for the sake of God's glory. What is His glory? It is the fulfillment of His will by all that He created. And in particular, it is when man, with his own free will, does God's will....God created the world with an infinite amount of differences and distinctions. Man has to unite them and make them one. His task is to create harmony and peace in time: between day and night, between seasons, years, decades and lifetimes; harmony and peace in places: between warm climates and cold climates, between highlands and valleys, lands blessed with produce and lands which are barren and bare. And man has to create harmony and peace in all forms of creation: between man and animal, animal and plant life, and so on; and especially between all the differences and distinctions that are mankind. Only with peace, only with harmony and a purpose of unity, can these differences be overcome. Seeking the truth, the One God, and fulfilling His will, illuminates the world with God's glory. When this illumination is complete, all the different parts of Creation will compliment each other (*Likutey Halakhot, Birkhot HaR'iyah* 4:2-4). Then, universal peace shall reign.

ATTAINING PEACE

Now that we know what to avoid in our search for peace and we know what peace is, the question remains: How do we attain it?

Torah and prayer. Rebbe Nachman teaches: How can we be at peace with the bad as well as the good, in all that happens to us? Through the Torah, which is called shalom (*Likutey Moharan* I, 33:1). Torah is called peace. It brings peace. The best solution for the person who has no inner peace — whose thoughts and counsel are forever split, whose decisions are uncertain and divided, whose mind is at war — is to study Torah, especially the legal codes. Just as each person experiences conflict within himself and disagreement with his family and friends, so too, there are debates and arguments in the Oral Law. By working to clarify the law, to make peace between the different opinions, you attach yourself to the peace of holiness. This helps you resolve your own inner conflicts (*Likutey Moharan* I, 62:2). Just as the disputes of Torah are settled through such principles as compromise and the search for truth within the texts, your personal conflicts can be solved through the practice of this very same code of conduct within your life.

Besides, the Torah also promotes peace, especially inner peace, by keeping those who study it away from the constant bombardment of the mass-media. Newspapers, radio and television reports of stock-market crashes, violence, war, and political back-stabbings (and front-flatterings), have a way of placing a good helping of turmoil on the breakfast plate together with the morning coffee. It usually comes just in time to ruin what might have started out as a nice, peaceful day. It does much the same when we are ready for a pleasant night's sleep. How much more peaceful it would be to read a few pages of Chumash or Mishnah and to recite some chapters of the Psalms at the start of the day.

Above all else, peace can be attained by your praying for it. Just as in your *hitbodedut* you asked God to keep you from the obstacles to peace, from the negative, ask Him also for the positive. "Please, God, let me find an inner peace. Let me be at peace with myself, my family and everyone I know. And, let the world, with all its differences and distinctions, attain universal peace." Realize that this takes time. You must have an abundance of patience to strive for inner peace. And, you must believe, no matter how it seems, that your every prayer does bring the world closer to universal peace.

Dialogue and truth. As we've seen, peace is the mutual cooperation that exists between different and differing parties, within any given unit. This unit may be smaller or greater, yet the same rules apply. For there to be peace, there must be a dialogue and rapport between the conflicting components of one personality. Between husband and wife, parents and children, between neighbors, business partners and so on. A more expanded peace requires dialogue and rapport between the members of a synagogue, a neighborhood and even a city. Taken still further, there is the greater peace that exists when there is dialogue and rapport between different factions in a nation and between different ethnic groups and countries. The ultimate peace, universal peace, will only come as a result of a dialogue and rapport which our world has yet to taste.

Reb Noson writes: When there is strife between people, they are not open with one another. This makes it impossible for either of them to speak to the other and draw closer to the truth. Even if people talk to each other, their main concern is to win the argument, which means that neither side is open to the words of the other (*Advice*, Peace 8).

There can be no real peace without dialogue. Without real peace there can be no honest dialogue. So where does one begin? When peace is what you want and you don't know how to get it, open a dialogue in search of the truth.

With yourself, this dialogue is *hitbodedut*. With someone else, this dialogue — even if it's not yet honest dialogue because peace is lacking — should be directed towards the truth. Make certain you differentiate between peace and cease-fire. A cease-fire is a mutual agreement between embattled parties to cease hostilities, whereas peace is harmony. Peace is understanding that both sides come to their dialogue on an equal footing. They do not have to be equals, but each one does have to see the other's desire for truth as equal to his own. Neither party seeks to dominate the other, but rather, to work together in their search for peace and truth.

*

Silence. We find in the Holy Zohar: King David says, "God saves man and beast" (Psalms 36:7). Is there a connection being made here between man and beast? Yes. This refers to a man, a wise man, who, despite being embarrassed, maintains his silence. Why? By holding his tongue, though he's been hurt by another's insensitivity, he is like the beast which cannot speak. This is the wisest of all acts, for he knows how to succeed in life. And, above all, he knows how to maintain peace (*Zohar* III:91a).

In a similar vein, Rebbe Nachman teaches: The essence of repentance is when a person hears himself being insulted and nevertheless remains silent. He hears himself ridiculed yet does not reply in kind. This indicates that he is unconcerned by affronts to his honor (*Likutey Moharan* I, 6:2). The result, as the Rebbe goes on to explain, is peace. When you can keep your silence despite being embarrassed you will see your enemies, both internal and external, eliminated. You can then come to achieve both an inner and a [albeit modified] universal peace.

Reb Yisroel Abba Rosenfeld (1882-1947) was very concerned that there be peace among his children. In his will, he stressed his desire that they all overlook each others' faults. His words were, "*zohl mein's ibber gein* (let mine be overlooked) [be silent. Forgive and overlook anything that might lead to strife within the family, even if you sustain a loss because of it]" (*Rabbi Zvi Aryeh Rosenfeld*).

However, the thing to watch out for is that your remaining silent is only for the sake of repentance — i.e. you realize that the insult and indignity actually come from Heaven and accept them as such. Sometimes, a person remains silent because he really doesn't have a way of answering and is afraid of putting his foot in his mouth any further. Or perhaps, his silence is an attempt to cover over something else. Worse, is the silence of someone who knows that the person who insulted him is waiting for a retort and he won't give him that satisfaction. In all of these cases, there is no reward for his silence (*Likutey Moharan* I, 82). The reason is simple. Silence meant as a retort or which has some ulterior motive, leaves a person angry, looking for revenge. Such silence does not bring peace. Only the silence which is motivated by repentance brings peace.

* * *

SPREADING PEACE

The real meaning of peace is to bring together two opposites. So, you shouldn't be annoyed when you come across someone who is the exact opposite of yourself. Even if his viewpoint is the exactly opposite of yours, don't be put off. Don't assume you'll never be able to live amicably with such a person. Similarly, if you see two types of people who are completely opposite types, don't decide that it's impossible to make peace between them. Quite the contrary! Perfect peace is achieved by making peace between two opposites, just as God makes peace in His high places between Fire and Water, which are two opposites (*Advice*, Peace 10).

Elsewhere, Reb Noson writes: Aharon, the High Priest, was the personification of peace. He pursued peace and sought to spread harmony through all of Israel. When a couple would have marital difficulties, Aharon would seek to mediate. He would go to the husband and explain the wife's position and then explain the husband's position to the wife, until he succeeded in bringing them back together again. (Domestic problems existed even then!) He would do the same when neighbors disagreed. For his peacekeeping efforts, Aharon merited the priesthood for himself and his descendants (*Likutey Halakhot, Netilat Yadayim li'Seudah* 6:59).

Therefore, it is by no means coincidental that the Sages incorporated the Priestly Blessing (Numbers 6:24-26) into the daily service precisely in the place of the *Amidah* prayer where we ask for peace. Nor is it surprising that the Blessing itself concludes: "May God turn His countenance to you and grant you PEACE" (*Ibid., Avadim* 2:12).

*

With each day that dawns, universal peace seems further and further away. Yet, our Prophets foresaw the time when Mashiach will come and bring this longed-for peace to the world. It is up to us to strengthen ourselves in faith, prayer, joy and Torah study, as well as in friendship, kindness and consideration. Look for the good points in ourselves and in others and intensify our search for the truth. By doing this, we *will* merit the coming of Mashiach, the rebuilding of the Temple and the ingathering of all the exiles, speedily in our days. Amen.

* * *

11

DAY AND NIGHT

> In the beginning...The Earth was chaos and desolate, with darkness...God said, Let there be light...God called the light "Day," and the darkness He called "Night" (Genesis 1).

Creation. In the beginning God created the heavens and the earth. He created chaos, He created desolation and Darkness. He created Night.... And, He created Day, He created Light. This is the history of man, a microcosm. Man encompasses all of creation within himself. All his thoughts and acts mirror, in one manner or another, the Creation and the current state of the world (cf. *Rabbi Nachman's Wisdom* 77).

* * *

The darkness of night and the light of day are much more than changes that occur when the sun either sets or rises. Conceptually, Darkness and Light manifest in many different aspects of our lives. We have good days and dark days. We have times when everything seems to be going our way; when whatever we do works out, and whatever happens to us is right. When this happens, the Day never seems long enough. But we also have times when everything goes the other way; when whatever we do goes wrong, and whatever happens to us is trouble. Then, the Night never seems to end. In this, we are experiencing the process of Creation — and our own creation — over and over again.

Night falls. And so, "creation" begins. Chaos and confusion, troubles and difficulties, beset a person. His life is suffused with Darkness, a Darkness which seems eternal. Yet, this Nightfall is actually the *beginning* of Day. It is the *beginning* of a new stage in life. When we experience the onset of Night, with accompanying Darkness and indecision, we must look upon it as a fresh opportunity to learn something new, to experience something different. The Day starts off Dark and depressing, but it ends with Light. Thus, trouble should not be seen as a chance happening, nor as an excuse for depression. It should rather be viewed as an opportunity for a new beginning. If we can understand that this trouble is only temporary, just another stage in life, we can face it better. God gives us the Night, with its confusion and chaos, however, He never intends it to continue forever. Daylight, joy and happiness will follow afterwards. Indeed, without this Night, Day cannot emerge. So, with each Night, with each new trouble, a new age is opening up in our lives. Creation is beginning again.

Another area of life where conceptual Darkness and Light are manifest is our thoughts. "Creation" as an ongoing process also occurs in our minds, as the things we think are always passing through periods of Day and Night. Thus Rebbe Nachman teaches: Day suggests wisdom. Night indicates a lack of knowledge (cf. *Likutey Moharan* I, 1). Darkness and Nighttime are symbolic of man's questions and doubts — his state of confusion. Light and Daytime are symbolic of solution and clarification — his resolving of personal chaos.

Understandably, Daylight — wisdom and knowledge — is preferred. Who wouldn't want all his personal questions answered, all his personal problems solved? In fact, given the chance, wouldn't we all jump at the possibility of being completely free from life's periods of confusion and moments of chaos? But things just don't work that way, neither in Creation at large, nor in the particular creations of our daily

lives. "The Earth was chaos and desolate, with darkness...."
First came Darkness. First came Night. Only afterwards did
God say, "Let there be light."

* * *

THE POWER OF THOUGHT

More than anything or anyone else, our thoughts are our
constant companions. They don't even leave us when we
sleep. Our minds — which is where we spend most of our lives
— experience alternating periods of Darkness and Light, of
turmoil and resolution. What's more, as Rebbe Nachman
said, wherever your mind is — that's where you are! (*Likutey
Moharan* I, 21:end). If your mind is experiencing confusion and
a lack of knowledge, it's Night, no matter what your watch
shows. You're "in the Dark." On the other hand, if your mind
is alert and filled with clarity and wisdom, aren't you seeing
the Light of Day? In fact, Light is always being associated with
creative problem-solving: viz. "the light bulb" which turns on
when you have a bright idea.

Realizing that our thoughts are so much a part of us and
make so much of a difference in how we live life, Rebbe
Nachman saw fit to focus so many of his teachings on
precisely this area. What the Rebbe was saying is: It all
depends on your attitude. Do you see Night as a threat, or as
a creative challenge? Are you cowered by Darkness, or does
it motivate you to greater heights? Consider the following
sets of teachings taken from Rebbe Nachman works. The
first, which is called "Night," focuses on the positive struggle
to remove Darkness (evil) from our thoughts. The second,
which is called "Day," focuses on how through our thoughts
we can create Light (good).

*

Night... You should know that when you find yourself
confronted by evil or confusing thoughts and you overpower

them, God takes great pleasure in this. It is very precious in His eyes. This can be likened to the sporting competitions that were held in stadiums to entertain the king. These battles between beasts were observed by the king and his entourage who took great pleasure in the victory of the conqueror. It is similar with our thoughts. Our evil and confusing thoughts are like the impure beasts, our good thoughts are like the pure beasts. The "beasts" of our minds are made to combat each other. It pleases God greatly when we overcome the impurities (*Likutey Moharan* I, 233).

Rebbe Nachman teaches: We have always to strengthen ourselves to overcome evil and confusing thoughts. These thoughts come to a person constantly, daily. The consciousness of man rises to do battle with the forces of the subconscious. It does not help to shake our heads back and forth, thinking maybe this will shake off the bad thoughts. We have to oppose them, as if in battle. This is accomplished by creating a diversion, by thinking other thoughts — as if moving the battle to a different arena. By thinking other thoughts, we can overcome the Darkness which leads us to passions and desires (*Likutey Moharan* I, 72). Thus Rebbe Nachman once remarked: Controlling the mind is as easy as leading a horse. You only need to grab hold of the reins (*Likutey Moharan* II, 50).

The Rebbe therefore teaches: It is impossible for two thoughts to occupy the mind at one time. It is easy to push away the evil thoughts if one wishes. All we have to do is divert our minds to Torah, prayer, business, whatever; as long as it is permissible. For it is impossible for two thoughts to be in one's mind at the same time. Then, the bad thoughts will eventually go away (*Likutey Moharan* I, 233).

But aren't we capable of thinking a few things at once? Yes... but. Although a few things may enter the mind at the same time, only one of them can remain there. Rebbe Nachman once remarked that the Evil One is a sly character.

He comes knocking on your mind. If you allow him to enter, he comes in and takes over, and if you repel him, he goes away and comes knocking again later on. But if you keep up the battle and not give in, he will eventually go away and not return (*Likutey Moharan* II, 51). Take some time to follow your thought process. See how one thought leads to the next, and how that one takes you to the one after it, and so on. Thoughts enter and leave quickly — very quickly. If they are given credence, they remain, but, if they are shrugged off and considered of no value, they will have been successfully chased away.

Reb Noson writes: The "battle of the mind" is compared to the battle that the Jews had with Amalek. Amalek would come stealthily, in a rear-guard action, launching sneak attacks at different intervals. So too, "Amalek" infiltrates our mind, planting seeds of atheism, of immorality, etc. The Torah therefore commands each and every Jew constantly to remember the battle of Amalek, and never forget it (Deuteronomy 25:17-19).

Furthermore, Amalek (עמלק) has the same numerical value as doubt (ספק), 240. All the doubts that pervade our minds, all our uncertainty in how to proceed in life, and especially in serving God, stems from "Amalek." We must constantly strive to control our thoughts. Where these doubts exist, we must pour out our hearts with prayer, asking God Himself to wage His war with "Amalek" and destroy them (Exodus 17:16; *Likutey Halakhot, Minchah* 7:19, 30).

*

Yet another very important aspect of Night and Darkness with respect to our thoughts has to do with the concept of *hastarah* (the hidden) and *hastarah* within the *hastarah* (hidden within the hidden).

Rebbe Nachman teaches: There are times when we feel distant from God. God is hiding Himself from us because of something we've done. We are within a *hastarah*. Though it is difficult enough to find Him at this time, at least we know that we must search for God until we merit finding Him. But, there is a worse case of hiddenness, the *hastarah* within the *hastarah*. In such a situation, it never dawns upon us even to think that we are distant from God. However, by studying Torah, we acquire the knowledge to awaken ourselves out of our *hastarah* and out of our *hastarah* within the *hastarah* (*Likutey Moharan* I, 56:3).

We walk around, everyone of us thinking that there is no *hastarah* in our lives; that in one way or another we have found God, we have "seen the Light." But have we? We talk about Him. We mention His Name. We even pray to Him. But are we *aware* of Him? Have we really searched for God? Or are we calling the Night "Day"? Are our minds so befuddled by Darkness that we no longer make any effort to truly find Him? We must bring the light of Day — awareness — into our lives. We must awaken ourselves with Torah study and with *hitbodedut*.

*

...Day "*VaYeetzer* — and God created man..." (Genesis 2:7). Why does the letter *yod* (י) appear twice in the word *yeetzer* (וייצר, created) when once would have been sufficient? Because there were two creations — the good inclination and the evil inclination (*Berakhot* 61a).

When God decided to create the world, He constricted Himself, as it were, and first created the Vacated Space. [That is, God was everywhere. There was no room for the Creation. So He constricted Himself, as it were, to create the Vacated Space.] Within this Vacated Space, He designed and created the world and everything in it. The entire creation was for man, that man should have the free will to choose between good (Light) and evil (Darkness). This way, God's Kingship can now be revealed to all (*Etz Chaim* 1).

Rebbe Nachman teaches: Man is a microcosm of the Creation itself. His mind and heart are the source of all his thoughts and all the actions he will perform. In this sense, his mind, being the source of his ideas and goals, is like the Vacated Space. These thoughts convey the ideas to the heart (the source of one's emotions), which then dictates to the body what to do. Thus, to perform good deeds, one must have a pure heart. In order to have a clean and pure heart, one must think good thoughts. And, whereas thinking evil thoughts literally creates evil within oneself, thinking good thoughts actually gives rise to a "good creation." He creates a clean and pure heart in which Godliness can be revealed; his heart then burns with great desire to serve God. Man's duty is to control this burning desire and keep it within his power to perform the mitzvot according to his capabilities, without reaching too high for his own good (*Likutey Moharan* I, 49:1).

Reb Noson writes: The battle between good and evil thoughts is the main reason for the Creation. The confusing thoughts in our minds correspond to the chaos and desolation that were created at the very beginning. We have to overcome these evil thoughts, and we can — by thinking positive thoughts, by concentrating on good thoughts and constantly thinking of ways to come closer to God. Through this process, we are, in a sense, re-creating Creation itself. And, all of us *can* do this. Every day, each of us has the ability to create new worlds. Each day is unique. It has something new, fresh and different, that never was before. And so, each day we should seek new thoughts and ideas about how to come closer to God.

And remember: even if we are overwhelmed by evil thoughts, even though we have tried many times to run away from the bad ideas that converge upon us, we always have the power to overcome them. For each day is a new creation, each and every day brings with it the concept of renewal. Start again.

Start over. If we encounter difficulties and seemingly endless obstacles to good thoughts, then we must cry out to God for help. Pray, appeal and plead to God to reveal Himself to us, to guide us on the right path.

From the Kabbalah we learn that God created the Vacated Space to make room for Creation. If you think about this, you'll realize that this in itself is a great paradox. God, as it were, withdrew His Godliness; however, without Godliness, nothing can exist. Yet we see that Creation certainly did take place, the world certainly does exist. So God *does* exist in the Vacated Space. The Vacated Space may look absolutely void and vacated, but it's not. Just as, by looking really hard, we can always find God even in the Vacated Space, so too, we can find Him even in the tumult and confusion that beset us in the Darkness of our lives.

This teaches us that although there are things we cannot understand, things which remain paradoxical no matter what, we must strengthen ourselves each and every day to think good thoughts. We are important enough in God's eyes to be considered mini-creators. Each and every one of us is entrusted with these powers to create. Our thoughts, our desires create Day, they create the good that exists in this world (*Likutey Halakhot, Minchah* 7:2).

*

Another means for "creating Day," i.e. creating good, is through the expression of one's holy thoughts and desires verbally. Not only should we think good thoughts, we should also enunciate them, speak them out and pronounce them, whether in prayer or by way of conversation.

Rebbe Nachman teaches: The [Hebrew] letters in Torah have no vowels. Like a body without a soul, they have no movement. (For example, the word ישב, *yshv*, can be read: yOshEv, yEIshEIv, yAshAv, yAshOv, yAshUv, and so on.) Inserting vowels gives meaning to the word. This can be seen as the connotation of the phrase (Song of Songs 1:11): "*Nekudot hakasef* — the vowels come from desire." [*Nekudot* are vowels and *kasef* is Aramaic for desire.] (*Likutey Moharan* I, 31:6-8, end; also see *Ibid.* 66:4).

From this we learn that our desire gives meaning to the letters and words that we speak. If we have good desires, we will speak good words and thereby create good letter and word combinations. This will, in turn, eventually lead us to perform good and kind acts. If however, our desires are for evil, we create evil combinations and bring these into the world. We should therefore always speak good, always speak out and declare positive desires. By doing this, we "create" a positive attitude towards good deeds and actually benefit the world through the Light which the expression of our holy thoughts and desires brings.

* * *

IMAGINATION

As we've said, our thoughts are our closest companions. The better part of any day we spend inside our own heads — in our ideas, images and impressions, in our designs and recollections, and so on. One of the concepts which Rebbe Nachman discusses in connection with our thought processes is what he calls the *medameh* (מדמה). The root of this Hebrew word is *damah* (דמה), which means to be like or resemble, and connotes the comparison of one thing to another. Therefore, the Rebbe's use of the word *medameh* might best be translated as the mind's imaginative faculty. Yet this would not give us a complete picture, because, depending on the context, Rebbe Nachman uses the word to mean either creative visualization or as what is generally termed illusion (דמיון). *Medameh* as creative visualization is a quality we associate with Light and Day; *medameh* as illusion, however, we associate with Darkness and Night.

*

Imagination as illusion. Who hasn't, at some time in life, let his imagination run wild? When we allow this to happen, our thoughts become subject to all sorts of confusion and chaos, our minds see everything as Night. Take, for example, what happens when we let our imaginations focus on something we fear. Rebbe Nachman teaches: Most things that people fear cannot harm them. We may even clearly realize that what we fear cannot harm us, yet, we have these phobias which we cannot overcome (*Rabbi Nachman's Wisdom* #83). How many of us spend our time fretting over and fearing imagined danger? We say things like, "My entire world is black," and we really think it is, just because we've imagined the worst possible scenario and convinced ourselves of its reality. The Darkness of illusion has shut out the Light, it has closed our minds to the wisdom and understanding which would normally help us see past the situation and even resolve it. We must do everything we can to avoid such anxiety and the ensuing depression, because it is the worst mental state possible.

And it's not only through fears and phobias that illusion plays havoc with our lives. Rebbe Nachman, after delivering a lesson in which he referred to one's desires and evil inclination as illusory and dreamlike, said, "We should give the Evil One a new name. From now on he should be called Imagination" (*Likutey Moharan* I, 25:end).

We imagine ourselves different than we really are: we might think we are indispensable and this leads to arrogance and strife; we might imagine our family life as okay when it is sometimes falling apart right in front of our eyes; we delude ourselves into thinking that we have, or can achieve, financial security, something which is virtually impossible. And sometimes, we even create illusions about our spiritual achievements and religious commitments. Are we really as devoted to God and to being a good person as we tell ourselves, and would have others believe? When we do the things we do, are we really being true to Judaism? Our forefathers offered the supreme sacrifice, their very lives, to remain true to our faith. If called upon to do so, would we do the same?

This is the illusory side of our imagination that Rebbe Nachman calls the Evil One. It is the *medameh* from which we must flee. As Rebbe Nachman said: The world deceives you. Accept this from me. Do not let yourselves be fooled! (*Rabbi Nachman's Wisdom* #51).

*

Imagination as creative visualization. There is, however, another side to imagination which, rather than deceiving us into Darkness, brings Light, wisdom and understanding into our minds. This is the quality of imagination through which we can turn even our darkest Nights into the brightest Days; it is *medameh* as creative visualization. Our Sages tell us that when Yosef was a servant in Egypt and his master's wife attempted to seduce him, he had a vision of his father's image and this saved him (*Sotah* 36b). Rebbe Nachman commented on this: How it happens that an image appears to a person is a very hidden mystery (*Likutey Moharan* I, 150).

Indeed, Rebbe Nachman himself made considerable use of the *medameh*. He told many stories, revealed numerous dreams, visions and innovative ideas — all of which display a prolific imagination and challenge even the most fertile and creative minds. And, he inspired his chassidim to follow suit. There can therefore be no doubt that the Rebbe also recognized the positive features of imagination and how it is to be used to our benefit.

Throughout the Rebbe's writings, there are references to imagination. Here are but some of his suggestions for making use of its positive aspects:

Human thought has tremendous potential. When we concentrate our thoughts on something and really imagine it to be, we can actually force the thing to happen. To accomplish this, we must visualize every step of the desired result in great detail. Diffused and generalized thought will not work. But when every faculty of the mind is intensely focused on that which we wish to see happening, we can genuinely exert great influence on all sorts of matters in the world (*Rabbi Nachman's Wisdom* 62).

When studying Torah, imagine and plan a schedule for your studies. Picture in your mind exactly how you will go about this course of study. Visualize yourself doing it, succeeding at it, until you actually do manage to fulfill your plans (*Ibid.*).

Rebbe Nachman teaches: When we are disturbed and unhappy, we should at least *imagine* ourselves as being joyous. Deep down we may be depressed, but if we act happy, we will eventually come to genuine joy (*Rabbi Nachman's Wisdom* 74).

Developing original insights is a most desired goal of all Torah study. To be worthy of such innovative thinking, Rebbe Nachman tells us that we must use the power of imagination — comparing item to item, thought to thought (*Likutey Moharan* I, 54:5,6).

*

We can conclude that any aspect of our power of imagination which we use to serve God and better ourselves, has to be a positive quality. The imagination that Rebbe Nachman refers to as the Evil One, the imagination which needs to be repressed and stifled, is not the creative power that is an innate quality and asset in each of us. Rather, it is the illusory imagination that lets us fool ourselves and others, the delusive thinking that allows us to waste away our lives.

And it's worth recalling once more Rebbe Nachman's teaching: Wherever your mind is — that's where you are! Thus, it all depends on what we really want. If we really desire and think about Godliness and genuine personal growth, we can attain it. If we desire something else, and that is where our mind is, then that's what we'll achieve. If we think Night, it is Night. But if we think Day, if we think good, positive thoughts, and continue to do so, we will find ourselves emerging into the Light.

* * *

THE TWENTY-FOUR-HOUR CYCLE

Just as every person's life has its periods of Night and Day, so each and every day has its "Nights and Days," its moments of Darkness and Light. This becomes especially clear when seen in terms of the set of daily prayers which take a Jew through the twenty-four-hour cycle.

It was the Patriarchs who introduced the three daily prayers. Avraham initiated the Morning Prayer, Yitzchak the Afternoon Prayer, and Yaakov the Evening Prayer (*Berakhot* 26b). Our Sages taught that the morning and midday prayers are compulsory, whereas the nighttime prayer is optional (*Berakhot* 27b). Nowadays, the Evening Prayer has also been made compulsory (*Orach Chaim* 237:1).

*

Ma'ariv, The Evening Prayer. Rebbe Nachman teaches: We should try to make "one" out of our prayers. This is done by our keeping in mind the very first letter we utter until we finish saying the very last word. Then the prayer is one unit. By doing this, we can remove our gaze from this world completely and be unified with the One, with God. We will then always be able to overcome our troubles, because we can see beyond the physical world and gaze upon the "end," the goal, which is The One. Then we will recognize that all is good and will merit being happy (*Likutey Moharan* I, 65).

The Jewish twenty-four-hour cycle begins at night. Night is confusion and difficulty, which in the terminology of the

Kabbalah is known as judgments or *dinim* (as opposed to Day which refers to kindness or *chesed*). The Evening Prayer, which is the first of the daily prayers, is therefore recited at the onset of the judgments. When these *dinim* abound — when Night falls — one must be able to see beyond the Night, beyond the difficulties and confusions that beset him (*Likutey Halakhot, Arvit* 4:1,2). This is how prayer gets us "through the Night."

Reb Noson writes: Seeing that there is no commandment to recite the Evening Prayer, and that one offers a prayer at night out of an inner desire and not as a fulfillment of one's obligation, why did Yaakov have to initiate it? Would anyone have assumed that it is forbidden to pray at night, that Yaakov had to establish a precedent to show that nighttime prayer is permissible? Besides, of what value is the implementation of an optional custom or devotion? However, Yaakov foresaw the forthcoming exiles, the long Nights and the ever-increasing obstacles to serving God. He anticipated the extended Darkness created by the power of the resistance to spirituality. Therefore, Yaakov established the Evening Prayer. He initiated Ma'ariv to show that even in our darkest moments, we have a path by which we can always return to God.

He also foresaw that because of the great Darkness which the long exile would generate, it would be impossible to force someone to pray. The bitter exile, Night, is a concept of silence. It is as if a person is intimidated by his surroundings, bound into a long silent suffering, where he sees no end and cannot raise his voice to cry out over his situation. Indeed, were it not for the great Tzaddikim — whose spiritual strength and foresight prepared various means and counsels to guide us through this long Night — we would never have been able to withstand the pressures and oppression of the exiles. People would long ago have given up all hope of praying to God and returning to Him. Thus, Yaakov "came to the place and spent the night there... He dreamt a dream in which he saw a ladder standing on the ground, and its top reached up to heaven" (Genesis 28:11,12). By spending the Night there and descending to where he descended, only to then rise up all the way to Heaven, Yaakov did indeed set the precedent that even in the darkest Darkness of the longest Night we have to awaken with strong desires to pray and return to God. This is the Evening Prayer. We must never despair!

But if the Evening Prayer is so important, then why, indeed, was it originally left optional? We can understand this by looking at the reason why the daily liturgy was established in the first place. This was done to help those who would not be able to entreat God without the aid of a formalized rite for presenting the prayers. However, the most productive and complete prayer is one that a person says straight from his heart; the private, secluded prayer known as *hitbodedut*. This is what Yaakov had in mind — a spontaneous prayer, one that a person can always offer, no matter where he is or what he has done in the past. This is the optional prayer introduced by Yaakov as the Evening Prayer. His intention was to instill in us the courage never to give up — never — even in the darkest moments (*Likutey Halakhot, Minchah* 7:89).

*

Chatzot, The Midnight Lament. Conceptually, one of the major reasons for interrupting our sleep and getting up in the middle of the night to recite the *Chatzot* Prayer (see Chapter 8, "Prayer") is to break the Darkness that surrounds us in our daily lives. Reb Noson writes: One who is distant from God is likened to someone who is sleeping. The deeper the sleep, the harder it is to arouse oneself to serve God. Furthermore, sleep is compared to "lesser" wisdom, an unconscious existence. Awakening is awareness. Thus, rising for *Chatzot* is akin to becoming aware of one's situation in order to make good use of the life he's been granted. It is also likened to finding the good points in oneself, within the Darkness one feels he is in. This is the great value in rising for *Chatzot,* for it "breaks" the sleep of unawareness and shortens one's distance from God (*Likutey Halakhot, Hashkamat HaBoker* 1:12).

This "sleep of unawareness" is a cyclical occurrence in our lives, as practically every day we fall into lethargy, whether in the midst of our prayers, our studies or even during our work. We have always to try to strengthen ourselves, no matter how weak we feel, to overcome our inertia and our lethargic stupor. This is the lesson of *Chatzot.*

*

Shacharit, The Morning Prayer. Reb Noson tells us that, conceptually, the Morning Prayer alludes to that part of our twenty-four-hour cycle which is associated with Light, with the new beginnings we make, and with the time when everything is going our way — Day (*Likutey Halakhot, Minchah* 5:5).

Rebbe Nachman teaches: Night denotes uncertainty. Day, on the other hand, denotes clear counsel. Why does life work out when one has faith? Because when one has faith he can attain clear counsel, symbolic of the Day which follows the Night (*Likutey Moharan* II, 5:2).

Day and Light connote clarity — clear, precise thought. They are synonymous with clean thoughts, the ideal of Creation and the goal of man. The goal of Torah study, of prayer, of proper desires. This is why most devotions and commandments are performed in the daytime, during the Light of Day, for they correspond to the consciousness of man, not the subconsciousness. A person has to be awake. He has to be alive! He has to *want* to do. With daylight, with Light, with proper guidance, he can. We all seek guidance. We all seek proper Light to lead us on the right path. This is the significance of Day (cf. *Likutey Moharan* I, 1).

Reb Noson writes: An newborn infant has no knowledge whatsoever. But he learns little by little as he grows through life's different stages. With each new area of development that he begins, it is as if he's starting over again. And, every time he learns something new, he begins the cycle once more. This is Shacharit — the Morning Prayer. It starts new every day. It is also the longest of the daily prayers because it signifies the need for a person to strive for continual growth and enlightenment (*Likutey Halakhot, Minchah* 5:1).

*

Minchah, The Afternoon Prayer. Reb Noson writes: Our Sages tell us that we have to very careful about the Afternoon Prayer (*Berakhot* 6b). This is because as the twenty-four-hour cycle progresses, Minchah corresponds to the time when the Light begins to wane. Day begins to ebb, and we tend to feel that we've squandered yet another golden opportunity to free ourselves from the chaos and confusion — the Darkness — that has remained with us from the previous Night. But the truth is that we must never, never, feel lost. Never despair! Never give up! Night falls, but it is the start of a new Day. A new point in Creation. A fresh start. We have to remember that life will always regenerate. Darkness is inevitable, but Light will always follow. One can find solace too in the fact that although Night is almost upon us, the Day will soon return (*Likutey Halakhot, Minchah* 4:1).

Reb Noson expresses another thought about the waning of Day. He relates the midday prayers to the mid-life crises that befall a person. Middle age is the time in a person's life when he has passed the zenith of youth. He finds himself beset with family problems, marrying off his children, and so on. In looking back upon his accomplishments to date, upon what he's done with his life, he also reflects upon his spiritual achievements. Many times, this leads to feelings that are so overwhelming, that a person may think that it's too late for him to strengthen himself to repent and turn back to God. Never for a moment should he entertain such thoughts, God forbid. Rather, he should always strengthen himself to accomplish whatever he can. This is why the Sages warned us to be very careful about the Afternoon Prayers (*Likutey Halakhot, Minchah* 5:5).

* * *

YOUR FAITH IS AT NIGHT

Night is chaos, confusion. Yet, as King David tells us, "Your faith is at night" (Psalms 92:3), for Night and Darkness are also a concept of faith. How so? As opposed to understanding and knowledge which, as mentioned earlier, Rebbe Nachman connects to Day, faith only applies when there is no Light of understanding and knowledge (cf. *Likutey Moharan* I, 1; *ibid.* 62). Therefore, just as Night affords us no Light with which to see, so too, faith is what one must have when coming up against the unknown. Who has seen God? Who can understand Him or His ways? Yet, Night is always followed by Day, Darkness is always followed by Light and understanding. Through faith, one can come to understand. And the more one believes in God, the more one comes to an understanding of Him, to see that He exists everywhere, and that we *can* find Him.

We have good moments in life as well as difficult ones. Sometimes Light fills our Nights, other times Darkness fills our Days. It is up to us to make use of what we have. We can feel overwhelmed by our Dark moments and let ourselves despair over our confusions, or, we can take the Darkness, the Night, the confusion, and turn to God, saying: "I am beset with troubles, with problems and doubts. Help me turn to You. Help me have faith in You. Help me strengthen myself in Your goodness and kindness. Even though at this moment I feel distraught, I shall, nevertheless, strengthen my faith in You. Rebbe Nachman taught us: 'Never give up! Never despair!' Therefore, please, help me to renew my faith in You."

One of Rebbe Nachman's most famous stories, *The Lost Princess,* illustrates this idea most graphically:

There was once a king who had six sons and a daughter. The daughter was very precious to him and he loved her very much. He spent much time with her. Once, when they were alone, he became angry at her. He inadvertently said, "May the Evil One take you away!" At night she went to her room. In the morning, no one knew where she was. Her father was very distraught. The viceroy, seeing the king's despair, offered to look for her.

The viceroy searched and searched for the princess for a very long time. He searched through deserts, fields and forests until, finally, he found her.... She was in a beautiful castle off on a side path, somewhere. "How did you get here?" he asked her. "My father said that the Evil One should take me. This is the place of evil." "How can I get you out of here?" the viceroy asked. She said, "You must choose a place and remain there for an entire year. All that time you must long and desire to get me out. On the last day you must fast and go without sleep for the twenty-four hour period."

The viceroy did as he was told. On the last day of the year, he fasted and did not sleep. Then he got up to go to the castle. On the way, he saw a tree with very beautiful apples. It was very desirable. He ate an apple and immediately fell asleep. He slept for a very long time, for many, many years. When he awoke he asked, "Where in the world am I?"

The viceroy returned to the princess and asked if he could have another chance. She was very upset and lamented, "You have been searching for such a long time. And then, because of one day, you lost everything. But it is too difficult not to eat. Therefore, find a place for another year and long to take me out from here. On the last day you are permitted to eat, but not to sleep. Do not drink any wine on that day, so that you will not fall asleep. The main thing is to avoid sleep."

The viceroy again went and did as he was told. On the last day of the year, he arose to go to the castle. On the way he saw a spring. It was red in color and smelled like wine. "It is a spring and should contain water," he reasoned, "but it has a red color and smells like wine." He took a taste of the spring and immediately fell asleep. He slept for a very long time, for many, many years. He remained asleep for seventy years. When he awoke, he asked, "Where in the world am I?" And once again he began to search for the princess who, in the meantime, had left him a note that she could no longer be found in the same castle. He was to look for a golden mountain and a pearl castle....

He again searched for her for many, many years. Eventually he came across a giant who tried to discourage him, telling him that no such place exists.... The viceroy wept. He was certain that somewhere there had to be a golden mountain and a pearl castle. The giant, who was the ruler of all the animals in the world, summoned the animals and asked them if they knew of such a place. They all said no. The giant told him, "See! I told you it does not exist!" and again tried to discourage him. But the viceroy insisted, so the giant then sent him to his brother who was in charge of all the birds. "Perhaps they, who fly high in the sky, know of this golden mountain and pearl castle."

The viceroy traveled again for many, many years. He finally encountered the giant's brother and requested his help. This giant also tried to discourage him, saying, "Such a place does not exist." The viceroy wept bitterly and pleaded, "But it does exist!" The giant then summoned all the birds and asked if any of them had ever seen a golden mountain and pearl castle. They all replied that they knew of no such place. "Don't you see that there certainly is no place with a golden mountain and a pearl castle?" asked the giant. But the viceroy would still not give in. "But it certainly does exist! Somewhere in the world." The giant said to him, "Further on in the desert you will find my brother who is in charge of all the winds. They cover the entire world. Go to him and tell him that I sent you. Maybe the winds know of this mountain and castle."

The viceroy again traveled for many, many years. He met the third brother and again requested help. This giant also tried to discourage him, saying, "It certainly does not exist." The viceroy pressed his case, weeping and pleading, "But it does exist!" The giant then summoned the winds and asked if they knew anything about the golden mountain and pearl castle. They all said that they did not. The giant said, "Don't you see that it certainly does not exist? People have told you foolish tales!" The viceroy wept very bitterly, "But I know for certain that it does exist!"

Just then, another wind came and the giant asked angrily, "Why didn't you come together with the other winds when I summoned them?" The wind replied, "I was detained because I had to carry a princess to a golden mountain and pearl castle." The viceroy was overjoyed.

The giant then commanded the wind to carry the viceroy to the golden mountain and gave him other assistance to help him in his quest. In the end, the viceroy redeemed the princess (*Rabbi Nachman's Stories* #1, pp. 31-54).

*

The king in this story is God. The princess in whom He delights is prayer, mitzvot and devotion. The viceroy, who tried very hard to find the King's beloved daughter, is each and every one of us. Like us, the viceroy was always being sidetracked by confusion, distractions and opposition. Some of his obstacles were self-induced, others weren't. He experienced countless lifetimes of Nights, enough to discourage him many times over. Yet he persisted, he kept searching and searching, so that he not only extricated himself from his difficulties, but also redeemed the princess in the end.

Why was the viceroy successful? He succeeded because he would not relinquish his faith. He remained firm in his belief that he *could* find the princess — that Day does follow Night. Rather than discouraging him, his faith enabled him to use the Darkness and Night, the uncertainty and confusion, to increase his desire and determination. Even when it seemed that all was lost, that he had tried the last possible resort and was told outright that no golden mountain and pearl castle — no World to Come, no Day, no resolution of life's problems, no goal worth working for — existed, he knew, he just knew, that such a place did exist. But how? He had no knowledge of it. Neither, for that matter, did anyone else. And yet, he still knew. He knew because he had faith. His faith was so strong, it gave him the wisdom and understanding — the Light — to realize the truth. If the princess said that a golden mountain and a pearl castle do exist, then, despite all obstacles and in the face of all "knowledge" to the contrary, he would find them. His faith was so strong, that through it he would attain a clear and perfect knowledge of what previously he could only believe in, but didn't know. And in the end, he did find her. In the end, because of his great and unwaivering faith against all odds, he succeeded in his mission.

Thus, Rebbe Nachman teaches: One should know that in Darkness itself, God can be found. "And the Jews stood from afar. Moshe approached the fog wherein God was found" (Exodus 20:18). Moshe Rabeinu excelled, specifically because he approached the fog, the unknown, the uncertainty, the confusion. He knew that he would find God. He knew that even in this Darkness he could find the Light of God that would radiate the way. He never shirked nor shied away from attempting. Therefore, he rose way above the levels of even the very great Tzaddikim (*Likutey Moharan* I, 115). And in the same way that Moshe was able to find the Light of God in the very Darkness itself, we, in the very darkest moments of life, if we but strengthen ourselves with faith, will also find Light — God Himself.

* * *

12

DAILY NEEDS

Rebbe Nachman teaches: Show great compassion for your body. Help it delight in all the spiritual insights and perceptions which the soul perceives. Your soul is always seeing and comprehending very exalted things. But the body knows nothing of this. Have compassion for the flesh of your body. Purify it. Then the soul will be able to inform it of all that she is always seeing and comprehending (*Likutey Moharan* I, 22:5).

Our physical needs are many. We all have to eat and sleep, take care of our health and make sure we have what to wear. At least half the hours of most people's lives are spent catering to these needs — sometimes more (cf. *Shabbat* 88b). Now, if we compartmentalize and separate these physical needs from our spiritual ones, we might conclude that half our lives concentrate on things other than serving God. The time we spend sleeping, eating, working...what value does it have for our souls? However, there is another way to look at it.

Noam HaElyon (Upper Delight) is the source of everything pleasing and enjoyable in this world. Whatever feelings of delight and pleasure we experience stem from this quality of God. This is even true of the pleasure associated with the physical necessities of this world, such as eating, sleeping, etc. As long as we perform them in holiness, we draw from *Noam HaElyon*. However, when we give in to our physical appetites and seek to gratify them, our desires descend to the level of lust. In that case, we are no longer attached to Upper Delight, but to the bittersweet delights and pleasures of this world. To atone for this loss of *Noam HaElyon,* we fulfill the five afflictions of Yom Kippur. We fast and limit our physical pleasures to remind ourselves of the need to avoid deriving our pleasures from this world. Yet, even this is not perfection and completeness. After all, we must sustain ourselves with food and care for our physical needs. On the other hand, perfection and completeness can be learned from the holiday of Sukkot. On Sukkot, we spend seven days in the *sukkah,* eating, drinking and sleeping. In doing this, we bring all our pleasures into holiness; reminding ourselves that food and all of our desires have their source in Upper Delight. This is perfection and completion with regard to the physical necessities of this world: learning to appreciate the pleasure and delight they afford, but recognizing that their source, *Noam HaElyon,* stems from God Himself (*Likutey Halakhot, Minchah* 6:8,9).

* * *

SOUL FOOD

Food — it's what keeps you alive. Food — it's what binds your body to your soul. Food is the very life of man. Or is it? Eating can either be a very great mitzvah or the antithesis of a mitzvah. Sometimes, it can be a lust — one of the three major lusts that prevent you from reaching out for Godliness. It all depends on you!

When he was young, Rebbe Nachman tried extremely hard to free himself from all physical lusts. As this required tremendous effort, he began by drawing all his physical desire into his appetite for food. He ate a lot, even more than most people, while at the same time he made every effort to rid himself of all his other desires. Only after suppressing all of these, did he begin to work on subduing his lust for food as well. He fasted frequently and repeatedly, until he no longer desired food at all. Eventually he had to force himself to eat in order to stay alive (*Rabbi Nachman's Wisdom* pp. 18,23).

Later on, the Rebbe said, "If I had known the greatness of *hitbodedut* earlier in life, I would never have wasted my body through fasting. The body is too important a vehicle with which to serve God, to have been subjected to such strenuous self-abnegation" (*Hishtafkut HaNefesh, Introduction*).

Through this lesson, Rebbe Nachman teaches that you *can* eat, as long as you keep your mind on serving God. You can break the desire or lust for food, and it can be accomplished without anorexia or self-destruction. "Eat and sleep. Just watch your time," the Rebbe told his follower, Reb Dov (*Kokhavey Or,* p.25). Make sure that you use all your time — even time spent getting, preparing and eating your food — in the service of God.

Reb Noson noticed someone studying Torah after the Morning Prayers. The man seemed to be pained by hunger, yet he persisted in studying. Reb Noson said to him, "That's enough! It's time to desist from your craving desire for food" (*Aveneha Barzel,* p.65 #37). The message is clear: Eat when you have to. Just don't make a big deal out of it.

*

FOOD, GLORIOUS FOOD...

According to the Kabbalah, Pharaoh is symbolic of the neck and throat (see *Likutey Torah, VaYeshev*). His enslavement of the Jewish people signified his control over the power of holy speech, which he silenced by keeping it trapped in the throat. Hence, only when the Jews were finally able to cry out, were they redeemed from Egypt. Now, Pharaoh had three servants: the *sar hamashkim* (chief wine steward), the *sar haofim* (chief baker) and the *sar hatabachim* (chief butcher); corresponding to the windpipe, the foodpipe, and the [jugular] veins, all located in the throat. These are the "chiefs," the heads, of all desires and they draw their strength from Pharaoh, the source of impurities (*Likutey Moharan* I, 62:5). Therefore, contact with these servants (which happens whenever we eat) brings us into direct contact with Pharaoh himself. Seeing that this is anything but desirable, might it not be better for anyone wishing to grow spiritually to stay away from eating altogether?

However, we know that this is impossible. What's more, it's forbidden, because denying ourselves nourishment leads to death — not at all the desired result of our spiritual yearnings! So we should eat, we have to eat. The question is: Where do we draw the line? How is it possible to eat, yet keep our eating holy? Is there a way to eat and avoid contact with Pharaoh's henchmen, thereby saving ourselves from the dangers of a spiritual death?

The answer is yes. How? By showing compassion for our bodies, by purifying ourselves, by not compartmentalizing and separating our physical needs from the spiritual. "You are *what* you eat," the saying goes, and it's true. It's also true, as Rebbe Nachman shows us, that we are *how* we eat (below) and *why* we eat. Taken together, they have the power to keep us from being enslaved in Pharaoh's clutches.

What we eat. Rebbe Nachman teaches: The nature of the food a person eats, gives rise to a similar temperament within him (*The Aleph-Bet Book, Da'at* A:4).

The most obvious requirement concerning what we eat is that we eat kosher food. Non-kosher foods and products lead us right into Pharaoh's hands. The Torah tells us (Leviticus 11:43,44): "Do not *titam'u* (defile yourselves) with them, because it will *v'nitmeitem* (make you unclean).... You must sanctify yourselves and be holy." Rashi states (v.43): This refers to eating. If one defiles himself in this world, one will be defiled in the World to Come. The Talmud comments (*Yoma* 39b): The word *v'niTMeiTeM* is written to teach us that not only does it defile the person, but it even makes him *m'TuMTaM* (foolish and spiritually insensitive). The very act of eating non-kosher food, even a little bit, defiles the person who eats it and, as Rashi explains, closes off all the channels of wisdom from him.

Rebbe Nachman also warned against eating unhealthy foods. Of course, in his day there were no packaged fast-foods, chemical dyes and preservatives, but two foods which the Rebbe specifically mentioned as unhealthy were raw onions and unripe fruits. This prohibition applies even on Shabbat. There are those who maintain that because eating on Shabbat is a special mitzvah, one can eat anything, even unhealthy foods, but Rebbe Nachman warned very strongly against this (*Rabbi Nachman's Wisdom* #265; see *Likutey Moharan* II, 88).

Why we eat. Eating kosher and healthy is not enough. A lot depends on why you're eating. Is your eating motivated by a lust for food? Of course, before you try to answer that, you'll want to know what exactly is a lust for food? Is it the same as gluttony? Rebbe Nachman explains lust as a desire for that which is unnecessary. He indicates that a person who can eat a lot, is free to do so. This would not be considered a lust for food (*Rabbi Nachman's Wisdom* #193). However, eating even a little, if motivated by desire rather than need, would be considered lust for food. Some people eat large amounts because physically, their body chemistry demands this of them. Others don't have a need for much food. Every person is different. If you need to eat a lot, go ahead. If not, don't.

It's your attitude towards food that makes the difference. Why are you eating? Do you want nourishment, or a full belly? Are you eating because your body needs to replenish its strength, or because the food tastes so good you just had to take another helping? One of the best ways to check this out is your attitude towards the way the food tastes.

Rebbe Nachman says that being fussy about what you eat is considered a lust for food (*Aveneha Barzel* p. 21). Are you particular, does your palate have to be pampered? Or will simple foods do? Do you require fine cuisine? If the food is not "just right," how do you respond?

The *Shulchan Arukh* points out that on Shabbat it is a mitzvah to eat fish, meats and various delicacies. But, one should eat only what he likes (*Mishnah Berurah* 242:2). The Rebbe never intended that we should feel obligated to eat unappetizing foods. What he meant was that when you are served your normal meals, eat them with joy and happiness, even if they could use improvement (see *Siach Sarfei Kodesh* 1-10). [Who knows? Either your cook will get better, you'll get a better cook, or you'll get used to it!] The main thing is not to be picky. We can all learn from Reb Nachman Chazan, Reb Noson's closest follower, who, when served his meal, didn't season his food (*Aveneha Barzel* p. 21).

We all know that eating too much is harmful, but most of us don't know there are spiritual reasons for this. Rebbe Nachman explains in spiritual terms what is generally assumed to be a purely physical matter: Like everything in Creation, food has a source from which it draws its spiritual vitality. When you eat and draw nourishment from your food, you are, in turn, giving spiritual nourishment to the food itself. This is because the appetite in man is a spiritual force. As you satisfy your appetite, its energy transfers into the food, giving it the vitality it seeks. This is why eating a proper amount brings health to a person: you nourish the food, it nourishes you. The problems start when you've already satisfied your appetite and continue eating. The extra food you eat has nowhere to draw its vitality. So it draws it from you — from your vitality and strength. This is physically very harmful and why over-eating (stuffing one's face) causes illness and sickness (*Likutey Moharan* I, 257). (Also see *Likutey Moharan* I, 263; *Rabbi Nachman's Wisdom* #143.)

Elsewhere, Rebbe Nachman teaches that eating excessively gives strength to the body, while at the same time weakens the soul (*Likutey Moharan* II, 8:1). So excessive eating causes double trouble. It drains your body and vitality, and it strengthens the Other Side at the same time, by weakening your soul.

How we eat. How to eat? The main thing is to realize that it matters. "A man's table is like an altar, it purifies him of all his sins" (*The Aleph-Bet Book,* Eating A:7). If that's the case, then how we eat certainly is important. Rebbe Nachman teaches: Get into the habit of eating without haste, calmly and with manners. Avoid grabbing a quick bite while on the run. Even when you're alone, eat with the same dignity and respect you would show if someone important were sitting at the table (*Tzaddik* #515).

This same point is emphasized when the Rebbe speaks about the value of fasting. "The main value of a fast is in how you end it. Don't gobble the food, but eat it calmly and without haste" (*Siach Sarfei Kodesh* 1-82).

It's also important not to eat when you are angry. Don't sit down to the table if you're really upset, and do your best to avoid getting angry during the meal. The seat of anger is the liver, the organ most associated with blood. The liver is also connected to Esav. His power is in the sword, in the spilling of blood. Because of this, anger gives strength to Esav, the Other Side incarnate. Conversely, controlling this anger gives strength to your intellect (*Likutey Moharan* I, 57:6).

There are positive things we can do to ensure that Pharaoh and his henchmen have no influence over our eating. We can add holiness to our eating habits with such things as washing our hands prior to the meal, reciting all the appropriate blessings, engaging in Torah study and conversations (between portions), and so on. Here is a selection of Breslov teachings related to these practices:

After washing your hands for bread, the custom is to raise them up so as to receive holiness (see *Orach Chaim* 162:1; *Sha'ar HaMitzvot, Ekev*). Rebbe Nachman explains that this holiness can only be attained if you *believe* that this act of raising the hands brings holiness. It is faith in one's own actions that actually brings holiness into a person. Every person has the power to do this (*Likutey Moharan* I, 91). "There will yet come a time," the Rebbe once remarked, "when a person who washes his hands before eating bread will be as big a *chidush* as the Baal Shem Tov was" (*Sichot V'Sipurim* p. 76, #6).

Reciting the blessings is also of major importance. Rebbe Nachman teaches: Offering praise to God is the joy of the World to Come (*Likutey Moharan* II, 2:1). Reb Noson comments: A person should constantly attach himself to the World to Come. He should always think about it and try to bring the joys and delights of the Future into the present. This can be accomplished through the blessings we recite before and after eating. When reciting a blessing over the food, we are taking a physical object and using it to praise God. This is a concept of the World to Come (*Likutey Halakhot, Betziat HaPat*, 2:1). See how great a level is reached just by reciting a blessing — and over something physical at that!

Reb Noson writes: The Torah, which comprises the Names of God, is life. By speaking words of Torah at your meal, you draw Godliness to your table (*Likutey Halakhot, Netilat Yadayim Li'Seudah* 1:3). It's easy to understand that when engaged in any of the spiritual activities, such as studying Torah or praying, we have the power to draw holiness upon ourselves. Reb Noson reveals that the same levels of holiness can be drawn into a physical act. This is not an analogy; it is for real. You can draw Godliness into every morsel of food that you eat, by thinking and speaking words of Torah [and by reciting the blessings].

*

EATING ON SHABBAT AND FESTIVALS

Over Shabbat, a person should eat three meals: on Friday night, on Shabbat morning, and one more on Shabbat afternoon (*Shabbat* 117b).

Rebbe Nachman teaches: Eat on Shabbat for the sake of Shabbat itself. Don't eat because you didn't have a chance to eat on Friday, or so you shouldn't be hungry on Sunday. Eat only for today, in honor of Shabbat itself. Honor Shabbat with the finest cuisine and as many delicacies as your budget will allow (*Likutey Moharan* I, 125). Don't even think that delighting in fine foods and wines is being extravagant and indulgent. All the foods that you partake of on Shabbat are considered holy. Besides, dining on Shabbat brings peace (*Likutey Moharan* I, 57:5,6).

Not only is eating the Three Meals the best way to honor Shabbat, but it can also rectify any Shabbat desecration one may have inadvertently committed (*Likutey Moharan* I, 277).

Celebrate the Shabbat and holiday meals with song and good food (*Likutey Moharan* II, 17; *Ibid.* II, 104). As far as the holidays are concerned, the *Shulchan Arukh* states that we should honor the Festivals with food and drink, just as on Shabbat (*Orach Chaim* 529:1). Thus, all the teachings that apply to celebrating and enjoying Shabbat are applicable to the holidays as well.

*

FOOD FOR THOUGHT

There are numerous Breslov teachings which discuss the importance of bringing holiness into the way we eat and making it a holy act. Perhaps without exception, they focus on what great spiritual levels a person can attain when his intentions are focused on Godliness.

Rebbe Nachman teaches: When you eat, it is possible to experience a revelation of the great spiritual light, the Light of Desire (*Likutey Moharan* II, 7:10). Man, by definition, implies limitation. He can desire great things, great levels, but he is limited by his physical reality. The one aspect of man's makeup which can be boundless is his desire for holiness. This level of desire for the spiritual is revealed to a person when he sanctifies the way he eats — so much so, that Rebbe Nachman teaches: One can attain such a level whereby his eating is in the same category as eating the Showbread in the Holy Temple (*Likutey Moharan* I, 31:9).

Eating kosher and in a dignified manner, is considered as having rectified the altar of the Holy Temple (*Likutey Moharan* I, 17:3).

Breaking one's desire for food encourages God to show favor and kindness to the world (*Likutey Moharan* I, 67:2).

Eating plays a vital role in refining and purifying Creation. The food we eat can be transformed into prayers, blessings and Torah study. This is akin to the greatness of the incense offering and brings great joy, lovingkindness and happiness to the world (*Likutey Moharan* II, 16; see *Advice*, Eating, 17).

Though a person steeped in the lust for food is distant from the truth, if he subdues this lust, he merits having miracles performed on his behalf (*Likutey Moharan* I, 47:1).

* * *

INDULGING

Aside from his encouragement to sanctify the way we eat, Rebbe Nachman also warned against certain excesses in which people indulge; vices which lead to physical and/or psychological dependencies. The three which he specifically pointed out were smoking, using snuff and drinking alcohol (*Tzaddik* #472, and n. 44). If anything, his warning needs to be heeded even more so today; with snuff having been replaced by "harder stuff," and the attachment to tobacco and liquor being no better than it was in the Rebbe's time.

In the early days of Chassidut, the chassidic leaders realized a value in having their followers come together to exchange words of Torah and talk about the fear of Heaven. At these gatherings, the chassidim would spark their enthusiasm with a little *bromfin* (liquor), though their objective always remained spiritual growth. But in time, priorities changed. Gradually, the drinking of *bromfin* became more and more the focus of these gatherings, while the discussion of the fear of Heaven all but disappeared. Thereafter, Rebbe Nachman rejected the custom of spending time at such gatherings. "I can't stand their [self-made] holidays, any more!" he complained. Rather, he wanted his followers to spend their time on their devotions to God (*Aveneha Barzel*, p. 51, #9; *Siach Sarfei Kodesh*, 1-92).

This does not mean a total disavowal of occasions when Breslover Chassidim get together. On Rebbe Nachman's yahrzeit (18 Tishrei, the fourth day of Sukkot), on Reb Noson's yahrzeit (10 Tevet, the evening prior to the fast), and on the yahrzeits of more recent leaders of the Breslov movement, the chassidim gather for a meal. However, liquor is not served, and the main thrust of the celebration is the exchange of Torah insights and the encouragement of one another in the service of God. The focal point of these gatherings is always a lesson from Rebbe Nachman's teachings.

The *Shulchan Arukh* tells us that Purim is the one time in the year that imbibing alcohol is encouraged (*Orach Chaim* 695:2). Some Breslover Chassidim fulfill this mitzvah to the fullest, others exercise caution and drink only a little wine or liquor. Celebrating Purim is serving God in a joyous and hearty manner. Even so, the halakhah states that getting drunk on Purim comes with certain responsibilities. We must take care that neither damage nor harm comes to anyone as a result of our drinking. A Breslover Chassid told me of how, one Purim, while completely intoxicated, he struck someone. As a result, he has never drunk again on Purim.

Another responsibility which accompanies drinking on Purim is the ability to fulfill the other halakhic requirements. Not being able to pray in the morning because of a hangover means that your reward (for having fulfilled the mitzvah of getting drunk on Purim) is outweighed by your loss (for having failed to pray).

Reb Shmuel Shapiro was known as the "Tzaddik of Jerusalem." His entire day was spent in Torah study and concentrated prayer, which he performed with an intensity known only in previous generations. On Purim he would pray, read the Megillah, distribute the Purim charity and send his Purim presents. Then he would start drinking, and wouldn't stop until he had gotten good and drunk. Yet, despite being totally inebriated, he talked of nothing else but serving God. In paticular, he loved to talk about traveling to Uman (to Rebbe Nachman's gravesite). And, no matter how plastered he got, Reb Shmuel would always sober up for the Afternoon Prayers. It was one of the most incredible things to watch.

Reb Noson scoffed at those chassidim who used to sleep with a bottle of liquor under their pillows. Someone once tried to justify this action to him. "If, when these chassidim wake up, Mashiach hasn't yet come, they put the evil inclination to sleep with a drink." "That won't help," Reb Noson said. "Better to sleep with a book of Psalms under the pillow. If, when you wake up, Mashiach hasn't yet come, then begin reciting the Psalms one more time" (Aveneha Barzel, p. 68, #46).

We all have our share of problems to face, but the means for overcoming them is not in the bottle. Prayer helps, meditation and inner strength help. Use your own spirit, not someone else's bottled version.

Long before the Surgeon General and the American Medical Association issued their warnings about the harmful consequences of smoking, Rebbe Nachman issued his own warning. "Is there such a lack of evil desires that we need this one too?!" he exclaimed (Siach Sarfei Kodesh, 1-3). He also warned that being addicted to tobacco can lead a person to commit a serious sin (*Ibid.* 1-4). The Rebbe understood — well in advance of the sociologists and psychologists — how dependency upon tobacco or alcohol (or drugs) completely conquers a person's willpower and destroys his life.

* * *

CLOTHING

Style and quality. The *Shulchan Arukh* has certain guidelines about what constitutes proper dress for Jews, male and female, and these should be adhered to. As far as the Breslover Chassidim are concerned, there is no outfit or uniform. They have always dressed according to the local Jewish custom, whether they lived in the Ukraine, Poland, Jerusalem or anywhere else. Rebbe Nachman did caution against dressing in the style particular to non-Jews (*The Aleph-Bet Book,* Clothing A:9).

Rebbe Nachman did not agree with wearing expensive and stylish clothing. Quite the opposite: Wearing stylish and expensive clothes leads to haughtiness (cf. *The Aleph-Bet Book,* Clothing B:3).

Reb Nachman Shpielband, who was a fairly successful merchant, once had a fine winter coat made for himself, but when Reb Noson saw it, he was not pleased. "Reb Nachman," Reb Noson remarked, "that's a very beautiful coat you're wearing. It wouldn't be proper to hang such a fine garment in your old closet. Shouldn't you buy a new closet for it. And certainly, once you change your closet you'll want to upgrade the quality of the rest of your furniture. This of course means that you'll probably consider redecorating the whole house, or even better, buying a newer and nicer one. Well, that much money you don't have! It therefore seems that you can't possibly afford all the expenses that come with this coat!" (*Siach Sarfei Kodesh* 1-642).

Ultimately, it comes down to what Rebbe Nachman described in the story of "The Master of Prayer." Though he had a diverse group of followers, the Master of Prayer was able to guide each one along the path that most suited him. So, when the Master of Prayer understood that a particular follower required expensive clothing in order to serve God, he would provide him with these garments. Likewise, when he understood that another follower was better off wearing humble clothing, he would instruct him to do so (*Rabbi Nachman's Stories* #12, p. 283).

Care. Rebbe Nachman teaches: Always make certain that your clothing is clean and cared for. Avoid wearing anything that is torn (*Likutey Moharan* I,127). The garments themselves will demand judgment from the person who doesn't care for them properly and keep them clean (*Likutey Moharan* I,127).

The importance of clean garments has already been mentioned in the Talmud: A Torah scholar whose clothing is soiled deserves the death penalty (*Shabbat* 114a). Rashi explains that, upon seeing the Torah scholar's soiled clothing, people will view him as despicable and then come to despise the Torah itself and for this he deserves to be severely punished. Rebbe Nachman extends this requirement to all Jews. He explains that every person, each according to his particular spiritual level, has an obligation to keep his clothing clean. The greater the person, the greater his responsibility. Furthermore, he explains that conceptually, clean clothes implies clean from sin. Keeping one's clothing clean of sin is a measure of how one keeps *oneself* clean from sin (*Likutey Moharan* I, 29:3).

*

Again focusing on the deeper nature of the physical necessities of this world, Rebbe Nachman said: Happy is he who "eats" a few chapters of Mishnah, "drinks" some verses of the Psalms and "clothes" himself in mitzvot (*Rabbi Nachman's Wisdom* #23).

* * *

SLEEP

Rabbi Avraham Chazan used to say: How can a Jew say that he's going to sleep? How can he waste his precious time sleeping? And yet, we have to sleep. Therefore, when you lay down and close your eyes, talk to God — engage in *hitbodedut*. Then, when you fall asleep, it is out of "duress" (*Rabbi Eliyahu Chaim Rosen*). Here again, we have to fulfill our physical need (in this case sleep), yet avoid separating it from the spiritual. If we don't, then indeed, how can we willfully go to sleep? If we do, we bring holiness into this aspect of our lives as well, and sleep also becomes a means of coming closer to God.

*

Sleep is important. It renews your body and your soul. It also instills and renews faith: just as your soul was returned to you this morning when you awoke, believe that it will be returned to you at the Resurrection of the Dead. The way to assure that your faith is renewed while you sleep is by reciting the *Kri'at Shema* before retiring for the night. The Shema itself is an affirmation of faith, and so it is most appropriate that this be your last conscious act prior to going to sleep. This will bring holiness into your sleep and it will also help you guard the Covenant (*Likutey Halakhot, Kri'at Shema al haMitah, 2*).

Talking about making sleep spiritual, Rebbe Nachman also had some advice for insomniacs. Many people take pills while others drink warm milk. The Rebbe advised a person having trouble falling asleep to "concentrate on your faith in the Resurrection of the Dead" (*The Aleph-Bet Book,* Sleep B:4). This is also a renewal of faith. Interestingly, Rebbe Nachman points out that prior to falling asleep, a person is shown the souls of all his dead relatives. This is also known to happen prior to death. Sleep, being one-sixtieth of death, also affords the possibility of seeing these souls, though only vaguely and in passing, in comparison to when one passes away (*Rabbi Nachman's Wisdom* #90).

*

As is well known, the need for sleep varies in each individual. Some can do well with four hours, others need six or eight hours sleep. Get as much as you need. "Sleep and eat," the Rebbe told one of his followers. "Just watch your time!" (*Kokhavey Or* p. 25). The main thing is to be awake when you're awake! As Rebbe Nachman teaches elsewhere: There are people who seem to be God-fearing and appear to be spending their days studying Torah and praying. Yet, God has no pleasure from their devotions, because they do not put life into them. It's as if they were *asleep*. This "spiritual sleep" happens when a person eats without holiness. The food produces a heaviness and his mind goes to sleep (*Likutey Moharan* I, 60:6).

Some obstacles automatically arise when we want to serve God. In addition, there are other difficulties which we create for ourselves. Indulging in food is an example of the latter. We get groggy and can't think straight. Not getting enough sleep does the same thing. We end up walking around in a fog, thinking we're serving God, when in truth there's no way we can concentrate on our prayers or studies. My Rosh Yeshivah used to say, "It's better to be a *mentsch* for two hours, than a *b'heimah* (animal) for ten" (*Rabbi Eliyahu Chaim Rosen*).

*

One of Reb Noson's followers asked him to interpret a dream he had had. Reb Noson cut him short. "Don't tell me what happens to you when you sleep. Tell me what is happening to you when you're awake!" (*Rabbi Eliyahu Chaim Rosen*).

*

In the s .nmer of 1806, Rebbe Nachman told his famous story, "The Lost Princess" (*Rabbi Nachman's Stories* #1). A few weeks later, on Rosh HaShannah, Rebbe Nachman gave a lesson (*Likutey Moharan* I, 60) in which he explains how telling stories, especially those of Ancient Times, can arouse people from their "sleep." After giving the lesson, the Rebbe said, "The world says telling stories helps one fall asleep. I say, telling stories wakes people up!" (*Tzaddik* #151). Some Breslover Chassidim read from *Rabbi Nachman's Stories* before going to sleep. Obviously, their intention in doing this is not to stay awake. Rather, they read from "The Stories" so that when they do wake up, they should be *really* awake.

* * *

HEALTH AND DOCTORS

Rebbe Nachman said: When you're healthy, devote all your strength to "do and do" in serving God. But, when you're not well, fulfill the mitzvah of "guard your soul" (cf. Deuteronomy 4:15). When you are not well, do only as much as your health will allow (*Aveneha Barzel* p.44 #64).

But, what if you're really sick? Should you call the doctor? Rebbe Nachman said that many people act irrationally when sickness strikes. They feel that they have no choice but to rush off to the doctor. What they do not realize is that the physician cannot give life. In the end, you must rely upon God alone. If that's the case, then why not do so right from the beginning? Why do so many people choose to place themselves in the hands of even the most outstanding physicians, who are closer to death than to life — agents of the Angel of Death himself? (*Rabbi Nachman's Wisdom* #50).

A pretty powerful statement. Ask the medical profession what they think of this one. *And then ask for a second opinion!* One of the most often asked questions about Rebbe Nachman has to be, "Why does he berate the medical profession with such a passion?"

Medicine is a very ancient profession. Doctors are mentioned in Genesis (50:2) and were probably around long before that, too. However, until this century, medicine was not much more than a "quack practice," with most doctors having little, if any, knowledge about the internal functioning of the human body. Rebbe Nachman's opinion was also based on firsthand knowledge. After visiting Lemberg (Lvov) in 1808, he told of a medical convention which had been in progress while he was there. "At the convention, there were two groups of doctors disputing the treatment of a serious disease. One group recommended a bland diet, saying that anything spicy was highly dangerous. The other group had the exact opposite opinion. They said that only spicy foods should be eaten, because sweet and bland foods were detrimental. Each group cited cases, claiming that the others' treatment was a death sentence" (*Rabbi Nachman's Wisdom* #50).

Rebbe Nachman continued, "These were among the world's leading experts, and even they could not determine the truth. Experimental evidence is useless, for sometimes it supports one view and sometimes it supports the opposing view. Since even the physicians themselves are not sure of the truth, with a person's life hanging in the balance, how can he place himself in their hands? The slightest mistake can destroy life....

"Medicine, especially internal medicine, has many fine points. The body is comprised of many intricacies and details" (*Rabbi Nachman's Wisdom* #50). What might be good for one part of the body is harmful to another, and can result in terrible side effects. Even with those medicines which have proven suitable for general use, there are no guarantees. Some medicine may produce negative reactions in only one in ten thousand, and that's great odds. But who wants to be that one? For these and similar reasons, Rebbe Nachman warned: Stay away from doctors!

*

And there we have it. Or do we? Even if all this is true, haven't we advanced into twentieth-century medicine? Hasn't what took place nearly two hundred years ago been improved upon? Rebbe Nachman himself said, "God now directs the world much better than ever before" (*Rabbi Nachman's Wisdom* #307).

First, let's put everything in perspective. Rebbe Nachman's polemic was primarily directed against the primitive medicine of Eastern Europe in his time. This was some sixty years before Pasteur's discovery of infectious diseases and even eleven years before the stethoscope was invented. Obviously, medicine at that time was quite primitive.

Yet, this was after Edward Jenner's discovery of the smallpox vaccination in the late 1790s. Regarding that vaccination, Rebbe Nachman said: "When a person does not innoculate his child against smallpox as an infant, it's as if he murdered the child. Even if he lives in some distant village, and even in the freezing cold of winter, he must bring his infant child to the city for a vaccination" (*Aveneha Barzel* p.29 #34). This seems to contradict openly the Rebbe's previous statements about medicine. Or does it?

Certainly not. From the way Rebbe Nachman spoke about vaccinations, it is clear that where there are *proven* positive results, we should consult a doctor and employ the appropriate healing methods. The real question is, what constitutes proven positive results? To answer this we must first analyze another of the Rebbe's statements.

Rebbe Nachman once said, "There are two whose job is nearly impossible: Satan and the Angel of Death. Each has to oversee the entire world. There are many, many people, and their task is very burdensome. Because of this, each has his assistants. Satan employs false leaders to 'kill' people spiritually, and the Angel of Death uses doctors as his messengers. This makes their jobs a lot easier" (*Aveneha Barzel* p.43 #64).

Since the Rebbe makes a connection between doctors and leaders, it would be wise to focus on the qualities they have in common. Look at the leader of a community. His position is by no means enviable. As their spiritual guide, he must direct the people who come to him, answering their questions on a steady basis. Quite literally, their lives — their emotional well-being, their religious and general outlook — are in the hands of this leader.

However, leaders can be true or false. A true leader, when faced with a difficult situation, frets over every decision. He worries that his advice might not be correct for *this* individual, in *this* specific case. It may have worked previously with someone else, but this person might be different. He has his unique qualities. Because of this, the true leader will pray to God for direction in each and every case. He knows that he is only human and can make mistakes, sometimes serious ones. He prays and prays hard, realizing that the person who came to him for advice is actually placing his life in his hands.

A false leader does none of this. His pride, arrogance and brazenness, which he displays to the "nth" degree, fools him into thinking that he can direct a community. In fact, he is not qualified at all (*Likutey Moharan* I, 10:4). When a person places his life in the hands of a false leader, he is placing his life in the hands of an incompetent adviser who thinks he knows it all and will advise according to his limited knowledge. Ask yourself: Would you place your life in the hands of an ignoramus? But if you don't know he's ignorant, if you think he's wise and knowledgeable, how can you protect yourself? You can't.

The same is true of doctors. When you turn to a doctor for healing, your life is in his hands. His choice of treament and medicines have a direct effect upon your life. Now, if your doctor were God, you'd have no problem. It goes without saying that He is perfectly competent. But most doctors don't even recognize Him. On the contrary, too many of them think of themselves as perfectly competent — godlike — and play the role accordingly. Our Sages teach: The best of doctors go to Gehennom (*Kiddushin* 82a). Rashi explains: This is because they do not turn to Heaven; and because sometimes they kill people; and because they refuse to heal the poor. The Maharsha explains: The best of doctors means a doctor who considers himself the best. He relies only upon his own wisdom. There are times when his haughtiness and conceit cause him to diagnose an illness mistakenly and as a result, his patient dies. He should make it a habit always to consult another physician, because a life has been placed in his hands (*s.v. tov*).

Arrogance. This is what Rebbe Nachman objected to. He understood that, like leaders, doctors were especially prone to the dangerous lure of pride and arrogance. And, while it is true that we are all subject to the frailties of our humanity, doctors and leaders, by the very nature of their special positions, are even more vulnerable. What's more, the harm they are in a position to cause can be lethal. The question which has to be asked is: Into whose hands are you placing yourself? This was Rebbe Nachman's question.

It is obvious that Rebbe Nachman's advice still contains lessons applicable to the relatively advanced medicine of today. Sure, we've come a long way and many lives have been saved by the tremendous progress made over the past two centuries. It seems natural that with all the advances of medical science, that doctors' diagnoses should be very accurate; their success rate should be phenomenally high. Unfortunately, the facts speak for themselves. Who doesn't have a story to tell about themselves or someone they know? A mistaken reading of vital statistics...an unexpected allergic reaction...a bungled operation.... The list is endless. It should be remembered that the title of doctor does not make one infallible, and physicians still make costly mistakes. Even in the highly computerized medical laboratories, there is always the human factor. And, if that factor is mixed with a little arrogance, a little uncaring and feigned knowledge.... This, apparently, was Rebbe Nachman's opposition. It stems from a defiance of faith in God.

In a similar vein, the Rebbe teaches: It is written (Ecclesiastes 1:18), "Increase knowledge, increase pain." As a result of each generation's increase of "knowledge" — in the form of new philosophies and heresies, there is a corresponding increase of "pain" — new illnesses which afflict mankind (Rabbi Nachman's Wisdom #291).

How then should you apply Rebbe Nachman's teaching to today? Apparently, if your physician is someone who realizes his shortcomings, someone who is humble and understands himself as God's messenger of healing, then you can at least turn to him as someone who is sincerely "trying to be helpful." This, as long as you yourself rely only on God. However, the bottom line has to be what the Rebbe himself said: "If you do go to a doctor, make sure he's the best!" (Siach Sarfei Kodesh 1-8).

As far as medicines are concerned, Rebbe Nachman's wariness of doctors would dictate that you should be very careful what you allow into your body. Most prescriptions are given in the spirit of choosing the "lesser of two evils." For every pill listed in the Physician's Desk Reference (a listing of all medicines manufactured in the United States, in pill, capsule and liquid form), one finds some side-effect, some other symptom to beware of. Therefore, it would seem only logical to stay away from doctors whose prescriptions are given out freely. Keep your intake of uncertain substances — something which applies to almost all medicines — to an absolute minimum. And above all, don't become dependent upon a drug. You can tell a Breslover Chassid by his medicine cabinet. Unlike the rest of the world, his medicine cabinet is not full.

*

It is known that Reb Noson did not use doctors at all (*Aveneha Barzel* p.43 #64). Apparently, neither did Reb Naftali. Once, when Reb Naftali was not well, Reb Noson wrote to him: "I understand that you are suffering from an illness which has affected your eyes. I will pray that you get well. I am also preparing a prescription for you: A) don't take medicines! B) don't take medicines! C) don't take medicines!" (*Alim Litrufah* #3). It is also known that Reb Avraham Sternhartz would not use medicines (*Rabbi Moshe Burstein*). When he passed away in 1955, he was ninety-three years old.

Over the years, many of the leading Breslover Chassidim have had to undergo surgery. And when they *had to*, they did. But they were very careful to choose a doctor with a top-notch reputation. And, they would try to speak to the doctor and encourage him to rely upon God to help him during the operation. Of course, they themselves prayed that this doctor be God's true messenger of healing, for they knew that it is all in His hands anyway.

And, if all else fails and you do go to a doctor, or find yourself facing a medical emergency, unable to check references and so on, remember Reb Noson's classic statement: God is so great, He can help a person, even if he has already called the doctor! (*Alim Litrufah* 176; *Siach Sarfei Kodesh* 1-63).

* * *

13

IN THE HOME

"A home is erected with wisdom; and with understanding it is established" (Proverbs 24:3).

It takes both wisdom and understanding to erect and establish a home. The male principle — wisdom — constructs and the female principle — understanding — provides permanence. Without either of these two qualities, a house can't possibly be turned into a home. This chapter focuses on three areas where wisdom and understanding come together for the very purpose of creating a home: the relationship between husband and wife; the raising of children; hospitality.

* * *

FOUNDED ON PEACE

The Zohar teaches that husband and wife are actually one soul. When this soul descends from above, it is separated into male and female, only to be brought together and reunited in this world (Zohar III, 283b). This reunion, which we call marriage, is meant to achieve very great things. As Reb Noson points out, the purpose of marriage is to enable the couple to bring into this world yet another soul — a soul that emanates from the highest levels, from the Very First Thought of Creation (Likutey Halakhot, Minchah 7:93). In so doing, the union between husband and wife brings Creation one step closer to its completion and perfection (cf. Nidah 13b). Understandably, when two people unite for such an exalted purpose, they are bound to encounter all kinds of difficulties and obstacles.

Rebbe Nachman teaches: The Evil Inclination hates man [and seeks to harm him] physically and spiritually. There's nothing it won't do to spoil his life (Rabbi Eliyahu Chaim Rosen). Nowhere is this more evident than in the home. The force of the Other Side will go to great lengths, leaving no stone unturned, just to prevent the soul from reuniting. How else can it hope to keep the world from its perfection? Therefore, it takes a lot of wisdom to build a home, and a great deal of understanding to know how to keep it together.

*

Reb Avraham Chazan used to say: Rebbe Nachman always exhorted his followers to marry young. Aside from the principal purpose of guarding the Covenant, there is another important reason. Rebbe Nachman's lessons are the most effective prescriptions against spiritual illness. A healthy person can pass a drug store feeling indifferent. He has no need for it. But a person who is not well looks to the drug store as his salvation. A single person cannot feel the need for Rebbe Nachman's "medicines." He sees himself to be healthy and sound, but a married person will have already tasted life's difficulties. He will have already discovered that not all is well. Therefore, he can find his salvation and necessary direction in the Rebbe's teachings (Rabbi Eliyahu Chaim Rosen).

Reb Noson's magnum opus, the Likutey Halakhot, is an eight-volume, three-thousand-six-hundred double-columned-page work on how to be a Jew. In his writings, he touches upon every area of life, including the relationship between husband and wife. Yet Reb Noson once said, "Had I wanted to write about the goings-on between husband and wife, I would have had to double the amount of Likutey Halakhot that I wrote (Siach Sarfei Kodesh 1-740).

*

They start off together. They end up separated (*Zohar* II, 95a). My Rosh Yeshivah would say that this refers to evil. Wicked people start off in total agreement about whatever they wish to carry out, but end up in disaccord and separated. Holiness, however, starts off separate, but ends up united. This is especially true of a Jewish marriage.

Two people who seek to live a truly Jewish life together have need of much adaptation. Adjusting to each other as newly-weds, adjusting to living their own lives away from their parents, adjusting once again when children arrive and so on. With all this adjusting, there are reasons aplenty for separation, as happens all too often these days. But, if the couple maintain their commitment to each other, and are truly committed to Judaism, they will always be able to find a way to overcome their difficulties. They may start out separate, but in the end they will unite as one (*Rabbi Eliyahu Chaim Rosen*).

My Rosh Yeshivah continued: "The Talmud teaches that if a man is deserving, his wife will assist him in everything he does. If not, then she will oppose him (*Yevamot* 63a). What most people don't realize is that this help/opposition can change back and forth hundreds of times *each* day. It depends on the person himself."

*

When they were first married, Reb Lipa and his wife got along very well. She had been raised in a home where the teachings of the Baal Shem Tov were taught and the spirit of the Chassidic movement filled the air. Reb Lipa's wife was very happy when her husband joined Rebbe Nachman's following. But after Reb Lipa stopped visiting the Rebbe, things became very bad between them. They were constantly fighting and their relationship turned sour.

What happened to Reb Lipa and his wife was just the opposite of what took place between Reb Noson and his wife. At first, Reb Noson's wife was very much against his travelling to Rebbe Nachman. She had actually been raised in a home in which there was a good deal of opposition to all the *rebbes* and their teachings. A divorce even seemed imminent. However, in time, Reb Noson's wife recognized her husband's greatness and she came to appreciate what Rebbe Nachman taught him.

Once, Reb Lipa met Reb Noson. The two friends began talking and Reb Lipa mentioned the talmudic teaching that if a man is worthy, his wife is turned into his helpmate; but if not, she is against him. Reb Lipa explained that it should have been enough to say that if he is worthy she is his helpmate and if not, then she is against him. "What is the meaning of *turned into?* Isn't it superfluous?" Reb Lipa asked.

Then Reb Lipa said, "But now I know the answer. If the husband is worthy, then even if she was against him — she is *turned into* his helpmate. This is what happened to you Reb Noson! But if the husband is not worthy, then even if she was a helpmate — she is *turned into* his opponent. This is what happened to me!" (*Kokhavey Or*, p. 55, #30).

*

The importance of peace in the home cannot be overstated. "Without peace in the house, you have no home" (*Rabbi Eliyahu Chaim Rosen*). Reb Noson, when he first came to Rebbe Nachman, was advised by a friend to totally disregard his wife's opposition to chassidut. He did not follow this advice, but instead tried to assure her that her fears were unfounded. Years later, he remarked, "Had I listened to my friend's advice, I would never have had peace in my home. And I would never have been able to draw close to the Rebbe" (*Aveneha Barzel*, p.7).

If the key to peace in the home can be summed up in one word, that word is consideration. When you are considerate of your spouse, and your spouse is considerate of you, there's peace. If each of you can say: "I am important, but then, so is she (he)," then all obstacles to peace, material and spiritual, can be overcome. In the chapter entitled "Peace," we've already seen that one of these obstacles is *nitzachon*. This need to feel victorious manifests itself in the home more than anywhere else. "Am I master of the house? Am I the boss? Then I must prove it!" And, as mentioned above, the desire to "prove it" can be so strong that it leads us to deny the truth. Yet the truth is that if a battle royal ensues, nobody wins. It takes real wisdom and understanding to know how and when to compromise and how to be forever considerate, without which no home can exist for very long.

Rebbe Nachman often warned us to honor and be considerate of our wives. He said: Women have much anguish from their children. They suffer in pregnancy and childbirth. Then there are the problems of raising the children, in addition to the many other areas in which they suffer for you. Take all this into consideration and respect your wives (*Rabbi Nachman's Wisdom,* #264). The Talmud even teaches: Honor your wives that you may have wealth! (*Bava Metzia* 59a).

*

Rebbe Nachman teaches: God is my light. God is truth (*Likutey Moharan* I, 9:3). Therefore, whenever things happen in my home — things which require my making a decision with wisdom and understanding — in order to determine my true path, to know which direction to take, I must seek out God. I must turn to Him for everything I need, in everything that I do. If I pray to Him for my needs, if I turn to Him with my doubts and seek His guidance, then I will find the correct answers, and then I will have peace in my home.

* * *

CHILDREN

That wisdom and understanding are absolute necessities for raising children is something clearly known to anyone who's had them. The problem is, knowing you need these qualities and having them aren't one and the same thing. Rebbe Nachman's *Advice* and *The Aleph-Bet Book*, both contain much wisdom and understanding in the art of child-rearing. Anyone who wants a full picture of the Rebbe's advice in this area should study these works. The following few general suggestions will, nevertheless, give us a good idea of Rebbe Nachman's approach.

*

Rebbe Nachman teaches: An angry parent begets foolish children (*The Aleph-Bet Book,* Children A:107). In addition to the positive effect which it has upon the relationship between husband and wife, a home founded on peace has a tremendous positive influence upon the children. As the most observant and perceptive creatures on earth, children quickly learn from their parents and absorb their parents' values. If their parents are loving and easy going, the children pick it up. If their father is diligent in Torah study, in prayer and performing mitzvot, the children learn the importance of religion in their lives. If their mother is generous and hospitable, the children learn good traits. But, if their father is aggressive or exacting towards others — his wife, his children — then the children learn this. And if their mother is slovenly or a yenta, they learn this too. The same is true of anger, *nitzachon* and all the other negative character traits. On the other hand, the compromise, compassion and consideration which the children see in the home will help them develop into strong, vibrant individuals, devoted to the true service of God.

Rebbe Nachman teaches: Don't show favor to one child over another (*The Aleph-Bet Book,* Children A:53). Our Sages learn this from the story of Yosef, whose father Yaakov openly favored him and gave him a multi-colored cloak (Genesis 37:3). This favoritism eventually led to the descent of what was then the entire Jewish people to Egypt (*Shabbat* 10b). Favoring one child is sometimes necessary and has its temporary advantages. But the long-term effects are generally negative. Only the very rare child will overcome the feelings of jealousy which favoritism shown to a sibling engenders.

Rebbe Nachman said that a child must be taught to behave properly right from the start (*The Aleph-Bet Book*, Children A:64). Respect for elders, self-restraint, the importance of kindness and the like, are all necessary ingredients for a child's development. These and all other character traits must be implanted in the child from infancy, or as soon as a child can begin to respond to these ideals. Never mind that the child does not understand their significance. Any delay until the child can "intelligently" behave properly usually results in insolence and an already molded personality which is very hard to change later on in life.

Children are very attentive human beings. They may not understand everything, but precious little escapes their observant eyes and questioning minds. And so, the Talmud teaches: Do not tell a child that you'll give him something then not deliver. This teaches the child to lie (*Sukkah* 46b). They are also extremely sensitive to their parents' moods and can detect inconsistencies in the way we act. Discipline yourself, the Talmud insists, then discipline others! (cf. *Bava Metzia* 107b). Our problem is the double standard we maintain between the way we ourselves behave and the way we want our children to behave. Rebbe Nachman also warned against our employing double standards and being inconsistent, and showed how we do both all the time in a fairly subtle way.

Children have been known to become stubborn. Your child wants something. You say no. The child insists. Yells. Screams. You get upset. You hit the child, as if that's going to make him quiet. Now you're the one yelling and screaming, but the child whines on. Finally, when you can't take it any longer, you give in and "make it up" to him. Rebbe Nachman said: "I say, don't *patsch* (slap) the child. And don't give in"

(*Siach Sarfei Kodesh* 1-91). After displaying our double standard by doing exactly what we insist our children stop doing, we then show them how inconsistent we can be by giving in to their demands.

Rebbe Nachman did not approve of parents hitting their children (*Aveneha Barzel*, p. 50 #4). On the other hand, he also said, "*Sometimes, we do give a patsch.*" This is because there are times, when a slap is the best medicine, a necessary disciplinary measure. Even so, the Breslover Chassidim used to say: Always try to push off "sometimes" to "another time" (*Siach Sarfei Kodesh* 1-212). For the truth is, that most times the slap is coming from the parent's anger, and not as a disciplinary measure to teach the child. Children know this; they learn to ignore the slaps and the intended discipline serves as no more than a temporary restraint. As Rebbe Nachman once said, "With anger, you won't accomplish what you want [from the child]. And even if you have accomplished something with anger, you would have accomplished a lot more with love" (*Rabbi Levi Yitzchak Bender*).

*

Nor are Rebbe Nachman's suggestions on the subject of children limited to how to raise them. In fact, most of what the Rebbe says on this topic in *Advice* and *The Aleph-Bet Book,* as well as in his other works, has to do with having children and all that's associated with what is essentially the very first mitzvah given to man. The following samples show that the Rebbe had some very insightful teachings on this subject.

Praying. It's important to start off on the right foot. This doesn't mean waiting till the baby is born and the *mazel tovs* have begun arriving. Starting off on the right foot begins with the many different prayers written for couples to recite before they even conceive the child. The Zohar teaches that the parents' thoughts at the time of cohabitation have a direct bearing on the child's character (*Zohar Chadash* 15a; see *Likutey Moharan* I, 7:3, n.39; *Likutey Moharan* I, 10:4, n.35).

Then there are prayers to recite during the pregnancy, for the birth, and of course, during the child's lifetime. Success requires constant prayer; beseeching God to grant us the wisdom, finesse, understanding and diplomacy needed to raise a child. Then, maybe, we'll succeed. Without prayer, the odds of this happening are far less. Thus, Rebbe Nachman tells us that praying with great effort is a *segulah* for children (*Likutey Moharan* I, 48).

*

Mashiach will not come until all the souls that were created will be born into this world (*Nidah* 13b). There are many people walking around today with the mistaken notion that there's no point bringing children into the world. Some say simply that the world is so messed up that they wouldn't want their children to have to live in it. Based on what we know from the Talmud's teaching, this is "Catch-22." Others use a different reasoning. They say, "What good is my having children — or many children — if there's a good reason to believe that they will not turn out the way they should. How will I have contributed to Mashiach's coming quickly?" And, unfortunately, it appears so. There are children who fail to be a source of *nachat* to their parents. Even so, Rebbe Nachman said: "A Jew should pray to have a lot of children. When Mashiach comes, he will rectify the generations all the way back to Adam" (*Aveneha Barzel*, p. 21 #4).

Da'at. Rebbe Nachman teaches: See to it that the world is inhabited by humans, not animals in the form of humans. To accomplish this, you must leave your *da'at* over in this world. *Da'at* is knowledge of God. Your *da'at* is *your* knowledge of God. It is transmitted from parent to child. It can also be transmitted by teaching others Torah, which is knowledge of God; for then it is as if you gave birth to that person and have transmitted *da'at* to the next generation (*Likutey Moharan* II, 7:3,4).

We toil. We sweat. We work away our lives so that our children will have. Yes, they were entrusted to us, and we are responsible for giving them the best we can. But, taught Rebbe Nachman and Reb Noson, it's also important to make sure that we have *what* to give them. We have to take the necessary time to serve God and fulfill *our* lives. We have to acquire *da'at*. Then we will have what to transmit, what to give our children. Living a true Jewish life will set the best example for our children to follow, so that they too will carry on our glorious heritage of Torah. After all, this is the greatest treasure we could ever hope to give them.

Good deeds. Someone once came to Rebbe Nachman asking the Rebbe to pray on his behalf for children. Rebbe Nachman answered, "Our Sages taught that the main 'offspring' of the righteous are their good deeds!" (Rashi, Genesis 6:9). Ask that you be a good Jew — that you be worthy of following the true path. If you are worthy of physical children, all the better, but your main offspring are born when you let your heart come close to God." This follower stopped asking for children and concentrated on his devotions. Afterwards, Rebbe Nachman told him, "Still, it would be good if you did have children," and he eventually had a son (*Rabbi Nachman's Wisdom* #253).

Our Sages taught that a person has three friends: his possessions, his family and his good deeds. When he nears his last days, the possessions leave him, for they are of no use to him any more. When he passes on, his second group of friends, his family, accompany him to the cemetery, but no further. After the funeral they leave him, and return home. Only the third group, his good deeds, go on with him to the World to Come (*Pirkei d'Rebi Eliezer* #34).

Children are important. Very important. They alone guarantee the perpetuation of our heritage and holy faith from generation to generation. But you are also very important. You also have an obligation to yourself, an obligation to see that you, too, turn out to be a good Jew. For in the end, you alone will have to account for all your years and deeds. In the final analysis, only your good deeds will accompany you and be permanently by your side. In connection with this, Reb Noson once said: It seems that everyone feels the need to leave over something for his children. This itself is a debt. Ask anyone who's ever lived why they work so hard and he'll tell you, "I do it for my children." "You'd think," said Reb Noson, "that since everyone is working for his children, you'd see such wonderful children. I'm still waiting to see that flawless child! [The one that everyone sells their lives for!]" (*Rabbi Eliyahu Chaim Rosen*).

So, Rebbe Nachman's advice would be: Pray for your children, whether you already have them or are hoping to have them, but make sure that you also pray for yourself. Your children will grow up and move out. Maybe they'll even provide *nachat*. You have to pray for your eternal offspring — your Torah and mitzvot; see that they remain intact. Doing so also gives you a better chance that your children will remain together with you in our faith.

* * *

HOSPITALITY

Aside from *shalom bayit* (peace in the home) and raising children, there are numerous other things which when practiced are capable of turning a house into a home. Welcoming guests is perhaps as good an example as any. The consideration, generosity and concern for others which hospitality displays are qualities necessary for all aspects of building a home. Knowing how to receive visitors and understanding how best to treat them can be a fine art in itself, and yet, as Rebbe Nachman points out, we are not to make so much of this "art" that we either end up nervous wrecks or feeling incapable of doing anything.

The greatness of hospitality, as exemplified by the patriarch Avraham, is well known. The Talmud and Midrash are replete with teachings on this mitzvah and Rebbe Nachman also stressed its importance. Once, the Rebbe was speaking of hospitality's great value to his daughter Sarah, encouraging her to acquire this trait. "If that's the case," she questioned with a good deal of concern, "is it even humanly possible to fulfill the mitzvah properly?" Rebbe Nachman replied, "What do you think? A guest [comes! You bring out] another piece of bread! Another drop of tablecloth!" (*Aveneha Barzel*, p. 21 #2).

It would seem that Rebbe Nachman understood the need for practicing hospitality the way he suggested we do everything else: placing simplicity above all else. A guest should be made to feel comfortable. If you try to overdo it, then sometimes the guest feels he has placed an extra burden upon the host and hostess. Keep it simple, taught Rebbe Nachman. Do the best you can with what you have. Don't be excessive and don't look to impress by going beyond your means.

Reb Noson felt this way too. Many of Reb Noson's followers would come to spend the Shavuot holiday with him in Breslov. Once, shortly before Shavuot, a woman came to Reb Noson asking him to pray on her behalf for children. Reb Noson answered, "For this, you must be hospitable to my followers." Then he added, "This means another bite of challah. Another drop of water in the soup!" (She readily added: "Fish and meat, too!") (*Rabbi Eliyahu Chaim Rosen*).

Reb Noson said that he did not understand anything from the *Burned Book* when he transcribed it from Rebbe Nachman's dictation. The one thing he did remember was that the Rebbe spoke about the greatness of preparing a bed for one's guest (*Rabbi Eliyahu Chaim Rosen; Siach Sarfei Kodesh* 1-

699). (The lessons in the *Burned Book* were even greater than those found in the *Likutey Moharan*. It was burned at Rebbe Nachman's behest in 1808, when he was ill. See *Until The Mashiach*, p. 294).

One of the primary expressions of the mitzvah of hospitality is to welcome Tzaddikim and/or rabbis into your home. This strengthens your faith and brings kindness to the world. It will also protect you from becoming an opponent of the true Tzaddikim (*Likutey Moharan* I, 28).

When Rebbe Nachman was in Lemberg (1807-1808; see *Until The Mashiach* pp.151-158), he had occasion to eat in the home of a very hospitable man. The Rebbe later said: "I was very envious of that man. He sat at his table like a 'rebbe with his followers.' However, the difference was that when followers take their leave of their rebbe, they give him money. But this man did not have to receive. On the contrary, he gave money to all those who ate at his table!" (*Aveneha Barzel* p.26 #18).

Hospitality also includes welcoming Shabbat and the festivals into your home. Rebbe Nachman teaches: Receive the festivals with great joy and happiness. Honor them as much as you possibly can (*Likutey Moharan* I, 30:5). Likewise, the Rebbe said that the main way of honoring Shabbat is with food. Even if one abstains or eats little during the week, he should honor the Shabbat with festive meals (*Likutey Moharan* I, 277). And, he should have a festive mood to match (*Likutey Moharan* II, 17).

Reb Noson adds: By welcoming and honoring the Shabbat with joy, you can merit binding yourself to the Tzaddik and attaining true repentance (*Likutey Halakhot, Shabbat* 7:69).

* * *

14

EARNING A LIVING

"Love God with all your heart, all your soul and all your possessions" (Deuteronomy 6:5). Rebbe Nachman teaches: Whoever conducts his business honestly and with faith, fulfills the mitzvah of loving God with all his possessions (*Likutey Moharan* I, 210).

It is told that the Reb Yaakov, the Dubno Magid, visited Rabbi Eliyahu, the Vilna Gaon. The Gaon asked Reb Yaakov to "give him musar" (ethical rebuke). "Reb Eliyahu!" Reb Yaakov began, "You think you are pious. But you spend your entire day locked away in your room, immersed in your studies. Go out into the street, engage in business, and then see if you are still so righteous!"

For most people, earning a living is the most time-consuming part of their lives. They leave early in the morning, work right through the day, and often bring some part of the work home with them at night — even if only in thought. And, this is if they live within their means and do everything according to the law and the Halakhah.

Nowhere are temptations so strong as when dealing with money. Most sins take only a few moments, and they're done. Sins connected with money often consume a person's time and tax his emotional and intellectual stability. Avarice leads to a whole host of temptations, everything from outright embezzlement to the more subtle overpricing and under-providing. "It's only a small amount"; "He'll never miss it anyway, he outdid me already" and so on. The Talmud refers to this dishonest rationalization as *moreh heter*.

All our business activities and work must be conducted with honesty and integrity. The Torah warns of the absolute need for keeping the scales, weights and measures exact. Lying, cheating, stealing are unequivocally forbidden. Above all, one's word should be kept, even if it means taking a loss. Our Sages tell us that breaking our word is akin to idolatry (*Sanhedrin* 92a). On the other hand, Rebbe Nachman teaches: Conduct your business honestly and with faith. Doing this will vitalize your soul, renew your faith and bring about the same rectifications as were achieved in the Holy Temple by the daily sacrifices and the incense offerings (*Likutey Moharan* I, 35:7,8).

* * *

WHAT KIND OF LIVELIHOOD

Rebbe Nachman very much wanted his followers to have a source of income. [There are those who spend their time only on study and prayer. This requires a tremendous amount of faith and trust in God that He will provide sustenance.] The Rebbe said: Better to have a means of income and direct your energies into several devotions, than to have to work on the devotion of *bitachon* (trust) and experience anxiety over your financial situation (*Tzaddik* #501). A person can easily maintain his faith that God will provide for him through the means of his business. He will then be able to concentrate on prayer and Torah study without wondering where the next dollar is coming from. This way, whatever he works at or trades in, he has put in his effort. Whatever success God has in mind for him, he has made his "vessel," his means, with which to receive Heaven's blessings.

As for what type of livelihood, in Rebbe Nachman's time the possibilities were very limited, especially for a pious Jew.

In today's world, the opportunities are vast and virtually endless. Let us examine some of Rebbe Nachman's statements regarding work, with an eye to understanding where one should concentrate his efforts in the contemporary world.

Teaching. Rebbe Nachman did not want his followers to be *melamdim* (religious teachers). He said: Our Sages taught that every person has his moment of success (*Avot* 4:3). If someone engages in business, when his moment comes, he's in a position to reap a great profit. Not so if he's a low-salaried worker. All he can look forward to is a possible bonus — "a nice pie" or something similar (*Tzaddik* #465). Elsewhere, the Rebbe said: If you make an error in business, corrections can be made and the client will probably excuse you. But, if you err in teaching or waste the time of your pupils, you may never be forgiven (*Rabbi Nachman's Wisdom* #240). (*Tosafot* opines that a teacher is always subject to being fired without warning for teaching incorrectly and wasting the pupil's time; *Bava Metzia* 109b, s.v. *v'sapar; Bava Batra* 21b, s.v. *u'makrei.*) This is an amazing statement! The Rebbe placed so much emphasis on honesty, integrity, fear of Heaven, Torah study and prayer. If not his followers, who then should be instructing the young?

First, let us compare the teaching profession as it was in Rebbe Nachman's era to that of today. In the Rebbe's time, day schools for young children were non-existent. The Jewish community, if large enough, would engage a teacher for their children. This was done generally on a semi-annual basis. Many times, different age groups had to be taught together, something which made the teacher's job quite taxing. If one lived in a small village or town, the individual parent, or a few parents, would hire a teacher for their young. This teacher would occasionally come from the village itself, but most often he would have to be brought from the surrounding areas (or even from farther away). For such a *melamed,* accepting a teaching position necessitated leaving his own home and moving to the village without his wife and children. Though these arrangements were highly undesirable, there was little choice. Not so in today's modern world; we have day schools, transportation and all the necessary conveniences to run a sophisticated educational institute.

In addition, Rebbe Nachman teaches: When among non-Jews, take great care not to fall from your spiritual level. We are in a very low world, the lowest world in existence, where even angels do not have the strength to overcome physical temptation. A Jew has greater power than the angels and can overcome all obstacles. But, the further we are from our spiritual reservoirs, the harder it is to maintain control over ourselves (*Likutey Moharan* I, 244).

When compared with the current situation, working away from home, the way teachers of two hundred years ago did, resembles more a travelling salesman than a teacher. Salesmen who spend a good deal of time on the road are subject to all kinds of temptations and are in constant spiritual danger. This is aside from the strain which constant travelling puts on his family relationships. Conversely, working close to home has a positive affect on *shalom bayit* (peace in the home) and in *Shmirat haBrit* (guarding the Covenant). On the other hand, today's teachers can work near their homes, in a structured educational system with working conditions that greatly benefit the student. Of course there are varied circumstances, but in the main, Rebbe Nachman would probably view today's religious teaching in a positive light.

However, the second objection raised by Rebbe Nachman, that of wasting a child's time, is still very relevant and of paramount importance. The aim of religious education is to instill in the children a fear of Heaven and a love for Torah and Judaism. If a person cannot do this, then he obviously has no business being a *melamed*. He's been hired and is being paid a salary to infuse faith and Torah in his students' hearts. If he does not do this, he is stealing; stealing from the children, their parents, and even the school. Worse, much worse, he is actually deterring his students from ever achieving true Judaism. Our Sages comment on this: Causing another person to sin is worse than killing him. Killing him deprives him only of this world. Causing him to sin also deprives him of his World to Come (*BaMidbar Rabbah* 21:4).

As for teaching secular subjects, Rebbe Nachman spoke very critically of those secular subjects that draw a person away from faith. These, unquestionably, should not be taught, nor should they even be studied by the person himself. This does not, however, include those subjects which have absolutely no bearing on faith, e.g. mathematics.

From the above, we can cull what would presumably be Rebbe Nachman's advice in selecting a means of income today. Choose a business, profession or trade that will enable you to be near home. If at all possible, work in surroundings that benefit your spiritual growth and at the very least, make sure that the atmosphere of your place of work is not incompatible with Judaism.

City or suburbs. Rebbe Nachman said: When it comes to earning a living, residing in a big city is best. Our Sages taught that everything has its place of success (*Avot* 4:3). Better business opportunities present themselves in cities (*Tzaddik* #465). Rebbe Nachman also said that he did not approve of a chassid living in a small town (*Tzaddik* #591) because he could easily become conceited, realizing that he would be the most pious among the town's dwellers.

In light of modern transportation and communications, and the easy access to large business centers which they afford, one should look to choose a community which offers both himself and his family those facilities required for religious growth. This includes opportunities for Torah study, religious schools and facilities, such as a mikvah for family purity, and synagogues.

As for conceit, if one can fall prey to it, which is unfortunately quite easy to do, then one should certainly take care not to live in a place which fosters it. This would apply whether he is wealthier or smarter or in any way capable of exercising power over others. One must conduct oneself humbly even, or especially, when engaged in business. He should bear in mind that the One Who bestows him the wealth and power can easily take it away.

The Chofetz Chaim said that because of today's spiritually weakened generations, God granted us different means of transportation that were unheard of in previous generations. These time-saving devices were given to enable us to have more time for Torah study. The horse and buggy provided not only a rugged ride, but also guaranteed that the traveler would feel his journey for quite a few days afterwards. By contrast today's modes of travel leave one rested and with considerably more time than he would have had years ago.

Go tell it to someone who has to travel every morning and night on the Long Island Expressway, the San Diego Freeway, or the M1 Motorway. With bumper-to-bumper traffic, horns blasting and so on, get someone to believe you that today's improved travel is for the betterment of mankind. However, if you think about it, you'll see that the Chofetz Chaim was right. Today is the age of the "Walkman" and tape-decks in the car. It is also an age in which we have thousands upon thousands of hours of cassette Torah lessons at our fingertips. We can conceivably travel from "coast to coast" and learn every minute of the day. There are tapes on Tanakh, Mishnah, Talmud, Jewish History, Ethics and so on. There are also many tapes of Rebbe Nachman's teachings and all these tapes are available in Hebrew, English, Yiddish and other languages. So, whether we commute by car, bus, train or plane, we have the opportunity to utilize our travel time for positive eternal profit.

Travel. A follower once expressed anxiety about undertaking a particular trip. He was worried that his long journey away from home would have negative consequences, spiritually. Rebbe Nachman replied: "If you have occasion to travel, there's no reason to remain at home and stubbornly refuse to go. Each person is destined to be in a particular place at a given time. Wherever a Jew travels, he corrects something. He makes a blessing, recites a prayer, or carries out a different mitzvah. Just watch yourself that you do not commit a sin. Thus, wherever you go you will make a rectification" (*Rabbi Nachman's Wisdom* #85).

In today's world, many people have to travel for business, sometimes to foreign lands, sometimes for weeks at a time. It's up to the person to make the most of it spiritually, even though he is distant from home. As Rebbe Nachman said, "God now directs the world much better than ever before!" (*Rabbi Nachman's Wisdom* #307). Anyone who has traveled over the past couple of years knows how much easier it is nowadays to adhere to Judaism when away from home. Kosher food is available almost everywhere. Frozen, canned and vacuum packed dinners, though not always the most appetizing, are quite easy to come by. Calendars with the times of sunrise and sunset for most places are available, enabling the traveler to know when to pray and when to begin Shabbat. And, as anyone who travels knows, there are two things you can find even in the most far-flung corners of the world: Coca Cola and a Jewish heart.

Borrowing. Rebbe Nachman teaches: A person who does not lust for money — living within his means, using his own money and not borrowing to [greatly] expand his business adventures — fulfills the mitzvah of (Deuteronomy 6:5): "You should love God with all your might/possessions" (*Rabbi Nachman's Wisdom* #289).

To borrow, or not to borrow? That is the question. In today's world of buy-now-and-pay-later, credit cards and plastic money, the question is only too real for nearly all of us. And it's by no means an easy one to answer. What exactly did Rebbe Nachman mean by living within one's means? What precisely is it to use one's own money and not borrow to [greatly] expand in business? Is there room for leeway, borrowing a little when necessary? Or, can we only buy the things we need, even our daily bread and milk, when we have ready cash? Can we only develop our businesses when we already have enough of our own money to do it? For those who follow Rebbe Nachman's advice, is all borrowing to be absolutely proscribed? Elsewhere, the Rebbe teaches: Whoever wishes to repent should avoid falling into debt (*The Aleph-Bet Book*, Repentance A:46). At first glance, this would seem to spell out the Rebbe's position on borrowing quite clearly.

Nevertheless, we find that Reb Noson, the Rebbe's closest follower and the one who understood more about Rebbe Nachman than anyone else, did occasionally borrow money (see *Yemey Moharnat*, 17b). Also, when my Rosh Yeshivah, Reb Eliyahu Chaim Rosen, undertook to build the Breslover Yeshivah in Jerusalem, he had to borrow money in order to begin. When asked how he could do this considering the Rebbe's strong objections to going into debt, he answered, "My teacher, Reb Avraham Chazan, said that when it comes to a mitzvah, jump in!"

Since, we have to consider the Rebbe's teaching beyond its face value, let's see if we can't come up with a guideline which will enable us to apply Rebbe Nachman's advice to ourselves and our daily situations. Looking at what Rebbe Nachman says: "One who does not lust for money...within one's means...not borrowing to [greatly] expand..." we can draw a number of conclusions. Fundamentally, what the Rebbe rejects is avarice: the insatiable desire for wealth or gain. This is by no means a denial of the need for a livelihood. We all need money. The problem is that we all *want* extras. Living within your means shows control over the lust for money. Borrowing just to survive, truly a rarity in today's world, is not at all what the Rebbe frowned upon. But, borrowing in order to purchase the extras or to increase the chances of [greatly] expanding your income, that's another matter. Fulfilling the desire for more and better material possessions by going beyond your present means, or borrowing to expand quickly — that's what Rebbe Nachman objected to.

In this sense, if borrowing to expand a business or make an investment (or even fix up a home) produces such heavy financial constraints that all your time is taken up with borrowing from Peter to pay Paul, then it should absolutely be avoided. A person's time is far too important to be spent on "juggling." Of course, borrowing the extra investment money with interest would certainly be forbidden. People who fall into this trap rarely come out of it unscathed.

However, the Rebbe's strong warning against borrowing would not seem to apply where the need for cash is short-term; such as when funds are tied up, your pay check is late in coming, or unforeseen repairs and unexpected expenses suddenly need tending. Knowing that you have from where to take to pay back your loan makes all the difference. You might even be permitted to borrow money if you see prospects of a good investment, for even though this will "tighten your budget," you will be able to manage the loan payments.

Even so, Rebbe Nachman teaches: Decrease expenditures. It's best to be satisfied with a minimum and not to be in debt at all. Better to owe yourself (a new suit, a new car and so on), than to owe someone else (*Rabbi Nachman's Wisdom* #122).

* * *

THREE POINTS TO REMEMBER

Having a profession or business of your own has many advantages. However, it also carries an assortment of obligations. Being a boss necessitates paying wages on time. Owning a business means being concerned with product quality vis-a-vis the pricing. Working for someone else requires doing an honest job and really earning one's wages. There are numerous responsibilities in Torah law connected to all these areas.

Three points which should be uppermost in a Breslover Chassid's mind are as follows:

1) Rebbe Nachman said: *"Meh darf zein zeier u'gehit mit yenem's a kopke"* (One has to be very careful with the other guy's money; Rabbi Nachman Burstein). Respect for the property and possessions of another person is emphasized throughout the Rebbe's teachings.

2) *Hitbodedut.* For all his opposition to his followers being teachers (in his time), Rebbe Nachman remarked: "If you're going to be involved in business and not practice *hitbodedut,* then it would already be better to take a job as a *melamed.* A businessman without *hitbodedut* can too easily err in financial transactions" (Siach Sarfei Kodesh 1-702). The importance of praying to God, asking Him for guidance in business and investments, for protection against wrongdoing when dealing with someone else's money and so on, cannot be stressed enough.

Rebbe Nachman teaches: When you suddenly find yourself with a thought of repentance, then turn to God right then and there. Sometimes, these thoughts are sent to a person at a specific place, therefore, remain rooted to that spot and grab in a few moments of prayer and *hitbodedut.* Waiting till you come to a more "appropriate" place, like a synagogue or a private room, may be too late (Likutey Moharan II, 124).

Reb Efraim (Reb Naftali's son) was a jeweler. Another Breslover Chassid once saw Reb Efraim in his booth at a convention in Kiev with his face washed in tears. "What's wrong?" the chassid asked, to which Reb Efraim replied, "Is this the purpose of my life? Was I born for this?" "Then why not go to the synagogue and pray there?" the chassid insisted. "That would not do," Reb Efraim countered. "Rebbe Nachman taught that wherever you receive a thought of repentance, even in the middle of the marketplace, turn directly to God and pray to Him. Before you get to the synagogue, the thoughts may well be gone" (*Aveneha Barzel*, p. 67 #43).

3) Set aside time for Torah study during the day. Actually, Rebbe Nachman taught that a certain type of stealing is very praiseworthy: "Steal *time* for learning even during a very busy day!" the Rebbe advised (*Likutey Moharan* I, 284).

Anyone with any sort of financial dealings must learn the Torah laws pertaining to business. Rebbe Nachman said, "It is impossible to conduct business honestly and with faith, without a comprehensive knowledge of the Torah's laws on these matters" (*Likutey Moharan* I, 35:6). The laws of commerce, real estate, employee relationship and so on are found in the fourth section of *Shulchan Arukh, Choshen Mishpat* (passim). Laws of interest and investments are found in *Yoreh Deah* (159-177). However, these laws are very detailed and difficult. One would do well to study the *Kitzur Shulchan Arukh* (Code of Jewish Law) to pick up the basics. With this as your foundation, you can then add to your knowledge from other works which discuss these laws.

* * *

THE DOS AND DON'TS

There are numerous dos and don'ts in earning a living. The list may well be endless, but here are a few, together with what Rebbe Nachman had to say about them.

Don't worry. Rebbe Nachman teaches: Anxiety and distress over one's income drains one's strength (*The Aleph-Bet Book*, Money, A:60). Rather than contributing to your peace of mind, all the worries and headaches that you carry around with you only serve to drain your strength. Instead of improving your ability to make a living, your fears and concern actually cut down your earning power. There is a better choice. You can always be joyous. Rebbe Nachman teaches: He who is constantly joyous, succeeds (*The Aleph-Bet Book*, Joy B:1).

Reb Noson had a childhood friend who lived in Moheliv. This friend over-expanded his business and eventually went bankrupt. With none of today's bankruptcy laws to save him, he had no choice but to run away from home. He decided to turn to a wealthy relative who lived in a distant city, hoping that this relation would help him out of his dire straits.

On his way, the man passed through Breslov. He remembered his old friend Reb Noson and elected to pay him a visit. As the two friends were talking, the man began to pour his heart out to Reb Noson, telling him all about his pressing financial woes. Hearing the problem, Reb Noson said to him, "You are truly in trouble, but your advice is not good. When you arrive at the house of your wealthy relative, your troubles will be written all over your face. His greeting will be halfhearted at best, and I doubt he'll give you more than a day or two of hospitality. Then what? You'll be a stranger in that city. Where will you stay?

"Take my advice and 'run away' — directly to God! Return to Moheliv. But, instead of going home, go straight to the House of Study. In your hometown people know that you are not a thief. There you are respected as a businessman who worked hard but met with hard times. When your family discovers that you've returned, they'll come demanding and yelling, but you be silent. Do not answer. Just run to Torah and prayer. If you follow this advice, you'll see that in a few days, God will help you straighten out your mess."

Reb Noson's words, spoken with true feeling and concern for his friend, entered the man's heart. He returned to Moheliv and headed straight for the House of Study. He began studying Torah and prayer, and remained silent in the face of all opposition. A few days later, the townspeople gathered to discuss the situation. His friends and acquaintances, realizing this was no more than his having fallen upon hard times, decided to lend him the money he needed to set up a business and get back on his feet.

Reb Noson's friend began to divide his time between Torah, prayer and work. He was blessed, and his new business grew steadily until he was able to return that loan and pay off the rest of his debts. He later wrote a letter to Reb Noson, thanking him profusely for his foresight and advice (*Aveneha Barzel*, p.82ff).

The need to find the time in your day for Torah study and prayer is essential. So, too, is the importance of joy. Both provide a haven of security — a sanctuary — in times of trouble. Sometimes, maybe too often, we face Blue Mondays, Black Tuesdays and so on. But if we have our time and place of refuge ready for us, if the tools necessary to "overturn a loss" are prepared and in place, we will be better equipped to absorb the difficulties and bounce back that much sooner.

Do keep the law. As we've mentioned, it is very important that we adhere strictly to all the Torah's laws while engaged in business. But what about secular law? What about "the law of the land"? Rebbe Nachman was strongly opposed to contravening these laws. He said: Remain steadfast in the faith that God will help you, and under no circumstances should you violate the laws of either the Torah or the government. Such tactics may seem worthwhile, but the advantage they offer are only short-lived (*Siach Sarfei Kodesh* 1-135). In the long run, only following the law will prove successful.

Don't lose your money. Rebbe Nachman strongly
cautioned us to safeguard our money and take good care of
our possessions. He said: A man takes time from Torah study
and prayer, struggling to earn some money. Then he doesn't
take care of it! Honest Jewish money must be guarded like
the eyes in your head. Rebbe Nachman was not sympathetic
to those who were careless with their money (*Rabbi Nachman's
Wisdom* #281). This also applies to spending or investing one's
money unwisely.

Rebbe Nachman teaches: Money, in its root, stems from
the same place as the soul. It is a person's *CHoMaH* (his wall)
and protection. He should keep that wall complete. However,
there is a particular character trait that is innate to a person
and grows as he does. This trait is *CHeiMaH* (anger). He has
to control this anger and prevent it from damaging his wall.
Furthermore, if he finds himself suddenly getting angry about
something, he should understand that he is about to receive a
blessing for wealth. The situation which angers him is a test.
He should then double his efforts to control his anger (*Likutey
Moharan* I, 68). Thus, one of the best solutions for protecting
one's money and possessions is controlling one's anger. This
way, a person can safeguard whatever he already has, while
looking forward to additional blessings.

Do have faith. Above all, have faith. Have faith in God
that you'll receive whatever you're supposed to. "Business
is faith" (*Likutey Moharan* I, 35:7). In today's pressure-filled and
highly competitive world, a person who comes home at the
end of a day's work with his faith intact is really very unique.
A person who remembers faith in the midst of the business
day, in the heat of it all, is even more extraordinary and
unique — an even bigger *chidush*.

The Talmud states: On Rosh HaShannah, God decrees the
exact amounts a person will earn and profit during the year
(*Beitzah* 16a). This decree is made official on the night of Shemini

Atzeret, as one recites the prayer of *Emet V'Emunah* (after the Shema; *Siach Sarfei Kodesh* 1-55). No amount of work or overtime will change this amount. If you think you can profit more by working longer hours, remember that God can easily "grant" you a corresponding amount of expenses or losses. For the Talmud also states: Just as one's income is decreed on Rosh HaShannah, so too, are his losses. If he is worthy, the charity he tithes from his earnings will be his "losses." [If not, his losses will be taken directly from his income] (*Bava Batra* 10a). Therefore, how much better it is to have faith and spend your "free" time in prayer and study — with guaranteed returns on your efforts — than exerting yourself for questionable gains.

On the other hand, "prayer can change a decree" (*Rosh HaShannah* 17b). If you want to increase your income, honestly, then spend time in prayer, recite the Psalms and talk to God in *hitbodedut*. Tell Him that you need more money. Explain your reasons. Plead. Your continuous prayer has the power to alter any decree of poverty and change your fortune for the better.

Torah study also has the power to bring wealth (*Shabbat* 63a). Rebbe Nachman told a story of two childhood friends who studied together. After they married and entered their own businesses, one succeeded while the other suffered constant poverty. Heaven's shining on his one-time friend particularly bothered the poor man, especially because he had actually seen his friend commit a grave sin. "Why should he have such success? I myself saw him commit a sin!" He was constantly upset, complaining against what he saw as God's injustice. He finally received his answer in a dream. "From the day you entered your businesses, your friend has consistently set aside times for Torah. He has taken upon himself to study a given amount each day. Come what may, he keeps to this schedule. But you are not involved with the Torah.

Consequently, your companion is worthy of riches despite his great sin. For "though it can extinguish a mitzvah, sin cannot extinguish Torah" (Sotah 21a). To this the Rebbe added that *"We'ain Averah M'khabeh Torah"* (sin cannot extinguish Torah) is the acronym for *MAoWT* — money (Likutey Moharan I, 204; Rabbi Nachman's Wisdom #137). Thus, not only does diligent and consistent Torah study not detract from your earnings, it actually adds to your profits and provides security to your income. (Charity provides the best protection and insurance for one's business, as is explained later on, in the chapter entitled "Charity.")

*

In short, engage in business, learn a profession, work to have a steady income. But don't forget that a person's time in this world is limited. There is much more to work for than just one's physical and material needs.

Our Sages teach: An unborn child is taught the entire Torah while in its mother's womb (Nidah 30b). The Zohar asks, "Why are newborn babies unable to see?" The answer is that in the womb, they are taught the Torah and are shown what beautiful lights and treasures await them in the World to Come. However, arriving in this world, these lights are hidden from them....Whoever does not seek the Torah is "blinded" from searching for the World to Come, whereas one who does seek a life of Torah, then God says (Genesis 1:3): "Let there be light!" Seeking the Torah opens one's eyes to the delights of the World to Come (Tikkuney Zohar 70, p.137).

The Talmud teaches: As huge as the world is, it is but 1/3200 of the Torah (Eruvin 21a). Thus, the Torah is many times greater in size than the entire earth. Rebbe Nachman asks: If the Torah is so great and huge, why don't people see it? He answers: Compare it to a great mountain in front of one's eyes. If a person places nothing more than a small coin in front of his eyes, he can no longer see the mountain

(*Likutey Moharan* I, 133). The message is clear: Don't let yourself be blinded by the "coins" of earning a living.

* * *

YOU WANT IT? PAY FOR IT!

Rebbe Nachman teaches: Pay for the mitzvah. Any mitzvah which a person does without incurring costs, is [still] considered a righteous deed. But, paying a price for a mitzvah — incurring expenses in order to perform the mitzvah correctly and as well as possible — breaks one's lust for money and is considered an act of pure faith (*Likutey Moharan* I, 23:5)

For the living room we buy an expensive couch. The beds are top quality and the washing machine is one that's guaranteed not to break down. Our clothing is practical but nice. How about our mezuzot and tefilin? How much are we ready to spend on a beautiful sukkah or special matzot for Pesach? And how much are we willing to put out so that our kids get the best Torah education they possibly can? Just as there is no need to go overboard when buying furnishings and clothing, there is no need to overspend completely when paying for a mitzvah (cf. *Bava Kama* 9b). Even so, Rebbe Nachman tells us that we should not try to get away with paying for the mitzvah altogether or looking for an inexpensive way out.

Reb Noson was once considering the purchase of a particularly beautiful etrog, and he brought it to the Rebbe for his approval. Rebbe Nachman looked at it carefully, but did not seem too impressed. Finally, the Rebbe very matter-of-factly nodded his assent and Reb Noson went off to pay for the etrog. When Reb Noson returned he encountered a complete about-face in attitude, for now the Rebbe greatly praised the etrog and exclaimed how beautiful it was. When asked why he didn't show any emotion earlier, the Rebbe replied, "It is truly an impressive etrog. However, had I shown

266 / CROSSING THE NARROW BRIDGE

any enthusiasm before, it would have shown on your face when you negotiated with the dealer. He most certainly would have raised the price on you. By hiding my feelings, you got a beautiful etrog without overpaying for it" (Oral Tradition). Mitzvot are our true possessions. The money we spend on them is money well spent.

* * *

15

CHARITY

Our Sages teach: If you see that your livelihood is limited, give charity! All the more so, if you have sufficient income. Compare this to two sheep, one shorn and the other laden with wool, which try to swim across a river. The shorn sheep has no problem crossing. But the wool of the laden one absorbs the water and soon, when the weight becomes too heavy, she drowns (Gittin 7a).

Interesting. You see your income dwindling. You find budgetary constraints closing in on you from all sides. What should you do? Give some more away! Yes, from the little bit that you have, take some and give it away. To charity. Go on, have less than you have today. That way, you'll be able to "cross the river." And not only this. Our Sages also give a *promise*: Do this — give charity — and you'll no longer experience dwindling resources!

We will soon see that the most guaranteed way to earn a living is to give charity. The Talmud, Midrash, Zohar and virtually all the Holy Writings, speak extensively about the greatness and the power of charity. Numerous Breslov teachings on the value of this great mitzvah appear throughout Rebbe Nachman's and Reb Noson's writings, and have been compiled in concise form most notably in *Advice* and *The Aleph-Bet Book*. Here, we will attempt to convey to the reader some of the Rebbe's more important teachings on giving charity, as well as offering his suggestions on how to make our charity most effective.

* * *

OPENING THE DOORS

"Pato'ach, tiphtach et yadkha — Open, you should open your hand..."* (Deuteronomy 15:8). Why does the verse use the redundant wording, *"Pato'ach, tiphtach"*?

Rebbe Nachman teaches: All beginnings are difficult. All devotions, all repentance...anything and everything we begin, we must encounter enormous difficulties and obstacles. Just as a woman giving birth must undergo the travails of labor before she can bring her child into this world, so too, anything we wish to accomplish — give birth to and create — we must first experience the "pains of labor." The hardest part is making the *petach* (the opening), the beginning. Charity is called a *petach*. It is the *first* opening — the one which widens all the cracks, and opens all the other doors. Therefore, the verse reads: *"Pato'ach, tiphtach* — Open you should open," because charity opens all the doors, it creates all the opportunities (*Likutey Moharan* II, 4:2).

Actually, charity in itself is also very difficult to begin. The verse teaches us that charity also requires an open door, so that we can begin to give. If our nature is to be compassionate, we encounter little resistance within ourselves when we donate to charity. But if it is our nature to be miserly or stingy, if there are streaks of cruelty within our personality, we must turn the cruelty into compassion — force open the opening of charity inside ourselves! (*Likutey Moharan* II, 4:1).

The power of charity is absolutely phenomenal. It can open the gates of great yearning and desire so that we can serve God constantly. Through charity we can draw upon ourselves such an influx of God's kindness, that we will no longer have to struggle earning a living. A blessing of kindness will descend, bringing abundance for all (*Likutey Moharan* II, 4:9).

This teaches us that charity can break open all barriers, including the obstacles and difficulties we experience while earning a livelihood. This is not to say that we should give all our money to some worthy cause in the hope of being rewarded with this great kindness and abundance. Indeed, the Talmud forbids the giving of more than twenty percent of one's possessions to charity [there are exceptions; see below] (*Ketubot* 50a). However, through Rebbe Nachman's lesson we can appreciate the value which charity has for the person seeking an opportunity to earn a prosperous living. Giving is truly receiving.

* * *

THE BUSINESS RECTIFICATION

In all the areas of our lives, proper conduct is important. Yet, the frailties of our humanity dictate that we cannot help but fail in some aspect of our conduct. No one can go through life without "blowing it," at least sometimes. Even so, there is always the possibility of rectification. We can make amends for the things we've done wrong and remedy the situation. The same holds true for improper "conduct" in thought and personality. There are ways to fix these things too.

For example, what happens when we hurt someone's feelings? We can always apologize. This is a rectification. Or, what if we borrow something from a friend and then break it? We can pay for it. This remedies the situation. If we're mean, we can be kind. If we get angry, we can make sure to keep our cool. And, if we have negative or improper thoughts, we can work on this too; each negative characteristic has its rectification.

The same is true when a person hasn't conducted his business honestly. He can pay back the person he's overcharged or return the money he hasn't recorded. But what happens when this has been going on for a long time, when he no longer has any idea of whom or what he owes? What if he's been honest in his business dealings, but is trapped in a lust for wealth? If, no matter how much he has, he never feels enough and always desires more? How can he correct these blemishes? Is there any way to rectify the past and improve the future? The answer is yes: He can employ a General Remedy.

Rebbe Nachman teaches: Charity is the General Remedy for business. Have in mind that in every aspect of your dealings, in everything you say and do in your work or business, your desire for profit is so that you will then be able to donate to charity. This is the General Remedy which rectifies business at its source. All the specific areas where you may have failed to conduct your business properly are then rectified automatically (*Likutey Moharan* I, 29:4,9).

*

Earning a living has to be based on faith. This means believing that whatever God wants to provide us with, that's what we are going to get. It's not easy! In fact, it's quite difficult truly to attain this level of belief. Too much of what happens in our daily lives seems to go against this; especially when a person thinks that all his efforts, and only his efforts, provide him with his livelihood. Actually, this attitude is a blemish in the way we go about making a living and engaging in business. It is also indicative of a great lack of faith.

As Rebbe Nachman tells us, the General Remedy for this is charity. If we keep in mind that a share of our profits will go to charity, then our every action in doing business is a reaffirmation of our faith. What better show of faith is there, than when we take what is ours, our hard-earned money, and give it away to others — because God commanded us to do so? This is a general rectification for all we do in business, because our every thought, our every word, our every action, is calculated with one specific aim: that charity benefit from whatever we accomplish.

This is why Rebbe Nachman teaches: Charity helps a person break his lust for money (*Likutey Moharan* I, 13:1).

One thing must be made absolutely clear: it is totally forbidden to rationalize that, because a part of the profits will be going to charity, it is permissible to cheat and steal for the sake of giving this charity. Rebbe Nachman's teaching on the General Remedy for business applies to a person who has erred in the past, mistakenly or otherwise, and who at present wishes to rectify his wrongs. In no way whatsoever is he suggesting that a person can commit a sin, knowing that the charity he gives later on will rectify his misconduct.

* * *

GUARDIANS OF THE WEALTH

"There will be no poor among you" (Deuteronomy 15:4). "The impoverished will never cease to be among you..." (Deuteronomy 15:11). Our Sages comment on this contradiction: When the Jews adhere to the Torah, there will be abundance and blessings. When not, poverty will prevail (Sifri, R'eih; Rashi, ad. loc.). What happens to Heaven's blessings and abundance when the Jews do not adhere to Torah? It goes to the nations. The Jews receive only the remains and scraps (Zohar II:152b).

Reb Noson writes: Certainly, each person has his own individual "pipeline" of shefa (blessing), so that if shefa descended commensurate with the mitzvot which a Jew performs, each pious Jew would be independently wealthy. But we are in exile and the channels of shefa are confused, even among the Jews themselves. As a result of these pipelines getting crossed, many wealthy people receive their blessing of abundance through pipelines that really belong to others.

Therefore, Reb Noson explains, the Torah warns of the need to give charity. People blessed with good fortune have, so to speak, been appointed to act as the guardians of God's monies. A prosperous person who understands that he has been blessed to oversee the needs of the poor, should be very happy to perform the mitzvah of charity. Unfortunately, there are those who believe that the wealth is their own, that they "earned" it. They do not accept that they have been blessed by God. So, these people become oppressors of the poor, not only do they not give charity, but they even begrudge the impoverished their basic sustenance.

However, by giving charity, we rectify these pipelines which channel the abundance. We "return" the poor man's *shefa*. And by doing so we open up even more pipelines, thereby bringing ourselves and others even more blessings, until, ultimately, full *shefa* will return to the Jews (*Likutey Halakhot*, Pikadon 5:35).

*

The story is told of a wealthy chassid who came to the Magid of Mezritch, announcing that he had taken upon himself to fast and mortify his body. The Magid grabbed him by his lapels, saying, "You must eat fish and meat every single day!" After this follower left, the students asked the Magid, "What would be so terrible if that wealthy man denied himself the pleasures of the body?" The Magid answered: "If he eats fish and meat, he'll understand that the poor must be given at least the basics, bread and the like. But, if he himself eats only hard bread, what will be left for the poor?!" (*Rabbi Eliyahu Chaim Rosen*).

* * *

THE GREATNESS OF CHARITY

Rebbe Nachman's lessons and conversations abound with references to the efficacy of charity. Presented here are a few of the teachings that direct us to the importance of charity and its unique influence on our daily lives.

Rebbe Nachman teaches: Giving charity reveals the greatness of God to the world (*Likutey Moharan* I, 25:4).

The difference between man and beast is the power of speech. Charity creates the power of speech (*Likutey Moharan* I, 225).

Giving charity generates all the blessings and engenders knowledge (*Likutey Moharan* I, 31:1,2).

Be generous and you will move up in the world (*The Aleph-Bet Book*, Charity A:28).

Charity to the poor in the Holy Land brings prosperity (*The Aleph-Bet Book*, Charity B:17).

Give charity and you will be blessed with children (*The Aleph-Bet Book*, Charity A:32).

Charity saves from sin (*Likutey Moharan* I, 116). It saves from the worst impurities (*Likutey Moharan* I, 242).

Charity brings peace (*Likutey Moharan* I, 57:7).

Charity helps guard the Covenant. Desecrating the Covenant involves giving nourishment to that which is forbidden, to the forces of evil. Charity rectifies this by giving sustenance where it is needed. One should therefore be careful to give charity to worthy places. Otherwise, even one's charity gives nourishment to unworthy places (*Likutey Moharan* I, 264).

Charity sweetens harsh judgment (*The Aleph-Bet Book*, Charity B:6).

Charity hastens the Final Redemption (*The Aleph-Bet Book*, Charity A:2).

* * *

CHARITY AND GLORY

Rebbe Nachman teaches: One has to elevate God's Glory from among the contemptuous. These brazen-faced people "capture" the Glory of God and use it for themselves —

unworthy people become "leaders" of the Jewish communities. This further debases the Glory of God and the glory of the Jewish people themselves. Such debasement is compared to death, but "charity saves from death" (Proverbs 10:2). Giving charity strengthens the soul and reveals wisdom on earth. This elevates God's Glory and brings Lovingkindness to Creation (*Likutey Moharan* I, 67:4-8).

Charity is more than just a mitzvah; it has an enormous power to sweeten harsh decrees. It can bring peace. It also elevates God's Glory so that He is recognized throughout the world.

However, because philanthropy is so closely bound with glory and honor, it brings with it a multitude of motivations. Some give for the sake of the mitzvah itself, while others give because they feel compassion for the poor. Still others because someone is at the door and "I don't feel like turning anyone away," or because a business associate hit me for a contribution, and so on. Then, there are those who give because of the honor they receive. Their names "go up in lights" and they become the talk of the town. "What a charitable person! What a great philanthropist...."

Giving charity for charity's sake is incontrovertibly the greatest level. Few attain it. Like intense prayer and deep Torah study, it is the goal all aim for. Those who give for compassionate reasons are also very praiseworthy, for they are a pillar of support to those who really need help. But what about those who seek and receive honor for their deeds? What can be said of their charity?

There are differing views in the *Shulchan Arukh* (*Yoreh De'ah* 249:13) about whether one should have his name placed upon a mitzvah, such as donating a Torah scroll or a window to a synagogue. Some take the position that contributions and acts of kindness are best left completely anonymous. Others posit that it is permissible and should even be encouraged. Even so, giving solely for one's own honor would seem to call into question the validity of the deed itself, for, in fact, such a person is giving to himself — giving in order to receive.

In a related vein, our Sages taught: A person should always do a mitzvah with a full heart. Had Boaz known that the Torah would later report that he gave Ruth six measures of barley, he would have fed her fattened calves! In the past, when one did a mitzvah, a prophet reported it in the Torah. But today, who records the mitzvot which a person does? Elijah the Prophet writes it down, while God and Mashiach bear witness (Ruth Rabbah 5:6).

Our Sages advise that a person should always seek to do his best, whether or not it will be written down for posterity. Lest it ever cross our minds that our charitable deeds might go unnoticed or be forgotten, the Midrash informs us that the Heavenly Tribunal has as its secretary none other than Elijah the Prophet, with Mashiach and God Himself signing as the witnesses.

So, we ask again: What about those who seek and receive honor for their deeds? What can be said of their charity? It is said that charity is unique among the mitzvot because no matter what the donor's intention — good, bad or horrid — he is still rewarded with having performed a mitzvah. The reason? No matter what his intention, the poor were helped. Even so, we would do well to listen to our hearts instead of our egos. "So what if I'm honored by having my name on a room, a building, a book, and so on. My intention was to give to charity. That's what counts. And maybe, just maybe, others will follow suit." Then our mitzvah is even greater. As our Sages said: Getting others to give is even greater than giving oneself (Bava Batra 9a; The Aleph-Bet Book, Charity A:15). This way, even more people become involved with the mitzvah.

Therefore, Rebbe Nachman teaches: One should see to increase God's Honor, while diminishing one's own (Likutey Moharan I, 6:1). The main intention in giving charity should be to elevate God's Honor, to spread His Glory in the world.

* * *

HOW MUCH?

The Laws of Charity are set out in *Yoreh Deah* 247-259. These include how much to give, to whom, priorities, etc. Our obligations are determined according to income, taking into consideration many of the same variables our accountants would, including: salary or business, profits or losses, taxes, investments, annuities and so on. Often, it is necessary to consult a competent rabbi. However, the generally accepted figure supported by most authorities is *ma'aser* (ten percent). The Talmud teaches: A person is not obligated to give more than a *chomesh* (twenty percent), lest he himself end up needing charity (*Ketubot* 50a). However, even this figure is negotiable (see *Yoreh Deah* 249:1).

Rebbe Nachman teaches: By giving twenty percent of your income to charity, you fulfill the mitzvah (Deuteronomy 6:5): "Love God with all your possessions" (*Rabbi Nachman's Wisdom* #299).

One *can* give more. Certainly the poor won't object. It's also hard to imagine how anyone with a few million and a healthy salary besides, would actually feel "threatened" with poverty were they to give more than twenty percent. Rebbe Nachman said that charity has two facets: A person who doesn't have much but is very generous should give commensurate with his generosity; while a person to whom God has granted wealth but is not particularly generous should give commensurate with God's blessing (*The Aleph-Bet Book*, Charity A:65).

Reb Dov of Tcherin, a businessman, was a follower of Rebbe Nachman. The Rebbe told him to give a *chomesh*, twenty percent of his income, to the poor. He fulfilled this mitzvah his entire life. Prior to his passing away he was heard to say, "With my *chomesh*, I have no fear of the [judgment of the] Heavenly court! I will come out [meritorious]" (*Kokhavey Or* p. 24, #19).

Rebbe Nachman teaches: By giving *ma'aser* you will be saved from your enemies (*Likutey Moharan* I, 221).

It has been noted: Were *all* our people to give ten percent, the poor would never want, neither would any organization lack funds for maintenance or building projects!

* * *

WHEN?

"Give, you should give him [the poor], and do not feel bad about giving it" (Deuteronomy 15:10).

It's good to set aside your charity money as soon as you receive your wages. This way, you "kosher" the money you keep for yourself, knowing that the portion belonging to the poor has already been set aside. The balance belongs to you (*Rabbi Zvi Aryeh Rosenfeld*). Some people even deposit their *tzedakah* monies in a separate checking account, keeping it specifically for the charities they wish to support.

Reb Eliyahu Chaim Rosen used to re-phrase the above verse: "Give what you gave already (have already set aside), then you will not feel bad about giving it." Having already set the money aside, you won't feel the pinch when asked for a contribution.

*

Rebbe Nachman teaches: One should give charity daily, before praying (*Orach Chaim* 92:10; *Likutey Moharan* I, 2:4).

"When beginning anything, give charity" (as above, "Opening the Doors"). Whatever objective you wish to pursue — be it Torah study, prayer, other mitzvot, even travel, business, or whatever — precede the act with charity (*Likutey Moharan* II, 4:2).

Rebbe Nachman teaches: Before an illness is allowed to afflict a person, it is made to take an oath that it will not leave him except on such and such a day, at such and such a time, and only because of a particular medicine and a particular person (*Avodah Zarah* 55a). If so, what does it help to call a doctor? Why bother, if the medicines will anyway not take effect until a certain date and a specific hour? But the answer is that charity has the power to nullify the oath. It sweetens and mitigates harsh decrees. Thus, by giving charity when we fall ill, we can sweeten the decree of illness which is upon us. Then, any doctor and medicine can assist in our cure, even before the time of the decree's end has come (*Likutey Moharan* II, 3; *The Aleph-Bet Book,* Sweetening Judgment A:1).

* * *

PRIORITIES

Every Jewish community shall set up a welfare fund to tend to the needs of the poor and the needy. Some communities had only a fund, others also had a free kitchen. These were entrusted to *gabbai tzedakah* (charity supervisors) who were responsible to the community (*Yoreh Deah* 256). This was the Jewish way of life in all communities, Sefardic and Ashkenazic, wealthy or not. The fund provided for food, clothing, shelter, the sick, the elderly and so on (the priority of recipients is listed in *Yoreh Deah* 251). Most synagogues today run a similar fund, used in caring for their membership and other charitable disbursements.

Priority. An important word in charity. *The* most important word. Ask any group of people about their priorities and you're bound to get a varied reply: supporting the sages, feeding the homeless, caring for the sick, assisting earthquake victims, medical research.... This section will provide a guide to what Rebbe Nachman viewed as the priorities of charity and how the Breslover Chassidim in the succeeding generations adopted his approach.

*

Stretching the contribution. Rebbe Nachman teaches: King Solomon says in his Proverbs: "Wealth adds many friends" (19:4). "Wealth" alludes to charity, particularly the charity which you give to the true Tzaddikim. It "adds many friends." Why? Simple, when you give charity to someone, you've created an air of harmony and friendship between yourself and that person. Obviously, the more you give to greater numbers of people, the more goodwill you are spreading. Therefore, when you give charity to these Tzaddikim — whose souls are inclusive of many Jewish souls and many followers — it is like giving charity to many, many people. It creates a wider circle of friendship and this spreads harmony and tranquility further. For this reason, it is best to give charity to the true Tzaddikim (*Likutey Moharan* I, 17:5).

When it comes to donating charity, we should always try to give it where it will do the most good. This does not mean "Don't give elsewhere!" It means, we have to weigh our priorities and see where our charity money will be most beneficial. If giving to an individual will support just that individual, whereas giving the same amount to an institution will support many, then logically we should give the money to the many. This might be thought of as "stretching" our charity dollar, getting more "mileage" for our money.

The Tzaddik himself is known as "many," because he teaches others and guides them through life. They are dependent upon him. Sometimes this is even a material and financial reliance, but most often they look to him for spiritual support — for the nourishment of their souls. By providing for the Tzaddik we provide for all those dependent upon him. By giving him our charity, we enable the Tzaddik to tend to the needs of those who rely upon him. Therefore, in essence, we are giving to many, many people. (This does not excuse us from helping any individual who is impoverished. We should not think that by giving to one place, even the most important charity, exempts us from helping what might be considered a lesser charity. We must weigh very carefully our contributions, and even more so our intentions.)

The right path. Rebbe Nachman teaches: There are three elements necessary for repenting: the first is seeing the Tzaddik; the second is giving charity to the Tzaddik; and the third is confessing and speaking to the Tzaddik and asking him for a path to serve God. Seeing the Tzaddik breaks one's tendencies for depression and bad desires. Giving charity to the Tzaddik breaks the tendencies for idle chatter, slander and haughtiness. By speaking to the Tzaddik, the Tzaddik directs one to the proper path so that he might rectify his soul (*Likutey Moharan* I, 4:8).

Charity has always been an important key for anyone desiring to return to God and repent. In this lesson, Rebbe Nachman emphasizes the importance of giving the charity to the Tzaddik, as this enables the donor to derive the greatest benefit from his mitzvah. The Rebbe compares charity given to a Tzaddik to the light of day. This light allows a person to "see" where he is going, it offers him direction in life, while at the same time helping him to break his undesirable traits.

Reb Nachman Goldstein of Tcherin writes: Even when the Tzaddik is no longer alive, it is still possible to fulfill these three elements of repentance.

A) Seeing the Tzaddik can be fulfilled by studying his teachings. This is because "the Tzaddik's books have in them [in their letter and word combinations] the face and soul of the Tzaddik" (*Likutey Moharan* I, 192). (This is explained in more detail in Appendix A).

B) Giving charity to the Tzaddik can be fulfilled by donating to any of the following: to those dependent upon the Tzaddik; to synagogues and institutions that further the Tzaddik's teachings; to the printing and publication of the Tzaddik's works. Any of these brings with it the rectification of giving charity to the Tzaddik (explained below).

C) Speaking to the Tzaddik can be fulfilled by making the pilgrimage to the Tzaddik's gravesite and praying, asking the Tzaddik to intercede on one's behalf to lead a spiritual life (explained in greater detail in the chapter "Tzaddik") (*Parparaot LeChokhmah* 4:5).

*

Rebbe Nachman teaches that we should bring *da'at* — true knowledge — into this world. We must share this knowledge with others, so that Planet Earth is inhabited by *human* beings. True knowledge is knowledge of God. Even when someone passes away, he can leave this knowledge in the world. The knowledge of God which he's attained can be transmitted to the next generation by teaching it to either his children or his students. Even if he is not a teacher, by sharing this knowledge with someone else, that person becomes a "student" by virtue of that bit of knowledge that was imparted to him (*Likutey Moharan* II, 7:2-4).

The purpose of Creation is to recognize God. This can be accomplished by studying more about God's ways until we come to some degree of knowledge of Him. This was the greatness of Moshe Rabeinu. His recognition of God reached higher levels than any other man who walked the face of this earth. He was also able to enlighten others, even the smallest child, with a knowledge of God. What about us? Can we attain this knowledge? Yes. By using the tools that Moshe Rabeinu left us — the knowledge which he passed on to his student, Yehoshua. For this very same knowledge has been passed on to us, generation after generation, until today.

*

These introductory teachings should help us in understanding how giving charity to the Tzaddik can be performed even today.

The Tzaddik's followers. We see that passing on *da'at*, knowledge of God, is an ongoing process. It begins with the Tzaddik and continues throughout the generations, through the Tzaddik's followers. By following the advice and teachings of the Tzaddik, they are continuing the process of revealing knowledge of God to the world, thereby making it a more habitable and a better place to live in. Thus, giving charity to the followers of the Tzaddik, is like giving to the Tzaddik himself.

Synagogue/institution. The same reasoning applies to those synagogues and institutions that bear the name of the Tzaddik. In these places, prayer and Torah study are practiced in accordance with the teachings of the Tzaddik; again revealing a knowledge of God that is transmitted by the Tzaddik through his followers. The added advantage of giving charity to an institution is that it is clearly the "many." Synagogues and educational facilities provide classes and lectures where large groups of people benefit from the Tzaddik's teachings and his *da'at*. This makes a larger segment of the world that much more "human."

Tzaddik's publications. King David said: "His charity remains forever" (Psalms 112:3). The Talmud asks: Which charity is forever? He that writes Torah books for others (*Ketubot* 50a). The person who contributes to producing Torah teachings in the world, books that promote knowledge of God and guarantee a means of transmission of this knowledge to future generations — this person's charity remains forever.

If ever there was a way to reveal the *da'at* of the Tzaddik throughout the world, publishing is it. There can be no doubt that disseminating the Tzaddik's teachings in book form is by far the greatest and most powerful method for reaching the widest possible audience. This, especially, can be appreciated in two aspects, time and impact.

Charity to the hungry is very great, but the next day, the poor man is hungry again. Funds have to be provided again and again. Today's donation is gone by tomorrow. Building a synagogue, by comparison, is a long-term charity that also carries with it an extremely large-scale reward because it ultimately supports group prayer and Torah study. Even so, the impact of the donation is limited to the people who attend the synagogue, benefitting the neighborhood in which the building was built.

In both time and impact, the money donated for publishing a book goes a lot further than other forms of charity. Once published, a book can be studied in every new generation. Torah scrolls, the Talmud and many Jewish writings have at one time or another been burned or destroyed by our enemies. But, having already been published, the same versions of these texts still survive. Therefore, the same *da'at* of God which these books revealed and promoted when they were first written, remains with us today. A book is forever. And, as Rebbe Nachman teaches: Each Torah book published has an important role to play in the world (*Likutey Moharan* I, 61:5).

Books can also go anywhere in the world. Thus, the impact of a holy book means that knowledge of God can reach any corner of the globe. A book can travel (or be shipped) from Aberdeen to Zurich, from Zion to Alaska, bringing with it its message and spreading the knowledge of God everywhere. Books therefore have a tremendous power to bring each part of Creation that much closer to fulfilling its purpose.

Indeed, there are numerous stories told of people who happened upon a Breslover publication and were moved to come closer to God, to improve their lives, because of it. And no doubt there are countless more of these stories which have never been told; stories about people who may never have gone on to study any of Rebbe Nachman's other teachings or become his followers, but who, because of the time they spent reading a publication which they inadvertently came across, did come that much closer to their purpose in life.

Of the stories which have been told, there's one that particularly stand. out. It happened in Warsaw, at a time when Breslov Chassidut was a growing force throughout Poland. The Jew in question had been having a very hard time. Life seemed no longer worth living. Depressed and dejected, he decided that it was time to end it all. He acquired some poison, intending to use it at the very first opportunity. As he reached up to the top of his bookshelf, where he wanted to put the poison for safekeeping, he knocked over a book entitled *Meshivat Nefesh — Restore My Soul*. Picking up the publication, a collection of extracts from Rebbe Nachman's writings on how to combat hopelessness and depression, his curiosity was aroused and he began to read from it. "No situation is so desperate that it cannot be turned to good." "God has spread good throughout Creation, even in the darkest places." Pretty soon he was devouring page after page of advice on how to draw from the wellsprings of joy and spiritual strength. Needless to say, he had no need for the poison after that (*Rabbi Yitzchok Gelbach*).

*

Rebbe Nachman teaches: There are Elders of Holiness whose knowledge is knowledge of God, and there are Elders of Impurity whose knowledge is the knowledge of atheism. Giving charity subdues the Elders of Impurity and reduces the negative influence of their teachings (*Likutey Moharan* II, 4:7-9).

Emphasizing the importance of giving charity for spreading the Tzaddik's teachings, Reb Noson writes: Charity, given for the purpose of revealing knowledge of God by publishing the works of the Tzaddikim who transmit this knowledge, has the power to subdue the Elders of Impurity, the root of atheism itself. This is because the Torah teachings that are revealed in these publications all have in them the power to instill knowledge of God, and to undo the questions and doubts that linger in the mind. In so doing, they draw the light and holiness of the Elders of Holiness into the world.

Aside from the Bible, God's Word was supposed to be transmitted orally. Eventually, permission was granted for all of it to be written it down because people were forgetting the Oral Torah. Questions arose for which no one had answers. Doubts multiplied, without teachings to resolve them. The publication of the Oral Torah became a necessity. There was no other way to stave off these doubts and clarify the questions that arose — and still arise. Each new work, each additional publication provides further clarification, thereby revealing more knowledge of God to the world.

Fortunate is he who contributes towards the publication of the Tzaddik's writings, giving charity to help bring them out into the world. He brings merit to many by helping to clarify all the questions and doubts. There is no end to his reward, and his charity certainly remains forever, for he brings merit and clarity, not only to his generation, but to all ensuing generations. He perpetuates the Torah. Fortunate is he! (*Likutey Halakhot, Birkhot HaShachar* 5:38).

* * *

GIVING TO THE TZADDIK

Rebbe Nachman once said: "*Zu mir, hot keiner nit derleigt* — No one has ever lost by contributing to me" (*Siach Sarfei Kodesh* 1-28). Elsewhere, Rebbe Nachman said: "My taking is actually giving. Whenever I take something from someone, I am actually giving to him" (*Rabbi Nachman's Wisdom* #150). There is a special blessing in giving to the Tzaddik: the giver gets! Though this applies to all true charity — whoever gives can see that the money finds its way back to him — it is especially true when donating to the Tzaddik.

This is taken quite literally by the Breslover Chassidim — not only in matters of charity, but also for any expense which a person puts out for the sake of Rebbe Nachman and his teachings. Chassidim of limited means readily undertake the expense of travelling to Russia to visit Rebbe Nachman's burial site, in order to pray there. Those who've made the pilgrimage can testify that, in one way or another, their expenditures have always been returned to them.

* * *

A GREATER MITZVAH...

Rebbe Nachman once said: "*Epes tut ihr gur kein mitzvos nit!* — It seems you are not involved with doing good deeds." The good deeds which Rebbe Nachman was referring to were acts of kindness for others: favors and collecting charity on their behalf (*Rabbi Nachman's Wisdom* #258).

The mitzvah of charity has an additional beneficial quality built into it. Though it appears to be a mitzvah only for those who can "afford" it, it can actually be performed by all, even daily. How? By getting others to contribute. Our Sages taught: Greater than the one who gives charity is the one who gets others to give. His deed brings peace (*Bava Batra* 9a). Thus, even someone of limited means has a way of performing the mitzvah of charity to the fullest: he can collect charity from others, for others. His reward for collecting a thousand dollars is far greater than the reward he receives for giving it. (A miser, too, can earn himself great rewards by raising a lot of charity from others. Even so, he is still not exempt from giving charity.)

*

AVOID TAKING

Our Sages, Maimonides and the *Shulchan Arukh,* all agree that one should make every effort not to accept charity for oneself. Better to work at a demeaning job than to be dependent upon the mercy of others (*Pesachim* 113b). Rebbe Nachman concurred.

Know! There is a ministering angel above. He has a number of deputies. These angels hold *shofrot*. They blow their *shofrot* and are constantly seeking lost items. There are many lost items. These things are lost due to sin (*Likutey Moharan* II, 88). Rebbe Nachman then said: It is very difficult [if one has] to receive alms. It appears that a person who accepts charity does much damage, making it difficult to recover what is lost (*Rabbi Nachman's Wisdom* #180).

Thus, we should make every effort to avoid being in a position where we must accept charity. Nevertheless, circumstances do change. Difficult financial situations arise, sometimes overnight, which are not always possible to avoid. At such times, we must not stubbornly refuse charity or financial assistance. In fact, it is forbidden to refuse the help of others when in dire straits. But, whenever possible, we should always try to be the benefactor, rather than the recipient, of charity.

* * *

CHARITY TO ISRAEL

Giving charity to the poor in one's own family takes precedence over giving to strangers and charity to one's community comes before charity to distant places and causes. All this is explained in the *Shulchan Arukh*. There are, however, certain commentaries that maintain that the poor of the Holy Land must be our first priority (see *Yoreh Deah* 251:3).

Rebbe Nachman teaches: Charity for the Holy Land is far greater than charity for the Diaspora. Contributing to Eretz Yisrael causes a person to be included in the "air" of the Holy Land. [That is, the air around him is purified in the sense that he is drawing the air of holiness, the source of which is in the Holy Land.] This holiness causes the merit of the Patriarchs to be revealed and brings Lovingkindness into the world (*Likutey Moharan* I, 37:4).

Noam HaElyon (Upper Delight) is the source of everything pleasing and enjoyable in this world. Whatever feelings of delight and pleasure we experience stem from this quality of God. A flow of this *Noam HaElyon* descends daily to the world. As it descends, it provides rectification for the lower level Intellect, known as the Intellect of the Diaspora, by raising it to the level known as the Intellect of the Holy Land. This latter Intellect implies a great understanding and knowledge of God. However, in order to be able to draw from the *Noam HaElyon,* it is necessary to have a vessel. This vessel is created by giving charity to the Holy Land (*Likutey Moharan* II, 71).

Reb Noson writes: I heard from the Rebbe that the [best] time for giving charity to the Holy Land is in the month of Adar (*Tzaddik* #562). Though it should be understood that the people in the Holy Land will gladly accept it the whole year round, Adar is the most propitious time for giving. One can, and should, give even during the rest of the year.

* * *

IT'S YOUR CHOICE

Worthy causes. Rebbe Nachman teaches: Wicked people also contribute to charity. However, charity itself fools the wicked and they give their money to the undeserving and the unworthy. This is because giving charity brings great merit, and the fear is that the wicked might use their merit to oppose even great Tzaddikim. Therefore the wicked are directed to donate their charity to unworthy causes and only seemingly righteous individuals. This saves the righteous from their wickedness (*Likutey Moharan* II, 15).

Never before in the annals of Jewish history has there been a more baffling and confusing situation facing the individual who wants to give to charity. Aside from our local obligations, we are inundated with letters, phone calls and "visitors" all seeking to have us share this mitzvah — with them. And all (or most) appear legitimate. Hospitals, schools, the impoverished, the elderly, the wise, the fool, widows and orphans, the battered, the homeless, the victims of man-made tragedies and natural disasters, alike. There are even organizations that are out to save animals, trees, stones and what not.

In late 1988, three whales were trapped in ice near the Alaskan coast. The United States, the Soviet Union and others, foundations and individuals alike, all joined forces with the media to bring the whales' plight into everyone's living room. Icebreakers were sent to cut the ice, helicopters dropped food and volunteers flew in to aid in whatever way possible. In short, *a few million dollars* and about a week's time were spent in the attempt to save three whales! You name it. There is always someone out there ready to pick up a cause.

Jeremiah the Prophet was thrown into a clay pit, abused, tormented and tortured by his opponents. These were the very same people he had tried so hard to help. His prayer to God was: "When they give charity, let it be to the unworthy, so that they receive no reward for their deed" (*Bava Kama* 16b). When a person contributes to an unworthy cause, not only is he not rewarded for his deed, but he even ends up losing his money for nothing.

Rebbe Nachman teaches: When we contribute to charity it is like passing judgment. We are taking money from a "wealthy" person (one who has what to give) and giving it to the "poor" (*Likutey Moharan* I, 2:4). Thus, charity is a true gauge of one's sense of fair judgment. The Torah forbids cruelty to animals. One who sees them suffering is obliged to relieve it wherever possible, but who in his right mind would challenge the priority of compassion for human beings — that man comes first?!

But which cause is the most important? Or more important? Or at least, legitimate? "Charity," Rebbe Nachman taught, "seeks the truth" (*Likutey Moharan* I, 251). Thus, if we truly seek to be charitable, we will spend the necessary time and effort to investigate the true value of the causes to which we donate. We will seek the truth.

*

Beautiful gelt. Rabeinu Asher ben R. Yechiel, the *Rosh* (1250-1327), was one of the greatest of all talmudic scholars and halakhic codifiers. Living in Europe during the dark Middle Ages, he fled Germany because of false accusations against him, and eventually became rabbi of Toledo, Spain. Concerning city taxes collected for protection against enemies he writes: Even in time of war, when life is threatened, taxes for the city's protection are levied according to overall wealth, and not by a poll tax. This is because most wars are ultimately a means of seeking money and possessions, and the wealthy must pay more to protect their share (*Bava Batra* 1:22).

It is interesting to note the obsession which the nations have always had with Jewish wealth and money. Even today we hear accusations, "The Jews control this...they own that...Jewish money, and the like." Why?

Rebbe Nachman teaches: Divine qualities manifest in this world in different material forms and shapes. So, for example, the Divine quality of grace and charm appears in the form of money. When Jews give charity, the charm in the money radiates out and the money appears beautiful. This is why money is so desirable. The nations then desire the money of a Jew. As our Sages taught (*Bava Batra* 9a): The continuous taxation imposed upon the Jewish communities by the authorities in their host countries can also be considered a form of "charity." Yet, as soon as the money leaves Jewish hands, it loses its grace and attraction, for the inner luster of the money (its grace) has become hidden (*Likutey Moharan* I, 25:4).

This lesson is certainly very applicable to what took place throughout the Middle Ages and even in Rebbe Nachman's time. Tax after tax was placed upon the Jewish communities in Europe and the Middle East in order to satiate the appetite of the local authorities and landowners who controlled the economies in their individual regions and states. No matter how much money was paid out, there were always demands for additional sums. Every decree brought with it another tax.

Yet, this lesson can be applied in our generation too. Today, instead of imposing various taxes (which would not be a "democratic" way of doing things), many causes come knocking at the Jewish door, asking for "Jewish involvement" and "Jewish funds." Accordingly, the Talmud teaches: If a person merits, his charity goes for good [causes]. If not, then he has the nations beckoning at his door (*Bava Batra* 9a).

As we've seen, there are many, many charitable causes nowadays. It can be very confusing. But, we've also seen that if we seek the truth, the truth will assist us. We will be able to evaluate, clearly, the pros and cons of each charity and give accordingly with clear consciences. Evaluate. "Weigh the gains of the mitzvah, *vis-a-vis* the loss" (*Avot* 2:1). And, above all, pray. Pray to God that He lead you to the better and more (or most) important charities.

Rebbe Nachman quotes a teaching of the Sages: God makes certain that a person who is eager to give charity receives the money to donate, and worthy causes are sent his way so that he will be rewarded for his benevolence (*The Aleph-Bet Book,* Charity A:19). Pray to God that He give you a more than adequate income, so that you have the opportunity to give charity in a large way. If money is a bit tight, then at least pray that you will be able to give charity continuously. And, pray that you find the right places to which to give, places that increase recognition of God in the world.

Zealousness. Rebbe Nachman teaches: Charity is compared to zealousness (*Likutey Moharan* II, 65). All of us have some streak of zealousness lurking within us. Some channel it into their work, some into their home lives or hobbies. Let us set aside pettiness, jealousies and strife, and let us choose to be zealous in charity.

* * *

16

THE SEVEN CANDLES

Rebbe Nachman teaches: There is a level of intellect one attains by means of numerous introductory explanations. This knowledge, once your mind has already comprehended and embraced it, is known as the Inner Intellect. There is also a greater knowledge, one which is at present beyond your capability to attain, known as Transcendent Intellect. When you are found worthy, this level of intellect comes to you without any introductory explanations, but by means of a Godly influx. And the only way to become worthy of this Godly influx is by sanctifying your mouth, nose, ears and eyes — the seven apertures of the head which allow the influx into the mind. These apertures are known as the Seven Candles. They correspond to the seven lights of the Menorah, with the head — the mind — corresponding to the Menorah itself (*Likutey Moharan* I, 21:1-4).

*

LIGHTING THE MENORAH

The Seven Candles, the seven apertures of the head, are the passageways through which information is fed into the mind. They are also the means by which the mind "feeds back" and interacts with all that is outside it. If the Seven Candles themselves are kept holy, they bring holiness and Godliness to a person's mind — sanctifying it so that it advances in spiritual knowledge and merits receiving the greater knowledge of Transcendent Intellect. However, if the reverse is true, if the Seven Candles are profaned, then the mind will reflect this. Rather than advance spiritually, it will be distracted by its attachment to the physical. Likewise, the sort of knowledge that is sent out from the mind will parallel the knowledge that has been filtered into it. This will be reflected not only in the individual's manner of speech (the obvious and readily observable means of expression) but also in that which emanates from the eyes, nostrils and even the ears.

Although this may seem somewhat abstract and very spiritually advanced, it does have clear practical aspects to which we all can aspire. Take, for example, the means for sanctifying our Seven Candles. These are very straightforward. Rebbe Nachman teaches: You can sanctify your mouth by not speaking falsely; your nostrils by having fear of Heaven; your ears by believing in the Tzaddikim; and your eyes by shutting them in the face of evil (*Likutey Moharan* I, 21:2).

Similarly, Reb Yitzchok Breiter explained the sanctification of the Seven Candles this way: Sanctify your eyes by not looking at evil; sanctify your ears by listening to the words of the wise; sanctify your nostrils by taking a long breath of patience, no matter what, thus showing love to the person with whom you were about to be angry; and, sanctify your mouth through speaking words of Torah and prayer and refraining from saying anything forbidden (*Seder HaYom* 21).

Rebbe Nachman teaches: The mind is the Chief-of-Staff of the body; the body's organs are the soldiers under the mind's command (*Likutey Moharan* I, 29:7). Furthermore, he said, a person's thoughts are determined by his personality traits. At any given time, the thoughts which pass through your mind parallel the particular characteristic then dominant in your personality (*Likutey Moharan* I, 29:end).

Thus, ideally, the body should be run by the mind, and not by the heart's emotions. Yet, as the Rebbe tells us, the leadership role which the mind assumes will ultimately be determined by the nature of the "soldiers" which it commands. In particular, it is the soldiers which interact directly with the mind — the seven apertures of the head — which have the greatest influence. Thus the Seven Candles are the keys to the mind and its thoughts. As Rebbe Nachman has explained, they are the soldiers of the mind, doing the mind's bidding. At the same time, they control the input to the mind, and can elevate a person to the highest levels of spirituality and knowledge.

Sanctification of the seven apertures has more power than simply elevating us personally to ever higher levels of holiness. Sanctifying the Seven Candles in this world enables us to rectify any blemish we may have caused in the Upper Worlds. As messengers of the head (the mind), these Candles permeate our very beings with their sanctity, helping to lead us on the path to Godliness.

*

The mouth. In order to sanctify the mouth, Rebbe Nachman counsels us to avoid falsehood and speak the truth. Reb Yitzchok Breiter, while emphasizing the need to distance oneself from saying anything forbidden, also advises speaking words of Torah and prayer. Actually, their advice is identical. Torah is truth, prayer to God is truth and offering words of kindness and sympathy to one who is ill or troubled — is also truth. These are all mitzvot and serve to bring a person closer to God.

Speech — its powers and potentials — is one of the recurring themes of Rebbe Nachman's lessons. Speech is what differentiates man from animal. Used properly, speech is the vehicle which can bring man to the highest spiritual levels (see "Hitbodedut"). Not only is it the means by which we most clearly express our feelings, but it is also the tool which creates and promotes peace. These aspects of speech all fall into the category of truth and speaking the truth.

On the other hand, there is speech which is false: slander, talebearing, mockery and all other forms of forbidden speech. If not false themselves, speech of this nature will inevitably lead to falsehood. For example, the gossip which one initiates might in itself be true, yet, as it spreads, it takes on all sorts of additions and embellishments. People rarely repeat anything exactly as they hear it. Each person garnishes and spices the details according to *his* taste. The same applies to other misuses of speech, one way or another they all lead to falsehood.

We must realize the importance of truth and the power of truthful speech. Rebbe Nachman says elsewhere that when a person wants to attach himself to the Holy One — so that his thoughts travel to the Upper Chambers (of Transcendent Intellect) — he has to avoid speaking falsely, even by mistake (*The Aleph-Bet Book,* Truth A:1). In order to attain these lofty levels, it is necessary always to seek and engage only in truth. Truth is "God's Light." Thus, if in everything we say, we take care to say it truthfully, then we assure ourselves an attachment to the One who is truth.

*

The nose. Rebbe Nachman equates fear of Heaven with the nostrils, as in the verse (Isaiah 11:3): "*V'haRiCHo* (והריחו; [Mashiach] shall be filled) with the fear of God...." *Rei'aCH* (ריח) is the sense of smell. The nose thus alludes to the fear of Heaven. As we've seen, Reb Yitzchok Breiter interprets this to mean: Sanctify your nostrils by taking a long breath of patience, no matter what, thus showing love to the person with whom you were about to be angry.

Again, these interpretations are analogous: the fear of Heaven and the long breath of patience are one and the same. Life is a series of confrontations and problems, most very minor, some major indeed. It is impossible to eliminate all problems from life. Even so, how we respond to these problems and annoyances makes all the difference in the world. In each case, our response is always an indication of how much we fear Heaven. If we understand and accept that everything is from God, that whatever happens to us happens because He has made it happen — this is true *yirah* (fear of God). Responding to life with such an attitude brings patience. We learn forbearance and develop great tolerance for all the lessons of the human condition. No matter what the circumstances, we realize and are aware that we are being tested and that we must solve the problem now facing us through our faith in God.

In addition, showing love and compassion for someone who angers us is the highest level of "turning anger into compassion" (*Likutey Moharan* I, 18:2). When we transform our anger into compassion, we cause a sweetening of the Heavenly decrees, and we, as it were, force God to change His anger into compassion.

You'll sometimes hear people who are feeling their way around an unknown situation say, "It doesn't *smell* right." With our power of smell, our nostrils can detect a pure fragrance or a foul odor. This applies to spiritual smells as well. A person who has fear of Heaven despises evil, for he can sense its foul odor when confronted by it. Conversely, the fear of Heaven enhances his power of smell so that he can sense purity, he can smell the fragrance of good and the aroma of a positive situation (see *Likutey Moharan* I, 2:end).

*

The ears. Rebbe Nachman teaches that sanctifying the ears entails believing in the Tzaddikim. Reb Yitzchok Breiter translates this as "listening to the words of the wise" (Proverbs 22:17). Indeed, would we listen to the wise if we did not believe in them?

We tune into what we want to hear. We tune out what we don't. Even so, relative to what our ears hear, we listen to precious little. This is because hearing and listening are not one and the same. Quite simply, listening is hearing when it is accompanied by one more ingredient: concentration.

In our case, listening to the wise includes concentrating on their teachings and words of advice. In addition, it includes one more ingredient. Listening to the Tzaddikim requires wholeheartedly accepting and following their counsel — believing in them. Without this belief, concentrating and learning their lessons, though certainly better than hearing, cannot be considered truly listening to them. Even when we are unable to fulfill the Tzaddikim's advice, if we continue to believe in them and at least "want to" follow their counsel — this is considered listening to the words of the wise.

The importance of faith in Tzaddikim has been discussed above, in the chapter on faith. To detail its importance fully would take many pages and still it would not suffice. My Rosh Yeshivah used to say: "One who has faith has no questions. One without faith has no answers." Part of understanding that the Tzaddik has attained the Transcendent Intellect involves believing that the Tzaddik can inculcate that knowledge into us. This fills us with an everpresent hope. We can always strive for Godliness, for we know that there is a Tzaddik who is willing to share his knowledge of this Godliness with us; a Tzaddik who is able to instill knowledge of God in every person, no matter how far that person may have fallen and been distanced from God. Our ears — when they tune into the Tzaddikim and are attuned to faith — provide us with every reason to hope.

In addition, our ears have to tune into Torah. Listening to the words of the wise can be interpreted to mean: Study Torah. Say the words. This way, you will hear *words* that were once spoken by wise people. Conversely, this means avoiding any conversation which includes slander, talebearing and the like. Our Sages warned of how terrible it is just to listen to such words passively. Belief in our Sages would encourage and help us avoid these sins.

*

The eyes. How do we sanctify our eyes? Rebbe Nachman tells us that we have to shut them in the face of evil. There are a number of ways to analyze this.

First and foremost, in its simplest interpretation, this entails not looking at anything evil or anything that may cause temptation. Evil can mislead us. We have to put "blinders" on our eyes, so that we "see no evil." We have to avoid looking lustfully, and avoid observing others transgressing. Censoring what we look at is one of the most important steps in achieving holiness.

Another way to understand Rebbe Nachman's teaching involves not observing others with an "evil eye." We need not even refer to the mystical implication of the "evil eye," but to the simple interpretation: looking critically at our neighbor; noticing with a jealous eye his affluence, his good fortune, his well-being, and so on. These "looks" have a very negative effect (cf. *Bava Batra* 2b; on both the observed and the observer).

There is a more subtle level of not looking at others which entails our not always looking to see how someone else is faring, even innocently. In his famous story *The Sophisticate and the Simpleton*, Rebbe Nachman describes how the Simpleton's wife asks him, "How come other shoemakers get three coins for a pair of shoes and you only get a coin and a half?" To which he replies, "What do I care? That is their work, and this is my work!" The Simpleton had no desire to eye the actions of others even harmlessly. Even without jealousy, plain curiosity can mislead us to look unfairly upon a neighbor or friend.

Still another way to shut our eyes in the face of evil involves closing our eyes to the evil of others. As Rebbe Nachman points out, judging others favorably brings even a wicked person onto the scale of merit, causing the wicked qualities we see in them to disappear (*Likutey Moharan* I, 282).

*

The head. Rebbe Nachman teaches: Guard your memory very carefully; protect it from forgetfulness. The essence of memory is always remembering that there are two worlds. Immediately upon awakening in the morning, focus on and attach your mind to the World to Come (*Likutey Moharan* I, 54:1,2).

The mind is a wonderful thing. It is far too important to waste, but, when we focus on this world, without thinking about the World to Come, then we are actually "wasting" our minds. This is because we are concentrating more than is necessary on the "waste" of this fleeting world. We have to face the mundane world daily; let us not fool ourselves into thinking otherwise. Even so, by always remembering the next world, the Future World, every mundane act we perform serves to prepare us for the World to Come. This is what Rebbe Nachman refers to when teaching that one should guard his memory.

Reb Noson writes: Acting in holiness, purifying the "vessels of the mind" (the Seven Candles), also serves to guard the memory; however, the main way to guard the memory is through speech. By speaking many words of holiness — Torah, prayers and supplications — we attach our minds to holiness and our memories to the World to Come (*Likutey Halakhot, Arvit* 4:5,6). As the Rebbe himself teaches: Faith and prayer actually improve one's mental abilities and power of recall (*Likutey Moharan* I, 7:excerpts).

* * *

THE COVENANT

We've seen that by keeping the Seven Candles holy, we perfect the vessels with which to receive the Transcendent Intellect from the Tzaddik. Yet there is something which, if we do it, is in itself on the level of Tzaddik. This something is known as Guarding the *Brit* (the Covenant). Throughout the Talmud and Midrash, we find references to the Tzaddikim and their greatness. But we do not find any succinct description of what qualifies one to be called a Tzaddik. How do we define Tzaddik? Is he someone who is knowledgeable in Torah? Or perhaps someone who prays fervently? Is he one who is very attentive to certain mitzvot? Or, perhaps is he only the one who fulfills all the mitzvot to the fullest?

The Kabbalah, however, does describe what a Tzaddik is. "Who is a Tzaddik?" the Zohar asks. "He is one who guards the Covenant" (*Zohar* I:59b). Rebbe Nachman's teachings make constant reference to this concept of *shmirat haBrit* and its implication for the here and now.

*

WHAT IS THE COVENANT

"This is My covenant between Me and you...you must circumcise every male child" (Genesis 17:10). God tells Avraham that He is making a covenant with him and all his offspring after him. This covenant is the sign that God will be true to the Jewish people and that the Jewish people will be true to God. Which covenant is this? "You shall circumcise your male child."

Rebbe Nachman teaches: All Jews are called Tzaddikim in that they are circumcised (*Likutey Moharan* I, 23:end). The merit of the *brit milah* (circumcision) is very great: it is enough to earn a Jew the distinction of holiness and the accolade Tzaddik. The Zohar illustrates this with the following:

Yishmael was given a *brit milah*. In fulfillment of God's commandment, Avraham circumcised his eldest son. As a result, for four hundred years Yishmael's guardian angel presented his claim for reward to the Heavenly Court. "Is it not true that whoever has been given a *brit milah* has a portion in Your Name?" the angel questioned. "Yes," God answered.

"If so," the angel asked, "then how come Yishmael has not been given a portion of holiness equal to Avraham's other son, Yitzchak?" "Yishmael's circumcision was not for the sake of the mitzvah," God replied. "Still," the angel demanded, "he was circumcised." To this God said: "Yishmael will be given a portion of holiness as his reward. But, just as his *brit milah* was without deeper meaning, so too, the portion of holiness which he will receive will be empty and void of meaning. The Holy Land will be Yishmael's reward. However, his possession of it will only come when it is empty of Jews. Indeed, his possession of the Holy Land will be the major factor in preventing the Jewish people from returning to their homeland, until such time that the merit of Yishmael's *brit milah* will terminate" (*Zohar* II:32a).

If this is the reward for *brit milah* when performed not for the sake of the mitzvah, then how much greater is the reward given to those who perform *brit milah* for the sake of doing God's will!

*

SHMIRAT HABRIT, GUARDING THE COVENANT

The Covenant — the *Brit* — is the pact which God made with the Jews. Were any mortal king to make a covenant with a people, would they not honor and cherish it and do their utmost to fulfill it at all times? Certainly, they would at least make every effort to safeguard it from being violated. Now, God, the King of kings, made a pact. He made this pact, this eternal Covenant, with the Jewish people. Isn't it therefore unthinkable that just by undergoing the *brit milah* in infancy, we should feel ourselves absolved of our part of the pact, exempt from guarding the Covenant and all that it stands for? Were a mortal king to expect us to honor and fulfill our covenant with him, how much more so should the Jewish people feel obligated to honor, fulfill and guard their eternal Covenant with God?

But what constitutes guarding the Covenant? What else is actually required of a person to heed this pact? Where in Torah is it mentioned that the Covenant must be guarded beyond what is actually written in the pact God made with Avraham?

The specific sign of God's Covenant with the Jewish people, the organ where the *brit milah* is performed, has been entrusted with the remarkable ability to initiate new life. But procreation can only be accomplished through a union. The Talmud teaches that there are three partners in a child: the father contributes the white parts of the body (bones, nails, etc.); the mother contributes the red parts (skin, flesh, etc.); and God breathes life into the child... (*Nidah* 31a). The three partners must function together. How does this happen?

The Talmud refers to marriage as *KiDuSHin*, from the Hebrew *KoDeSH* (holy). This is to teach us that marriage, the union between husband and wife, should be an act of holiness. Then the *Shekhinah* (the Divine Presence), the third partner, resides between them (cf. *Sotah* 17a). Sexual union, when performed in holiness, shows honor and respect to the God-granted powers of procreation. Thus, living within the framework of the Torah and adhering to its laws, ensures the guarding of the sign of the Covenant and hence the safekeeping of the Covenant itself.

(The laws of suggested and permitted marriages appear in *Shulchan Arukh, Even HaEzer* 1-17. The laws of Family Purity on the menstrual cycle and immersion in a *mikvah* are found in *Ibid, Yoreh Deah* 183-201; and the laws of marital obligations are found in *Ibid, Orach Chaim* 240. Many of these laws are also available in condensed form, in works such as *The Code of Jewish Law; Laws of Nidah* by Rabbi Shimon Eider; and *The Laws of Nidah: A Digest* by Rabbi A. Blumenkrantz.)

Rebbe Nachman teaches: As long as one marries according to Torah law and keeps his marriage within the Torah's boundaries, he is reckoned as one who guards the Covenant (*Likutey Moharan* I, 11:7).

In addition, Reb Noson writes: Having children whom you try to raise to recognize God, is in itself a very great rectification of the *Brit*. A person never knows what kind of offspring he may father; from his seed may come forth a Tzaddik, perhaps a very great Tzaddik. Even among the ancestry of the great Rabbi Shimon bar Yochai there were simple, very ordinary Jews. Yet, from them came forth this great Tzaddik who revealed such awesome levels of Godliness and holiness in the world. Rabbi Shimon was able to rectify all his ancestry and, what's more, he assumed responsibility for even rectifying the entire world (see *Sukkah* 45b; *Likutey Halakhot, Shabbat* 6:23).

The level we've been discussing until now is considered guarding the Covenant in its most basic form. It is worth noting the existence of a much higher degree of *shmirat haBrit* — that of conducting oneself with maximum purity and a stricter degree of holiness than the Torah generally prescribes. (Both levels are discussed in *Likutey Moharan* I, 11:5-7; and Lesson 31:5-6). In addition, there is a third and higher level. This is the level on which the Complete Tzaddik guards the Covenant. The awesome spiritual levels, greatness and power of the Complete Tzaddik will be discussed in the next chapter. Here we will continue to relate to the level depicted in Rebbe Nachman's teaching: One can be a Tzaddik even without being a scholar...even the simplest Jew can be a Tzaddik (*Rabbi Nachman's Wisdom* #76).

Thus, guarding the *Brit* — observing those Torah laws that pertain to guarding the sign of the Covenant — enables even the simplest Jew to attain the level of Tzaddik. Most likely, the average person will be skeptical of this. Is this all that's required to become a Tzaddik? The answer, Rebbe Nachman tells us, is yes.

There are 613 (תריג) mitzvot in the Torah. *Brit* (ברית) has the numerical value of 612. Torah (תורה) has the numerical equivalent of 611 (תריא). This teaches us that guarding the *Brit* is equivalent to all the other 612 mitzvot. Any attempt we make to guard the Covenant by attaining sexual purity will propel us into Torah and holiness. This is true even if we can only guard the Covenant on the most basic level, because we are "passing" these other levels on our way to attaining *Brit*.

*

P'GAM HABRIT, DEFILING THE COVENANT

Rebbe Nachman teaches that there is a dew of holiness whose drops descend into the world, bringing with them abundant blessing and prosperity. This corresponds to the "drops", the seed which emanates from a person's mind. If he guards himself (his mind) in holiness, then his "drops" draw this abundance into the world. However, when a person defiles the Covenant, just as he wastes his seed, so too, he wastes all blessings and abundance which revert to the powers of unholiness. (See *Likutey Moharan* I, 11:4, where this is more fully explained.)

As explained, the most basic level of *shmirat haBrit* entails adhering to the Torah's laws of marriage and Family Purity. This guarding of the Covenant is a process of sanctification. The reverse of this sanctity involves *p'gam haBrit* (defiling the Covenant), sexual impurity, of which the following are the most common examples: 1) having relations with a woman who does not adhere to the laws of Family Purity; 2) having relations with a woman whom the Torah forbids one to marry (e.g. a priest marrying a divorcee, or worse, relations with a married woman, incest, marrying a non-Jew); 3) homosexuality; 4) masturbation.

Any of these defile the Covenant, and represent the very opposite of honoring and sanctifying the God-granted powers of procreation. Each involves wasting seed, and the transference of all blessing and bounty to the Other Side.

Unfortunately, truly guarding the Covenant has never been an easy level to attain. The world we live in offers many, many enticements; man is exposed to all sorts of temptations long before he even considers marriage. Even so, the longer he waits the harder it becomes to guard the sign of the Covenant in purity. Rebbe Nachman therefore advises his followers to marry as young as possible, before being completely overcome by temptation. The Talmud teaches: One who marries before twenty can be saved from lustful thoughts (*Kiddushin* 29b). Though marriage at this age isn't always possible, parents should encourage their children to marry as early as possible.

Not that getting married solves all the problems. As many can testify, even after marriage, problems in the home cause all kinds of difficulties in *shmirat haBrit*. Once, a group of Rebbe Nachman's followers were seated around his table. Suddenly, the Rebbe said, "Who is it that has the *chutzpah* to sit at my table with impure thoughts!" One follower, whose homelife had been a continuous battle for a number of years, admitted that his mind had wandered to unclean places. He promised Rebbe Nachman that as soon as he got home, he would make peace with his wife (*Aveneha Barzel* p.28 #27).

*

WAYS TO GUARD AND RECTIFY THE BRIT

Rebbe Nachman teaches: There are ways to mortify the body which then diminishes the power of lust within a person. Sleeping very little is one example of this; however, this only tends to destroy the mind. Reb Noson added: I understood from the Rebbe's teaching that there is no easy way to diminish one's lust, without also breaking the mind [or body] at the same time. A person must attempt to strengthen himself and use all his inner powers to overcome his lusts (cf. *Likutey Moharan* I, 253).

Rebbe Nachman teaches: If you attain true joy, to the point where you are joyous enough to dance, then God Himself will guard your Covenant, your purity (*Likutey Moharan* I, 169). The "Serpent's bite" is depression. It leads to defilement of the *Brit*. Joy, on the other hand, is the best weapon against depression, and hence it is the best method for overcoming your lusts and guarding the Covenant.

Torah study is another way to guard the Covenant. Rebbe Nachman said that Torah study has enormous power. It can elevate a person from any abyss into which he has descended. When asked about a blemish in the *Brit*, Rebbe Nachman answered, "Torah (Tiferet, in the *Sefirot*) stands higher than *Brit* (Yesod)!" (*Tzaddik* #573).

Truth also protects the sign of the Covenant [from blemish] (*The Aleph-Bet Book*, Truth A:24).

Reciting the Haggadah on Passover Evening with fervor rectifies the Covenant (*Advice*, The Covenant 20).

Inspiring others to serve God is a rectification for the Covenant (*Likutey Moharan* I, 14:end).

Whoever performs kindness and charity rectifies his sign of the Covenant (cf. *The Aleph-Bet Book*, Charity A:54).

To rectify the Covenant, pursue peace (*The Aleph-Bet Book*, Immoral Behavior A:30).

And, of course, prayer and *hitbodedut* are also helpful. Prayer plays a major role in the quest for purity and rectifying the Covenant. In addition, Rebbe Nachman revealed the General Remedy as a means of combatting lust and rectifying the spiritual damage brought on by sexual transgressions. All these concepts are covered fully in the book entitled *Rabbi Nachman's Tikkun*.

*

WHAT IF...

And what happens if you've failed to guard the Covenant? If you've succumbed to temptations? For this, Rebbe Nachman revealed his General Remedy. Before speaking of the Psalms which comprise this *Tikkun HaKlali,* the Rebbe said, "First is mikvah. You must first immerse in a mikvah" (*Rabbi Nachman's Wisdom* #141).

Mikvah. The mikvah has always had an important place in Jewish life. Its primary purpose today is (as the key to Family Purity) for women after their menstrual period. Traditionally, men also immerse in the mikvah for purity and holiness (*Berakhot* 2a). Rebbe Nachman suggested immersing at least on those days associated with festivity (such as Rosh Chodesh, Lag b'Omer, Purim, etc.; *Rabbi Nachman's Wisdom* #185). Reb Noson writes: Prior to their being given the Torah at Mount Sinai, the Jews were required to purify themselves by immersion (*Kritut* 9a). A non-Jew, prior to conversion, must also immerse himself in a mikvah (*Yoreh Deah* 268:1). From this we can see that to enter any level of holiness, from the lowest to the highest, immersion in a mikvah is an absolute necessity (*Likutey Halakhot, Mikvaot* 1:4).

In the wee hours of the morning of Shabbat Chanukah, 1844, two weeks before Reb Noson passed away, word got out that the building which housed the mikvah in Breslov had collapsed. At first, people said that it had become impossible to immerse. But at daybreak, it was learned that the mikvah was actually still intact and only a distant part of the building had been destroyed. Reb Noson, who was quite ill at the time, began speaking about the importance of mikvah. "Had it been necessary," he said, "I was ready to go to the river, break the ice and immerse. The importance of immersing in the mikvah cannot be over-emphasized. Whoever is very resolute and consistent in immersing in a mikvah will certainly rectify everything."

He explained: In the Book of Ezra we find that the Jews intermarried during the Babylonian exile. When they returned to the Holy Land, they wanted to repent. The leaders came to him saying, "But is there no *MIKVeH* — no hope?" (Ezra 10:2). The word generally used for hope is *tikvah*. However the verse specifically chooses the word *MIKVaH* to teach us that no matter how terrible the transgression, there is always hope — there is always the tremendous powers of the mikvah to help bring a person to true repentance (*Kokhavey Or*, p. 80 #37).

Thus, the first step in rectifying any sin — and especially sexual transgression — is immersing in the mikvah. The next step is reciting the *Tikkun HaKlali* (the General Remedy).

*

The General Remedy. (Tikkun HaKlali). For each sin there is a specific *tikkun,* a specific deed which rectifies the spiritual harm caused by that sin. But what happens when we want to rectify many sins, or even one sin whose ramifications are many? Is it necessary to enact all the many specific *tikkunim?* Is such a thing really possible? It's not. And because it is not, Rebbe Nachman tells us that there exists a concept of general rectification, general remedy, for all sins (*Likutey Moharan* I, 29:4).

The general remedy which Rebbe Nachman revealed relates to the Ten Types of Song with which the Book of Psalms was composed (see *Pesachim* 117a; *Zohar* III:101a). Song has the power to sift the good from the bad and nullify the spiritual blemish which sin produces. Thus, the Rebbe advised us to recite ten chapters from the Book of Psalms. And although any ten psalms correspond to the Ten Types of Song, Rebbe Nachman revealed which ten specifically comprise the General Remedy:

16, 32, 41, 42, 59, 77, 90, 105, 137, 150.

Specifically, these ten chapters of the *Tikkun HaKlali* constitute a special remedy for the wasteful emission of seed. However, it is precisely because they rectify this sin — the defiling of the sign of the Covenant — that they also serve as a *general* rectification for all other sins. We've already seen that guarding the Covenant (the pact which God made with the Jewish people), demands sexual purity. We've also seen that *shmirat haBrit* is equivalent to all the other mitzvot. It follows that defiling the Covenant by sexual impurity causes a spiritual blemish of much greater import than that caused by an individual sin. *P'gam haBrit* is therefore a specific transgression with general ramifications. This is exactly why it requires a general rectification — a *tikkun klali* — in order to remedy it.

And so, Rebbe Nachman tells us that by reciting these ten chapters, we can rectify all the blemishes caused by wasted seed — and all our sins — and thereby come to true repentance (*Rabbi Nachman's Wisdom* #141).

*

It has to be emphasized that Rebbe Nachman advised the recital of the General Remedy as a rectification for an accidental nocturnal occurrence, and not the deliberate wasting of seed (cf. *Rabbi Nachman's Wisdom* #141). We should not mistakenly assume that intentional sinning can be taken lightly because we know about the General Remedy. Indeed, the Zohar teaches that for the willful emission of seed there is no repentance (*Zohar* I:188a).

And yet, despite the severity of defiling the sign of the Covenant, the Rebbe emphatically insisted that the Zohar's teaching could not be taken literally. He argued that repentance helps for all sins, even one as severe as this. True repentance involves never repeating the sin; being put in the same situation, having the same temptation, and yet not repeating the sin (*Rabbi Nachman's Wisdom* #71). As Rebbe Nachman said: Never Give up! (*Likutey Moharan* II, 78).

Reb Noson writes: There is a "point" within each and every Jew that is truly holy. This point is lost when one spills his seed needlessly, causing evil and even death in the world (Nidah 13a). Still, one can repent. He must regain his point of holiness. The way to do this is by attaching oneself to the Tzaddik and by revealing new levels of God's Lovingkindness through one's repentance. Having lost this point, he should, rightfully, not be entitled to repent. Therefore, if nevertheless he does repent, he causes new levels of Lovingkindness to be revealed (Likutey Halakhot, Tefilin 2:11).

*

Rebbe Nachman said, "Go out and reveal the Tikkun HaKlali to others. It may seem like an easy thing to recite ten chapters of the Psalms, but it will actually be very difficult in practice" (Rabbi Nachman's Wisdom #141). Whether because of outright opposition to Rebbe Nachman himself, or due to the belief that "greater" means (such as self-mortification and sorrowing despair) are necessary for rectifying the sins of sexual immorality, or simply because of a lackadaisical attitude on the part of even those who do follow his advice —time has proven the Rebbe's prediction to be only too accurate.

He also said: Saying these ten chapters of Psalms is a very wonderful remedy and rectification. It is entirely original. From the time of Creation, Tzaddikim have sought the remedy for this sin. God has been good to me and allowed me to attain this understanding and reveal this remedy to the world (Rabbi Nachman's Wisdom #141).

* * *

17

TZADDIK

"Tzaddik — the foundation of the world" (Proverbs 10:25).

No book about Rebbe Nachman's teachings would be complete without a chapter on the Tzaddik. Indeed, of all the concepts discussed in Rebbe Nachman's teachings, Tzaddik is arguably the most often cited. At the same time, it is the least understood.

The many questions always boil down to this: "What role does the Tzaddik play in Judaism? Is he a rabbi — codifier or general sage, is he a leader, an intermediary, a father figure and counselor, or what?" In this chapter, we will attempt to portray the clearest possible picture of what the Tzaddik is; the greatness of the Tzaddik; his role in Judaism; the meaning of binding oneself to the Tzaddik; the benefits of such an attachment; and the importance of praying at their gravesites.

* * *

AT CREATION

"...to differentiate between the light and the darkness" (Genesis 1:4). The Midrash comments on this verse from Creation: Light denotes the deeds of the righteous, darkness the deeds of the wicked (Breishit Rabbah 1:6)

In the physical world in which we reside, God created opposing forces and gave man the free will to choose between them: to choose light from darkness, right from wrong, good from evil. His purpose in Creation was that man should consider and define for himself which is the correct road before him and which route he will choose. Many attempt to follow the path of true righteousness, few are they that fully succeed.

An atheist once asked Rabbi Yehoshua ben Korkho: "Did not God foresee that man would not be able to overcome temptation?"

"Yes," Rabbi Yehoshua answered, "He certainly did foresee this."

"Then why did He grieve when He decided to bring the Flood upon the world?"

"Do you have a son?" Rabbi Yehoshua asked the atheist.

"Yes," came the reply.

"Were you happy when he was born?"

"Sure I was," answered the atheist.

"But didn't you know that your son would one day die?"

"Yes, I did."

"Then why were you happy?"

"In times of joy we rejoice. In times of sadness we mourn."

"Well then!" exclaimed Rabbi Yehoshua. "In times of joy God rejoices. And in times of sadness He mourns!" (*Breishit Rabbah* 27:4).

It is generally recognized that the average man does not overcome the attractions of this world. In fact, very few succeed. God knew that it would be so. He knew that most men would succumb to temptation, some more, some less; but He also knew that a few *would* succeed in battle and withstand all temptations. These few are the symbol of light, so at those times when all seems dark and the forces of evil seem fully triumphant, this too serves the purpose of Creation. Those who are symbolic of light, those who overcome enticement, rise above this evil.

When a person discerns the light from the darkness, he is a positive force in Creation. He is on the way to realizing the truth, the path of true righteousness. For the individual who completely triumphs in his endeavors to overcome his physical desires, God created the world. He is the Tzaddik.

* * *

EARNING THE TITLE

When God decided to create the world, He took counsel with the souls of the Tzaddikim (*Breishit Rabbah* 8:7). One might ask, "Which Tzaddikim? Could anything have existed before Creation? And, even if souls did exist, how could they have been Tzaddikim when they had yet to pass the tests of this world? Isn't it necessary to exercise free will in order to earn the title Tzaddik?"

In a number of instances in the Torah, we find that the souls of certain Tzaddikim were prepared long before they actually came to fulfill their special mission in life. Jeremiah was told, "Before you were created in the womb you were destined to be a prophet" (Jeremiah 1:5). At Creation, the verse states that "God created *ha'Adam* (the Man)" (Genesis 2:7). The Midrash tells us that "*the* Man" refers specifically to Avraham. But if the world was created for Avraham, why was he not created as the first man? The answer is that Avraham came later so that should man sin, there would always be Avraham to rectify these sins (*Breishit Rabbah* 14:6). And again, Moshe was prepared as the redeemer... Mordechai prepared for redemption (*Breishit Rabbah* 30:8). In fact, from the Talmud we know that Mashiach was created prior to the world (*Pesachim* 54a, see *Etz Yosef*).

The Tzaddik, the Complete Tzaddik, was chosen for his mission before his life even began. He was empowered with spiritual greatness to descend to this world and serve as leader and guide of God's Nation. Even so, man is always given free choice to choose his path in life. Though this unique Tzaddik was destined and chosen before his birth, he still had free choice. However, when he subdued his corporeality so much that he rose way above the simple choice of right and wrong, his freedom of choice moved to another plane entirely — to a much loftier level of free will (*Likutey Moharan* I, 190).

[God's Prior Knowledge of man's actions and man's ability to exercise Free Choice are mutually exclusive to us. While clothed in the physical, there is no way man can fully resolve this paradox intellectually; see *Rambam, Hilkhot Teshuvah* 5:5; *Likutey Moharan* I, 21:4.]

The Ari teaches: Moshe Rabeinu, as great as he was at the time of his birth, was not created on as exalted a level as the one he ultimately attained. His greatness came about because of his many good deeds (*Sha'ar HaGilgulim* #36). Elsewhere, the Ari points to Tzaddikim who not only had very lofty souls at birth, but during their lives were able to rise even higher than their soul's root. As an example, the Ari mentions Rabbi Akiva and his five main students: Rabbi Meir, Rabbi Yehudah, Rabbi Yosi, Rabbi Shimon bar Yochai and Rabbi Nechunya. These five students were rooted in a place in Heaven much higher than the World of the Souls (i.e. in the five *gevurot* of the *Da'at* of *Zer Anpin*). Of Rabbi Shimon bar Yochai we are told that he ascended to the level of *Binah,* the level which Moshe Rabeinu attained when he ascended Mount Sinai to receive the Second Tablets! (*Zohar* III:132b; *Shaa'r HaKavanot, Drushei Pesach* #12; see *Nitzutzei Orot, Zohar* III:287b). Thus, his soul had achieved — through his efforts in this world — an even more exalted level than the one it was given at birth.

Rebbe Nachman also emphasized the ultimate importance of effort in man's quest for righteousness. When someone suggested to the Rebbe that he had achieved what he had because of his exalted soul, the Rebbe seemed very annoyed. "This is the trouble. You think that Tzaddikim attain greatness merely because they have a very great soul. This is absolutely wrong! I worked very hard for all this. I put much effort into attaining what I did. But you think that because I have a great soul, because I am a descendant of the Baal Shem Tov (his great-grandson), that this is why I attained these levels. You are mistaken. It is because of the devotions and the efforts I put in" (*Rabbi Nachman's Wisdom* #165).

From all of this we see that the righteousness of the Tzaddik is generally determined by two distinctive factors. There are Tzaddikim who are destined to be so from the time of Creation. Their righteousness, which they in any case have to establish through their own good deeds, is given to them so that they perform a certain mission for God. And then there are individuals who rise to the level of Tzaddik by overcoming their physical desires. They literally earn the title.

The difference between these two types of Tzaddikim is somewhat similar to the difference between a *Kohain* (a priest) and a Torah scholar. We can't choose to be descendants of Aharon, it is a privilege which is either given or not given to us at birth. Not so the higher level of being a Torah scholar, which is available to everyone provided he is willing to expend the necessary effort and devotion. And indeed, the true greatness of any Tzaddik depends upon his devotions. Thus the Ari teaches that everyone can rise to the level of Moshe Rabeinu (*Sha'ar HaGilgulim* #1). This is exactly how Rebbe Nachman concluded his conversation with the chassid, mentioned earlier. He said, "Any person can attain my levels and become just like me. It all depends on how hard you try" (*Rabbi Nachman's Wisdom* #165).

* * *

THE GREATNESS OF THE TZADDIK

There is a widely held inaccuracy that the concept of Tzaddik was introduced by the founding fathers of the chassidic movement. While there are certain aspects of the Tzaddik's role which definitely did have their beginnings with the Baal Shem Tov and his followers — most of which in any case have no place in Rebbe Nachman's teachings (dynasties, dress codes and the like) — the concept of the righteous individual and his greatness has always been a part of Judaism and appears throughout the holy writings of our people. Thus, what is the greatness of a Tzaddik and the Tzaddikim? Our Sages taught:

For the merit of even one Tzaddik, the world was created (*Yoma* 38b).

The entire world stands upon one Tzaddik, as is written, "The Tzaddik is the foundation of the world" (*Chagigah* 12b).

God decrees and the Tzaddik has the power to nullify the decree. But, the Tzaddik decrees and God fulfills his decree (cf. *Moed Katan* 16b).

In the Future, the angels will behold the Tzaddikim and exclaim, "*Kadosh!* (Holy!)" — just as they now exclaim before God (*Bava Batra* 75b).

If the Tzaddikim would so wish, they could create worlds (*Sanhedrin* 65b).

So meritorious are the Tzaddikim, that they are able to placate God and nullify decrees (*Breishit Rabbah* 33:3).

Not only are Tzaddikim able to nullify decrees, but they are afterwards blessed for this (*Zohar* I:101b).

Tzaddikim draw down [and reveal] God's Divine Presence in the world (*Shir HaShirim Rabbah* 5:1).

All blessings in this world come about in the merit of the Tzaddik (*Zohar* I:189a).

Great are the Tzaddikim, for even though they have passed away, their merits last for generation after generation (*Zohar* I:183a).

Were it not for the prayers of the Tzaddikim who've passed on, the world would not last even for one moment (*Zohar* III:71a).

And so on. It would take literally a whole book just to quote from our Sages, from the Talmud, Midrash and Zohar, about the greatness and awesomeness of the Tzaddikim. The above is just a small sampling, to try to open our hearts and minds to what the True Tzaddik is; and how important it is that we try to understand this greatness.

*

Rebbe Nachman teaches: The Tzaddik is "all — in the Heavens and in the Earth" (1 Chronicles 29:11). Who is it that binds together Heaven and Earth — the Tzaddik! (Zohar III:257a). The Tzaddik unites the Upper World with the Lower World, and all that is in them. With this, the revelation of Godliness can be made (Likutey Moharan II, 7:7).

The Tzaddik is a bridge between the spiritual and the physical. He is above the physical and yet is not, nor can he ever be, as spiritual as God. What then is this "bridge"? Only when one understands this concept, can one begin to grasp the true nature of greatness and the Tzaddik. The Tzaddik has transcended the physical and is capable of grasping what spiritualism is really about. With his mastery, he can take the most wondrous aspects of Godliness and bring them down to a level to which the simplest person can relate.

Rebbe Nachman teaches: A person should pray extremely hard to find someone that can explain Godliness to him. Such a person is very difficult to find. It takes a truly great teacher to be able to explain the great wisdoms of Godliness (Likutey Moharan I, 30:2).

On three separate occasions, Moshe Rabeinu ascended to Heaven for forty days and forty nights. He neither ate nor slept and had no physical wants or needs to look after (Deuteronomy 9). Moshe — a man of flesh and blood. Even the angels were jealous (Shabbat 88b). He was able to keep his physical form in Heaven, because he had risen completely above its corporeality. Our Sages thus comment on the verse (Deuteronomy 33:1): "Moshe, the Godly man" — When he ascended to Heaven he was an entirely spiritual being (*Devarim Rabbah* 11:4).

Because of his greatness, Moshe Rabeinu was able to attain God's wisdom and knowledge, as it were. He was also able to encompass that knowledge in the "vessel" of Torah, bring it down to the physical world, and reveal it to us. The greater a person's spiritual level, the greater his access to higher wisdom, and therefore the greater his ability to convey this knowledge to this world.

Rebbe Nachman teaches: We find that our Sages were very well-versed in all aspects of this world (*Likutey Moharan* II, 58). Ask yourself this question: If these great rabbis spent all their time in Torah study, how were they able to grasp so completely the working principles of agriculture, textiles, finances, animal husbandry and horticulture, the design and construction of various tools, astronomy and astrology, and many other of man's physical enterprises and skills? The answer is that their understanding was based upon their spiritual perceptions and attainments. Knowledgeable in the workings of spiritual principles, they understood these working principles as they filter down into their physical forms (see *Likutey Moharan* II, 58).

Thus, when discussing the construction of certain tools and vessels, Rabbi Yochanan ben Zakai remarked, "Woe to me if I reveal. Woe to me if I don't reveal" (*Keilim* 17:16). Woe to me if I reveal its workings, maybe the dishonest will learn how to cheat with these ideas. Woe to me if I don't teach it, because people will say the rabbis were ignorant in these ways. Furthermore, as the *Maharsha* states: Do not say that the Talmud is lacking in any wisdom. In it, you can find a cure for every conceivable illness, if you but understand their language... (*Maharsha, Gittin* 68b, *s.v. l'dama*).

*

The soul of a Jew stems from the highest levels of Creation (see *Likutey Moharan* I, 17:2). It is sent down into this lowly physical world so that it can be purified through holiness and by letting the soul discover its level and route back to its spiritual source. But, because of the physical restraints imposed upon him by this world, man — almost without exception — finds it nearly impossible to perceive this spiritualism.

The Tzaddik is the exception. He does have a grasp of the spiritual. He can discover the level and the route — and not only his own, but those of others as well. Some Tzaddikim convey their knowledge to us through their teachings, others through their deeds. Observing the Tzaddikim, through either their active or written lessons, will convince us of their ability to see what is important. A Tzaddik knows on what to concentrate his energies and how to focus on it, and he knows how then to bring his understanding down to a level that even ordinary people can comprehend.

Actually, the ingredient for grasping all that knowledge is missing in us, while the Tzaddik has it. We need to work on ourselves and increase our belief that the Tzaddikim *have* attained the spiritual and can bring it as far down as need be to reach us.

*

Reb Nachman Chazan was Reb Noson's closest disciple and the leading Breslover Chassid after Reb Noson passed away. He was once asked if he would talk about a miracle which Rebbe Nachman had performed.

Reb Nachman Chazan's expression became very intense and he exclaimed with great fervor, "A miracle?! You want me to tell you one of the Rebbe's miracles?

"I! I am Rebbe Nachman's miracle!"

Reb Nachman Chazan felt his service to God to be insignificant and worthless. He felt too distanced from God to be of any consequence. Yet, God had seen fit to draw him close to Reb Noson, who fed him many dosages of Rebbe Nachman's "medicines." He eventually rose to a great spiritual position, and so he exclaimed, "I am Rebbe Nachman's miracle. What greater miracle could there be than taking a lowly person like me and getting me to serve God" (*Rabbi Eliyahu Chaim Rosen*).

* * *

LEADER, TEACHER, INTERMEDIARY?

Moshe received the Torah at Sinai and transmitted it to Joshua; Joshua to the Elders; the Elders to the Prophets; and the Prophets transmitted it to the Members of the Great Assembly (*Avot* 1:1). The entire body of Judaic Law, written and oral, came through Moshe, who received it directly from God. God did not give it directly to the Jews. Why not?

The Talmud relates: The Emperor told Rabbi Yehoshua ben Chananya that he wanted to see God. Rabbi Yehoshua took him outside and told him to look at the sun. "This is not possible!" exclaimed the Emperor, to which Rabbi Yehoshua answered: "If you cannot even look upon the servant of God, how can you expect to look at God Himself?!" (*Chullin* 59b).

With this in mind, we can attempt to examine the role of the Tzaddik. In Judaism, the Tzaddik is a leader, a guiding light to his followers. In general, people have a need for leadership. The average person is for the most part unsure of his responsibility in life and how to go about fulfilling it. He must learn this from the Tzaddik. Therefore, what is needed is true leadership; truly knowledgeable people with an understanding of what someone else's capabilities are and what is demanded and required of that individual.

Torah is the instrument which conveys God's Infinite Wisdom to man. Who among us can honestly say that he is wise enough to look at that medium and grasp what is required of him? The Talmud, Midrash and Shulchan Arukh stress the importance of receiving from a teacher, so that one's understanding of Torah be clear. Thus, a teacher or rabbi has to have received from his teacher, and so on, back to Moshe Rabeinu. To look directly into the Torah and say "I know and understand," is to say "I don't know and never will, because I consider myself capable enough to glance at God by *myself*." As the Talmud teaches: Even one who has studied, as long as he has not received from a *Talmid Chakham*, a qualified teacher, is still considered an ignoramus (*Berakhot* 47a). And: How foolish are those who stand up for the Torah Scroll, but do not stand up for the Sage (*Makot* 22b). The Torah can actually mislead a person who follows it, without the benefits of true guidance and leadership.

This does not mean that there are no exceptions to the rule. The Talmud speaks of those unique individuals who did succeed in Torah study, though they did not follow the prescribed approach to study outlined by our Sages (see *Avodah Zarah* 19a). But these singular human beings are very few and far between. One must receive at least the basics of learning from a rabbi, whose task it is to see that the material taught conveys its true meaning (*Bava Batra* 21a,b).

So, why didn't God give the entire body of Judaic Law directly to the Jews? Because the Torah's light would have been too blinding. Being an extension of nothing less than God's Infinite Wisdom, it is too great for the average person to receive directly. To be able to gaze upon this light, we need "sunglasses"; we need some type of filter which processes the light and distributes it in manageable quantities. This filter is the Tzaddik.

So, "Moshe received the Torah... He transmitted it to Joshua, and Joshua transmitted it...." Maimonides, in his introduction to the *Yad HaChazakah*, lists the nation's leaders in each generation until the redaction of the Talmud. The Ravad (Rabbi Avraham ben Dior), in *Seder HaKabbalah*, lists the leaders in each generation up until his own (c. 1000). And, all these leaders and teachers were followed by others. Throughout the generations the Tzaddikim have led the Jews by transmitting their knowledge of God to us. They've taught us what our responsibilities are in life and how to go about fulfilling them. They've also shown us how to turn to God and how to derive pleasure from His great light.

*

The Tzaddik is also an intermediary. He is an agent between God and ourselves. Yet, he is *not* an intermediary at all. God forbid that anyone should think he needs a medium between the Almighty and himself; not from his side, and certainly not from God's. Rather, because the Tzaddik is one who has conquered the physicality of this world and entered the spiritual realm, he serves as an agent and a catalyst for bringing spirituality to this world. Having attained the wisdom and understanding necessary for serving God in a true and proper manner, the Tzaddik serves Him by bringing His will to mankind and by getting people to recognize God in all aspects of their lives. The average person cannot perceive God's will, and therefore has to turn to someone who can. Thus, in *this* sense, the Tzaddik is an intermediary.

"Moshe took the Tent...whoever sought God would go to the Tent of Meeting..." (Exodus 33:7). Rabeinu Bechaya (1263-1340) asks: Shouldn't the verse have said, "whoever sought *Moshe* would go to the Tent of Meeting"? Thus we see that Moshe is called in God's Name. Yaakov was also called in God's Name (Genesis 33:20; see *Megillah* 18a). Mashiach is also called in God's Name... For whoever is truly attached to something is called by the name of that thing (*Rabeinu Bechaya, Ki Tisa*). Furthermore, this teaches us that one *cannot* go to God — be made aware of God — except through the Tzaddik (*Leket Amarim* p. 145ff).

The Talmud tells us that when God gave the Torah at Mount Sinai, He first offered it to all the nations of the earth. They refused. Then He offered the Torah to the Jews and they accepted it (*Avodah Zarah* 2b). As a result of what happened at

Sinai, if anyone now wants to enter the realm of Torah he must first convert to Judaism. Without embracing Judaism one cannot embrace the Torah. So too, Rebbe Nachman teaches, one cannot enter the realm of Torah and be a truly devout Jew, without being close to the Tzaddik (*Tzaddik* #299).

There is another aspect to the Tzaddik's role as intermediary. As God's children and chosen people, we have no need for an in-between twixt God and ourselves. But, do we know what to do? Can we, on our own, know what prayers to pray, what actions to take? And what happens when we have estranged ourselves from God by our misdeeds? Who will defend us? Who will speak out on our behalf? We need someone who will not only show us how to make amends, but also serve as our advocate. Our Sages teach: He who has a sick person in his family should turn to the wise man and ask that he pray for him (*Bava Batra* 116a). Reb Avraham Chazan explains it this way: To see the Tzaddik as a medium and a proxy of God is absolutely forbidden. However, turning to the Tzaddik for the sake of including oneself in the Tzaddik's prayers, for the sake of having more meritorious prayer, is not only permitted but even encouraged (*Biur HaLikutim* 10:17). In this sense, the Tzaddik is a spokesman, interceder, and even a peacemaker between Father and child.

*

We also find that the Tzaddik himself may be so far removed from our understanding that we need an intermediary between him and ourselves. Sometimes what the Tzaddik does or says is beyond the ability of the average person to comprehend, and then it becomes necessary to have someone else, someone who is closer to the Tzaddik than we ourselves are, to help us understand the paths of spirituality upon which the Tzaddik walks. Just as the Tzaddik is an agent in guiding us to understand God's will, this intermediary guides us to better understand the Tzaddik's will (which is in any case God's will, for he has made "God's will his will").

Rebbe Nachman teaches: A Tzaddik is like a rubber stamp. The letters on the stamp are all reversed. Unless we first impress it on paper and read what's written there, it's almost impossible to know what it says. So, too, the Tzaddik. It's impossible for us to understand his ways. But he leaves his imprint on his students and from them we catch a glimpse of his greatness (*Likutey Moharan* I, 140).

Torah Scrolls, tefilin and mezuzot must be written on the hides of kosher animals (*Shabbat* 108a). Reb Noson writes: Even something so physical as the hides of animals can be elevated to the highest levels of holiness by inscribing the letters of Torah on them (*Likutey Halakhot, Tefilin* 5:35; see *Tefilin: A Chassidic Discourse* where this is explained in detail). The Tzaddik has done the same with his body. He has taken his "hide" and purified it (*Tzaddik* #234).

Therefore, in examining the role of the Tzaddik, we must understand that his spiritual position is far beyond what we even can imagine. True, every Jew has the possibility of attaining a level where he can serve God without any advice or guidance from the Tzaddik, becoming a Tzaddik himself, but, except for a unique few, this is rarely the case. Therefore, we need the Tzaddik as an intermediary.

Unfortunately, the term intermediary has been used too often by those who do not, or cannot, understand that they have no grasp of the Tzaddik. They cast aspersions on and question the validity of his role. In so doing, they mislead people and draw them far away from the Tzaddik. This did not begin with the advent of chassidic Tzaddikim. Already in biblical times, we find that "the people mocked the messengers of God" (2 Chronicles, 36:16). These "messengers" were none other than the Tzaddikim and Prophets of that generation. Then, as now, people had no conception of how great these leaders were. They thought themselves capable of choosing the correct path for serving God on their own, and it was this which caused the destruction of the Temple and the exile.

The concept of the Tzaddik has always been with us. Generation after generation has seen its spiritual giants, men who would lead, teach and act as intermediaries for the people. However, just as our understanding and perception of the Torah has diminished down the ages, so too has our understanding and appreciation of the role of the Tzaddik. We must, therefore, bind ourselves to the Tzaddikim and turn to them as our guides for understanding God's will. By accepting their advice and counsel, modeling our own service to God after theirs, we can all draw closer to God through the Tzaddik.

* * *

BINDING ONESELF TO THE TZADDIK

Reb Yitzchok Breiter taught: A person must bind himself to the Tzaddik at the beginning of each day. He must accept upon himself that during the forthcoming day he will attempt to live by the advice and direction of the Tzaddik (Seder HaYom 1).

Having established that the Tzaddik himself has attained an understanding of God's will and therefore knows which direction each of us should take while in this world, the question naturally is: What does this do for me? What does this mean to me?

Rebbe Nachman teaches: Fear and Love of Heaven are attainable only through the Tzaddik. The Tzaddik can reveal the beauty and grace that exist in the Jewish soul. This soul comes from the loftiest of places: it is rooted on high, in the Thought of God and it stems from the Very Source of Creation. The Tzaddik reveals this beauty, thereby revealing what Fear and Love are (Likutey Moharan I, 17:1,8). Perhaps, the following parable from Rebbe Nachman illustrates this best.

One May evening, Reb Shmuel of Moscow, a poor and impoverished Jew, dreamt of a great treasure under a certain bridge that crosses the Danube River in Vienna. He immediately traveled there, hoping to dig up the treasure for himself. But when he arrived, Reb Shmuel saw an officer standing alongside the bridge and he was afraid to search for the treasure. Before he could make up his mind what to do next, the officer became suspicious of the loitering stranger.

"What do you want here?" the officer called out as he approached the frightened Jew.

Reb Shmuel concluded that it would be best to tell the truth and perhaps he could at least split the treasure with the officer. "I dreamt that there was a treasure here," he responded. "I've come to dig it up."

"Ha! You Jews! All that concerns you are dreams!" chuckled the officer. "I too had a dream. One night, maybe two weeks ago, I dreamt that there was a treasure at such and such an address, in the yard of a certain Reb Shmuel of Moscow. So what! You don't see me hurrying off to Moscow, do you?!"

The Jew was astounded. The officer had mentioned his city! His address! His name! And they had both had their dream on the very same night. Reb Shmuel rushed home, searched his yard and found the treasure. "Look at that," he exclaimed. "The treasure was right here next to me all along. But in order to find it, I had to travel to Vienna!"

"This is true for all of us," taught Rebbe Nachman. "Each person has a treasure inside him, but in order to find it, one must travel to the Tzaddik. The Tzaddik will show him how and where to look" (*Rabbi Nachman's Stories* #24).

Each and every Jew has incredibly great treasures hidden within himself. With these treasures he can excel to the greatest heights. This explains why the Jews have always been so successful, no matter the field of endeavor. Despite all the unfavorable conditions, the Jew has succeeded and prospered at everything he put his hand to and in every place his wanderings have taken him. But what are these treasures? Is it sharp minds, incredible memories, creativity, etc? Rebbe Nachman teaches: Each person has at least one trait in which he excels, one point in which he far surpasses his friend (who may be superior in many other areas) (*Likutey Moharan* I, 34:4). Which trait and characteristic do I excel in? Which is my area of excellence?

For this, you need advice. You need proper counsel. This is where the need for binding yourself to the Tzaddik is important. To find your point of excellence — your hidden treasure — being attached to the Tzaddik has no equal.

What is the purpose of this binding?

Quite simply, binding is what you need to do to "assure" yourself that you will follow the Tzaddik's advice through thick and thin and to the best of your ability.

How is it done? Can it be done?

*

Get a Rav.... The Talmud teaches: Bind yourself to God's Attributes. Just as He is compassionate, so should you be compassionate. Just as He is kind, so should you be... (*Shabbat* 133b).

The bond which we seek to create with the Tzaddik is a spiritual one. In this sense, it is like the bond each Jew wants to create between himself and God. Obviously, that too is something spiritual. So, how is it possible to be spiritually attached to the Holy One? From our Sages we see that by following God's "example" — assuming His Attributes — we form this bond, this connection and attachment between ourselves and God. By being compassionate and kind we become attached to Him spiritually, and we ourselves become Godly.

Well, the same holds true when binding ourselves to the Tzaddik. By following the Tzaddik's example and attributes, i.e. accepting his counsel and advice, and following it, we become bound to the Tzaddik. By doing what he says and as he does, we become attached to him spiritually, and we ourselves become Tzaddik-like. As Rebbe Nachman teaches: Receiving counsel from the Tzaddik creates a bond between the giver and the receiver. In a sense, this is like a marriage. Through the transmission of his advice, a union occurs between the Tzaddik and the person receiving from him (*Likutey Moharan* I, 7:4).

The Rebbe also teaches that the key for achieving spirituality is listening to the Tzaddik — to everything that he says — and not swaying from it even so much as a millimeter. Just accept his teachings with full simplicity (*Likutey Moharan* I, 123).

You may be tempted to ask, "Well, why? Why shouldn't I understand what I'm doing?" Simple. Do your children understand the reasons for all the things you tell them to do? Of course not, you expect them to accept and do. They can always question later. Presumably, as they grow, they'll find less and less reason to question. And if they do, they'll be better-equipped to understand what you tell them. Well, it's no different in terms of the Tzaddik. He is someone with a far greater perception of what is really necessary for you to do in life. Later on, after having been consistently bound to the Tzaddik, you'll also come to understand.

Now we can understand the Mishnah: Get yourself a *Rav* (a rabbi) and remove yourself from doubt (*Avot* 1:16). If a person is attached to his *Rav,* his leader, he can get all the direction he needs. All he has to do is ask. Whereas, if he thinks that he has already achieved the heights of wisdom and doesn't need direction, then either he is a *Rav* or he's in big trouble. So, get yourself a *Rav.* Get yourself a Tzaddik to whom you can turn for counsel and advice. Not only will this free you from doubt and uncertainty, but the Tzaddik to whom you are bound will also guide you onto the correct path for the rectification and perfection of your soul. How? The Tzaddik knows the source of each person's soul and the place in Heaven to which it has to reach, so the Tzaddik can give you proper direction. He can reveal the Fear and Love that already exist within you, and he can reveal the inner beauty and grace of your soul, causing it to rise to its source.

Rebbe Nachman teaches: Whoever refuses to listen to the words of the wise can literally go crazy. And, even the most insane person, were he to listen to normal people and do exactly as they say, he, too, would behave normally and be accepted as such (*Rabbi Nachman's Wisdom* #67). The same can be said of someone who does not accept the Tzaddikim as his leaders. Lacking their advice, he can go insane. If he's on the wrong track — and without true and proper guidance the vast majority of people are inevitably on the wrong track — then whatever he attempts will be the wrong thing.

Furthermore, Rebbe Nachman teaches: It is impossible to grasp even a bit of the Tzaddik's teachings unless the person has completely rectified his *Brit*. That is, he himself must be very pure and holy. [He must be a Tzaddik in his own right.] If not, the Tzaddik's teaching can mislead him (*Likutey Moharan* I, 36:5). In his commentary to this teaching, the *Parparaot LeChokhmah* questions if there is anyone who can say this about himself. Who can claim that he is pure enough to understand the Tzaddik's teachings? Who can honestly claim to be completely free of any blemishing of the Covenant? And if there is no one, or almost no one who can make such a claim, then who are his lessons for? What purpose do the Tzaddik's teachings serve if no one can grasp them?

The answer which the *Parparaot* gives is a long one. Basically, it is similar to what is said of the teachings of Torah in general. Ideally, our aim has to be to learn Torah for its own sake. Does that mean that if our learning is mixed with a desire for honor or for some other ulterior motive, that we shouldn't study Torah? Won't these impure motives cause us to be misled? Our Sages tell us that despite this we are to study. Eventually, we will come to Torah study for its own sake. But if the intention is much more sinister, such as mastering Torah to use it as a means for mocking others and becoming arrogant, then it would be better were we not to study at all. The same is true in studying the Tzaddik's teachings. A person who rejects the Tzaddik's teachings because he considers them unacceptable, will indeed be totally misled, and he will use (misuse) the Tzaddik's teaching eventually as a means to reject other facets of Torah. If, however, someone truly desires to come closer to God but cannot understand the Tzaddik's teachings on how to achieve this, then he will blame all shortcomings on himself. He will accept the Tzaddik's lessons as being correct and work on himself to rectify his personal faults (*Parparaot LeChokhmah* 36:2).

Reb Yisrael Karduner once said, "A person's actions are like the spokes attached to the hub of a wheel. If the hub is straight, then the spokes that turn with it will be straight. But if the hub at the center is crooked, then all the spokes will be crooked" (*Rabbi Eliyahu Chaim Rosen*). Attaching yourself to the Tzaddik allows your center hub to straighten out. Then, all your actions will be set right.

*

Rabbi and student. As we've seen, receiving advice from the Tzaddik and thereby becoming bound to him is the key through which a person attains his true path of spiritual growth. Rebbe Nachman refers to visiting the True Tzaddik as "something upon which all one's Judaism depends" (*Likutey Moharan* I, 66:4). However, a person might say to himself: "What do have I to do with such an extraordinary Tzaddik? I'm not looking for such great things that I should need an outstandingly pious and holy teacher. Let me be on my own level, or at most let me first reach the level of my local religious leader. Then, if I can grow spiritually, I'll try to seek a greater leader. Why should I look now for such a great Tzaddik?"

Rebbe Nachman teaches: A person should never be satisfied with a less accomplished teacher. He should never think that it is enough to be like this rabbi, teacher, etc. The more insignificant a person is, or thinks he is, the greater a leader he needs to guide him. A person with a minor illness seeks advice from a general practitioner. A person with a more severe illness will seek a cure from a specialist. An extremely sick person will only want to consult with the best doctors available. The same applies to spirituality. The more a person is distant from God, the more he is steeped in physicality, the greater is his need for a leader to pull him out of his spiritual illness and provide him with the Heavenly wisdom necessary for his cure (*Likutey Moharan* I, 30:2).

We are tempted to think that it's quite enough to have a good local person as our spiritual guide. But if we were to evaluate our knowledge and recognition of God honestly, we would readily accept that we need a great person to elevate us from the depths to which we've lowered ourselves. And the more we realize this, the more we would understand that we have to bind ourselves to the greatest spiritual leader available so that he might heal us from our spiritual malaise.

Another advantage of following a great Tzaddik is explained by Rebbe Nachman: The construction of the letter *aleph* (א) consists of two points, an upper and lower *yod*, with a *vav* in between them. The Tzaddik, the *Rav*, is compared to the upper point — the crown. The student is compared to the lower point — the footstool. The two points allude to Moshe and Joshua. "Moshe is like the sun, Joshua like the moon" (*Bava Batra* 75a). The moon has no light of its own, only that which it receives from the sun. Between them stands the sky, the firmament. This is the letter *vav* which functions as the channel for conveying the upper light, the sun, to the moon, the lower light (*Likutey Moharan* I, 6:5).

There is a great distance between the Tzaddik, the upper point, and the student, the lower point. The distance is the entire length of the firmament, a world of difference. Yet, this student can reflect all the great wisdom of his teacher, by willingly following his advice. He can be the recipient of great light and knowledge. In addition, just as the moon catches the sun's light and then reflects it to the world so as to benefit others, the follower of the Tzaddik, by absorbing his teachings, will automatically be a contributor of good advice and counsel to those near him.

In the story of "The Rabbi's Son," Rebbe Nachman tells of a Jew who performed one certain mitzvah and because of this acquired the attribute of the "lower light," the moon. The Tzaddik himself was the "greater light." Had these two been able to come together, their meeting would have brought Mashiach (*Rabbi Nachman's Stories* #8, pp. 154-159). Just like the Rabbi's son in the story, at any given moment, any one of us has the potential to perform a certain mitzvah in a certain manner and thereby acquire the attribute of the lower light. Thus any Jew, no matter where he is, if he binds and attaches himself to the Tzaddik, has it in his power to hasten the coming of Mashiach.

*

Easy advice. People expect the advice and *tikkunim* which the Tzaddik prescribes to be severe and demanding. They think that rectification can only be achieved through long periods of self-mortification, fasting and the like. Rebbe Nachman teaches otherwise: When Na'aman, the commander of the Assyrian army, was stricken with leprosy, he traveled to Elisha for a cure. Elisha told him, "Wash seven times in the River Jordan and you will be healed." At first he refused to listen, thinking this cure to be too simple to be effective. Eventually, his servants persuaded him to follow the prophet's advice and he was cured (2 Kings 5).

The same is true, perhaps even more so, today. Sometimes, we shy away from the counsel which the Tzaddik prescribes, just because it looks too easy. We expect marvels and mortifications. We get "applesauce." The main thing is to accept the Tzaddik's teaching with simple faith (*Tzaddik* #492).

* * *

THE TZADDIK AND HIS FOLLOWERS

The holy Ari writes that the souls of most people are actually like leaves on the branches of the greater souls, those of the Tzaddikim (*Sha'ar HaGilgulim* #38). Thus, each Tzaddik has his "leaves," the souls for which he is responsible. The greater the Tzaddik, the more souls he has in his care. And the True Tzaddik, the leading Tzaddik, has all the souls under him. Rebbe Nachman teaches: There is a Tzaddik who is the foundation of the world. In him are rooted all the other souls, even those of the Tzaddikim. Some are [main] branches. Some are branches of these branches (*Likutey Moharan* I, 70). The Ari comments on the verse: "Six hundred thousand souls are those at my foot" (Numbers 11:21) — that all six hundred thousand Jewish souls were but parts of Moshe's soul (*Sha'ar HaPesukim* 2:3; see *Likutey Torah, B'ha'alotkha* that Elijah the Prophet attained a similar level).

But, all people are different. How can the Tzaddik reach out to each individual differently? Especially the True Tzaddik, the leading Tzaddik, how can he reflect each person's needs? However, the answer is that the Tzaddik is a man of many faces. In Rebbe Nachman's classic story, the Master of Prayer was a sort of expert chameleon, able to adapt his words to all manner of *thinking* — no matter with whom he was speaking (*Rabbi Nachman's Stories* #12).

Despite all the advances science has made, despite all the modern technology that we possess, mankind has yet to make appreciable strides in subduing negative character traits. Yet, the Tzaddik is one who, in every aspect, has risen above all his basic instincts. His approach to life reflects neither a need for honor or possessions, nor any type of physical pleasure. He has divested himself of these "human" wants and, by seeing in everything its relationship to God, rises above the feelings of the average man.

The Tzaddik is also a true representative of his Creator. His worship of God has a depth which the average person cannot even comprehend. He has so totally subjugated his corporeality that, "even though he has a human body, he is totally different" (*Rabbi Nachman's Wisdom* #14). He has attained a [type of] spiritual body (see *Zohar* III:169b; *Likutey Moharan* II, 83). This "nothingness" enables him to reflect all the diverse moods and feelings in his followers and appeal to each one on an entirely different level. Rebbe Nachman's famous parable illustrates this very well.

Once there was a prince who thought he was a turkey. He removed his clothes and sat beneath the table, pecking at crumbs. All efforts to cure him were of no avail. His father, the king, was terribly distraught.

A wise man came and offered to help. The king consented. The wise man removed his clothes and also sat beneath the table, pecking at crumbs.

"Who are you?" asked the prince. "What are you doing here?"

"I'm a turkey," replied the wise man.

"I'm also a turkey," replied the prince and welcomed him.

After they'd gotten to know each other a bit, the wise man signalled for shirts be thrown to them under the table. When he donned his shirt the prince asked, "Why are you doing that?" to which the wise man replied, "One can wear a shirt and still be a turkey." The prince also put on a shirt.

Some time later the wise man motioned for the king's servants to throw them pairs of pants. Again the prince asked what was the point in putting on pants if he was a turkey.

The wise man answered, "It won't diminish your status as a turkey. You can wear pants and still be a turkey."

The wise man continued in this manner until they were both completely dressed. Then he signalled again, and they were given regular food from the table. When the prince questioned this, he was reassured that it would in no way detract from his being a turkey.

Finally, the wise man said, "What makes you think a turkey must sit under the table? Even a turkey can sit at the table."

They then sat at the table. The wise man convinced him he could dress as a human, eat what humans eat, sit with them and still be a turkey. And, continuing in this manner, by mimicking what humans did, the prince was finally cured (*Rabbi Nachman's Stories* #24).

*

The Tzaddik can appear like a regular person, no different from anyone else. On the other hand, he can appear strange and different. Even as a turkey. To each individual he can be something else. The greater the Tzaddik, the greater amount of "faces" he can present to instruct each follower on the path which is correct for him to follow. And, each person has the freedom to look at the Tzaddik as he truly wishes to perceive him — with the respect due a leader or with mockery. Thus Rebbe Nachman teaches: The Tzaddikim are called "the eyes of the community" (*Horiyot* 5b). Through the Tzaddikim our eyes are opened and we are given to see our true appearance, a picture of how we really look (*Likutey Moharan* II, 67).

*

The Talmud teaches: When an ignoramus first meets a righteous man, he values him as gold. In time, he sees him as silver. Still later, he thinks of the righteous man as pottery. When pottery shatters, it cannot be repaired (*Sanhedrin* 52b).

When Reb Noson first came to Rebbe Nachman, he was extremely impressed with the Rebbe's teachings. Yet, Reb Noson still wondered whether the Rebbe could direct him to the path in Judaism which his soul was seeking. As Reb Noson was thinking this, Rebbe Nachman addressed him: "When Reb Mechel of Zlotchov first met the Baal Shem Tov he was moved to a feeling of incredible awe for the founder of Chassidism. But then he began having second thoughts. With each passing minute he began to think less and less of the Baal Shem Tov. "Perhaps I'm an ignoramus," Reb Mechel wondered to himself, recalling the talmudic teaching. Just then, the Baal Shem Tov grabbed him and said, "Mecheleh, you're an ignoramus," impressing upon him that he [the Baal Shem Tov] knew Reb Mechel's every thought. Reb Noson was thinking those exact same thoughts about himself when Rebbe Nachman told him this story, hinting to him that he [the Rebbe], too, could read the thoughts of others. From this, Reb Noson understood the power of the True Tzaddik. He can reach out to the person, read his mind, and offer him the helping hand he needs to cross the threshold into holiness (*Aveneha Barzel* p.11 #6).

* * *

FINDING THE TZADDIK TO FOLLOW

Well, now that you've accepted that you need a *Rav,* how do you find him? How do you locate the Tzaddik you should follow? Only by searching for him; just as you would pursue the perfect mate, hunt a top job, search out the right home, so must you expend effort upon effort in trying to find your true leader. Rebbe Nachman advises: One must search and seek very much for such a great teacher... (*Likutey Moharan* I, 30:2).

This can only be accomplished by searching and seeking, again and again, for the spiritual teachings that quench the thirst of the soul. Even when you've found something that alleviates your thirst, you must still strive to attain the full value of this teaching and get whatever you can out of it. If you find yourself growing spiritually with this, fine. If not, then you must seek again. Only in this manner can you find what you lack in true spiritual development.

One must pray to God to direct him to the truth, to find this True Tzaddik. The means for seeking the Tzaddik is limited by one's knowledge. Whatever one understands of spirituality — this will guide him to what he thinks is right. Yet prayer can bring a person to a higher level — to the highest levels. It can elevate him far above his capabilities and enable him to find the True Tzaddik.

Reb Noson illustrates this in one of his discourses. There is much confusion in the world about finding the Tzaddik, especially the True Tzaddik. First of all, there are many false leaders, those who teach Torah based upon philosophies and atheism. They are not leaders at all. (In fact, Rebbe Nachman once said of one such person, "He caused at least one thousand people to lose their portion in the World to Come"; *Tzaddik* #537). There are also many who are righteous, even Tzaddikim, but who are not the True Tzaddik. How then can I find the True Tzaddik, the leading Tzaddik? Who and where is that Tzaddik for whom I should search?

Any Tzaddik who teaches us to come closer to God, who instills in us a fear and love of Heaven, who bases his teachings upon our Sages — from the Talmud, Midrash, Zohar, Ari, Shulchan Arukh, etc. — that Tzaddik is worthy to be followed. But it's still confusing! Since I'm to search for the *greatest* Tzaddik, how can I get to him? Where is the True Tzaddik?

The Talmud teaches: Whoever is lost in the desert and has forgotten which day it is, should count six days and consider the seventh day Shabbat. He must keep all the laws of Shabbat on that day which he's chosen, with the exception of the minimal amount of work needed to keep himself alive.

During his "weekdays," he must also keep each day as though it were Shabbat. The sole difference between his Shabbat and his weekdays is that he makes Kiddush and Havdallah on what is his Day of Rest (Shabbat 69b). Thus, until he finds out which day is the true Shabbat, he must apply the laws of Shabbat to every day.

Reb Noson compares this law to our dilemma in finding the True Tzaddik: The Tzaddik is compared to Shabbat (Zohar III:144b). Whoever seeks the True Tzaddik and cannot find him, should accept all the Tzaddikim. However, he should choose one Tzaddik as his "Shabbat," his leader, but this is only until he can find the True Tzaddik. In the meantime, he must engage in a minimum of work in order to use whatever time he has to searching for the Tzaddik. It's not easy. He is likened to one lost in the desert. Yet, ultimately, it all depends on how much he's willing to search. With a strong enough desire, nothing can stand in his way (Likutey Halakhot, Shabbat 5:13).

* * *

THE TZADDIK'S POWER

Rebbe Nachman teaches: Every good thought or deed performed by any Jew, anywhere, is another "brick" in the rebuilding of the Holy Temple. Each brick serves a different purpose. Some are foundation stones, some are for the framework and so on. Every mitzvah performed by a Jew, every word of Torah and prayer, has to be brought to the Tzaddik of the generation. The Tzaddik will elevate it and place it in its correct place. Only the True Tzaddik knows how to place each and every part in its right position (Likutey Moharan I, 2:6).

Reb Noson was once asked, "Who is greater? A simple person who binds himself to the Tzaddik or a learned individual who is not bound to the Tzaddik?" Reb Noson replied:

"Examine the chapter about the building of the Tabernacle (Exodus 35-40). If a prominent Jew contributed an ark, a table or any other valuable object for the Tabernacle and tried to have this item used without first bringing it to Moshe, it would not have been accepted. But, when even the simplest Jew made a small contribution to the Tabernacle through Moshe Rabeinu, it was considered most valuable and was readily accepted" (Aveneha Barzel p.74 #62).

Reb Noson writes: The main hope of Israel is its reliance upon the great Tzaddikim. A person can falter, his strength may wane, but the great Tzaddik has enormous spiritual strength. He is always searching to locate every drop of good that a Jew performs. This good is immediately taken by the Tzaddik and arranged in its proper place (Likutey Halakhot, Minchah 7:63).

*

During one's life. Rebbe Nachman teaches: The Tzaddik has the power to elevate all souls, including those who have not made even the slightest move in the direction of spirituality (Likutey Moharan I, 13:2, end). He can rectify the souls of his followers even if they have not completed their deeds, even if they were negligent. Even if they were malicious in their deeds, the Tzaddik has the power to elevate them.

*

...and after one's passing. The Talmud teaches: King David elevated his son Absalom from the seven levels of Gehennom into Gan Eden (Sotah 10b). Rebbe Nachman said, "I can also do this. I can raise a person out of the seven levels of Gehennom and place him in Gan Eden" (Tzaddik #298). He also once said, "It is easier to rectify the souls of one thousand people who have already passed away, than to rectify the soul of a living Tzaddik — for he still has free choice" (Tzaddik #94).

Rebbe Nachman teaches: The Tzaddik has the power to intervene in a Heavenly judgment. By sending the one being judged on a mission, he can save him. In Jerusalem there is a synagogue to which all the dead people on earth are brought. As soon as someone in this world dies, he is brought there at once to be judged as to where his place should be. There are people who die in Eretz Yisrael who are taken outside the Land. Others who die outside may be brought to Eretz Yisrael. It is in this synagogue that the court which hands down these judgments sits and allocates each person the place he deserves. There are even cases where the verdict is that there is no place at all for the person concerned and he is to be destroyed and cast into the Hollow Sling.

When the dead are brought there, they are brought in clothing. Sometimes a dead person's clothes are incomplete: one person might be missing a sleeve, another a piece from the edge of his garment, and so on. Everything depends upon a person's actions in his life time (because his clothing after death corresponds to his deeds). The verdict depends on the clothes he has when he is brought there, and his place is allocated accordingly.

Once a dead person was brought there completely naked. He had no clothes whatsoever. The verdict was that he should be cast into the Hollow Sling and destroyed, God forbid, because he was completely naked. However, a certain Tzaddik came and took one of his own garments and threw it over this person.

The court asked him, "Why are you giving him one of your own garments?" The court took exception to this, because why should the dead man be given a garment and be saved with clothing that was not his? The Tzaddik answered: "I have to send this man on a mission for my own purposes, and for this reason I am entitled to dress him in my own garment. Surely you are aware that on occasion a nobleman may send his servant to another nobleman and the servant delays carrying out his bidding. His master asks him, 'Why have you not left yet as I ordered?' The servant replies, 'Because I don't have the right clothes for going to the nobleman in question. He is very great and it is impossible to go there in clothes which are not respectable.' The master answers, 'Quickly. Take one of my garments and put it on and hurry to the nobleman to do my bidding.' Similarly I need to send this dead person on a mission of my own. For that reason I am giving him one of my garments." This is how the Tzaddik saved the dead man from the bitter penalty of the Hollow Sling. The Rebbe told this story to show the tremendous power of the True Tzaddik to save his followers in the World of Truth (*Tzaddik* #228).

Therefore, Rebbe Nachman teaches: One should pray very hard to be able to bind himself to the True Tzaddik. Happy is he who becomes bound to him in this world and happy is his portion, because afterwards (after one's passing), it is extremely difficult to become attached to the Tzaddik (*Likutey Moharan* II, 78).

*

Reb Noson writes: What is the meaning of the verse (Psalms 16:10): "You will not abandon me to the abyss (Gehennom), for You will not allow Your chassid to see the pit (Gehennom)"? If one is a pious chassid, why should he descend to Gehennom? And if both parts of the verse refer to the same person, why the redundancy?

Reb Noson answers: Someone who is attached to the True Tzaddik will not stay in Gehennom. If he must suffer punishment, it will not last forever, for the Tzaddik will take him out. Why? Because, "You, God, will not allow Your chassid — the Tzaddik — to suffer Gehennom." Since I am attached to the Tzaddik, the Tzaddik must come to take me out. He cannot remain, "for You do not wish him to see Gehennom." Thus, my attachment to the Tzaddik is my after-life insurance policy against Gehennom (*Likutey Halakhot, Hashkamat HaBoker* 4:4).

*

And after the Tzaddik's passing. Tzaddikim are greater after their passing than when they were alive (*Chullin* 7b). The power and ability which the Tzaddikim possess to rectify souls is even greater after the Tzaddik passes away from this world. Our Sages teach: Abraham takes the Jews out of Gehennom (*Eruvin* 19a). Isaac pleaded the case of the Jews and saved them (*Shabbat* 89b). During the Babylonian exile, it was Rachel who forced God, as it were, to take an oath regarding the Redemption of the Jews (*Peticha d'Eichah Rabbati* 24). Moshe defended the Jew from Haman's assault against them (*Esther Rabbah* 7:18). And so on.

When he was on his deathbed, Rabbi Yochanan ben Zakai began to weep. His disciples could not understand why such a great and holy man would have to cry. "There are two paths before me," Rabbi Yochanan told them, "one to Gan Eden, one to Gehennom. I do not know which path I will be led upon" (*Berakhot* 28a).

Rebbe Nachman asked: "Do you really think that Rabbi Yochanan was afraid of being sent to Gehennom?" The answer is this. Rabbi Yochanan did not know whether he had reached the level of being worthy to enter Gehennom and remove some souls from there while he himself was on his way up to Gan Eden (*Tzaddik* #602). The *Tikkuney Zohar* adds: The Tzaddik enters Gehennom to remove all those souls which considered repenting but did not. The Tzaddik intercedes on their behalf (*Tikkuney Zohar* 32). The Ari also writes that the Tzaddikim work to correct, rectify and elevate all the souls of those who need rectification, even after they themselves have passed away (*Sha'ar HaKavanot, Mizmor Shir L'Yom HaShabbat*). In fact, this is their main objective, to see that every soul is

344 / CROSSING THE NARROW BRIDGE

rectified. Rebbe Nachman added: "When Mashiach comes, he will rectify everyone" (*Aveneha Barzel* p. 21 #4).

On the night before he passed away, Rebbe Nachman told his followers, "What is there for you to worry about, seeing that I am going before you." Reb Noson added: Even those who did not have the privilege of knowing the Rebbe during his lifetime can still rely on him, provided they come to his holy grave, put their trust in him, learn his holy teachings and accustom themselves to following his ways" (*Tzaddik* #122).

* * *

THE NAMES OF TZADDIKIM

Rebbe Nachman teaches: Both man's destiny and mission in life are determined by the name he is given (*Rabbi Nachman's Wisdom* #95). The Rebbe also taught that every person's essence is defined by some combination of the letters of his name (*Rabbi Nachman's Wisdom* #44).

As we've seen, the Tzaddik is given a special mission in this world and his name indicates this task. When the Tzaddik accomplishes his mission, his name includes his accomplishments as well. Thus, Reb Noson writes: Even the mere mentioning of the names of Tzaddikim arouses their achievements and therefore their merits. What's more, mentioning the names of the Tzaddikim causes their merit to be drawn upon us (*Likutey Halakhot, Netilat Yadayim Li'Seudah* 4:6).

To facilitate this, Reb Noson compiled a book in which he listed the names of the Tzaddikim until his generation. He called it *Shemot HaTzaddikim,* and whoever wants to draw the holiness of the Tzaddikim upon himself can recite these names.

The Rebbe teaches that mentioning the names of Tzaddikim can bring about a change of nature (*The Aleph-Bet Book, Tzaddik* B:20). Indeed, from the Rebbe's time, Breslover Chassidim have seen how reciting the *Shemot*

HaTzaddikim has brought them God's help in the most amazing ways.

* * *

GRAVESITES OF TZADDIKIM

There is an ancient Jewish custom to visit the gravesites of Tzaddikim and pray there for God's salvation, from their personal difficulties and for all of Israel (*Orach Chaim*, 581:4). Yosef did this when he was sold into slavery. Passing by the tomb of his mother Rachel, he stopped to plead his case (*Seder HaDorot* 2216). Kalev went to Hebron to pray at the Tomb of the Patriarch, so that he would not be drawn into the spies' evil plot against entering the Holy Land (*Rashi*, Numbers 13:22). The Talmud teaches: Why was the grave of Moshe Rabeinu hidden? The answer is that if the location of his grave was known to man, the Jews would go there to pray — and they would be forthwith redeemed from exile! (*Sotah* 14a; see *Eyn Yaakov, Sotah* #54). In fact, throughout the Talmud, Midrash and Zohar, we find similar stories about the efficacy of visiting the burial site of the Tzaddikim.

What is the reason for these prayers at the gravesites? The Zohar asks the same question: Rabbi Chizkiyah and Rabbi Yeisa were travelling together. Rabbi Yeisa asked, "When the world needs rain, why do we go to the graves of the Tzaddikim to pray?" To support his argument he quoted the verse, "Do not seek of the dead" (Deuteronomy 18:11). Rabbi Chizkiyah answered, "Yes, but the dead mentioned in the verse refers to those who are truly dead, the wicked. As for the Tzaddikim, they are always alive" (*Zohar* III:71b).

Our Sages say: He is Satan, he is the Evil Inclination, he is the Angel of Death (*Bava Batra* 16a). They are one. Whoever follows his Evil Inclination joins with Satan and is thereby given a taste of death. The Tzaddik, however, has nothing to do with the Evil Inclination. He is pure and holy. Because of this, Tzaddikim do not taste death, they are always alive. Thus, our Sages teach that the Patriarch Yaakov did not die (Ta'anit 5b). The Zohar adds: Moshe did not die. How can this be when the verse clearly states, "And Moshe died"? (Deuteronomy 34:5). True, but his death is only vis-a-vis our understanding and level of perception. From our human perspective he is indeed gone, but actually, he lives on. This is true not only of Moshe Rabeinu, but of all the Tzaddikim: they do not taste death. Whoever is completely holy, death [as we know it] has no effect over him (Zohar II:174a).

Rebbe Nachman advises: It's very good to go to the grave of the Baal Shem Tov and pray there. The burial site of a Tzaddik is as holy as the Holy Land. The verse reads (Psalms 37:29), "Tzaddikim will inherit the Land." This means Tzaddikim merit that their burial sites have the same degree of holiness as the Holy Land itself (Likutey Moharan II, 111).

Reb Noson writes: The Tzaddik is one who devotes himself to revealing God and His Kingship as much as he possibly can and his entire lifetime is dedicated to achieving this. Thus, even when he passes away, he still desires and strives to achieve his aim. But, in the Upper Worlds, there is no way for him to do this. Therefore, the Tzaddik waits for someone to come to his grave and pray there. When this person asks to repent and return to God, the Tzaddik continues his life's work: elevating people to God and revealing His Kingdom even further (Likutey Halakhot, Minchah 7:80).

Thus it is a very great mitzvah to seek God's salvation by visiting the graves of the Tzaddikim. Praying there enables us to bind ourselves to the Tzaddik and we even acquire some of the holiness of the Tzaddik himself. Being there also opens a more direct line for our prayers — they are more easily elevated to heaven, as the Tzaddik now has more power than ever before.

Reb Noson writes: Rabbi Shimon bar Yochai was a phenomenal Tzaddik. In authoring the Zohar, he was the

first Tzaddik ever granted permission to speak openly about
the esoteric wisdom we call Kabbalah. His departure from
this world was, and is, an overwhelming loss. Yet, instead of
declaring his *yahrzeit* — Lag B'Omer — a day of remorseful
mourning, we celebrate and rejoice. Why?

The answer, Reb Noson tells us, is that when a Tzaddik
passes away his powers increase manifold. This is what the
Talmud says (*Chullin* 7b): "Tzaddikim are greater after their
passing than when they were alive" and this gives us great
cause to celebrate. Since Rabbi Shimon was so outstanding
during his lifetime, it stands to reason that now, after having
shed his corporeality, his ability to work the rectifications he
labored to achieve during his life has become all the more
potent (*Likutey Halakhot, Hekhsher Keilim* 4:4). Is this not something
for us to rejoice over? Today, nearly two thousand years
later, Rabbi Shimon's power to intercede on our behalf and
help us come closer to God is even greater than when he
was alive. As Rabbi Shimon himself said, "I have the power
to correct the entire world; I can exempt the whole world from
Heavenly judgment" (*Sukkah* 45b). And, Reb Noson writes, this
is true of all the other Tzaddikim as well.

While Rebbe Nachman was still alive, he made a promise
in front of two witnesses (Reb Aharon of Breslov and Reb
Naftali). He said: "Whoever comes to my gravesite, recites
the ten psalms of the General Remedy and gives something
to charity for my sake, even if his sins are many and grave,
I will do everything in my power — spanning the length and
breadth of creation — to cleanse and protect him.... By his
peyot (sidelocks) I'll pull him out of Gehennom. It makes no
difference what he did until that day, but from that day on,
he must take it upon himself not to return to his foolish
ways" (*Tzaddik* #122; *Rabbi Nachman's Wisdom* #141). (At Rebbe
Nachman's gravesite, one should first set aside the coins for
charity, and then recite the Ten Psalms; *Rabbi Yaakov Meir
Schechter*).

"You can rely upon me!" Rebbe Nachman insisted (*Tzaddik* #88). Before he passed away he said, "I have finished... and I will finish!" (*Tzaddik* #126).

* * *

THE TZADDIK IN TODAY'S WORLD

To conclude, it remains for us to consider how the role of the Tzaddik is viewed in this generation by various Breslover Chassidim. First though, we have some important concepts from Reb Noson, who covered this topic at great length in his *Likutey Halakhot*.

*

Tzaddik of the generation. Reb Noson writes: During the Revelation on Mount Sinai all the Jews were brought to a level of prophecy. This prophetic quality gave them clarity of imagination, which in turn meant that they would always have the ability to renew and increase their faith. It was Moshe Rabeinu who brought the Jews to this level. Without his direction they would not have been worthy of receiving the Torah, prophecy or faith.... This teaches us that we must always seek the True Tzaddik in each and every generation. He possesses an aspect of this prophecy and, by guiding us to clarity of imagination, he helps us renew our faith.

There seems to be a paradox here. Our Sages tell us that all Jews were present for the Giving of the Torah: our souls were there and we all attained the level of prophecy needed for clarity of imagination and faith. If so, why is it necessary to seek the Tzaddik? We've already undergone this purification at Sinai, and our faith has already been made pure. Actually, this question is quite similar to the often raised objection: What need is there ever to travel to the Tzaddik? If the Torah, which we received at Sinai, can clarify our faith, why bother travelling to the Tzaddikim for this? We can get it from all the books of Torah, just by studying them in our homes. Yet, doesn't the Rebbe stress that we *must* travel to the Tzaddik, for without attachment to the Tzaddik we cannot have pure faith?

But, answers Reb Noson, Rebbe Nachman's teachings are everlasting truth, and they are clear to anyone who seeks wisdom. True, complete faith is something which we must draw upon ourselves on a daily basis. Each day in creation, each day in a person's life, is something entirely new and different that never before existed. Accordingly, each day, God's Kingship and Glory manifest themselves in an entirely unique and original manner and this necessitates that our search for God be a continuing and ever-developing process. Therefore, each day must see a renewal of faith. It's not enough that we had faith, even pure faith, yesterday — or many yesterdays ago.

What's more, we were all created with free will. In other words, as long as we live we face the ongoing challenge of choosing right from wrong. And since each day is different, the Evil Inclination is always finding new ways and means to overpower us and destroy our trust in God. This means that we must constantly overcome new tests and obstacles that have the power to distance us from God and undermine our faith. To overcome these unprecedented hurdles and obstructions, and to remain absolutely firm in faith, our having already received the Torah together with our own personal study of its teachings proves insufficient. Only the True Tzaddikim of our generation can provide the original lessons and Torah interpretations necessary for battling and defeating the new doubts and uncertainties which each new day brings. Only through the Tzaddik can we come to *new* revelations of Torah and faith.

This can be better understood in light of what happened with the sin of the Golden Calf. The Jews had been miraculously redeemed from Egypt, they witnessed miracle after miracle at the crossing of the Red Sea and in the desert, culminating with the Revelation of God Himself at Mount Sinai. They were purified of their pollutions and they were endowed with prophecy. And forty days later — lo and behold, they made an idol! We have to ask ourselves this: Is there anything more powerful than man's ability to exercise free will?! Just imagine how compelling the Evil Inclination must be if it was able to mislead the people after so many wonders!

The Talmud teaches that the making of the Golden Calf was prompted by Satan's showing the Jews that Moshe had died (*Shabbat* 89a). Thrown into panic by what they assumed was the loss of the Tzaddik of their generation, they saw themselves as leaderless and hurriedly made an idol to guide and protect them. As soon as Moshe reappeared, he destroyed the idol and later brought the Second Tablets. By doing this, he was able to reinstill faith in the hearts of the Jewish people. The lesson we learn from this is clear: we must constantly strengthen ourselves with renewed faith, faith drawn into us by the power of the Tzaddik.

Reb Noson continues: As it was for the Jews in the desert, so it is for us today: Faith in the Tzaddikim is the main battleground between Satan and the Jewish people. In each age the Evil Inclination renews its attack, specifically against the True Tzaddik of that generation. Usually, this is done by rousing human opposition — often from the most prominent individuals of the Jewish communities — against the True Tzaddik. By doing this, Satan hopes to conceal and isolate the generation's Tzaddik much as he convinced the Jews in the desert that their True Tzaddik, Moshe, had died.

This has been borne out historically. A certain Tzaddik appeared in a generation, only to be questioned, challenged and criticized. Years later, often after the Tzaddik and his critics were no longer alive, people would look back and see that he really was a Tzaddik and his teachings were really new revelations of Torah and faith. They would not, however, say this about the Tzaddik who appeared in their own generation. He would be ridiculed and doubted, just as the Tzaddik of the previous generation had been. Of course, afterwards — when he is no longer the Tzaddik of the current generation — he too is accepted. But then, the generation has questions about the Tzaddik of its own age and so on.

Today, who doesn't recognize the holy Ari as the greatest Kabbalist of modern times, as unquestionably the True Tzaddik of his generation? Yet, in his own time, he encountered great opposition. His contemporaries refused to accept that in their day and age it was possible for a Tzaddik to appear with such awesome levels of prophecy, holiness and insights into the esoteric teachings of the Kabbalah. Years later, when the generation had been given a new Tzaddik, Satan no longer sought to conceal his greatness and the Ari was accepted by all. The same is true of the Baal Shem Tov. He was such a wondrous, awesome light, yet he was opposed and persecuted endlessly. His detractors had already admitted to the Ari's great qualities and uniqueness, but they could not accept the Tzaddik of their own generation — the Baal Shem Tov. Yet, years later, he too was recognized as having been the True Tzaddik.

Since the True Tzaddik faces constant opposition, unfortunately, his light is kept concealed from the world. His attempt to reveal the truth from the darkness is an ongoing battle. Our attempts to recognize, accept and attach ourselves to the True Tzaddik is also an ongoing battle. All sorts of camouflage, in the form of strife and argument, stands ready to prevent us from connecting with him and thereby renewing our faith. Therefore, we have no choice but to search constantly for the truth. We must seek and seek again for where the truth lies, there the True Tzaddik can be found *Likutey Halakhot, Birkhat haRei'ach* 4:31-33).

*

Elsewhere, Reb Noson goes into greater detail in discussing the mistake which the Jews made when they approached Aharon to make the Golden Calf. They said to him (Exodus 32:1): "Make a god to lead us. For the man Moshe, the one who brought us out of Egypt, we know not what has become of him." Reb Noson writes: Now, those of you who wish to study the Torah with an eye of truth, come see that the entire error which the Jews made came about because they did not seek Moshe Rabeinu. They briefly entertained the thought that he disappeared, and as a result ended up committing idolatry.

This is what is meant (Deuteronomy 31:29), "I know that after I die, you will become corrupt..." But haven't we seen that the Tzaddik never dies? (see above). The answer is that the Tzaddik dies from our side — we feel that the Tzaddik is no longer with us.... As long as we are bound to the Tzaddik, we can benefit from him and his teachings. But, when the Tzaddik is no longer part of our reality, then we become corrupt.

Thus our pursuit of the True Tzaddik has to be a continuous search, an unending quest. Even after the Tzaddik passes away, there always remains an individual, and sometimes many, who have received the teachings of the Tzaddik and are qualified to pass them on to others. No generation is orphaned, the Tzaddik leaves over his blessings — his teachings — in this world and they can be found with his followers (Likutey Halakhot, Shluchin 5:10-12).

*

Seeking the truth. Rebbe Nachman always taught: Seek the truth. Search for it. Rise above your *nitzachon,* your desire for victory. Rise above the silliness of pride and anger. Just pray to God that He open your eyes. Reb Noson himself, throughout his *Likutey Halakhot,* expresses the importance of always seeking the truth —the True Tzaddik. As we've seen, it is a search which is ongoing and perpetual, and we have to be persistent and never-tiring in our efforts.

Someone asked Reb Moshe Breslover: "You are always talking about the True Tzaddik. Where can I find him?"

"Apparently Pharaoh was smarter than you," Reb Moshe replied. "When Yosef predicted that there were going to be Seven Years of Plenty and Seven Years of Famine, he advised Pharaoh to appoint a wise man to oversee the stockpiling of the harvest of the seven good years. Pharaoh answered that if Yosef was smart enough to foresee the need to appoint a wise man, he must be that man.

"So, too, in our case," concluded Reb Moshe. "Rebbe Nachman always talked about the True Tzaddik. He must have known what it's all about!" (*Rabbi Nachman Burstein*).

Reb Noson sincerely sought the True Tzaddik. He found Rebbe Nachman. And he followed the Rebbe to the end. He gave his life for Rebbe Nachman and his teachings. Yet, despite all of this, Reb Noson repeats over and over, "Search for the truth, again and again." Who's he talking to? Who is Reb Noson telling that we have to keep looking and looking for the True Tzaddik? It can't be the Breslover Chassidim — they study Rebbe Nachman's teachings. And it can't be the non-Breslover — they don't read Reb Noson's *Likutey Halakhot* and don't even know of his advice. So who was Reb Noson talking to? The answer is that there is always a part of us which has questions, many questions — especially as Rebbe Nachman is not here today in the flesh to answer them for us. Therefore, the search for truth becomes an endless search, even for those who think they've already found it. Even for those who've found Breslov teachings and are convinced that they've finally come to the truth, the search must go on, the search for *real* truth.

Undoubtedly, every Breslover Chassid would say that the True Tzaddik of today is Rebbe Nachman. But then, every chassidic group would say the same about their *Rebbe*. For that matter, every Yeshivah student would probably feel the same way about his Rosh Yeshivah or a leading rabbinical authority. Our purpose in this book is to explain the Breslov viewpoint.

Reb Noson writes: Why do we see that those who choose truth are despised? For truth is trodden upon. The main reason for the delay in Mashiach's coming is the strife and opposition to the True Tzaddikim (*Likutey Halakhot, Netilat Yadayim li'Seudah* 6:74).

Ultimately, truth will speak for itself, making itself known to those who sincerely search for it. Therefore, let everyone seek his own truth, for if the real truth — the *emeser emes* — is our goal, we will soon realize that we have no choice but to pray extremely hard for it. We will plead with God to be able to find the real truth, and by virtue of this, God *will* ultimately lead us to it.

*

The Breslover view. Rebbe Nachman said: Rabbi Shimon bar Yochai was a unique figure, as everyone knows. From the time of Rabbi Shimon (2nd century) until the time of the Ari (1534-1572), the world was quiet. (In other words, there were no new revelations of Torah comparable to those of Rabbi Shimon.) Then the Ari came and revealed entirely new and original teachings. From the time of the Ari until the time of the Baal Shem Tov (1700-1760), the world was again quiet. Then the Baal Shem Tov, a totally unique figure, came and revealed completely new teachings. Then once again, from the Baal Shem Tov until the present, the world has again been quiet. But now I am beginning to reveal awesome and exalted teachings, teachings which are entirely new and original (*Tzaddik* #279). The Rebbe added: And from myself until Mashiach, there will be no more original figures (*Rabbi Eliyahu Chaim Rosen*).

In the mind of every Breslover Chassid, Rebbe Nachman is truly the Tzaddik, not only of his generation — but until Mashiach comes. His teachings are universal, covering the entire spectrum of Judaism. They maintain their freshness and are inspiring; they give hope and encouragement, assurance and motivation to anyone and everyone, from all walks of life. And, Rebbe Nachman said: "I did not come to the world for myself. I came to the world to bring the Jewish souls closer to God. But, I can only help someone who comes to me and tells me what he needs" (*Tzaddik* #307).

Ask anyone who has been touched by Rebbe Nachman's teachings what inspired him and he'll answer, "Rebbe Nachman speaks to me directly." One present day Breslover summed it up this way: "I find it absolutely amazing that the words of someone who lived in the late 18th and early 19th centuries in Eastern Europe can, two hundred years later, relate directly to someone such as myself, a product of 20th century western civilization." Or, as Reb Avraham Sternhartz once remarked, "I have proof that Rebbe Nachman was a truly wise and remarkable person. He was a young man. Yet he could relate to and advise even elderly people."

Open any book of Rebbe Nachman's teachings and you'll find advice for countless situations. The Rebbe always seems to have something to say for what you're going through right now. Review that same material some time later, when other concerns occupy your thoughts, and you'll find in it an entirely new set of directions — advice specifically applicable to your new situation and circumstances. This is hard to explain to anyone who has never experienced Rebbe Nachman nor had the good fortune to study the Rebbe's works. His teachings are bottomless wellsprings, everflowing brooks of life and vitality. We need only avail ourselves of them to benefit from their amazing resources.

You need only look around yourself to see the growing interest in Rebbe Nachman and his teachings. Of all the great leaders and Tzaddikim we have had in the past, who else foresaw these generations and prepared so much material to advise and strengthen people, regardless of their situation? (*Rabbi Moshe Kramer*).

Rebbe Nachman said: "I am a river which cleanses from all stains" (*Tzaddik* #332). Whoever has taken the Rebbe's advice and spoken to God in *hitbodedut* knows the wonderful sensation of being able to open one's heart and pour out his innermost feelings. He knows that no matter where he is, God is with him, waiting for him to repent and come closer. He also knows that no matter how bad things get in life, when the time comes and his days in this world are done, he can always rely on the strength and power of the True Tzaddik to argue his case before the Heavenly Court. And he knows that in the end, the True Tzaddik — Rebbe Nachman — will rectify and cleanse his soul.

"Yes, Rebbe Nachman speaks directly to me."

And, as much as we might feel an affinity toward Rebbe Nachman and his teachings, rest assured that Rebbe Nachman feels the same way towards us. As Reb Noson once said, "Whoever just attaches himself to the Rebbe, the Rebbe will not leave that person until he's been rectified" (*Siach Sarfei Kodesh* 1-713).

*

For today. "So, we have to bind ourselves to the True Tzaddik. So, we look to him for advice and spiritual direction. We have just one more question for the Breslover Chassid: So, whom do you go to for advice?"

This is a question often asked of Breslover Chassidim today. It's a very good question. Rebbe Nachman, though here in spirit, is unfortunately not here in the flesh. What does a Breslover do when he has a question or problem and needs counseling?

Reb Noson mentions that each and every age has in it a Tzaddik of that generation. After Rebbe Nachman passed away (1810), the Breslover Chassidim were divided; however, the majority became followers of Reb Noson and went to him for advice. After Reb Noson's passing (1844), Reb Nachman Chazan (d. 1884), Reb Noson's closest follower, became the leader for most of the chassidim. In his time, Reb Nachman of Tcherin (d. 1894), a leading halakhic authority and a recognized genius in Torah, also gave counsel to many of the chassidim. Until then the center of Breslover Chassidut had been either in the city of Breslov itself or had just moved to Uman. In both places there was easy access to the Breslover leaders when one wanted to ask advice. As the movement grew, so did the requirement to have additional leaders who were knowledgable in Torah and Rebbe Nachman's teachings — luminaries who could disseminate this treasure to future generations.

The next generation of leaders which emerged came from those Breslover Chassidim who had received the tradition and had greater knowledge of Rebbe Nachman's teachings and were able to convert them into advice and practice. This included such prominent figures as Reb Yitzchok Breiter (1886-1943?), Reb Avraham Chazan (1849-1918) and Reb Avraham Sternhartz (1862-1955), to mention but a few. In this latest generation, we have been fortunate to receive guidance from various leaders, each a Tzaddik in his own right, who themselves received from those mentioned above. Thus, the chain of capable leaders continues until today.

As to why Breslov Chassidut (after the Rebbe's passing) has always had several leaders and not any single one — why there has never been another *Rebbe?!* — we return to what was said earlier about the Master of Prayer: he was able to appear differently to each individual. In today's world, Breslovers come from and live in all walks of life. Rebbe Nachman could sit with the great Tzaddikim and Torah

scholars of his generation, the followers of the Magid of
Mezritch and the leading rabbinical authorities; he could sit
with Reb Noson and Reb Naftali and others of his inner
circle; he could sit with the simple folk who came for advice
and blessings; and he could sit and match wits with leading
aristocrats, including the leaders of the *Haskalah* movement
in the Ukraine. Today, no single personality could span such a
spectrum as Rebbe Nachman did. Thus, whoever joins Rebbe
Nachman's following, no matter what his family background
or level (or lack) of religious education, always has someone
whom he can relate to and from whom he can receive — i.e.
the Rebbe himself. As Reb Noson said: "There are a few
who have received the Tzaddik's teachings and are qualified
to pass them on" (*Likutey Halakhot, Shluchin* 5:12).

So, to those who ask if Breslov wouldn't be better off
if it had a "unified command," the answer is, "Yes. But!"
Our weakness is our strength. Other groups, chassidim and
mitnagdim alike, have their hierarchy and structure. It has
many benefits, but not everyone can join and not everyone
relates. Breslov, on the other hand, because it is not rigidly
structured, is much more open. Anyone can find a place. And
even so, the search for *the* leader, the True Tzaddik, must
still continue.

*

Rebbe Nachman once spoke about the achievements of the
Baal Shem Tov and other Tzaddikim. He said: They succeeded
in improving the world. But after they passed away, the effects
of their work did not endure. I wish my "thing" to continue.
That is, my followers should make additional followers; those
followers should make other followers... (*Tzaddik* #373).

The truth which the Baal Shem Tov came to reveal to the
world has to a large extent lost its effect, because it was
changed from its original form. Notice that Rebbe Nachman
said to "make followers..." — followers not leaders. The

great Tzaddikim know their awesome levels and what can be accomplished if their teachings are followed properly. But when the followers make amendments and try to fit the "Rebbe" into their own ideas and perspectives, then the effect of the original teaching becomes distorted and cannot accomplish its original intention. In this, Breslover Chassidut differs greatly from the other chassidic groups. They have never changed, nor distorted, the teachings of Rebbe Nachman. There are no leaders in Breslov — just followers of the Rebbe (Rabbi Nachman Burstein).

As the Rebbe himself said, "My fire will burn until Mashiach comes" (Tzaddik #126).

* * *

Rebbe Nachman said: Surely the main struggle a person has in life is to reach the ultimate goal. In this life, one cannot really savor the true meaning or feeling of being close to the Tzaddik owing to the gross physicality of the body and all the other obstacles.

Therefore, the main thing is to strive for the ultimate goal. Then, when you leave this world after a long and full life, you will understand what you heard long before. More than this, there will be the spiritual joys each one will attain. Happy is he who remains strong in his faith in God and the True Tzaddik, and who fulfills what the Tzaddik says. He will never be disgraced or put to shame either in this world or in the World to Come (Tzaddik #227).

* * *

18

ROSH HASHANNAH

"My very essence is Rosh HaShannah!" (*Tzaddik* #403).

Anyone even slightly familiar with Rebbe Nachman's teachings knows of the paramount importance attached to this holiday within Breslov circles. From near and far, people came to Rebbe Nachman for Rosh HaShannah, to spend the beginning of each year with him. Even after his passing, this practice continued. Breslovers flocked to Uman to pray at Rebbe Nachman's grave on the eve of Rosh HaShannah and to attend the *kibutz*, the gathering of his followers, on the holiday.

When Breslover Chassidut spread throughout Poland, the chassidim would cross the border into Russia before Rosh HaShannah. Even some of those who lived in Israel at the turn of the century made the long and arduous journey to Uman. When the Bolshevik Revolution closed the Russian border, other *kibutzim* arose where the chassidim gathered together. The first was in Lublin, in the Yeshivah of Chakhmei Lublin, headed by Rabbi Meir Shapiro. This continued until Nazi Germany exterminated Polish Jewry. Then two other *kibutzim* were established in the Holy Land: one in Jerusalem and one in Meron at the gravesite of Rabbi Shimon bar Yochai. After the Second World War, a third *kibutz* began in New York for those chassidim who had made their way to the "New World."

The thought of not being present at the *kibutz* for Rosh HaShannah never entered the mind of the committed chasid.

The reasons, though many, really boil down to faith in the Tzaddik and his teachings. The Rebbe himself put it this way: "My Rosh HaShannah is greater than everything... No one should be missing! My very essence is Rosh HaShannah!" (*Tzaddik* #403).

* * *

WHAT IS ROSH HASHANNAH

The head. The year is a complete construct. It has a head, a heart, arms, feet and so on. The individual parts correspond to the twelve months. For example, the first day of the year is the head — the *rosh* — of the year. Just as the head directs the body, so too, one's Rosh HaShannah will determine the outcome of the rest of the year. Thus, our Sages teach: On Rosh HaShannah it is decreed what will be at the end of the year (*Rosh HaShannah* 8b). Whatever takes place at the very end of Elul, the last month in the Jewish calendar, was already decreed at its "head," at the very beginning of the year.

Rosh HaShannah is not one of the three festive holidays. It is, as it is otherwise called, the Day of Judgment. Our health, our wealth — indeed, our very lives — are at stake. In a sense, it is a repeat of Creation. In order to create something new, we need a sense of judgment. Should we go ahead? Will we be successful? Rosh HaShannah is no different. It requires, from God's side, a new creation: a New Year. The year to come has not yet been, and needs to be brought into existence. Creation.

Just as construction of a building requires a blueprint, so too, the construction of the year needs a specific plan. Just as an architect draws up the blueprints for the building, so is God the architect of the year. His plans are prepared and drafted on Rosh HaShannah.

Reb Noson writes: I heard from Rebbe Nachman that he had a lesson about Rosh HaShannah and the importance of travelling to the Tzaddik for Rosh HaShannah. There are three *roshim* (three heads) that gather together at that time: the Tzaddik is the *Rosh B'nei Yisrael* (the "head" of the Jews); *Rosh* HaShannah is the "head" of the year; and each and every Jew comes with his *rosh* (his "head") to be by the Tzaddik on Rosh HaShannah (*Likutey Moharan* II, 94).

So, Rosh HaShannah is not merely the first day of the Jewish calendar. It is the outline for the entire year. Aside from his many other considerations, Rebbe Nachman places paramount importance on Rosh HaShannah because he wants to impress upon us the significance of the "head" — what we can accomplish if we attempt to begin the year right and have our "heads" — our thoughts — in the right place.

Therefore, Rebbe Nachman teaches: We must be *wise* on Rosh HaShannah and only think good, positive thoughts: that God will be good to us and give us a good year. And, because Rosh HaShannah is associated with thought rather than speech, the Rebbe also counsels us to be very careful to speak as little as possible on Rosh HaShannah (*Rabbi Nachman's Wisdom* #21).

*

The shofar. Rosh HaShannah is also innately connected with the sounding of the ram's horn. The Talmud, Midrash, Zohar, as well as all the later writings, offer numerous insights to explain this connection. Rebbe Nachman's teachings are no exception. In one lesson, the Rebbe says that the blasts of the shofar sweeten the severity of God's judgment (*Likutey Moharan* I, 42). Elsewhere, he expounds on the interpretations given in the holy teachings that sounding the shofar is intended to arouse people from spiritual sleep and prevent them from idling away their days in slumber. The Rebbe shows how this is related to the concepts of starting anew and conceiving a child, both of which are linked to the New Year (*Likutey Moharan* I, 60:9).

Rebbe Nachman also associates the sound of the shofar with the sound of thunder. Anyone hearing the shofar's blasts on Rosh HaShannah from a man of true piety can be assured that he will not be afraid of thunder throughout the year. This is because his blowing of the shofar is in itself an aspect of thunder and it instills true fear — the fear of Heaven — in a person's heart. When his heart feels this thunder, it is moved to rejoice (*Likutey Moharan* I, 5:3). Thus, when we include the blowing of the shofar by a pious person into the blueprint of our year, we can look forward to fear of Heaven and a joyous heart throughout the entire year.

* * *

ROSH HASHANNAH WITH THE TZADDIK

Rebbe Nachman teaches: People travel to the Tzaddik for Rosh HaShannah. The reason is as follows: Decrees pertaining to the entire year are issued on Rosh HaShannah. As such, this is the main time for mitigating and "sweetening" any decree. Now, sweetening must take place at its source, in Thought on High, and can only be accomplished when we first purify our own thoughts. Yet, try as we might, the only way we can achieve this purity of thought is through the Tzaddik. So, we travel to Tzaddikim for Rosh HaShannah in order to purify our minds, and this brings about kindness and compassion for the entire year (*Likutey Moharan* I, 211).

On Rosh HaShannah, all of creation comes before God to be judged (*Rosh HaShannah* 16a). We are judged for every act, every word, even every thought. If we truly believe this, we know that we have cause for concern. Rabbi Levi Yitzchak of Berdichov used to say, "When Elul comes around, I feel it [the fear] in my shoulders" (*Rabbi Eliyahu Chaim Rosen*).

So what are we to do? Repent. But, if things are as bad as we think they are, what chance do we have? The charge sheet is a few pages long, maybe even a few reams long. The credit sheet is at best so-so. Is there really any hope of repenting for everything?

Rebbe Nachman teaches: Each judgment, each decree, is a constriction, having its own precise and specific means by which it can be mitigated. This is because a decree can only be sweetened at its source, and the source of each judgment is limited to a specific part of Upper Wisdom. Someone who wishes to set aside each and every judgment and transform it into compassion and kindness must rise to each one of these sources, individually.

There is, however, a *Seikhel HaKollel* (an All Inclusive Wisdom) which surpasses all individual Wisdoms. Someone who attains this *Seikhel HaKollel* is capable of sweetening all decrees, because all individual judgments emanate from this Inclusive Wisdom. This is why people travel to the Tzaddikim for Rosh HaShannah. Each person comes with his individual constriction, his own good and bad. Because the Tzaddik can rise to the highest of sources, he is the embodiment of the *Seikhel HaKollel*. He can take each constriction, each judgment and decree, and sweeten it (*Likutey Moharan* I, 61:6,7).

Rosh HaShannah is a day of judgment, when dire decrees can be issued against a person or his family, God forbid. Yet, it also contains its own antidote against strict judgment. Therefore, even if a person may not have been all he should have been during the year, he has a chance, a good chance, to make amends and begin afresh. The New Year brings with it an opportunity for a new start, so that even if the charge sheet is indeed long, the seemingly impossible task of setting everything right can be made much easier by travelling to the Tzaddik. As a "first class defense attorney," he is capable of arguing on our behalf by rising even to the All Inclusive Wisdom to sweeten any decree.

* * *

PREPARING FOR ROSH HASHANNAH

You might think that because Rosh HaShannah is so great and awesome, it requires tremendous preparations. And you know what? You're right! During the last month of the Jewish year, the month of Elul, all Jews begin anticipating the Day of Judgment. In one way or another, we all begin preparing ourselves for the New Year. Some buy tickets at their nearby synagogue, many start preparing festival meals and some even go so far as to actually contemplate repentance. They increase their study of Torah or they settle their "loose accounts" and request forgiveness from those they may have slighted. "Many recite Psalms" (*Likutey Moharan* II, 73), and extra efforts are put into praying. Chanah Tzirel, Reb Noson's daughter, once remarked, "Now that Elul is coming and everyone will begin thinking of repentance, remember that Elul brings with it its own set of obstacles and problems" (*Rabbi Michel Dorfman*).

*

Study. Rebbe Nachman suggested to some of his followers to read through the entire *TaNaKh* (Bible) during the days of Elul, the Ten Days of Repentance, and until Hoshanna Rabbah [the last of the intermediate days of Sukkot, the final day of judgment] (*Rabbi Nachman's Wisdom* #251; *Zohar* 2:142a).

Rebbe Nachman also said that after regular worship during the month of Elul, it is customary to recite the *Tikkuney Zohar,* as well as many prayers and petitions. The efforts put into these devotions are all valued on High and are made into great and lofty things (*Rabbi Nachman's Wisdom* #294).

Reb Noson once said, "Even just reciting the teachings of Rebbe Nachman — *Likutey Moharan, Sefer HaMiddot, Sippurey Ma'asiot* and his *Sichot* — is a tremendous *segulah* (potent power), similar to reciting the *Zohar* and *Tikkunim.*" He added: "It is a great mitzvah to recite them all in the month of Elul [and the Days of Awe]. It helps tremendously [to purify the soul, preparing it for the Days of Judgment]" (*Kokhavey Or*, p. 77f #26,27).

In Uman, the custom of those who studied Rebbe Nachman's works during Elul was varied. Some began on Rosh Chodesh Elul while others began on the Shabbat before Elul, when the New Moon was announced. Still others began on the fifteenth of Av (*Rabbi Eliyahu Chaim Rosen*).

*

Cleansing. Rebbe Nachman teaches: Elul connotes guarding the Covenant — *shemirat haBrit* (*Likutey Moharan* II, 87). This is why we should make every effort to cleanse ourselves and increase our level of holiness during the month of Elul. There is a dual advantage to working on *shemirat haBrit* during this month. First, the month itself, because it is the month of repentance, is intrinsically geared to assist us in our struggle. And secondly, the spiritual advances we make in Elul get us ready for Rosh HaShannah — the Day of Judgment.

The Kabbalistic meditations for the month of Elul center around the dire need to cleanse oneself of arrogance, haughtiness and pride (see *Likutey Moharan* II, 82). Therefore, the days (of Elul) themselves, provide extra support for the person who wishes to subdue and even eliminate these evil characteristics from his personality.

Rebbe Nachman also teaches: In addition to diminishing your pride, work on developing modesty. This should be developed to such a point that you can hear yourself being embarrassed and not retort. Such silence will cleanse you and bring you to true repentance — even to the highest levels of repentance (*Likutey Moharan* I, 6:1).

With regard to cleansing oneself through repentance, the Rebbe counseled: If a person merits to truly feel the pain and anguish of his sins, and he regrets these acts, then his offspring must also feel some of that regret. The best time for this is Elul (*Likutey Moharan* I, 141).

In addition, Rebbe Nachman said that the day before Rosh HaShannah is a very good time for presenting a *pidyon* (*Rabbi Nachman's Wisdom* #214), whereby one gives charity to the Tzaddik in the hope of redeeming oneself in the eyes of Heaven and cleansing the soul. Nowadays, Breslover Chassidim give their redemption money to an elder of the community on Erev Rosh HaShannah.

The prayers and devotions of the Breslover Chassidim prior to Rosh HaShannah were fulfilled with such great fervor that Rebbe Nachman once remarked, "Other Tzaddikim wish themselves a Rosh HaShannah as good as our Erev Rosh HaShannah" (*Imrot Tehorot*).

* * *

REBBE NACHMAN'S ROSH HASHANNAH

The following is a sampling of the statements by Rebbe Nachman and the chassidim after him, on the importance and great value of the Rebbe's Rosh HaShannah:

"My Rosh HaShannah is something completely new. God gave me the gift of knowing what Rosh HaShannah is" (*Tzaddik* #406).

"Anyone who has the privilege of being with the Rebbe on Rosh HaShannah is entitled to be very, very happy" (*Tzaddik* #403).

There were people who all through the year were unable to obtain their rectification. Even the Rebbe himself was unable to give them their *tikkun*. But on Rosh HaShannah, he could help them. He said that on Rosh HaShannah he was able to make certain *tikkunim* which he was not able to achieve throughout the rest of the year (*Tzaddik* #406).

"What other Tzaddikim work to accomplish from Rosh HaShannah until Hoshanna Rabbah, I achieve on the first night of the New Year" (*Siach Sarfei Kodesh* 1-75). On the first night of Rosh HaShannah, Rebbe Nachman would stand in silent *d'veikut* (cleaving to God) for four hours as he recited the *Amidah* Prayer. His followers would finish praying without him, go home to eat, then return to sit with him at his meal (*Siach Sarfei Kodesh* 1-304).

Reb Noson writes: There are many obstacles to overcome in order to be with Rebbe Nachman for Rosh HaShannah. These must be confronted. There were instances when people came to the Rebbe some time prior to Rosh HaShannah, complaining about their many difficulties and obstacles. The Rebbe told them to stay at home. However, the real truth is, if a person wants to rectify his soul, then he must make every effort to be with the Rebbe for Rosh HaShannah. The Tzaddik cannot tell a person to undertake something which involves supreme sacrifice, even though he wants the person to make the sacrifice and break all the barriers. Therefore, the person who wants to do what's right will make every effort to overcome all obstacles and be present among Rebbe Nachman's followers on Rosh HaShannah. This applies to all generations (*Tzaddik* #406).

When rejecting the suggestion of a chassid who thought it might be preferable if he came to the Rebbe at a less crowded time of the year, Rebbe Nachman said, "Whether you eat or don't eat; whether you sleep or don't sleep; whether you pray or don't pray [with proper concentration]; just make sure you are with me for Rosh HaShannah" (*Tzaddik* #404).

At one point, Rebbe Nachman gave each of his followers a list of fasts they should undertake for repentance and rectification. After a while he abolished this practice, saying, "Anyone who does not come for Rosh HaShannah should not fast. And anyone who does come, certainly has no need to fast" (*Tzaddik* #491).

On one Rosh HaShannah in Uman, after Rebbe Nachman's passing, there was a great and awesome arousal of emotions during the prayers. Reb Noson said: "I believe that the Rebbe is here with us now. And if the Rebbe is here with us, so are the Seven Shepherds (Avraham, Yitzchak, Yaakov, Moshe, Aharon, Yosef and David)." Those who witnessed Reb Noson saying this described him as if he were actually looking at these Tzaddikim at that moment (*Siach Sarfei Kodesh* 1-590).

*

Reb Noson once remarked, "Even if the road to Uman were paved with knives, I would crawl there — just so that I could be by Rebbe Nachman for Rosh HaShannah" (*Tovot Zikhronot* p.137).

Reb Abba Shochet and his son, Reb Shmuel, set out on their journey from Tcherin so that they could spend Rosh HaShannah 5570 (1809) with Rebbe Nachman in Breslov. As a gift for the Rebbe, Reb Abba had purchased a very beautiful silver goblet. On the way, they were caught in an abnormally heavy downpour and could find no wagon driver willing to travel in such weather. They soon realized that they were in danger of not reaching Breslov in time for the holiday. Finally, they found one driver who was willing to take them, but only if Reb Abba agreed to his price. Although he was being asked to pay an absurd amount of money to complete the journey, Reb Abba accepted. How could he not be with the Rebbe for Rosh HaShannah?! But much to the disappointment of the two chassidim, they soon discovered that the roads had become muddy and travel was very difficult. It was already noontime of the day before Rosh HaShannah when they reached Heisin (30 km. from Breslov), and the possibility loomed large that they might have to spend the holiday somewhere on the road. Reb Abba pressed the wagon driver, a simple Jew, to drive faster. After cracking his whip once or twice, the driver called to his horses, "*Nu, kinderlakh. Tzum Rebben!* —Children, hurry hurry. To the Rebbe." Suddenly, the horses began travelling faster and faster, and Reb Abba and his son arrived in Breslov during the Minchah Prayer. They had no time to greet Rebbe Nachman before the holiday.

Later that evening, with all the chassidim gathered around the Rebbe for the *tish* (the meal), Rebbe Nachman said to Reb Abba, "Abba! Tell us about your journey." Reb Abba told of the difficulties he and his son had encountered along the way, and he admitted he had had no choice but to pay the wagon driver with the silver goblet he had bought to give the Rebbe. "How can I praise you for this journey?" Rebbe Nachman said to Reb Abba. "For the goblet, I will knock out the eyes and teeth of Satan. As for you, Abba, there is no reward great enough in this world. And you, Reb Shmuel, you get the soup!" Shortly after Rosh HaShannah, Reb Abba passed away. His son, Reb Shmuel, turned his hand to business and soon became extremely wealthy. Everyone then understood the meaning of what Rebbe Nachman had said to Reb Abba and Reb Shmuel at his Rosh HaShannah *tish* (*Aveneha Barzel* p.48 #76; *Siach Sarfei Kodesh* 1-198).

The obstacles to spending Rosh HaShannah with the Rebbe's *kibutz* have always existed. They have a way of coming from anywhere and everywhere, not the least of which from the families of the chassidim themselves. Wives have always objected to their husbands going away for the holiday. Reb Noson once remarked about this, "It is one of God's miracles that Yom Kippur comes right after Rosh HaShannah. This way, the members of the family have to forgive each other!" (*Rabbi Eliyahu Chaim Rosen; Siach Sarfei Kodesh* 1-665). As for the financial difficulties which the long journey inevitably produced, the Rebbe said, "I have already made it my business to take care of the expenses of those who come to me for Rosh HaShannah" (*Siach Sarfei Kodesh* 1-27).

*

Reb Avraham Sternhartz, who led the congregation as the *baal tefilah* in Uman for fifty years (and for twenty more years in Israel), writes: The awakening and arousal that came upon us on Erev Rosh HaShannah left an unforgettable impression upon all those who had the merit of being there. Who can forget what it was like when we recited *Z'khor Brit Selichot* and the Morning Prayers afterwards; when we poured out supplication from the depths of our hearts while standing at Rebbe Nachman's grave during the day; while we made the preparations for Rosh HaShannah itself, which began with the Afternoon Prayer two hours prior to the Holiday; and finally when we fervently recited the Rosh HaShannah prayers themselves. Even today, our ears still tingle, our hearts are uplifted by these beautiful memories. So powerful was the experience that many people became Breslover Chassidim because of the impression it made upon them (*Imrot Tehorot* p.95).

From Rebbe Nachman's time until today, the Breslover Chassidim have always come together on Rosh HaShannah. It is a time for renewing ties, for rejoicing, for having made it through the past year and looking forward to the one that lies ahead. But, it is far more than that. Rosh HaShannah is a time when all our inner feelings and longings — which we've expressed throughout the year in *hitbodedut* — come together. On this special day, all our yearnings swell up from inside us and manifest themselves in prayer and supplication, in pleading with God to grant us only good and prosperity throughout the forthcoming year.

What is it that moves one to such inspiration and fervor? For the Breslover Chassid who comes to Rebbe Nachman's gathering, it is his awareness and appreciation that these are truly the *Days of Awe*. As Rosh HaShannah approaches, his fear of and trepidation towards the important judgment that is about to be rendered is coupled with his faith that in the Rebbe, he has the best possible "defense attorney" one could hope to have. He arrives at the *kibutz* with a mixture of awe and joy, with a reverence for the day and a gladness for having been able to cast his lot together with all those who've joined Rebbe Nachman's *kibutz*. Anyone who's ever spent a Rosh HaShannah with the Breslover Chassidim can never — and will never — forget it.

* * *

ROSH HASHANNAH IN BRESLOV TODAY

Asked to describe a taste of what it's like to be a Breslover Chassid, Reb Eliyahu Chaim Rosen responded in the same fashion Rabeinu Tam did when asked what it's like to be a Jew (*Sefer HaYashar*): "You want me to give over the taste of Breslover Chassidut? It can't be done! Can you give the taste of eating a scrambled egg? We can talk about it and even describe the experience, but giving over the taste is impossible." The same is true of the Rebbe's Rosh HaShannah. The only way to taste it is by trying it yourself!

Throughout the generations, all those who've joined the *kibutz* for Rosh HaShannah have been filled with the same feelings of awe and reverence which filled the hearts of the chassidim in the Rebbe's time. This, despite the fact that most of Breslover Chassidut was destroyed in the Holocaust and, as of around 1940, travel into Soviet Russia for the *kibutz* became impossible. Over the past forty years, with the number of Rebbe Nachman's followers continuing to grow and grow, three yearly gatherings were established: in Meron and Jerusalem in the Holy Land, and in Brooklyn, New York. Arrangements for food and lodging are available in each of these places, even for last-minute arrivals.

With the writing of this chapter (late 1989), the first full-fledged Rosh HaShannah gathering in Uman for decades has just taken place. Close to 1,000 people, roughly 750 from the Holy Land, were granted permission to stay in Uman by the Soviet authorities. The area around Rebbe Nachman's gravesite was expanded to accommodate the large crowd. A renovated factory complex was converted into a large synagogue, a dining hall and kitchen, and full dormitory facilities. Even a mikvah was built, almost overnight.

It might seem a bit odd that people would actually leave Eretz Yisrael and travel to Russia for the holiday. From America, England, France or any of the other places in the Diaspora to which Breslover Chassidut has reached, this might seem logical. But to leave the Holy Land? For the answer, we refer the reader to the above chapter on the Tzaddik. Rebbe Nachman taught that the holiness of the graves of the Tzaddikim parallels the holiness of the Land of Israel. Thus, "those who travel to the graves of Tzaddikim are actually travelling from the Holy Land, to a Holy Land!" (*Rabbi Shmuel Shapiro*).

Our fervent hopes and prayers are that Rosh HaShannah 5750 (October 1989), will prove to have been a watershed in the yearly return of Breslover Chassidim to Uman for *Z'khor Brit Selichot* and the Rosh HaShannah *kibutz* near Rebbe Nachman's gravesite. As Rebbe Nachman said: "The entire world is dependent upon my Rosh HaShannah" (*Tzaddik #405*).

*

Our Sages teach: On Rosh HaShannah, three books are opened; one for the completely wicked, one for Tzaddikim and one for those in between. Tzaddikim are inscribed immediately for good, the completely wicked for bad and those in between are given time until Yom Kippur to repent (*Rosh HaShannah 16b*).

Reb Noson writes: Those who are attached to the Tzaddikim are inscribed together with the Tzaddikim (*Likutey Halakhot, Nezikin 5:17*). May we all be granted this year — and every year — to be written and inscribed in the Book of the Righteous, Amen.

* * *

19

ERETZ YISRAEL — THE HOLY LAND

Reb Yitzchok Breiter writes: Every day of your life, yearn, pray and make a practical effort to live in the Holy Land, or, at the very least, to walk four steps there. By doing this you will achieve patience and be able to advance from level to level, attaining complete holiness. This is the ultimate holy victory a person wins in this world (*Seder HaYom* #27).

Our Sages teach: Whoever walks four steps in Eretz Yisrael is promised a portion in the World to Come (*Ketubot* 111a). Having spent his childhood years among the leaders of the Chassidic movement, particularly some of those who took part in the first *aliyah* in 1787, Rebbe Nachman was no stranger to the pride of place that Eretz Yisrael should have in the heart and mind of the Jew. He surely knew that Moshe Rabeinu prayed five hundred and fifteen prayers so that he might merit entry into the Land, and was familiar with the many talmudic teachings regarding its import. In addition, the Rebbe was certainly aware that his great-grandfather, the Baal Shem Tov, nearly sacrificed his life in order to walk those treasured four cubits in the Holy Land.

*

At the conclusion of a quite complex and esoteric lesson, Rebbe Nachman says: When one comes to Eretz Yisrael, he is called a "mighty warrior" (*Likutey Moharan* I, 20:end).

Prior to beginning this lesson, Rebbe Nachman said: "Whoever wants to be a Jew — which means going from level to level — can only succeed through the Land of Israel. When he wins the battle and arrives in the Holy Land, he is then called a mighty warrior." Then the Rebbe gave his Lesson. After he finished, Reb Noson asked him, "What did you mean when you said that the Land of Israel is so great that this is the main victory?" The Rebbe answered, "I mean this Israel — with these houses and apartments!" He wanted every Jew who wished to be a true Jew, to go to Eretz Yisrael. Even if one encounters many difficulties, many great and seemingly insurmountable barriers, one must make every effort to get there.

Rebbe Nachman then talked about the tremendous obstacles and great dangers he faced during his pilgrimage to the Holy Land (*Tzaddik* #141).

* * *

Rebbe Nachman's pilgrimage to the Holy Land took place in 1798 at the height of the Napoleonic campaign in the Middle East. His return in 1799 was fraught with even greater dangers. His travels and travails are detailed in *Rabbi Nachman's Wisdom* (pp.33-97), *Tzaddik* (#26-47) and in *Until the Mashiach* (pp.24-55). We offer the reader some highlights from Rebbe Nachman's journey to show the reader what is meant by sacrificing oneself for the sake of a mitzvah.

REBBE NACHMAN'S PILGRIMAGE

Prior to Rebbe Nachman's journey, his family tried to dissuade him. His reply was, "Most of me is there already. The minority must follow the majority" (*Rabbi Nachman's Wisdom* p.36). Together with one of his followers, Rebbe Nachman set out on his journey from Medvedevka on LaG B'Omer (May 4, 1798). He traveled by land and sea, reaching Odessa, a port on the Black Sea. From there, he sailed to Istanbul shortly after Shavuot.

While in Istanbul, he was mistaken by two emissaries from the Holy Land for someone else, and they heaped abuse upon him. They went so far as to tell the ship's agent not to allow Rebbe Nachman passage on any ship. (Naturally, when the agent found out who the Rebbe was, he assisted him.)

At that time, most people took the overland trip through Turkey, Syria and Lebanon, in order to reach Israel. However, the Rebbe wanted to travel by ship, as this made the journey much shorter. Hearing that Turkey had allied with England and declared war against France, the Jewish community refused to allow any Jew to set sail from Istanbul. Only out of respect for the entreaties of a visiting Jerusalemite rabbi, did the community finally grant permission for the hiring of a ship.

They set sail in the beginning of September, about ten days before Rosh HaShannah. During the journey, a violent storm threatened to capsize their ship, and a few days later, their supply of drinking water ran out, thus endangering all the passengers. They suffered for three days, until a strong wind arose carrying them to the port city of Jaffa on Sunday, September 9, the 28th day of Elul. Rebbe Nachman, so near yet so far, was forced to stay on board, because the Turks suspected him of being a French spy. That night, the ship drew anchor and sailed to the port of Haifa. On Monday morning, the 29th of Elul, Erev Rosh HaShannah of 5559, Rebbe Nachman fulfilled his long-awaited dream of walking four cubits in the Holy Land. The Rebbe said: "As soon as I walked those four cubits, I had attained my goal" (*Rabbi Nachman's Wisdom* p.54).

He spent Rosh HaShannah, Yom Kippur and Sukkot in Haifa, for the most part extremely happy and joyous. After the holidays, he wanted to return home, but his attendant insisted that having come so far they should at least go on to Tiberias. The Rebbe went there after Sukkot.

In Tiberias they met the leading Chassidic rabbis. Rebbe Nachman spent most of the winter there (until after Purim, March 1799). He made an occasional trip to Safed and Meron, visiting the gravesites of the Tzaddikim. During his stay, Tiberias was plagued with troubles from the city's overseer, the Turkish army, and severe epidemics. He made plans for a journey to Jerusalem, but was unable to complete it.

After Napoleon conquered Jaffa, it became extremely difficult to leave the Holy Land. Nevertheless, Rebbe Nachman decided to depart quickly, as Napoleon was advancing toward Acco and it seemed as though he might soon have complete control of the coast. The Rebbe returned to Acco where he booked passage on a neutral ship. But, due to the confusion and chaos that reigned in Acco at the time, the Rebbe and his follower accidentally boarded a bark that took them to a Turkish warship anchored in Haifa.

The ship departed the next morning, leaving no time for Rebbe Nachman to prepare provisions for the return voyage. It sailed to the island of Antalya near the Turkish coast, where it docked. At the time, the people there had a rule that any Jew falling into their hands would be swiftly offered as a human sacrifice. The Rebbe and his follower were in very great danger and they remained hiding in their cabin for three days.

Then, a sudden storm arose, snapping the anchor ropes. The ship was completely out of control and tossed about the sea all that night. In the morning it became obvious that they had been blown back towards Acco. That afternoon, another storm broke out, sweeping the ship along. For several days and nights the ship was buffeted about at sea. Then it sprang a leak and began filling with water. For the first time in his life, Rebbe Nachman prayed to be helped and saved on the merit of his ancestors, the Baal Shem Tov, Rabbi Nachman Horodenker and his grandmother Adil. The leak was then found and plugged. Rebbe Nachman recited the Psalms with great joy.

Pesach was drawing near and they were without provisions. On the day before Pesach, the ship docked in Rhodes. The captain considered selling the Rebbe and his follower at the slave market. When news of their predicament reached the leaders of the Jewish community, they arranged for matzot and wine to be brought to the ship so that the Rebbe could conduct the Seder, and then they redeemed Rebbe Nachman and his follower from the hands of the Turkish captain.

During Pesach, the Rebbe entered Rhodes. After Pesach, he made his way to Istanbul and from there he crossed into what is now Rumania. During the course of his return trip from Rhodes, he faced plague, imprisonment, temptations and other miseries. He finally arrived home after Shavuot, in June, 1799.

*

All through his life, Rebbe Nachman praised God for giving him the strength and endurance necessary to make the pilgrimage to Eretz Yisrael. He taught many lessons about the Land's holiness, encouraging his followers to make every effort to go there. He said: "I led the way. Now my followers will be able to make the journey with fewer obstacles" (*Tzaddik* #141).

* * *

THE GREATNESS OF ERETZ YISRAEL

Rebbe Nachman teaches: Torah is the essence of life. Separation from Torah is like separation from life itself! That being so, how is it possible for anyone to disengage himself from the Torah — even for one moment?! Yet, at the same time, it is impossible to remain attached to the Torah twenty-four hours a day, every day, without interruption. There are physical needs that we all must tend to. And what about those unable to study Torah at all? How can they draw life?

What's more, we can ask the same question about the world at large. Before the Revelation at Sinai, what sustained the world? How did the world draw life before the Torah was given? The answer is that it drew life from God's Eternal Kindness. This Kindness sustained the world prior to the Revelation... And the "path to Eretz Yisrael" is just like God's Eternal Kindness. It has the power to sustain life, even if one is distant from the Torah (*Likutey Moharan* II, 78).

Rebbe Nachman teaches: The Land of Israel is sustained by God's direct Providence. This Providence draws holiness and wisdom into the Land. Thus, our Sages say: The air of the Holy Land makes wise (*Bava Batra* 158a). This wisdom is drawn from the delight that God has with the Jewish souls (*Likutey Moharan* II, 40).

From these two lessons we can glimpse the unparalleled greatness of the Holy Land. Its powers are enormous, and they are manifest even in our daily lives. Eretz Yisrael brings life. Eretz Yisrael brings wisdom. Literally! And not only for us, but for the entire world.

Furthermore, Rebbe Nachman teaches: True faith, prayer, miracles and Eretz Yisrael are all one concept (*Likutey Moharan* I, 7:1). Each is connected to and strengthens the other. Faith motivates us to pray. We believe that there is whom to pray to and that our prayers will be answered. And by praying, by begging God to help us when we are in need, miracles occur. Such is the power of prayer, it can bring about the supernatural. And this is the concept of the Holy Land, which defies natural phenomenon.

Eretz Yisrael can cause the barren to be blessed with children (*Likutey Moharan* I, 48).

Eretz Yisrael is called the Land of Life. All prosperity is drawn to the world through it (*Likutey Moharan* I, 47).

In Eretz Yisrael it is possible to acquire the quality of *erekh apayim* (great patience), because the Holy Land has the power to help subdue the evil character trait of anger. Therefore, pray to God to bestow on you a yearning and desire to get there. Also pray that He plants a longing for Eretz Yisrael in everyone's heart (*Likutey Moharan* I, 155).

* * *

LAND OF MILK AND HONEY

"For God is bringing you to a good land — a land of flowing streams, of fountains and underground springs gushing out in valley and mountain. It is a land of wheat, barley, grapes, figs and pomegranates; a land of olives and honey-dates. It is a land that lacks nothing..." (Deuteronomy 8:7-9).

The Torah, Talmud, Midrash, Zohar, and virtually every other book in our holy writings, extol the beauty and wonders of Eretz Yisrael. Naturally, one might ask, "Where are all these wonders? Where is this land of milk and honey? Where are the fruits that conquered nations?" (see *Breishit Rabbah* 98:12). These seem to be very legitimate questions.

Rabbi Yehoshua ben Levi said: "Eretz! Eretz! Gather in your fruit! To whom are you giving them? To the Arabs who have taken over due to our sins?" (*Ketubot* 112a). The Talmud raves about the size and taste of the fruits produced in the Land of Israel. "One grape filled thirty barrels of wine, honey oozed from the dates until people waded in it..." (*Ketubot* 111b). Where is this fruit today? As Rabbi Yehoshua tells us, the Land of Israel is very loyal to its rightful owners. When the Jews dwell in the land, it yields its produce. If not, it dries up. Indeed, we have merited to see this with our own eyes in our generation. When the Jews began returning to Eretz Yisrael and working the land, the Holy Land began yielding its fruits.

But what about the talmudic teachings of fantastic fruits in both size and quality? Where are those? The Jews have toiled, tilled and tended. Where are the *blessed* fruits? This question becomes even more emphatic in light of Rebbe Nachman's teaching (mentioned above) that all prosperity is drawn to the world through the Holy Land.

To answer this we turn to yet another of Rebbe Nachman's teachings about Eretz Yisrael: The reason for settling [and building] the Holy Land should be spiritual. The intention should be to draw closer to God. Anyone who goes there for this aim, will certainly benefit. Merely by setting foot on the land, he will be merged with the Holy Land and transformed by its sacred character. On the other hand, if a person's motive has nothing to do with drawing closer to God, then the verse states (Leviticus 18:28), "...the Land will spit you out, as it vomited out the nation that was there before you" (*Likutey Moharan* I, 129).

The Jews entered the Holy Land for spiritual reasons, and they attained spiritual levels. They may have sinned, they may even have been punished, but, overall, they developed spiritually until they were worthy of building the Holy Temple. However, after a few hundred years, they were exiled. They returned after the miracle of Purim, but were driven out again. With them went the taste and value of their fruit since their spirituality had plummeted to great depths (*Sotah* 48a).

Even though today Jews are again living in the Holy Land, its holiness remains hidden from us. We have quite a way to go yet in improving our spiritual yield and only then can we expect the Land to improve its yield.

Rebbe Nachman teaches: God reciprocates man "measure for measure" (*Sanhedrin* 90a). Nowhere is this repayment more exacting than in the Land of Israel. However, this is really His Kindness. If we know that God repays us according to our deeds, then by thinking about the situations God sends us we can learn to better our ways (*Likutey Moharan* I, 187).

Living in the Holy Land is not easy. It is, however, a most gratifying feeling, one that every Jew should seek, yearn, desire and strive for. Also, we must understand that we are presently only at the threshold of revealing the holiness of Eretz Yisrael. If we cling to our spiritual desires, work hard at becoming involved with the Land and what it stands for — its spiritual value — then we will merit seeing the great physical transformation that awaits Eretz Yisrael. As the Talmud teaches: In the Future (when Mashiach comes), the Land of Israel will produce loaves of bread ready for eating and silk garments ready for wear. Even barren trees will produce fruits (*Ketubot* 111b).

Thus the Rebbe teaches: The holiness of the Land of Israel is the epitome of holiness, encompassing all other levels of holiness. It is there that we can free ourselves completely of the materialistic viewpoint which insists that events take place naturally. We can come to know that everything takes place through the Hand of God (*Likutey Moharan* I, 234).

* * *

EXILE FROM ERETZ YISRAEL

"Raise the banner to gather our exiles and gather us together from the four corners of the earth..." (*Amidah Prayer*)

In explaining this passage which we recite thrice daily, Reb Noson writes: To wherever it is that even a single Jew has been exiled, God considers it as if all the Jews have been exiled there. By virtue of Jewish presence in any particular place, the "sparks of holiness" which exist in that place are gathered together and rectified. Such rectification, in turn, brings about the Ingathering of the Exiles. This is the reason the Jews were dispersed throughout the world — to gather in these sparks of holiness.

Reb Noson then asks: If it is the mission of the exiled to rectify and gather in all the good that has been scattered in distant places, then logically, the only ones we should find in these far away places are the righteous — the ones whose deeds will bring about these rectifications. But this is not so. Quite the contrary, we find that most Jews who go to places far removed from any Jewish community are generally those not observant in Torah and mitzvot. How can these people, who seem to need a considerable rectification themselves, rectify the sparks of holiness? How can they bring about the Ingathering of the Exiles?

However, as Reb Noson tells us, the answer to this can be found in the exile itself. If, when the Jews were in the Holy Land, they were not observant, how then can they be expected to keep the Torah in the Diaspora? If in the place which embodies the very fulfillment of our spiritual existence we did not keep our contract with God, how much more so when subjected to the influences of the nations. But, the Torah states: "I will exile you among the nations... From there you will seek God..." (Deuteronomy 4:27-29). *From there,* from the exile, you will seek. Come again? From the exile we will seek God, but not from the Holy Land?

While they were in the Holy Land, the Jews felt very close to God. In fact, they felt they had already found Him. As a result, their search for Him ceased and their yearning for spirituality died. Had they been in the Diaspora this would have been bad enough, but, because they were in the Land of holiness, because they were in "the King's palace," each improper thought and every flawed act was considered a great blemish. And each blemish brought a still greater blemish, as in, "One sin begets another" (Avot 4:2). Eventually, this brought on the exile.

But all is not lost. On the contrary, now that the Jews are in exile, now that we are far from the holiness of the Holy Land, precisely now can we begin to feel how distant we are from God. We can now arouse and encourage ourselves to feel our Judaism, our Torah, our faith. Now, we can first begin to reach out to God for help, because precisely here — in the exile — every small thought, word or good deed, is very precious in God's eyes (*Likutey Halakhot, Birkhat HaRei'ach* 4:45).

Thus, from Reb Noson's words we understand that every notch a person registers on the scale of merit is an aspect of Ingathering of the Exiles. By being in exile, yet yearning for Eretz Yisrael, we elevate the sparks of holiness and, as it were, bring these sparks — and ourselves! — back to the Holy Land.

*

We see that *eReTZ* is like the word *RaTZon*, desire. Thus, *Eretz Yisrael* means *I want to be a Jew*! (*Rabbi Yaakov Gedaliah Tefilinsky*).

* * *

BRESLOV IN THE HOLY LAND

We find that many of the Breslover Chassidim made great efforts to make at least a pilgrimage to Eretz Yisrael. Some sought to live there, even in the early days of the *yishuv*, when life was extremely difficult. At that time, the majority who came as part of the Chassidic *aliyah* settled in Tiberias or Safed.

After Rebbe Nachman's passing, Reb Shimon, who had been the Rebbe's personal attendant, moved to Safed. He is buried in Safed near the Ari. Reb Yitzchak, Reb Noson's son, also moved there and is buried near Rabbi Yosef Caro, the author of the *Shulchan Arukh*. Reb Noson had a few other followers who lived in Safed and Tiberias, most notably, Reb Noson ben R. Yehudah Reuven, compiler of *Kuntres HaTzeirufim*. At the beginning of the twentieth century, a community of Breslover began to form in the Galil, with Reb Yisrael Karduner the outstanding chassid.

Reb Avraham Chazan was a fiery chassid possessing great knowledge and profound depth of soul. His father, Reb Nachman Chazan told him, "The Diaspora cannot contain your holiness. *Antloif* (run away) to Eretz Yisrael" *(Rabbi Eliyahu Chaim Rosen)*. Eventually (c. 1894), Reb Avraham moved to Jerusalem. On his yearly trip to Uman for Rosh HaShannah, he would urge others to follow his example and settle in the Holy Land. Later on, in the 1920s and '30s, there was a small influx of Breslover Chassidim from Eastern Europe, most of whom settled in Jerusalem and B'nei Brak. The decade which followed saw the near total destruction of Breslover Chassidut in Europe. Almost all those living in Poland and Russia were killed either during the Holocaust or under Stalinist rule. In time, the precious few who did survive came to settle in the Holy Land.

Breslover Chassidut in Jerusalem centered in the Old City, with a few pockets of chassidim living in Meah Shearim, Shkhunat Knesset and Shaarei Chesed. After the Israel War of Independence, those from the Old City were resettled in Katamon. In the early 1950s, Reb Eliyahu Chaim Rosen undertook to build the Breslov Yeshivah "Or HaNe'elam" (Hidden Light, a reference to Rebbe Nachman), which currently houses the main Breslov synagogue in Jerusalem.

As the communities grew, the chassidim spread out, so that one can now find Breslov synagogues in different areas of Jerusalem, B'nei Brak, Safed, Emanuel and other places throughout Eretz Yisrael.

Those Breslover Chassidim who have not yet had the opportunity to make the move to the Holy Land always yearn for the time when this dream can come true. It is always a part of their thoughts and their *hitbodedut* (aside from being a separate blessing in the *Amidah*). In the meantime, they make efforts, at least, to visit Eretz Yisrael as much as possible. Such visits are seen as opportunities for "recharging their spiritual batteries."

Rabbi Zvi Aryeh Rosenfeld, who lived most of his life in Brooklyn, was fond of saying that "a Jew should always have his passport updated and ready. You never know when the opportunity will present itself for a trip to Israel. How foolish it would be to be able to fly to Israel, only to have to cancel the trip because of an expired passport." (Today, the same reasoning applies to travelling to Uman, to Rebbe Nachman's gravesite. Now that the Soviet authorities have been allowing the pilgrimage, it is important to be ready for the trip by being able to submit one's passport for visa applications etc., on a moment's notice.)

* * *

THE HOLY LAND TODAY

One must understand that just as God's Holiness and Glory are hidden for the duration of the exile, so too, the holiness, beauty and glory of the Land of Israel cannot shine brightly until Mashiach comes. For five years, Reb Eliyahu Chaim Rosen struggled to leave Stalin's "paradise" and settle in the Holy Land. During that period, he suffered through a typhus epidemic, the famine of 1933 and imprisonment with a death sentence hanging over his head. Miraculously, he obtained an exit visa from Moscow at a time when he had been forbidden to leave the city of Uman. Permission granted, the man who was later to become my Rosh Yeshivah headed straight for Israel.

Reb Eliyahu Chaim arrived in Haifa port on Erev Shavuot. How happy he was finally to set foot in Eretz Yisrael, especially after nearly losing his life more than once for remaining committed to God despite Communism's ruthless insistence upon atheism. Disembarking, he expected to find Jews living a happy Jewish life in the Holy Land. But he was appalled by the Judaism — or lack of Judaism —which he encountered. "Is *this* Naomi?" (Ruth 1:19; *naom* implies pleasantness and beauty). "Is this what I sacrificed so much for? Was it for this that I risked my life and worked so hard to leave Russia — so that I could raise my children as Jews?!" The day after Shavuot he left Haifa for Jerusalem. Arriving in the Holy City, he liked what he saw and exclaimed, "*This* is Naomi!" This is what he had been seeking.

The physical beauty of the Land today is recognized by all. Anyone who visited here in the early 1960s can personally attest to the vast improvements in the *gashmiyut* (physical comforts) that have taken place in Israel over the years. From an impoverished country of settlers, it is now possible, with a sufficient bank account, to have all the modern comforts of the most technically advanced societies. But, to find the *ruchniyut* — the spiritual beauty of the Land — we still have to look very hard. It exists, yet it must be sought.

A person might step off the plane in Israel expecting to be inundated by a rush of spirituality. Rebbe Nachman taught differently. "From the way the Torah extolls the virtue of Eretz Yisrael, we might conclude that the Holy Land is not part of this physical world at all." Rebbe Nachman said that this is not so. "The Holy Land, as great as it truly is, is still part of the physical reality [a country on planet Earth like all the other countries]. Even so, the level of its spiritual greatness is beyond imagination. Its holiness is the very epitome of holiness" (*Likutey Moharan* II, 116).

And so, we should not be discouraged and disappointed when we visit the Holy Land and fail to find the holiness we came looking for. Getting off the plane in Tel Aviv is not like walking into outer space. What is prevalent in other cities around the world can be found in Israel, too. Perhaps it should not be this way, but it is. What we have to do is look for the "good points." As with judging people, we have to keep searching for the good points of the Holy Land. As King David wrote, "See the good of Jerusalem all the days of your life" (Psalms 128:5).

Let us hope and pray that we merit seeing the good of Israel — both of the Nation and the Land. Try to make a pilgrimage. Try to live there. "There is no obstacle that can withstand the will of a person" (cf. *Zohar* II;162b). Even if presently you cannot dwell or even visit Eretz Yisrael, you can still keep it in mind. Think about the Holy Land. Reflect on it. Who knows? You might even develop a complete mental picture of the Holy Land to carry with you at all times. As Rebbe Nachman once said, "My only place is Eretz Yisrael. Wherever I go, I am only going to Eretz Yisrael" (*Tzaddik* #53).

* * *

20

YOU CAN TOO

Breishit. In the beginning. The world was created for Israel, who is called *reishit* — first! (*VaYikra Rabbah* 36:4).

Rebbe Nachman, throughout his lessons and conversations, speaks about the greatness of the Jewish soul. Its source lies at the very beginning of Creation, prior to everything else. In fact, it is the *raison d'etre* of Creation itself (see *Likutey Moharan* I, 17:1).

Understandably, you might feel a bit bewildered by all of this. Is my soul really so great? *Me?* Is it possible that all the lofty levels Rebbe Nachman speaks about are really meant for me too?

The answer, in short, is — *Yes!*

"You, too, can reach for the highest levels." Rebbe Nachman teaches that man can be likened to an elephant standing before a mouse (*Likutey Moharan, Shir Yedidut*). He shivers, he quakes, he is frightened to death. Of what? A mouse. Ridiculous? Yes, but that is what man is. A powerful being, but scared to use his strength — his incredible, inherent, spiritual strength. Were we to reach for the highest levels and experience real spirituality, we would find it hard to imagine living any other type of life.

On the other hand, it sometimes happens that a deluge of Judaism overwhelms us. We might feel there is too much to do, and, because we don't feel capable or have the desire to do it all, we choose to do nothing. Judaism is demanding. Extended spirituality is even more demanding. "Who says if

I start I'll be able to continue. Maybe I do wish to begin. But there is so much to do, so far to go, I'll never make it." So we give up before we even start. Or we try a bit, and then call it quits (*Rabbi Nachman's Wisdom* #27).

When we experience such turmoil, Rebbe Nachman compares us to a pot of water. The sediment and impurities within are resting on the bottom. To purify this water, we have to boil it. As the water boils, the impurities rise to the top and can be siphoned off. The same is true of us. Whether just entering the realm of Judaism, or entering deeper than ever before, we bring along our many impurities. Time is needed to purify us and to siphon off our impurities. This process is a period of agitation and confusion. If we don't give up, we will eventually be cleansed — perfectly, positively and absolutely (*Rabbi Nachman's Wisdom* #79).

*

Reb Noson said: I find it easier to explain and comment on the hardest and deepest "Maharam Schiff" (a complex commentary on the Talmud by Rabbi Meir Schiff, 1605-1641), than to comment on a living person. The essence of a person is his broken heart, and who can know another's broken heart?! (*Siach Sarfei Kodesh* 1-623).

Besides, as long as we are alive we have free choice, and this free choice is forever presenting itself in so many different ways. Do I perform the mitzvah? What will my family think of me? What will my friends say? What about my boss?

Throughout his *Likutey Halakhot*, Reb Noson, time and again, focuses on the problems of indecision which people face. We should not be overwhelmed by what we see written in all the holy writings. Our tendency is to say: "How can I ever do these devotions? Mikvah every day! *Hitbodedut* for an hour! Regular Torah lessons! Simplicity! Truth! Joy at all times! Come on, when will *I* ever be able to reach these levels? I doubt if I'll ever be able to reach even the lowest level mentioned. Why talk to me about all these high levels?"

Rebbe Nachman teaches: Just as a person has to strive to reach the highest level, he has to keep himself from falling from even the lowest level! (*Siach Sarfei Kodesh* 1-70). Reb Noson writes that every word spoken by our Sages and Tzaddikim, every sentence and passage passed on to us, generation after generation — they are all meant for us. We *can* find ourselves in these words, if we but try hard enough.

Whether we are striving for the greatest heights or feel too insignificant to see ourselves reaching even the lowest levels, we must strengthen ourselves in faith. Faith means believing that every word of Torah, every word of encouragement spoken by the Tzaddikim, is actually meant for us.

When Reb Noson first came to the Rebbe, Rebbe Nachman gave him the *Shevachey Ha'Ari,* a book about the greatness of the great kabbalist the Ari and his main student Rabbi Chaim Vital. After Reb Noson returned it, the Rebbe asked him what aspect of the book he had found to be the most interesting. "Rabbi Chaim Vital's humility," Reb Noson replied.

Rabbi Chaim was very humble, yet, every time he came to his teacher, the Ari would praise him profusely. Rabbi Chaim was embarrassed, considering himself unworthy of such praise. When he mentioned this to the Ari, the great kabbalist of Safed said, "Prior to Mashiach's coming, with but a little effort one can attain the advanced spiritual level of Rabbi Akiva." Rebbe Nachman said to Reb Noson, "That's exactly what I wanted you to notice!" (*Aveneha Barzel* p.19f). From this we can see that today — even with only a fraction of the effort required in previous generations — it is possible to attain true spiritual heights. All we need to do is take the words of the Tzaddikim to heart and do our best.

If this still seems too much, then do whatever you can. Remember, every good thought, word and deed you do are taken by the Tzaddikim and cemented into the "holy buildings" being built from our mitzvot. This is true no matter who you are, no matter what the condition of the mitzvah. If you tried, if you put even a minimal amount of effort into it — as long as you performed a good deed — it is now a brick in the spiritual building being constructed by our mitzvot. Every mitzvah, every good thought, goes a long way towards building this structure, and when this structure is complete, then Mashiach will come.

Thus, Reb Noson writes: Even if a person is distant from God, the Holy One still shines His light into him, to bring him closer. What if the person only stays "closer" for a few days and then falls away? As far as those few days are concerned, it doesn't matter. They remain very precious in God's eyes. The verse reads (Isaiah 33:24, see Rashi): "The dweller shall not say 'I am ill'; for the people that dwell therein shall be forgiven their sin." The dweller is someone who comes even for a short period. Even he can attain mercy and forgiveness for his sins (Likutey Halakhot, Arvit 4:34).

So, if you feel insignificant — don't. If you feel you can't do it all, then know that whatever you can do, counts — and counts a lot. Don't ever let go of the little bit you can do. Provided your desire is real, the time will come when you will be able to do more. Our Sages teach: The Torah only demands of a person that which he is capable of doing (Avodah Zarah 3a; Zohar III:104a).

Rebbe Nachman teaches: There is no despair! Kain yi'ush iz gohr nit far handen! — There is no such thing as giving up! Never give up! (Likutey Moharan II, 78). So, don't give up. Just do your best. Do what you can. Whatever and wherever you can.

Ask God to guide you on the right path. Our Sages teach: Each and every mitzvah that a person does comes decorated in its spiritual beauty before the Almighty and calls out: "I am from so and so. Such and such a person performed me!" This mitzvah brings peace above and peace below (Sotah 3b; Zohar III:118a).

The following question was put to Reb Noson: Seeing that Mashiach hasn't yet come, despite all the efforts of all the very great Tzaddikim in all the previous generations, how can *we*, who are spiritually much weaker, expect to bring him? Reb Noson answered this paradox with a parable:

There was once a city that was very well fortified. It was enclosed by a thick stone wall, thought by everyone to be impenetrable. Many of the world's kings and rulers had tried to conquer the city but found it impossible. Their warriors and soldiers were killed before they could make even a dent in the wall.

Finally, a wise king came and decided to conquer this fortified city. After inspecting its fortifications, he sent his mightiest soldiers to bring down the wall and attack the city. They pounded and pounded on the wall, but were unable to breach it. Soon, these soldiers fell. The king sent a second wave of mighty soldiers, and then a third wave, and so on. Before long, his entire army had been depleted and the wall had not come down. But the king did not give up. Once again he circled the city, inspecting its walls.

"How can you expect to capture this city if all your mighty soldiers are gone?" he was asked.

The wise king smiled. "If you look closely, you will see that though the soldiers could not breach the wall, they did succeed in cracking it. It is no longer strong and impenetrable. Now, with even the weak and wounded, with the women and children, I can bring down the wall."

The king then sent his few remaining and weakest soldiers into battle and they were able to tear down the "impenetrable" wall and conquer the city.

Reb Noson concluded: Who captured the city? The old and infirm? How could they have even attempted the battle, if the mighty warriors had been destroyed to a man? Even if they had fought for a thousand years, they could never have brought down that wall! They won the battle because of the strength of the earlier, mightier and stronger soldiers.

The same is true of us. We are weak, tired and drained of spiritual greatness. But the earlier Tzaddikim — Moshe Rabeinu, Rabbi Shimon bar Yochai, the Ari, the Baal Shem Tov and Rebbe Nachman, indeed all the Tzaddikim — though they did not succeed in bringing the Mashiach, all the great Tzaddikim of previous generations did succeed in cracking the wall of obstacles which stand in the way. Now, even we can mount that final attack and bring Mashiach (Ma'asiot U'Meshalim p. 36-37).

May God grant that we merit to study and fulfill the Torah and bind ourselves to the true Tzaddikim, following their advice. If we do, we will merit seeing the Coming of Mashiach, the Ingathering of the Exiles and the Rebuilding of the Holy Temple. May it come speedily, in our days, Amen.

* * *

APPENDIX A

APPENDIX A: A GUIDE TO TORAH STUDY

Considering the paramount role which Torah plays in the life of a Jew, the following "Guide to Torah Study" is being offered as a suggested general study program for beginners and those on intermediate levels. We've already seen the great emphasis which Rebbe Nachman himself placed on Torah study and his desire that we "visit" in all the holy teachings. As mentioned, he stressed the need for a general and extensive knowledge of the Torah and accordingly favored a *seder limud* (a study-method) which produces a broad knowledge, rather than the approach which develops analytical prowess (see chapter 7, above).

There are subjects in the Torah which apply to everyone, and at all times. Others are seasonal and some apply only in rare situations. This, together with Rebbe Nachman's expressed preference for a broad *seder limud,* has resulted in the following guide being left general. Each individual should weigh his time carefully and place emphasis on the areas he will benefit from most. The *seder limud* can and should be planned out with one's rabbi and/or study partner.

The subjects that apply to all are: Bible (Torah, Prophets and Hagiographa) with Rashi; *Shulchan Arukh;* Mishnah; Talmud; Musar-ethics and Chassidut. These and their importance will be explained first; followed by those branches of Torah, such as Midrash and Kabbalah, whose importance cannot be questioned, but whose study generally requires greater skills. As for the books of Breslov, a guide to studying these teachings appears in Appendix B. It must be pointed out that the study program presented here is strictly the author's understanding, based on Rebbe Nachman's teachings. It might seem geared more towards the *baal teshuvah,* yet it is actually a balanced method, one suitable for a broad spectrum of backgrounds and interests.

CHUMASH. Alternately known as Torah (hence *Tanakh*), the *Chumash* (The Five Books of Moses), the first of the three parts of the Bible, is the basis of the entire body of teaching we generally call the Torah. It is also the first book of Jewish (and world) history.

As *the* source book for all branches of Torah knowledge, it is absolutely vital that one be familiar with the *Chumash*. Any law of Torah studied, any Jewish custom ever discussed, unquestionably has its root in a biblical teaching. The *Chumash* contains the source references for all the legal points of the Mishnah and Talmud, for all the homilies of the Midrash, the revelations of the Zohar and the insights of the Kabbalah and Chassidut. Without a clear understanding of the verses of the *Chumash*, one cannot hope to ever fully understand a page of any of these teachings. The Torah is divided into weekly portions, spread over the entire year. A person should study each week's reading with Rashi's commentary (*Orach Chaim* 285:2).

With the commentaries available to us today, especially that of Rashi, we can approach a chapter of the Bible and learn from it nearly all of the talmudic and midrashic teachings necessary for our understanding of that passage. Clearly and succinctly, Rashi provides us with the important background information and historical data relating to the events in the *Chumash*, and he gives the talmudic interpretations of the passages with regard to their halakhic implications.

Rebbe Nachman remarked: Rashi is like the Torah's brother. Little children study the *Chumash* with Rashi. So do the older boys, young men...all of Israel. Every Jew studies the Written Law and the Oral Law with Rashi's commentary. From this we can begin to appreciate Rashi's unique greatness (*Rabbi Nachman's Wisdom* #223).

Reb Noson added: Whoever spurns Rashi's commentary and studies the Torah commentaries based on philosophical ideas — separates himself from life itself and uproots himself from God and the Torah (*Likutey Halakhot, Tefilin* 4:7). Thus, if we are going to advance in our Torah studies, *Chumash* is of prime importance. But it needs the interpretation of the traditional commentaries, the ones whose goal it is to bring us closer to God.

TaNaKh. Although this acrostic stands for *Torah* (the Five Books), *Nevi'im* (Prophets) and *Ketuvim* (Hagiographa), the term is popularly used to refer to only the latter two. And there can be no doubt that of the different areas of Torah study which are generally neglected, *Tanakh* probably ranks as number one. This, despite the fact that when our Sages said: Children should be taught the Holy Writings (see *Avot* 5:21), they were referring to the Prophets and Hagiographa as well as the Five Books of Moses.

We are a holy nation. We have a long and proud history. The Talmud teaches that each Jew must ask himself, "When will my deeds be like those of my forefathers?" (*Tana D'Bei Eliyahu Rabbah* 25). If that's the case, then isn't it absolutely necessary for us to know that heritage? Don't we have to learn from the deeds and errors of our ancestors? We must recognize *our* heroes — King David, Samuel, Elijah, Boaz, King Hezekiah, Isaiah, Mordechai, Esther, Daniel, etc. — and follow in their footsteps.

This is not to say that the study of *Tanakh* is, God forbid, for the sake of historical or hero-worshiping purposes. *Tanakh* is a major branch of the Torah and, as such, requires study for Torah's sake. However, it cannot be denied that our past plays a very important role in contemporary Judaism and has much to teach us about our present. "History," the saying goes, "is the best teacher." Only with the knowledge of our forebearers, of their merits and their strengths, and the legacy which they bequeathed us, will we be able to continue forward as a Jewish Nation.

Rebbe Nachman once said, "My *musar* book is *Tanakh*" (*Sichot V'Sipurim* p.113 #21). The Rebbe was referring to yet another major benefit derived from studying *Tanakh* — faith. Reading about and taking to heart all that happened to our forefathers, we find ourselves instilled with a faith and trust in the One above. We are given encouragement to "wait out" the trials and tribulations that afflict us; all the while hoping for the salvation promised us by our prophets and righteous leaders. Thus, just before Reb Noson passed away he asked someone to bring him *kol tuv* (the very best). Asked what *kol tuv* he was referring to, Reb Noson replied, *"Tanakh."*

By studying only two chapters of *Tanakh* in consecutive order, or one chapter of Prophets and one of Hagiographa, a person can finish the entire *Tanakh* in just one year (*Yesod V'Shoresh Ha'Avodah*). *Tanakh* should be studied with Rashi. In addition there are the commentaries *Metzudat David* and *Metzudat Zion*. These explain the simple meaning of the verse and the more difficult words. Whatever commentary you choose, make sure that it is founded on the traditional sources and teachings of our Sages. Rebbe Nachman warned us against studying the Bible with commentaries that are based on philosophical ideas and calculations. Such works only confuse the mind and implant unsound beliefs. Their teachings are against all that we have received from the Talmud, the holy Zohar, the Ari and the Baal Shem Tov (see *Tzaddik* #407).

SHULCHAN ARUKH, THE CODES. Our Sages teach: Whoever studies the Codes of Jewish law every day is guaranteed a portion in the World to Come (*Nidah* 73a). In the time of our Sages, Codes of Jewish law meant the study of the Mishnah and Talmud. Today, it is the *Shulchan Arukh* ("The Code of Jewish Law"). The comprehensive outline for daily living which this work contains should be a major area of Torah study. More than any other area of learning, the Rebbe advised his followers to study *The Code of Jewish Law* with its commentaries (*Rabbi Nachman's Wisdom* #29). He further taught that studying the *Shulchan Arukh* actually *is* the "delight of the World to Come" (*Likutey Moharan* II, 2:2).

There are a number of lessons in *Likutey Moharan* which refer to studying Codes and some of the important reasons why one should do so. When a person sins, he is mixing up good with bad. (He was good, but has now let evil into himself.) Studying Codes entails learning all the differing opinions, clarifying them in one's mind and then concluding the correct halakhic decision. This is likened to clarifying the good from the bad. Thus, the person who studies the *Shulchan Arukh* undergoes the same clarification within himself: keeping the good he already has and dispelling the bad, the evil, from himself (*Likutey Moharan* I, 8:6).

Another reason which Rebbe Nachman gives for studying Codes has to do with something called strife of holiness. This is the differences of opinion between the Rabbis. They argue over the pathways of Torah, how best to reveal them in the world. The source of strife within a person — the evil inclination — emanates from the strife of holiness. Thus, rectifying the "differences," the arguments and inner strife that a person faces, can be accomplished by finding and clarifying the proper and correct path — studying and clarifying Jewish Law (*Likutey Moharan* I, 62:2).

Therefore, Rebbe Nachman teaches: Every Jew has an obligation to study Codes, every single day. One should try to study the entire set of Codes, in order, from beginning to end, even those laws that relate to financial agreements, marriage, etc. The very least one should do is to study those laws which apply to oneself directly, such as Shabbat, tefilin, prayer, family purity, kashrut, etc. Even when one is under duress and has no time, he should try to study at least one paragraph of Codes, even if not in (his) set order. Never let a single day pass without studying at least one law (*Rabbi Nachman's Wisdom* #29). However, one should bear in mind that the single paragraph studied when time is limited must be a paragraph which is accepted as law (not a halakhic dispute that remains undecided) (*Kokhavey Or* p.73).

It should be emphasized that what the Mishnah and Talmud were to previous generations, the *Shulchan Arukh* is for us today. The Mishnah is a compilation of all the laws taught at that time. The Talmud (*Gemara*), contains the explanation and reasoning behind the law. The *Shulchan Arukh,* compiled by Rabbi Yosef Caro, with glosses by Rabbi Moshe Isserles, consists of all the laws derived from Mishnah and Talmud that are applicable today.

Rebbe Nachman said that one should learn in the "big" *Shulchan Arukh* — the full set of Codes: The *Orach Chaim* (daily, Shabbat and holiday laws); *Yoreh De'ah* (personal laws of kashrut, family purity, oaths, interest, mourning, etc.); *Even HaEzer* (laws of marriage and divorce); *Choshen Mishpat* (monetary laws of financial transactions, damages, etc.). These should be studied with all the commentaries and codifiers (such as: *Magen Avraham, TaZ, SHaKH, S'MA, Bet Shmuel, Ba'er Hetev,* etc.). If one's learning ability is not up to such a level, he should learn in the "small" *Shulchan Arukh* (The Codes with the *Ba'er Hetev.* The *Ba'er Hetev* is a condensed review of the major commentaries on the *Shulchan Arukh*).

Reb Noson praised the halakhic work *Chayey Adam* ("The Life of Man"). He said that its author, Rabbi Avraham Danzig of Vilna, had a very keen ability for clearly and precisely clarifying the law (*Siach Sarfei Kodesh* 1-522). (The work covers the topics in *Orach Chaim* in condensed form, including the laws pertaining to the week, Shabbat and the festivals, with some other additions from *Yoreh De'ah*. A similar work, *Chokhmat Adam* by the same author, is a condensed version of *Yoreh De'ah*.) Rabbi Zvi Aryeh Rosenfeld added that the gloss on the *Chayey Adam* known as *Tosefot Chaim* ("Additional Life") should be included in one's studies as it futher enhances the halakhic scope of the text.

The "small" *Shulchan Arukh* that Rebbe Nachman refered to is today associated with the study of the *Kitzur Shulchan Arukh* by Rabbi Shlomo Ganzfried and translated into English as *The Code of Jewish Law* (*Rabbi Shmuel Shapiro; Rabbi Zvi Aryeh Rosenfeld*). Since the *Kitzur Shulchan Arukh* is available in a pocket format, many Breslover Chassidim keep a copy in their talit bag. This way they are able to study from it right after the morning prayers, while still wearing their Rabeinu Tam tefilin.

There is also a very simple and obvious reason for our studying the *Shulchan Arukh*: how else can we know what to do? Without knowledge, we cannot know our obligations and how to go about fulfilling them. Someone with easy access to his rabbi and halakhic authority might assume this convenience allows him to remain ignorant of Torah and its requirements. But this is not the case. Choosing ignorance is forbidden. Besides, no rabbi is on call twenty-four hours a day, three-hundred-sixty five days a year. Consider the following example. The *Shulchan Arukh* states: "One must be very well versed in the laws of use of medicine and healing on Shabbat. Should an emergency arise, one must be able to act immediately, rather than lose precious time trying to locate his rabbi. The time it takes to ask the rabbi could endanger another's life. This is forbidden" (*Orach Chaim* #328:2; *Mishnah Berurah* 328:6). This same reasoning can be applied to all laws. Each of us must try to have as much knowledge of Jewish Law as is possible. This is necessary so that we can live our lives without having constantly to ask, "Can I do this?"; "May I do that?"; "Is this permissible?" In addition, by studying Codes we at least have an idea of what we don't know, and are educated enough to know what questions to ask of the person who does.

At this point, a warning about "taking the law into one's own hands" is in order. We can presume that we are acting within the requirements of the halakhah when the law is clear and we have no doubts about our own understanding of it. But, under no circumstances should we ever make a halakhic decision where there are doubts about which authority should be followed, and certainly when we do not understand or know the law. The qualified rabbi is one who has studied the Talmud, the Codifiers and all the applicable commentaries. He is therefore suited to render an opinion. When in doubt, we *must* turn to him for a ruling.

Whenever anyone asked, "What is the Breslover custom in such and such a case?" the answer was, "Look in the *Shulchan Arukh*. Whatever is written there, that's what Rebbe Nachman did." However, there are cases where the Codes offer differing opinions. The best thing is for each person to follow his family's custom. Jews of Sefardic extraction should continue the Sefardic customs; Ashkenazic Jewry should maintain their customs, etc. Rare are the instances where there is a specific Breslov custom. When in doubt, consult your local rabbi.

MISHNAH. The Mishnah is the foundation of the Oral Law; the basis of the Talmud. It is also the source for the rulings in the *Shulchan Arukh*. Our Sages taught: The study of Talmud is above all. If that's the case, why is it taught that one should master the study of Mishnah more than to the Talmud? The emphasis was put on studying Mishnah because the students were [and still are] running towards mental calisthenics, directing their attention to sharp questions and answers. As a result, the basic laws themselves were being forgotten (*Bava Metzia* 33a,b). The Mishnah and the Talmud are basically one and the same, Mishnah is the law and Talmud is the discussion and clarification of the law. They go together and complement each other.

Yet, they are two different studies. The Mishnah is a series of laws, applicable to the tractate in question. The Talmud presents a wide-ranging discussion of the Mishnah's law, sometimes challenging the Mishnah's statement and offering differing, and often opposing views to the Mishnah being discussed. Often these questions arise from wide-ranging passages in the Talmud which at first seem to have no connection whatsoever with the subject under consideration. Indeed, this may well be why our Sages advised us to make a thorough study of the Mishnah before entering the deep and complex realm of the Talmud (see *Avot* 5:21). This is also the opinion of many of the Codifiers.

The author of *Sh'nei Luchot HaBrit* (*Mesikhta Shavuot*), states that today, since we have commentaries on the Mishnah which present the reasoning of the Talmud, such as *Bartenura, Rambam* and others, we should make Mishnah a major area of study. This way, we study the laws, the source for these laws, and the reasoning behind them, as they are discussed in the Talmud. These commentaries also clarify the law, indicating which opinion to follow. In our present generation we also have the commentaries of the *Tiferet Yisrael* and *Mishnayot Mevuarot* (*K'hati*) which are invaluable tools for truly understanding the Mishnah, as well as clear English translations, such as the Blackman Mishnayot and the Art Scroll series.

It would be especially beneficial for someone young enough, whether "frum-from-birth" or "baalei teshuvah," who finished school, but not yet married, and/or has the ability to spend long hours studying, to spend his time studying the Mishnah. First, this would introduce the student to many areas of the Torah, i.e. the laws of purity and impurity, permitted and forbidden, kosher and unkosher, which were hitherto unknown to him. Secondly, because the Mishnah is in Hebrew and the Talmud in Aramaic, the student sometimes finds it difficult to master both studies, in two separate languages, at the same time. It would be easier to concentrate on one of these studies together with learning its language, and Hebrew is easier to pick up than Aramaic. Thirdly, perhaps most important, it would allow him to study quickly — Mishnah being far easier to grasp than Talmud. This would allow for a considerable increase in knowledge in a relatively short period of time; studying one chapter a day allows a person to finish the Mishnah in less than a year and a half. As one gains familiarity with the system of logic employed in the Mishnah, one can increase his speed, learning two or more chapters a day. This would make it possible to finish the entire Mishnah in less than a year! (Study eighteen chapters a day and it can be finished in one month!) Then one should be ready to tackle the Talmud.

TALMUD. The Talmud is known as "the wine of Torah." As the focal point of all Jewish law and lore, the Talmud is perhaps the most important study in which one should engage. Our Sages said that the Talmud is all inclusive — containing Bible, Mishnah and Talmud (*Sanhedrin* 24a). However, not everyone has the foundation for studying the Talmud. This is especially true of the *baalei teshuvah*, who only begin studying at a later age, while at the same time being burdened with the yoke of earning a livelihood. Many are made to feel that they must stick to a rigorous diet of Talmud, even at the expense of their ever studying *Shulchan Arukh!*

Reb Nachman Chazan of Tulchin, Reb Noson's closest follower, was orphaned at a very young age and did not have the opportunity to study Torah in his youth. Once, Reb Nachman was traveling with Reb Noson who lectured him about the importance of Torah study. When they arrived at an inn, Reb Nachman took a *Gemara* and began to study. Reb Noson said to him, "What you are now is known as a *turbulent* student. [A turbulent learner is one who gets involved in studies above his true level; see *Likutey Moharan* I, 100.] The Baal Shem Tov said that he came to this world to eliminate the *turbulent* student. Better you should learn *Chumash, Mishnah, Eyn Yaakov, Shulchan Arukh, Midrash,* and the like." Reb Noson understood that were Reb Nachman to start studying Talmud at such a late stage in life, he could become a *lamdan,* but he would never reach the level of Tzaddik. He therefore started him off with the easier studies, and from this he eventually did become a great Tzaddik (*Aveneha Barzel* p.66).

We see from Reb Noson's advice that it is far better to begin with the basics — studying the "easier" areas of Judaism and gaining a broad knowledge of Torah ideas and ideals — in order to develop a firm foundation in Torah. Where there's a will there's a way, so that later on, if one so desires, he will have ample time to engage in a concentrated study of the Talmud. (Rabbi Moshe Chagiz, author of *Mishnat Chachamim* and *Leket HaKemach* agrees with this view.) This is especially true today (1989). There are many *daf hayomi* classes (daily page of Talmud study), as well as lessons on the entire Talmud recorded on cassette in English, Hebrew and Yiddish. It is very advantageous and even quite necessary for a person to study all of the Talmud. Each man was created in God's image. Yet, as Rebbe Nachman said, "Man's Godly image cannot shine until he studies and finishes the entire Talmud" (*Siach Sarfei Kodesh* 1-73).

The Rebbe also taught: We find that in earlier generations the study of Torah delayed the Angel of Death (cf. *Shabbat* 30b; *Moed Katan* 28a). Yet today, people die even in the middle of their studies! This has to do with the evil force known as *Lilit* (לילית) having the same numerical value as Talmud (תלמוד), 480. Proper study of Torah protects a person, but if the study is with impure motives, especially the study of Talmud, then one is actually giving more strength to the Other Side (*Likutey Moharan* I, 214).

For those capable, i.e. the advanced talmudic student, "studying Talmud with Rashi and Tosafot daily is an obligation as great as putting on tefilin" (*Chyda, Yoreh De'ah* 245). For those who are beginning or even on an intermediate level, the Maharal of Prague was extremely adamant that Talmud should be studied with emphasis on understanding the law that evolves from the talmudic discussion, not on *pilpulim* (*Netivot Olam, Netiv HaTorah* 5). Rebbe Nachman wanted us to study the Talmud with the commentaries and Codifiers so that we could learn the reasoning behind the law and clarify the proper way for it to be practiced. Reb Noson also wrote to his son: I am glad that you are studying Tractate Shabbat and the Laws of Shabbat in the *Shulchan Arukh*. If you can work it out with your learning partner to study the laws applicable to the page of Talmud as you study it, that would be even better" (*Alim Litrufah* #6).

MUSAR — ETHICS AND CHASSIDUT. Ethical guidance is one of the most important areas of Torah study. Without morals, Torah has no meaning. The Talmud teaches: The Torah can be compared to the inner gate, Fear of Heaven is likened to the outer gate. Without entering the outer gate of Fear, how can one ever hope to pass the inner gate of Torah? (*Shabbat* 31a). We must spend much time on acquiring Fear of Heaven. This can be accomplished by studying those Torah works which focus on moral values and ethical behavior. They help a person understand the importance of these values and of being a "mentsch."

Rebbe Nachman told his followers to study the *Mesilat Yesharim* (*Sichot V'Sipurim*, Manuscript of Tcheriner Rav p.167). The Rebbe himself studied the *Reishit Chokhmah*. He also said that studying the *Eyn Yaakov*, the homiletic passages of the Talmud, brings Fear of Heaven.

The *Reishit Chokhmah*, for instance, speaks about eliminating evil characteristics while rectifying and building the good traits. It details the rewards and punishments for many of the mitzvot and transgressions. However, lest we feel a bit shaken by the severity of certain punishments and become depressed, Reb Noson said, "The author of the *Reishit Chokhmah* never intended for you to become depressed by his work. If you can't study his *musar* without becoming depressed by it, then study something else" (*Siach Sarfei Kodesh* 1-601).

In today's generation there are many *musar* and chassidic books available. Each has its unique approach for guiding us and helping us develop Fear of Heaven. However, my rabbi taught me that "If you truly want to *know* and *experience* Fear of Heaven, study Rebbe Nachman's teachings!" (*Rabbi Zvi Aryeh Rosenfeld*). This was not, God forbid, intended to diminish the value of the other works. His point was to instill in us a feeling for the importance and greatness of Rebbe Nachman's teachings. The Rebbe's teachings go directly to the heart, touching our innermost feelings and arousing us to an awareness of God that is simply unparalleled in other works.

Rebbe Nachman once said, "Have you heard me lecture you with words of musar?" Reb Noson writes: "We were a bit amazed by this remark. It seemed to us that his every word was religious and moral guidance. All his words were literally like burning coals, capable of kindling a person's heart with fiery inspiration. Whoever heard him speak was immediately drawn to serve God. Even today, whoever studies Rebbe Nachman's teachings sincerely will be enflamed with a burning desire to come closer to God" (*Rabbi Nachman's Wisdom* #124).

Reb Noson often wrote to his son, Reb Yitzchak of Tulchin, encouraging him to study Rebbe Nachman's works: "Study them and continue to study them, for all is in them; look deeply into them; grow old and gray over them, and do not move from them, for there is nothing greater than them" (cf. *Avot* 5:22).

Our Sages tell us that when reciting words of Torah, a person should imagine the author of those words standing before him (*Yerushalmi, Shekalim* 2:8). Rebbe Nachman teaches: Each work of a Tzaddik has [in its letter and word combinations] the face and soul of the Tzaddik (*Likutey Moharan* I, 192). Thus, even in this day and age, by studying Rebbe Nachman's works it is possible to gaze directly at the Rebbe and draw from his holiness.

Rebbe Nachman once said, "It pays to spend an entire lifetime working to save yourself from even just one evil thought, as this will save you from one extra burn in Gehennom" (*Rabbi Eliyahu Chaim Rosen*; cf. *Rabbi Nachman's Wisdom* #236). My Rosh Yeshivah applied this to the Rebbe's teachings. "By studying Rebbe Nachman's works," he would say, "one is assured of being spared from many evil thoughts and even gaining numerous good thoughts and desires."

There is a saying among Breslover Chassidim about the talmudic teaching that whoever studies Codes of Jewish law every day is guaranteed a portion in the World to Come. They say that this also applies to studying the *Likutey Halakhot*. Reb Noson's "Collected Laws," his *magnum opus*, interprets the entire set of Codes into practical advice and guidance to which everyone can relate. Unique in its style and approach, this eight-volume classic teaches us how we can relate each aspect of Torah to every moment of life. A person just has to open any volume, to any page he chooses, and he will see that Reb Noson's words speak directly to him. There isn't a person, place or thing in this world which Reb Noson doesn't touch upon. His teachings bring the reader to levels of joy and happiness, prayer and repentance, which until now had been hidden from him. Fortunate is he who spends his days studying the *Likutey Halakhot*.

* * *

Other areas of study

MIDRASH AND EYN YAAKOV. The Midrash is a collection of homilies and analogies which focus on explaining the complete story and underlying significance of the typically terse biblical verse. As such, it is a treasure-house of musar, ethics and moral guidance. Similar to the Midrash, *Eyn Yaakov* is a collection of *musar* and stories drawn from the Talmud. Commentaries abound on both the Midrash collection and the *Eyn Yaakov,* many of which highlight how these provide direction and Torah knowledge to guide a person in his daily life. Both Midrash and *Eyn Yaakov* are also very important studies because they have tremendous power to instill Fear of Heaven into those who study them. English translations are available.

ZOHAR AND KABBALAH. Rebbe Nachman taught: The study of the Zohar is very beneficial for the soul. By studying the Zohar, you can acquire enthusiasm for all sacred studies. The very language of the Zohar can motivate a person to serve God (*Rabbi Nachman's Wisdom* #108).

The study of Kabbalah too, is extremely beneficial, both for the person who studies it and for the world at large. It affords man a microscopic glimpse of God's greatness and the greatness of the Torah and the Jewish soul. Rabbi Chaim Vital writes that one hour of studying Kabbalah is worth more than a month of studying the basics of the Torah (*Etz Chaim, Introduction*). The Zohar states: Studying Kabbalah, the depths of Torah, hastens Mashiach's coming. Those who do not engage in Kabbalah study cause the Torah to be considered "dry" (barren), and bring poverty, war and destruction to the world (*Tikkuney Zohar*, 30). Elsewhere the Zohar teaches that whoever studies Torah and does not study Kabbalah, would have been better off had he not been created. Such a person lengthens the exile. But, one who repents and studies Kabbalah, the mysteries and secrets of Torah — he draws blessings and abundance into the world" (*Tikkuney Zohar*, 43).

Moshe Rabeinu appeared to Rabbi Shimon bar Yochai and said, "Your teachings, the Holy Zohar, is rooted in the Tree of Life (as opposed to the study of Mishnah and the Codes which is rooted in the Tree of Knowledge). Because of it, the Jews will merit to go up from exile" (Zohar III:124b).

Though the Rebbe spoke very highly of the Zohar, and from the above passages we see the greatness and importance of studying the Kabbalah, not everyone is worthy of even perusing the Holy Zohar, let alone studying it in depth. The pre-requisites for studying Kabbalah, according to the renowned Kabbalist, Rabbi Moshe Kordevoro (the RaMak, author of the Pardes Rimonim), are: 1) being married [so one can study in purity], 2) being knowledgeable in the Codes, and 3) possessing Fear of Heaven (Or Ne'erav, Introduction; see Yoreh De'ah 246:4; Shakh 246:6). If a person is worthy, the Kabbalah will elevate him and give him an incredible insight into God's greatness and the immense spirituality which exists even in this world. If not, he must steer himself away from studying the Kabbalah, for fear of blemishing himself even more.

Rebbe Nachman was once visited by a person who was known for the angry and abusive way he treated others. "He does not guard the covenant," the Rebbe remarked. When Rebbe Nachman later discovered that this scholar studied kabbalistic texts, he said, "Such a person is not fit to study Kabbalah!" (Rabbi Nachman's Wisdom #249). Furthermore, Rebbe Nachman said: "Kabbalah (קבלה) is the same gematria as no'ef (נואף), immoral. Whoever is not worthy, yet studies Kabbalah, is considered immoral. One must pray to God asking that he be led in the proper path" (Tzaddik #526).

Anyone who has studied Chassidut, such as Toldot Yaakov Yosef, Meor VaShemesh, Tanya, Kedushat Levi, knows that the Zohar and Kabbalah are often quoted. Should a person shy away from these teachings too? Definitely not! The Codifiers — Beit Yosef, RaMa, Magen Avraham, TaZ, ShaKh, Mishnah Berurah and so on, all quote from the Zohar and the writings of the Ari. So do many other authors of works on the Revealed Torah. The warnings against studying Kabbalah, for those not worthy, refer to a straight and analytical study of a basic Kabbalah text. They do not apply to short passages quoted in other works (Rabbi Zvi Aryeh Rosenfeld).

Therefore, we differentiate here between studying basic Kabbalah, directly from the Ari's writings, and the terminology of Kabbalah that is often quoted in Chassidic works, especially in Rebbe Nachman's teachings. One should understand that the study of Divine Persona, the Tetragrammaton and the many mystical intentions in Torah are not, and cannot be, for the beginner. By their very nature, these concepts assume the would-be student already to have a good working knowledge of all the other branches of Torah. Otherwise, there is no way for them to be properly understood.

In another sense, Kabbalah is the depth, the inner beauty — the very soul of the Torah. It is what allows a person to "feel" a great attachment to God, discovering and knowing that God is everywhere. Towards this end, the study of Chassidut is extremely beneficial because Chassidut brings out the "soul of Torah" and transmits it in a format that applies to every Jew. This is especially true of Rebbe Nachman's *Likutey Moharan* and even more so of Reb Noson's *Likutey Halakhot*. Both these works present kabbalistic teachings in simple, layman's terms, and in simply applied approaches to daily life.

*

"Above all else, a person must understand in his studies a way that will bring him closer to God. He must "take out" from his studies proper advice on how to deal with himself and his colleagues, with his family and with those whom he has dealings. This can only be accomplished with faith in the Tzaddikim" (*Likutey Moharan* I, 61:1). Believing in the Tzaddikim and the Torah teachings they revealed, will imbue us with a true appreciation of the actual beauty of Torah and the important place that it has in our lives.

* * *

APPENDIX B

APPENDIX B: BRESLOV BOOKS

The following is a list of works authored by Rebbe Nachman, Reb Noson and other Breslover Chassidim, up until the present generation. It is divided into six sections: Rebbe Nachman's writings; Reb Noson's writings; the Tcheriner Rav; Reb Avraham b'Reb Nachman Chazan; Reb Alter Tepliker; other works (including music and cassettes).

This appendix is intended to serve as an introductory guide to Breslov publications, including a short history of each work, its content and its context within Breslov Chassidut. Though "every book is important" (*Likutey Moharan* I, 61:5), only the most often used works — the main body of Breslov teachings — will be discussed. Where a book has been translated into English or other languages, its name appears in parentheses next to the original Hebrew title. Anyone wishing further bibliographical information about these and other Breslov works is referred to *Nevey Tzaddikim* by Reb Noson Zvi Koenig; *Until the Mashiach* (pp.287-295), Bibliography; *Rabbi Nachman's Stories,* Bibliography.

At the end of this appendix, having already explained each work, a suggested order of study for the novice in Breslov teachings has been provided.

* * *

Rebbe Nachman's Writings

Likutey Moharan — Anthology of *MoHaRaN* (Morenu HaRav Rabeinu Nachman). This is Rebbe Nachman's *magnum opus* in two parts; Part I containing 286 lessons, Part II containing 125 lessons. Some of the discourses were recorded by Rebbe Nachman himself, marked *leshon Rabeinu*, but most of them were written down by Reb Noson. After hearing a lesson, Reb Noson would record it from memory and later on (usually) review it with Rebbe Nachman. The *Likutey Moharan* is the most often studied book in Breslov, containing Rebbe Nachman's major discourses. The lessons are generally begun with a quote from a Biblical verse or a teaching of our Sages which is then woven into a most beautiful tapestry of ideas and thoughts — exhorting the reader to strive for the lofty levels about which the Rebbe teaches. Yet, the work itself is quite a difficult one to study. Even advanced scholars have trouble keeping pace with the Rebbe's movements throughout each lesson. This makes a simple commentary impossible. One must have thorough knowledge of the Bible, Talmud, Zohar and the Kabbalah truly to enter this incredible palace of sublime teachings. However, even on a beginner's level, a novice has a good deal which he can glean from the lessons.

In 1960-61, Rabbi Zvi Aryeh Rosenfeld pioneered the use of tapes to record a running translation of the *Likutey Moharan*. These lessons have been transferred to cassette and are currently available. An English translation with a running commentary providing the necessary tools to weave one's way through the discourse, is currently underway. Three volumes are already complete, beginning with Reb Noson's Introduction through Lesson #22. The entire translation should be about 12 volumes.

Sippurey Ma'asiot — (*Rabbi Nachman's Stories*). These are thirteen mystical stories told by Rebbe Nachman. Originally transcribed by Reb Noson in Yiddish (the language in which the Rebbe told them), the book was published with the stories translated into Hebrew at the top of the page and the Yiddish at the bottom. Reb Noson writes that any commentary offered is not even a drop in the ocean in comparison with what the stories actually contain. At best, such a commentary only opens the reader's heart by giving it a glimpse of the brilliant Torah secrets contained in the stories.

An English translation of the stories by Rabbi Aryeh Kaplan, with extensive notes based on traditional Breslover works, was published in 1983. This was the first compilation of all the commentary material written on the stories. French (*Les Contes*) and Russian editions are also available, but without the accompanying commentary.

Sefer HaMiddot — (*The Aleph-Bet Book*). *Sefer HaMiddot* is a collection of aphorisms on the various character traits (good and bad), as well as other aspects of the spiritual life of the Jew. It is arranged in alphabetical order by subjects. The work is divided into two parts. Part A was written by Rebbe Nachman in his youth, in order to direct and encourage himself in his struggle to attain holiness. Part B is similar to Part A in form and structure, and the aphorisms are, in the main, on the same subjects as in the first section. However, it was written later on in life and Rebbe Nachman said that it was based on considerably deeper understanding of the sources than the first part.

Rebbe Nachman himself never disclosed the exact references for these aphorisms. Nevertheless, he did indicate that anyone who carefully studied the material would be able to discover these sources, be they from verses in the Bible or the teachings of the Rabbis. This prompted Reb Noson to include a number of source references in the second printing, in 1821, ten years after the first edition was issued. For the seventh edition (1873-74), the Tcheriner Rav prepared a full set of references and they have been printed together with the references prepared by Reb Noson in all subsequent editions. In 1907-08 a new edition of the book was published containing further sources by Rebbe Tzadok HaCohen of Lublin.

A new edition of the Hebrew version, with expanded references, was published in 1984. These references quote in full each and every reference, with a commentary showing how the aphorism can be understood from the source. English and French (*Le Livre Du Aleph-Bet*) translations are also available.

Tikkun HaKlali — (*Rabbi Nachman's Tikkun*). Rebbe Nachman first mentioned the concept of the General Remedy in 1805, however the exact ten psalms which comprise this remedy were only revealed later on, in 1809-10. The first time the *Tikkun HaKlali* was printed as a separate book was in 1820-21. It was printed in Reb Noson's house on the initiative of his son Rebbe Shachneh. The Ten Psalms were accompanied by an introduction, a related lesson from *Likutey Moharan* I:205, and the prayer composed by Reb Noson to be recited after the psalms themselves. Subsequent editions of the *Tikkun HaKlali* have been printed with additional material from *Likutey Moharan* II:92, and *Sichot HaRan* #141 (the account of how the *Tikkun HaKlali* came to be revealed), and in some cases with commentaries on and translations of the Ten Psalms, and additional prayers, etc.

English and French (*Le Tikoun de Rebbe Nachman*) editions containing translations of the Ten Psalms, transliteration of the Hebrew, translations of the introductory material and general insights, are also available.

Reb Noson's Writings

Reb Noson's works have been divided into two sections: those about Rebbe Nachman and his works, and those which contain his own original insights.

Part I: About Rebbe Nachman.

Shevachey v'Sichot HaRan — (*Rabbi Nachman's Wisdom*). The *Shevachey HaRan* is an account of Rebbe Nachman's spiritual attainments. It includes *Masa'ot HaYam* which is an account of the Rebbe's pilgrimage to the Holy Land in 1798-99. *Sichot HaRan* is a collection of conversations and teachings ranging from simple, everyday advice to the most esoteric kabbalistic mysteries. An authoritative English translation of these two works with full references and some explanatory notes by Rabbi Aryeh Kaplan, edited by Rabbi Zvi Aryeh Rosenfeld, was published in 1973 under the title "Rabbi Nachman's Wisdom." A French edition of the *Sichot HaRan*, the conversations (*La Sagesse de Rebbe Nachman*), is available.

Chayey Moharan — (*Tzaddik*). This book is divided into three parts. The first part, *Chayey Moharan,* includes: accounts of the way in which many of Rebbe Nachman's lessons came to be revealed together with the events associated with them; dates of many of the lessons, and other relevant material; accounts of some of Rebbe Nachman's dreams and visions and other mystical experiences; an account of his life including details about many of the major events and incidents at that time. The second part describes Rebbe Nachman's spiritual attainments and the third part contains additional conversations and teachings on a variety of subjects, similar to the collection of conversations in *Rabbi Nachman's Wisdom.* The book was written by Reb Noson in order to convey a sense of the unique vitality of Rebbe Nachman — as Reb Noson puts it, "a man who was truly alive" — and in order to preserve as many of Rebbe Nachman's conversations as possible. It was evidently written after 1824 but, because of the controversy and strife directed against Reb Noson at that time, it remained unpublished circulating privately among Reb Noson's pupils. It was published later on by the Tcheriner Rav in 1874. An authoritative English translation with explanatory notes and full references by Avraham Greenbaum was published in 1987.

Likutey Etzot — (*Advice*) and **Kitzur Likutey Moharan**. In 1805, Rebbe Nachman told Reb Noson to collect the practical aspects and advice contained in *Likutey Moharan* and present them in an abridged form. The result was the *Kitzur Likutey Moharan.* When he showed Rebbe Nachman the fruit of his labor, the Rebbe called it "*a shein tzetel* (nice work)." Later on, in 1826, Reb Noson began collecting the rest of the advice from Rebbe Nachman's teachings. These were then separated according to subject matter and called *Likutey Etzot.* Thus we list them together, though they are separate works.

Likutey Etzot is unique because it goes straight to the heart of the subject matter of Rebbe Nachman's lessons. However complex one may find the *Likutey Moharan,* this work brings out the essence of every discourse in a simple form and enables the reader to apply the advice directly to his life.

Likutey Etzot was translated into English as *Advice* by Avraham Greenbaum and published in 1983.

*

Part II: Reb Noson's Works.

Likutey Halakhot. This is the "Collected Laws," Reb Noson's *magnum opus*. A monumental, eight-volume work of Breslov thought, it follows the order of topics in the *Shulchan Arukh*. With *Likutey Moharan* as his basis, Reb Noson focuses on the inner aspects of halakhah through an ethical eye. He highlights many of the major concepts in Rebbe Nachman's teachings and in a completely unique and unparalleled way shows their practical application and their interrelationship with all aspects of life for a Jew.

People have been known to randomly open *Likutey Halakhot* and find Reb Noson speaking directly to them, on the topic closest to their hearts at that very moment. There is nothing quite like it in all our holy writings and the *Likutey Halakhot* discourses are easy to follow, provided one has a command of Hebrew. Though the structure of each discourse inhibits a literal English translation, parts of *Likutey Halakhot* have appeared in *Tefilin, Garden of the Souls, Azamara, Ayeh, Tsohar* and *Mayim*.

Likutey Tefilot. Taking Rebbe Nachman's advice to "turn Torah into prayer," Reb Noson composed *Likutey Tefilot*, "A Collection of Prayers," in two volumes. It uses Rebbe Nachman's *Likutey Moharan* as its foundation, and through the words of prayer expresses the ideas and concepts of each lesson in a systematic way (explaining the lesson). At the same time, the prayers are simple and sincere, with the reader being able to pour out his heart before God through them. The first volume contains 152 prayers; the second contains 58 prayers.

In many of the recent editions these prayers have been supplemented by *Tefilot v'Tachanunim*, "Prayers and Supplications." These were authored by the Tcheriner Rav and focus on some points in the individual lessons that were skipped by Reb Noson, or on other lessons and conversations.

For anyone interested in experiencing what true prayer is like, the *Likutey Tefilot* is the book to have. An English translation is currently underway, though it is clear that one can never hope to duplicate, or even approach, the eloquency of Reb Noson's poetic Hebrew.

Yemey Moharnat. "The Days of *MoHaRNat*" (an acronym for Moreinu HaRav Reb Noson) is Reb Noson's autobiography. It is presented in two parts: the first deals with his life, from his birth in 1780 until 1835; the second part records his pilgrimage to the Holy Land in 1822. Interestingly, Reb Noson reports on the first twenty-two years of his life (he was born, raised, married, etc.) all on the first page, as if to say that his real life began only after he met the Rebbe. His journeys, the obstacles he faced and his innermost feelings are revealed in this important autobiographical work.

Alim Litrufah. The "Leaves of Healing," or, "The Collected Letters of Reb Noson." Most of these letters were penned to his son, Reb Yitzchok, who lived in nearby Tulchin, though there are additional letters to his contemporaries and followers. Despite their having been written to specific individuals, the letters are full of general encouragement and spiritual support for any and all. Throughout his correspondence, Reb Noson often refers to the ideas taught to him by the Rebbe; therefore, the work can be studied as a synopsis of many of Rebbe Nachman's teachings. The letters also have important biographical and historical data, spanning the years from 1822 to 1844, when Reb Noson passed away.

These two books, *Yemey Moharnat* and *Alim Litrufah*, along with a number of minor works, will be used in an English language biography of Reb Noson — clearly the most colorful personality in Breslover Chassidut. The project has passed the drawing board stage and is due to get underway shortly, God willing.

Shemot HaTzaddikim. This work lists most of the Tzaddikim found in the Tanakh, Talmud, Midrash and Zohar, including the *Gaonim, Rishonim* and *Acharonim* until Reb Noson's time. It was compiled by Reb Noson in 1821, just before he set out on his pilgrimage to the Holy Land. In fact, he felt that it was the merit of this work that enabled him to get to Eretz Yisrael.

A Hebrew version is found in *Rabbi Nachman's Tikkun*, following the Ten Psalms, with an explanation in English about the greatness of mentioning the names of the Tzaddikim.

Until the Mashiach. *Rabbi Nachman's Wisdom, Tzaddik* and *Yemey Moharnat* form the basis for most of our knowledge about Rebbe Nachman's life. Collecting data from these and numerous other sources in Breslov, Rabbi Aryeh Kaplan compiled an authoritative chronology which carries the title, *Until the Mashiach*. Aside from biographical information about Rebbe Nachman, this work contains an historical overview of Eastern European Jewry until Rebbe Nachman's day. It also contains separate appendices on the Chassidic leaders of the Rebbe's time, history of the cities Rebbe Nachman was associated with, and brief life-sketches on his followers and family, including a family tree. It is *the* source book for anyone seeking historical data on Rebbe Nachman. (Note: *Until the Mashiach* is not a work by Reb Noson. However, its major sources are Reb Noson's writings, without which we would know next to nothing about Rebbe Nachman. It has therefore been included here among his writings.)

*

Reb Nachman Goldstein of Tcherin

Known affectionately, yet reverently, by Breslover Chassidim as the Tcheriner Rav, Reb Nachman Goldstein was a *gaon* (genius in Torah) with few equals. His writings have contributed much to understanding Rebbe Nachman's teachings, by exposing their depth and beauty. His works (some twenty tomes) include:

Parparaot LeChokhmah. This is an indispensable commentary for understanding many of the complex concepts and structures in the discourses of *Likutey Moharan*.

Yerach Ha'Eitanim. This work relates *each* lesson in *Likutey Moharan* to Rosh HaShannah, Yom Kippur and Sukkot.

Zimrat Ha'Aretz. Here the Tcheriner Rav relates *each* lesson in *Likutey Moharan* to the Land of Israel.

Yekara DeShabbata. In this work he relates *each* lesson in *Likutey Moharan* to Shabbat.

Nachat HaShulchan. This tome shows the connection between numerous chapters of the *Shulchan Arukh* and the first lesson of *Likutey Moharan*.

Likutey Etzot HaMeshulash. Here we have an expanded version of the *Likutey Etzot* (Advice), with additional material from Rebbe Nachman's teachings, plus collected teachings of Reb Noson from the *Likutey Halakhot*.

In addition, the Tcheriner Rav researched the sources for *The Aleph-Bet Book*, spanning the entire length and breadth of the Bible, Talmud, and Midrash. His works also include a commentary on *Rabbi Nachman's Stories*. Many of the English language translations have been made possible thanks to his having opened many a "closed door" in Breslov teachings.

*

Reb Avraham b'Reb Nachman Chazan

Reb Avraham was the son of Reb Noson's closest follower, Reb Nachman Chazan. Although he authored a number of works based on the Rebbe's teachings, relatively few remain extant, and even these not in their entirety.

Biur HaLikutim. This work contains a very deep commentary on the *Likutey Moharan,* and presumes a good deal of familiarity with the Rebbe's work on the part of the reader. Only a sampling of the work was printed in the author's lifetime. Reb Shmuel Horowitz (d.1973) published the first edition in 1935. Reb Mordekhai Frank has recently edited and annotated the work which has now (1989) been published in a fully amended edition.

Kokhavey Or and Sichot v'Sipurim. As a confidant of his father, then the major leader of the Breslover Chassidim, Reb Avraham had direct access to and knowledge of many stories and traditions from Breslov lore. He incorporated this information in this work. Primarily, it is a compilation of anecdotes and ideas, with stories about Reb Noson's early childhood and his first encounter with the Rebbe. He also writes about many of the Rebbe's other followers.

*

Reb Alter Tepliker

Reb Moshe Yehoshua Bezhilianski of Teplik, more popularly known as Reb Alter Tepliker, authored and compiled about ten works. He is perhaps best known for the following four:

Meshivat Nefesh — (*Restore My Soul*). A collection of passages from *Likutey Moharan, Likutey Halakhot* and other Breslover works, all of which focus on man's inner strength and how he can always find his way back to God — even in the darkest moments. This small work is imperative for anyone who wants to discover his own power to overcome his habits and desires, and to return to God. The English translation is by Avraham Greenbaum, and a French edition (*Courage*) is also available.

Hishtafkhut HaNefesh — (*Outpouring of the Soul*). This is a collection of sayings on *hitbodedut* and meditation, taken from *Likutey Moharan, Likutey Halakhot* and other Breslover works. It was the first comprehensive compilation on *hitbodedut,* and remains necessary reading for anyone who truly hopes to follow Rebbe Nachman's path in meditation. The English translation was done by Rabbi Aryeh Kaplan, with the role of meditation in Jewish history clearly explained by this prominent author. A French edition (*Hitbodedut — Le Porte Du Ciel*) has also been published.

Mai HaNachal. This is Reb Alter Tepliker's commentary on the *Likutey Moharan*, in which he clarifies many difficult points. It has proved to be a most helpful work for the English translation of the Rebbe's discourses.

Haggadah Or Zoreiach — (*The Breslov Haggadah*). Collected teachings from *Likutey Moharan, Likutey Halakhot* and other Breslover works which serve as a commentary to the traditional Pesach Haggadah. An expanded edition of Reb Alter's original compilation has been produced in Hebrew, as well as an original English translation. Accompanying the English version are: the Midrashic story of the Exodus; Pesach anecdotes from Chassidic literature; and teachings on Pesach, Sefirat Ha'Omer and Shavuot. A French edition is available.

*

Other Works

There are many other books in the Breslov library, including original Torah insights explaining Rebbe Nachman's teachings, collected letters of Breslover Chassidim to each other, and some bibliographical and index material. The works whose descriptions follow were originally either stories, conversations, or oral teachings which have been transmitted by the leading Breslover Chassidim of this past generation and committed to writing.

Seder HaYom. A small but powerful treatise compiled by Reb Yitzchok Breiter (d.1943 in Treblinka), the *Seder HaYom* formed the basis for this book. Reb Yitzchok shows how — by applying Rebbe Nachman's teachings — a person can get the most out of each day. It appears in English as "A Day in the Life of a Breslover Chassid," and is printed as an addendum to the *Seven Pillars of Faith,* and also as an addendum to *Questions and Answers about Breslov.*

Seven Pillars of Faith. Also compiled by Reb Yitzchok Breiter, this time in conjunction with other leading Breslover Chassidim in Poland. The *Seven Pillars* comprises the seven most important aspects of faith as they are understood in Rebbe Nachman's teachings. An English translation by Avraham Greenbaum is available.

Ma'asiot U'Meshalim. These are parables told by Rebbe Nachman which were found recorded in a notebook of Reb Naftali, Rebbe Nachman's disciple. They have been translated into English and appear as a separate section at the end of *Rabbi Nachman's Stories.*

Aveneha Barzel, Sipurim Niflaim. This work is a collection of stories and anecdotes about Rebbe Nachman, Reb Noson, Reb Nachman Chazan and other Breslover Chassidim. It was compiled by Reb Shmuel Horowitz (d.1973) during his visit to Russia in 1933. Over a period of a few months, Reb Shmuel would spend an hour each day recording the stories told to him by the disciples of Reb Avraham Chazan. These disciples were Reb Eliyahu Chaim

Rosen (1898-1984), Reb Levi Yitzchak Bender (1897-1989), Reb Moshe Glidman (d.1946), Reb Moshe Shmuel and Reb Yochanan Galant (d.1978).

Tovot Zikhronot and Imrot Tehorot. Both these works are by Reb Avraham Sternhartz (1862-1955). *Tovot Zikhronot* contains informative stories about how some of the lessons in the *Likutey Moharan* came to be revealed, as well as many stories about Reb Noson, all of which were transcribed by Reb Gedaliah Koenig from Reb Avraham's dictation. *Imrot Tehorot* is an essay about the greatness of spending Rosh HaShannah with Rebbe Nachman in Uman or, when this is not possible, spending it in Meron by the gravesite of Rabbi Shimon bar Yochai.

Siach Sarfei Kodesh. This work is a collection of stories, anecdotes and conversations of and about Rebbe Nachman, Reb Noson and other Breslover Chassidim. These were transcribed by Reb Avraham Weitzhandler in conversation with Reb Levi Yitzchak Bender. The first two volumes are about Rebbe Nachman and Reb Noson, and were published in 1988 by Agudat Meshekh HaNachal. Additional volumes about other Breslover Chassidim are currently being prepared.

Questions and Answers about Breslov. Compiled by Avraham Greenbaum, this pamphlet answers many of the most often asked questions about Rebbe Nachman and the teachings of Breslover Chassidut.

*

Music and Cassettes. The traditional music of Chassidei Breslov is currently being transcribed by Benzion Solomon and produced in book form with an English transliteration and translation of the Hebrew words to the songs. The first volume covers the Friday Evening synagogue and family tunes, while volume II contains Shabbat morning and Afternoon songs and melodies. Other volumes are currently in production. In addition, Shabbat songs as well as meditative and dance melodies have been recorded and are available on cassette.

Study Tapes. Many of the leading Breslover Chassidim have had their lectures and classes recorded in Hebrew, Yiddish, English and French. General subjects, all spiced with Rebbe Nachman's teachings, include: *TaNaKh*, Psalms, Talmudic lore, halakhah and a broad selection of contemporary subjects. Breslov teachings include: *Likutey Moharan, Rabbi Nachman's Wisdom, Meshivat Nefesh* and a wide range of coversations.

* * *

Suggested Order of Study

The following is a *suggested* sequence by which to approach the works of Breslover Chassidut. Three separate schedules have been provided, based on your background in Judaism in general, and your ability to understand Hebrew texts. What is common to all three is the recitation of the prayers in *Likutey Tefilot*, as these heartfelt prayers will open the way to all the rest.

A. For those with no (or limited) background:

1) Rabbi Nachman's Wisdom
2) Advice
3) Until the Mashiach
4) Outpouring of the Soul; Restore My Soul
5) Azamra, Tsohar
6) Rabbi Nachman's Stories
7) The Aleph-Bet Book
8) Mayim; Ayeh?
9) Tzaddik
10) Rabbi Nachman's Tikkun

*

B. For those with some background:

1) Rabbi Nachman's Wisdom
2) Advice

3) Outpouring of the Soul; Restore My Soul
4) Rabbi Nachman's Stories
5) Azamra, Tsohar; Mayim; Ayeh?; Tefilin
6) Likutey Moharan; Tzaddik; The Aleph-Bet Book
7) Rabbi Nachman's Tikkun
8) Until the Mashiach

*

C. For those with (some) knowledge of Hebrew:

1) Rabbi Nachman's Wisdom
2) Advice
3) Outpouring of the Soul; Restore My Soul
4) Rabbi Nachman's Stories; Yemey Moharnat
5) Likutey Moharan; The Aleph-Bet Book (Hebrew version with sources)
6) Tzaddik; Kitzur Likutey Moharan; Alim Litrufah
7) Rabbi Nachman's Tikkun
8) Until the Mashiach
9) Likutey Halakhot

*

Our Sages taught: "Lucky is he who comes here [to Heaven] with his studies in his hand" (*Pesachim* 50a). When our days on this earth have come to an end, we will all have to appear before the Heavenly Court. The "luggage" we will carry with us will consist of whatever Torah study and good deeds we performed during our lifetimes. Reb Noson said, "The study mentioned certainly applies to Rebbe Nachman's works" (*Oral Tradition*). Happy is he who "packs" Rebbe Nachman's teachings to take on this final journey.

* * *

APPENDIX C

APPENDIX C: BRESLOV BIOGRAPHIES

This book is a collection of the teachings and ideas of Breslov Chassidut, from Rebbe Nachman down to the current generation. We present here short biographies on some of the leading luminaries of the movement — the "chain of tradition" — whose lives and lessons have provided us with the material for this work. The biographies are listed alphabetically according to the chronological order of the generation in which they lived.

*

Rebbe Nachman

Rebbe Nachman was born on Shabbat, Rosh Chodesh Nissan, 5532 (April 4, 1772), in Medzeboz. His father was Reb Simchah, the son of Reb Nachman Horodenker, who was a leading disciple of the Baal Shem Tov. His mother was Feiga, daughter of Adil, the daughter of the Baal Shem Tov. He had two brothers, Reb Yechiel and Reb Yisrael Met, and a sister Perel. His uncles, Feiga's brothers, were the prominent Chassidic figures, Reb Moshe Chaim Efraim, author of the *Degel Machaneh Efraim,* and Reb Baruch of Medzeboz.

Rebbe Nachman was born at a time when the Chassidic movement was beginning to ebb. A week after his birth, a cherem of excommunication was issued against the Chassidim. About half a year later, the Magid of Mezritch, the Baal Shem Tov's successor, passed away.

Rebbe Nachman grew up in Medzeboz, and married Sashia, the daughter of Reb Efraim of Ossatin, when he was thirteen (as was then the custom). On his wedding day he attracted his first disciple, Reb Shimon. Though older than Rebbe Nachman, Reb Shimon remarked proudly, "I left all the older *guter Yidden* (good Jews; a euphemism for Tzaddikim), and attached myself to a *yunger man* (young man)!"

The Rebbe had eight children, six daughters and two sons. Of these, only four daughters survived him. They were Adil, the eldest, then Sarah, Miriam and Chayah. Miriam moved to the Holy Land in 1809 where she passed away childless. Adil, Sarah and Chayah had children and a comprehensive family tree appears at the end of *Until the Mashiach*. The Rebbe had no children from his second wife, whom he married after Sashia's death from tuberculosis.

Rebbe Nachman moved to his father-in-law's town, Ossatin, and lived there for about five years. From there he moved to Medvedevka where he began to attract a large following, some of whom were to become his closest followers: Reb Dov, Reb Shmuel Isaac, Reb Yudel, Reb Aharon the Rav and Reb Yekutiel, the Magid of Terhovitza.

From Medvedevka, Rebbe Nachman made his pilgrimage to the Holy Land in 1798-1799. In 1800, shortly after Adil's wedding, he moved to Zlatipolia. There, the Rebbe encountered major difficulties from Reb Aryeh Leib, the "Shpola Zeide," who became Rebbe Nachman's embittered enemy. Two bitter years of relentless opposition led to Rebbe Nachman's moving to Breslov in the summer of 1802.

As much as the Rebbe's move was a necessary flight from controversy, it was also the watershed for Breslover Chassidut. Not far from the city of Breslov, in the town of Nemirov, there lived a certain young man who was to become Rebbe Nachman's closest disciple and Boswell. This was Reb Noson. Coming from a family of Mitnagdim, Reb Noson was, nevertheless, very impressed by the devotions of the Chassidim and made many attempts to find his niche within the relatively young movement. If Medvedevka and Zlatipolia were distant and inaccessible for Reb Noson, Breslov was right around the corner. Reb Noson, together with his friend Reb Naftali, immediately visited the Rebbe. They were so inspired by Rebbe Nachman's devotions and teachings that they promptly joined his following and before long became the Rebbe's most intimate disciples.

In early spring of 1803, Rebbe Nachman's daughter Sarah was married. In 1805, Miriam was married. (Chayah married after the Rebbe passed away.) During those years, except for some set times when the Rebbe visited Medvedevka, Tcherin and Terhovitza, Rebbe Nachman remained in Breslov.

In the winter of 1807, Rebbe Nachman set out on a journey to Novoritch, Dubno, Brody and Zaslov. In Zaslov, where the Rebbe spent the Shavuot holiday (June), his wife passed away. Before Rosh HaShannah (September 1807), he married again, this time the daughter of Reb Yechezkel Trachtenburg from Brody. Shortly afterwards, he contracted tuberculosis, which finally took his life three years later.

In 1808, Rebbe Nachman made a journey to Lemberg (Lvov), where he sought treatment for his illness. During that year, while the Rebbe was in Lemberg, the first volume of his major teachings, the *Likutey Moharan*, was published. He had already begun telling his famous stories and had also revealed his *Sefer HaMiddot* (The Aleph-Bet Book).

After his return from Lemberg, the Rebbe spent the next two years in Breslov. During this period he revealed the General Remedy and many far-sighted teachings for the Chassidic group he had founded. The tuberculosis continued to consume his body and Rebbe Nachman became very weak and frail. Realizing that his death was near, he began to make arrangements to move to Uman, the place he had chosen in which to pass away. The Rebbe had considered travelling to the Holy Land, but feared that he lacked the strength for so difficult a journey. He also wanted his followers to have access to his gravesite, something which might not prove possible were he to be buried in the Holy Land. Therefore, he chose the city of Uman, where there had been a huge massacre of some 20,000 Jews by Ivan Gunta and the Haidemacks in 1768. Rebbe Nachman said: "There are many *kedoshim* (holy martyrs) buried in Uman and it would be good to lie there amongst them" (*Tzaddik* #114).

In spring 1810, shortly after Pesach, a major fire in Breslov destroyed the Rebbe's house. A day later, word arrived that negotiations for welcoming the Rebbe had been concluded and accommodations had been arranged. Hearing the news, the Rebbe's face turned red. He knew that he was being summoned to die.

Rebbe Nachman arrived in Uman on May 9, 1810. During his stay there, the Rebbe talked much about rectifying souls, those close to him as well as other souls. It was here that he issued his famous call: "Never despair!" and exhorted his followers to gather for Rosh HaShannah. He passed away on the fourth day of Sukkot, 18 Tishrei 5571 (October 16, 1810), and was buried the next day. His grave has remained a shrine, visited by Breslover Chassidim and many others, from all over the world, ever since.

A full chronology of the Rebbe's life can be found in *Until the Mashiach,* with much biographical data in *Rabbi Nachman's Wisdom* and *Tzaddik.* Rebbe Nachman said, "We will always be known as the Chassidim of BReSLoV, the letters of which are the same as *LeV BaSaR* (heart of flesh)" (*Tzaddik* #339). Though Rebbe Nachman passed away nearly two hundred years ago, his flame burns brightly and continues to bring light and happiness to thousands upon thousands of people. Rebbe Nachman himself said: "My fire will burn until the Mashiach comes" (*Tzaddik* #126). May this be speedily and in our days, Amen.

* * *

Reb Noson

Reb Noson Sternhartz was born in Nemirov, on 15 Shevat, 5540 (January 22, 1780). At thirteen, he married Esther Shaindel, the daughter of the prominent Rabbi Dovid Zvi Orbach, a renowned halakhic authority in Poland and the Ukraine. Reb Noson was twenty-two when Rebbe Nachman moved to Breslov, and Reb Noson promptly became his leading follower. He also developed into the Rebbe's scribe, writing down all of the Rebbe's teachings and conversations. Rebbe Nachman himself said: "Were it not for Reb Noson, not a page of my writings would have remained" (see *Tzaddik* #367).

After Rebbe Nachman passed away, Reb Noson moved to Breslov (1811). He printed all of Rebbe Nachman's writings, and wrote his own original discourses and teachings, some of which were published during his lifetime. He also traveled throughout the Ukraine, visiting Rebbe Nachman's followers and continuing to spread the Rebbe's teachings. In 1822 he made his pilgrimage to the Holy Land, a trip that in many ways rivaled Rebbe Nachman's in adventure and suspense. During those years, Reb Naftali Hertz's business failed and Reb Noson became subjected to poverty. He once said that when he began eating from wooden utensils, he felt no taste in the food. Around 1830, with the pronounced increase in the number of those coming to Uman for Rosh HaShannah, Reb Noson initiated the construction of a large Breslov synagogue (until then, they had rented a place in the city for the *kibutz* gathering.)

In late 1834, Rabbi Moshe Zvi of Savran, the Savraner Rebbe, instigated fierce and fanatical opposition to Reb Noson and the Breslover Chassidim. This opposition led to Reb Noson's temporary imprisonment by the authorities. After his release, Reb Noson fled from city to city in the Ukraine, only returning to Breslov in the spring of 1835. Shortly afterwards he was banished from Breslov, and was under court order to remain in the city of his birth. Though he obtained permission to travel to Uman for Rosh HaShannah and for other select occasions, he was virtually a prisoner in Nemirov. His confinement also put him at the mercy of his opponents, who seized every opportunity to torment him. With the Savraner's sudden death in 1838, the relentless opposition waned and Reb Noson returned to Breslov later that year.

Reb Noson had five sons and one daughter, all of whom survived him. Reb Shachneh (b. 1802) and Reb Yitzchok (b. 1808) were born during Rebbe Nachman's lifetime. Reb Noson's only daughter Chana Tzirel (b. 1820) and his third son, Reb Dovid Zvi (b. 1822) were also born to him by his first wife, Esther Shaindel (d.1826). Reb Noson then married Dishel, who bore him two sons, Reb Nachman (b.1827) and Reb Yosef Yonah (b.1829).

Despite great personal suffering from both poverty and opposition, Reb Noson was singlehandedly responsible for shaping the Breslov movement into the vibrant force it is today. This, in spite of the fact that there is no "living" rebbe. On the morning of his passing, 10 Tevet, 5605 (December 20, 1844), Reb Noson had the first two stories of *Rabbi Nachman's Stories* read to him. The second story ends, "...let us go home!" Hearing these words, Reb Noson nodded his head as if to say, "Yes, it is my time to go home." He passed away later that day in his home in Breslov, just before the onset of Shabbat. Reb Naftali, with whom Reb Noson had been very close ever since childhood, was then living in Uman. The next morning he said that he was certain that "Reb Noson passed away last night." When asked how he knew this, he replied, "I had a dream in which I saw Reb Noson. He was running. I asked him, 'Reb Noson, where are you running?' 'Me?!' he answered. 'Straight to the Rebbe!'" (*Oral Tradition*).

* * *

The Rebbe's Followers

From his many disciples, Rebbe Nachman had an inner group of followers — six giants among the many. They, together with Rebbe Nachman himself, are referred to in Breslov circles as the Candelabrum. These followers were: Reb Shimon, Reb Shmuel Isaac, Reb Yudel, Reb Aharon, Reb Noson and Reb Naftali. Biographical sketches about these and other followers of the Rebbe can be found in *Until the Mashiach,* pp.296-320.

* * *

B. The Second Generation

Chazan, Reb Nachman [of Tulchin] (1813-1884). Reb Nachman's grandfather was a follower of Rebbe Nachman. Born shortly after the Rebbe passed away, Reb Nachman was named after the Rebbe. Orphaned as a very young child, he grew up in his uncle's house, where he met Reb Noson on the latter's pilgrimage to the Holy Land in 1822. Reb Noson made such a deep impression upon him that the young Nachman decided to be close to Reb Noson forever. He indeed became Reb Noson's most intimate follower and eventually was leader of the Breslov movement.

Reb Nachman was the *chazan* (prayer leader) for the Musaf Prayer on Rosh HaShannah, hence the family name Chazan. His supplications were so intense, that those assembled felt he was "standing on air" while reciting the prayers. His great fervor was matched by his modesty. Though he was the leader of the Breslover Chassidim at that time, Reb Nachman did not consider it beneath him   serve others. Immediately after praying the daily prayers with great devotion, he would take the water buckets to draw water for the synagogue.

Reb Nachman published the first volume of his mentor's *Likutey Halakhot* while Reb Noson was still alive. Later, he edited and published the remaining seven volumes. Reb Nachman lived for eighteen years in Tulchin and then moved to Breslov after Reb Noson passed away so that he could continue Reb Noson's work. After eighteen years in Breslov he moved to Uman, where he lived an additional eighteen years. It was this move that shifted the focus of Breslover Chassidut to Uman. For all his greatness, he was extremely modest and humble, serving as *shamash* (sexton) of the Breslover Synagogue in Uman.

Goldstein, Reb Nachman [of Tcherin] (b.?-d.1894). Known affectionately and reverently as the Tcheriner Rav, Reb Nachman was the son of Reb Zvi Aryeh of Breslov. His father's father, Reb Aharon, was the Chief Rabbi in Breslov in Rebbe Nachman's time. In fact, the Rebbe said that he invoked his ancestral merits in order to bring Reb Aharon — whose clarity in rendering halakhic decisions was unparalleled — to Breslov. An erudite scholar even as a young boy, Reb Nachman, who grew up in Breslov, shied away from Reb Noson in his early years. Reb Noson once called him over and said, "You know, it's very possible that Rebbe Nachman used his ancestral merits to bring your grandfather to Breslov only because of you."

After Reb Noson passed away, the Tcheriner Rav regretted having distanced himself from Reb Noson and he became very involved with Reb Noson's works. He published the *Likutey Etzot HaMeshulash*, the expanded *Likutey Etzot* (Advice) and collected Reb Noson's teachings in the *Likutey Halakhot* on all the same topics which appear in the earlier work. He also was the first to begin writing a commentary specifically on Rebbe Nachman's works, thereby making these complex tomes somewhat more accessible to the layman. His personal level of scholarship defies description.

Known as a *matmid* (diligent in Torah study), he often remained awake all night while immersed in study. As Rabbi of Tcherin, he was always being invited to weddings by the local residents, though he did not always go. Once, his attendant decided not to pass on the invitation since he knew that the Rav in any case, was not going to attend. When he discovered this, Reb Nachman was upset. "Whenever I receive an invitation to a wedding, I know that I'm not going to get any sleep that night (he would always only sleep till midnight and then rise to study Torah until morning). So, even if I don't go to the wedding, I stay up throughout the night studying. By not giving me the invitation, you 'cheated' me out of a full night of Torah!"

After writing his commentary *Yekara DeShabbata*, explaining the holiness of Shabbat as perceived in each lesson of the *Likutey Moharan*, the Tcheriner Rav said that he could no longer sleep on Shabbat. He said, "Someone who keeps Shabbat is known as a *shomer Shabbat* (*shomer* means watchman or guard). Everyone knows that it is forbidden for a watchman to sleep on the job! How then can I sleep on Shabbat?!"

A younger contemporary of Reb Nachman Chazan, the Tcheriner Rav was highly respected and honored by the Breslover Chassidim. He, together with Reb Avraham Ber, Rebbe Nachman's grandson, was responsible for Reb Avraham Sternhartz being appointed prayer leader for the Rosh HaShannah prayers. Still, when making the pilgrimage to Uman for Rosh HaShannah, he would not expect or allow any preferential treatment because of stature. "In Uman, we are all alike," he said. "When I set out for the Rosh HaShannah *kibutz*, I leave behind my rabbinical status and authority."

All told, he authored about twenty books, several of which were only seen by Breslover Chassidim in manuscript form before they were lost. Of his major works that remain with us are the *Parparaot LeChokhmah* on *Likutey Moharan*, *Rimzey Ma'asiot* on *Rabbi Nachman's Stories* and the source references for the *Sefer HaMiddot*. He also compiled a two-volume collection of teachings on various topics from the Baal Shem Tov and his major disciples, entitled *Leshon Chassidim* and *Derekh Chassidim*.

Lubarski, Reb Moshe [Breslover]. Reb Noson was once confronted by a distraught woman who pleaded with him to bless her with children. Her two sons, Reb Moshe and Reb Zanvil Lubarski, were the fruits of Reb Noson's blessing. Reb Moshe was one of Reb Noson's closest followers and a leading Breslover figure after Reb Noson. Reb Yisrael Karduner was sent to him to learn about Breslov. The Tcheriner Rav who sent him, said, "Reb Moshe grew up by Reb Noson. He will plant Reb Noson's teachings in you."

Reb Moshe's faith in Reb Noson was beyond description. Once he was robbed. Instead of looking for the thief, Reb Moshe entered the house of study, took out Reb Noson's *Likutey Halakhot* and studied the laws and discourses on stealing. Shortly afterwards, his possessions were returned to him. After his marriage, Reb Moshe moved to Tcherin where he would converse daily about the Rebbe's teachings with Reb Avraham Ber, Rebbe Nachman's grandson and another of Reb Noson's followers. Reb Dov, the Rebbe's follower and Reb Avraham Ber's father-in-law, once asked Reb Moshe to speak to him. Reb Moshe stood in awe and said, "What can I say to you about serving God? You knew the Rebbe!" Reb Dov answered, "Believe me! You learned more about Rebbe Nachman through Reb Noson, than I know even from Rebbe Nachman himself."

Reb Efraim b'Reb [son of] Naftali (b.1800?-1883). Though Reb Efraim's father (Reb Naftali) was one of Rebbe Nachman's closest followers, his father sent him to study Breslover Chassidut from Reb Noson. A close follower who spent much time with Reb Noson, Reb Efraim later wrote two books patterned after his mentor's works. The first is *Likutey Even*, following the style of the *Likutey Halakhot* by explaining the Codes with Rebbe Nachman's teachings. The second is *Tefilot HaBoker*, prayers which are based upon Reb Noson's teachings. He was very modest and published both volumes without his name appearing as author. Reb Efraim was a very close friend of his contemporary Reb Yitzchok Sternhartz (q.v.) and both were held in high esteem by Reb Noson.

Sternhartz, Reb Yitzchok (1808-1871). Reb Yitzchok was Reb Noson's second oldest son. After his marriage, he lived in Tulchin (about nine miles from Breslov where his father lived after the Rebbe passed away). Reb Yitzchok was highly respected and honored, especially amongst the local authorities, who placed him in charge of the post office (which also served as a government bank in those days). Reb Noson said, "I had no time to write all the letters that I did to my son. The letters were written by Reb Yitzchok's burning desire to hear words of encouragement from me." These letters make up the *Alim Litrufah*, which has letters that Reb Yitzchok himself wrote appended to the book. Reb Yitzchok moved to the Holy Land in the summer of 1868 and passed away in Safed a few years later. He is buried right next to Rabbi Yosef Caro, author of the *Shulchan Arukh*.

* * *

C. The Third Generation

Breiter, Reb Yitchok (1886-1943?). Reb Yitzchok was born in Poland seventy-six years after Rebbe Nachman's passing, and he grew up without ever having heard about Breslover Chassidut. One day, while studying in Rabbi Tzadok's Yeshivah in Lublin, he came across a copy of the *Likutey Moharan*. He became engrossed in Lesson #64 of volume I, which opened entirely new worlds of thought and faith in the Torah for him. Hiding the book so he could easily find it the next day, he was most disappointed when he returned to discover that it had disappeared.

A few weeks later Reb Yitzchok came across a copy of *Parparaot LeChokhmah*, the Tcheriner Rav's commentary on *Likutey Moharan*. He used the information it contained to make contact with the Breslover Chassidim in Russia and by the following Rosh HaShannah made his first trip to Uman. After that, Reb Yitzchok became instrumental in spreading the teachings of Breslov throughout Poland, so that by the beginning of the Second World War, Breslover Chassidim in Poland numbered several thousand. In 1917, when the border between Soviet Russia and Poland was closed after the Bolshevik Revolution, he established the *kibutz* for Rosh HaShannah in Lublin. Reb Yitzchok was a recognized elder in the Warsaw Ghetto until he was sent in one of the transports to Treblinka, where he was murdered at the hands of the accursed Nazis.

Chazan, Reb Avraham (ben R. Nachman) (1849-1917). As a youth, Reb Avraham displayed incredible tenaciousness in his devotions. He would often leave home right after Shabbat with only a sack of bread and a stack of books, to disappear into the forest for an entire week. There he would meditate and study undisturbed. His profundity can be seen from his commentary, *Biur HaLikutim*, which dissects Rebbe Nachman's lessons point by point by delving into their depths. Even so, Reb Avraham himself said about the Rebbe's simple conversations: "I hope that ten thousand years after the Resurrection, I will be worthy of understanding even one of Rebbe Nachman's statements, the way the Rebbe himself understood it in this world."

The year after Reb Nachman Chazan passed away (1884), Reb Avraham began recording many of the stories and Breslov traditions that he had received from his father. This formed the basis for the *Kokhavey Or* (five sections), *Sichot V'Sipurim* and other books. Around 1894 Reb Avraham moved to Jerusalem, though he would travel back to Russia each year to spend Rosh HaShannah in Uman. He continued this until the outbreak of World War One left him trapped in Russia, where he remained until his passing on Chanukah, 1917. Among his students were Reb Eliyahu Chaim Rosen and Reb Levi Yitzchok Bender, some of the key individuals responsible for the development of Breslover Chassidut in Jerusalem today.

Halperin, Reb Yisrael [of Kardun] (d.1920). Reb Yisrael was born in Poland and was recognized as a prodigy. Finding a *Tikkun HaKlali*, he became enflamed with Breslover Chassidut and moved to the Ukraine, where he studied under Reb Moshe Breslover. In the end of the story of *The Spider and the Fly* (Rabbi Nachman's Stories #7), the Rebbe mentions a beautiful person. Having seen Reb Yisrael, the Tcheriner Rav said that this alludes to him. At the turn of the century, Reb Yisrael moved to the Holy Land, living in Meron, Safed and Tiberias. His prayers were legendary for their sweetness, and many people became attracted to Breslov Chassidut after hearing Reb Yisrael in his devotions. A number of melodies in the Breslov repertoire originate from him. Perhaps his most often quoted remark is, "There was someone [Rebbe Nachman] who called out 100 years ago, 'Never give up!' and we still hear that voice today." He lost his entire family during a plague in Tiberias, where he himself is buried.

Sternhartz (Kokhav Lev), Reb Avraham (1862-1955). Reb Avraham was Reb Noson's great-grandson and a grandson of the Tcheriner Rav. Orphaned at a young age, he was raised by his illustrious grandfather whose influence upon him was unmistakable. Even as a child, Reb Avraham showed great diligence in Torah study, a trait for which his grandfather was known. After the morning prayers he would seclude himself in the attic where he would study Rebbe Nachman's *Likutey Moharan*, not interrupting his studies until he knew the lesson of the day by heart. After completing the entire Talmud at the age of sixteen, he married. He was a scribe in Tcherin and at age nineteen was accepted as Rav in Kremenchug. At twenty-two he was appointed prayer leader for the Rosh HaShannah *kibutz*, a post which he also held after coming to the Holy Land, for a total of seventy years.

Reb Avraham arrived in Jerusalem's Old City in 1936, where he was received and recognized as the outstanding Breslover elder of his generation. In 1940 he established the *kibutz* in Meron for Rosh HaShannah. Exiled from the Old City during the War of Independence in 1948, he was resettled in Katamon together with many other Breslover Chassidim. Among his disciples were a number of the major Breslover leaders of the past few decades, including: Reb Moshe and Reb Nachman Burstein, Reb Michel Dorfman, Reb Shmuel Horowitz (d.1973), Reb Gedaliah Aharon Koenig, Reb Zvi Aryeh Lippel (1903-1979), Reb Zvi Aryeh Rosenfeld, Reb Shmuel Shapiro and Reb Yaakov Meir Shechter.

It was said of Reb Avraham that he was a "living" *Likutey Moharan*. Just by looking at him, one could see that his every action was based on some statement in Rebbe Nachman's teachings. When giving a lesson in *Likutey Moharan*, he would begin by reading from the text, divert to complementary material for an hour or two, and then pick up again from the exact word where he'd left off. What was amazing about this was that it was all done entirely by memory, without Reb Avraham's ever having to look into the written text! And what's more, he did this up until he passed away at age ninety-three and a half.

Tepliker, Reb Alter (d.1919). Though known affectionately as Reb Alter, his real name was Reb Moshe Yehoshua Bezhilianski. A leading Breslover in Uman (Teplik is near Uman) at the turn of the century, he was the brother-in-law of Reb Avraham Chazan. During the Cossack uprising in the Ukraine in 1919, Reb Alter was murdered in a synagogue while seated next to a Torah scroll. Reb Alter initiated the publication of Breslov teachings in the more popular format based on separate topics, such as *Hishtafkhut HaNefesh* on *hitbodedut* and *Meshivat Nefesh* on inner strength and so on. (A list of his works is found in Appendix B.)

* * *

D. The Fourth Generation

Bender, Reb Levi Yitzchok (1897-1989). Arriving in Uman in 1915, Reb Levi Yitzchok became a close student of Reb Avraham Chazan. Although his mentor passed away two years later and World War One had come to an end, he remained in what was then the center of Breslov Chassidut for the next twenty some odd years. It was not long before Reb Levi Yitzchok's special qualities were recognized and at the age of thirty he was appointed prayer leader for the Morning Prayer on Rosh HaShannah in Uman. In the early winter of 1936, he and Reb Eliyahu Chaim Rosen were imprisoned in the Ukraine as "subversive elements." Given a conditional reprieve, Reb Levi Yitzchok fled. He ran from city to city, never remaining long in any one place. The years of the Second World War he spent in Siberia, after which he emigrated to Poland. Finally, in 1949, he arrived in the Holy Land. Reb Levi Yitzchok was the recognized head of the Breslov synagogue in Jerusalem until his passing. Many Breslover Chassidim accepted him as their spiritual guide, especially the *baalei teshuvah,* who've joined the Rebbe's following in great number over the past two decades.

Reb Levi Yitzchok's personal study schedule was legendary. He gave himself over to following Rebbe Nachman's teaching of finishing many of the holy writings each year (see chapter 7). His diligence in following the Rebbe's advice to recite *Chatzot* and practice *hitbodedut* was also amazing. For some seventy-five years, he never missed a night of *Chatzot*. Yet, when someone once asked him, "Which of your accomplishments is most precious to you? Which are you going to present to the Heavenly Court?" Reb Levi Yitzchok answered simply and in true Breslov fashion: "I lived thirty years in Russia and I still believe in God!"

Rosen, Reb Eliyahu Chaim (1899-1984). Founder and dean of the Breslov Yeshivah in Jerusalem. Reb Eliyahu Chaim was born in Poltosk, Poland and orphaned as a very young boy. At five he was sent to study Torah away from home. Excelling in his studies, he was admitted to the famous Lomzer Yeshivah when only twelve. There he found a *Tikkun HaKlali* and met a Breslover Chassid who convinced him to travel to Uman. He arrived in Uman in 1914 and was extremely impressed that Rebbe Nachman's followers, though definitely chassidim, paid strict adherence to the Halakhah as delineated in the *Shulchan Arukh* — without what is commonly known as chassidic "twists."

While in Uman he heard that Rebbe Nachman had said: "The most difficult spiritual devotion is far easier than a simple physical transaction." Not understanding this, he sought an explanation from Reb Avraham Chazan. The then leader of the Breslover Chassidim replied simply, *"Hitbodedut* is the greatest spiritual devotion one can perform. All it takes is speaking with one's mouth. Even earning just a small amount of money requires more effort than that." From then on, Reb Eliyahu Chaim remained in Uman under Reb Avraham Chazan's tutelage.

A resident of Uman for twenty-two years, he was instrumental in the survival of many Breslover Chassidim in Uman and its environs during the famine which swept the Ukraine in 1933. He organized shipments from the breadlines in Moscow, mailing food back to Uman. He also applied to the Joint Distribution Committee for assistance. This last act caused him to be arrested by the NKVD (predecessor of the KGB) in November 1935, when both he and Reb Levi Yitzchok Bender were charged with making contact with foreign organizations. They were imprisoned, put on "trial," and were under threat of having the death sentence passed against them. However God was with them and a Jewish official in the Ministry of Justice in Kiev was put in charge of their case. Being close to the Breslover Chassidim, this official won them a reprieve. They were permitted to return home, but under "city arrest," forbidden to leave Uman.

Despite this, Reb Eliyahu Chaim returned immediately to Moscow. Even before the famine, in 1931, he had made a request to emigrate to Israel, so that upon his return he found his exit visa waiting for him. Reb Eliyahu Chaim fled to Jerusalem, arriving there in early summer 1936. He took up residence in the Meah Shearim quarter of "new Jerusalem" and established the Breslov Yeshivah in the Old City, in 1937. In early 1953, Reb Eliyahu Chaim initiated the construction of what is today the home of the Breslover *Shul* and Yeshivah on Meah Shearim Street in Jerusalem. For this, he was ridiculed even by some of the leading Breslover Chassidim. "For whom are you building such a large *shul?*" he was asked. (There were maybe 150 Breslover Chassidim in all of Israel at the time.) Today, nearly forty years later, his brilliant foresight can no longer be questioned. The synagogue, despite its size, is not quite large enough to house the growing numbers of Breslover Chassidim in our generation.

As an address for the brokenhearted, Reb Eliyahu Chaim was the number one stop. Anyone with a heavy heart who came to see him, walked away wondering why he'd been so troubled. It's not that the problems suddenly disappeared. Rather, they remained and were real, but with Reb Eliyahu Chaim's razor-sharp mind, all the accompanying pressures and anxieties had been analyzed, all the excess factors had been cut away. Now, all the person had to deal with was the one point around which the problem really centered and through which he would be able to correct his situation. He would always say, with a broad smile, "The Torah has Five Books. The *Shulchan Arukh* comprises four volumes. What happened to the fifth volume? This corresponds to one's common sense, knowing where and how to apply your knowledge."

Reb Eliyahu Chaim's inner strength and joy were ever-present. His level of *yishuv hada'at* (calmness and serenity) had no equal.

His body weakened by typhus and other illnesses during his early years, he was quite weak towards the end of his life. Yet, as the true Breslover Chassid he was, he never missed reciting *Chatzot* and practicing *hitbodedut*. When asked how he found the strength for such devotions, he replied, "If you get used to it when you are young, it comes automatically after so many years." He taught us, over and over again, never to do anything without *hitbodedut*. During his last year, when he was in bed most of the time, he said, "What would I be able to do now, if I didn't have Rebbe Nachman's advice of *hitbodedut*."

Rosenfeld, Reb Yisrael Abba (1882-1947). Reb Yisrael Abba was born to a Breslover family and lived most of his life in Kremenchug in the Ukraine. With the massacre of his family during the Bolshevik revolution, he made his way west, through Poland, arriving in the United States in 1924. Though there was barely a *minyan* of Breslover Chassidim in New York at that time, he helped establish weekly study sessions in Rebbe Nachman's teachings. Reb Yisrael Abba was also active in raising funds for the Breslov community in Israel.

Spector, Reb Elchonon (d. 1985). A descendant of the Chozeh of Lublin, Reb Elchonon was a child prodigy and an ordained Rav early in life. Even so, he wanted neither the honor nor the proprieties which he could have had due to his position and vast knowledge. And vast it was. He was said to know the entire Talmud, Midrash, Zohar and many other writings by heart. Later on, when he moved to Eretz Yisrael, Reb Elchonon shunned the possibility of a rabbinical position and supported himself as a scribe. He preferred to keep his great knowledge from the public eye.

Yet, there were rare times when, by engaging Reb Elchonon in casual conversation, he could be "caught off guard." On these occasions he would open up and one might have the good fortune to glimpse just how deep the wellsprings of Reb Elchonon's great wisdom really were. His humility was such, that one could see the awe-filled embarrassment which he felt before God written on his face. In Breslov circles he was recognized as an halakhic authority and his deep understanding of the Rebbe's teachings meant that his ideas were always valued by other leaders of Breslover Chassidut. Some of his original insights into Rebbe Nachman's teachings were published, though most still remain in manuscript.

* * *

D. The Fifth Generation

Koenig, Reb Gedaliah Aharon (1921-1980). Born in Jerusalem, Reb Gedaliah was a young man when he was drawn to Rebbe Nachman's following by Reb Avraham Sternhartz. When the war of 1948 ravaged the Old City, he moved, together with his mentor, to what is today Katamon. Aside from his efforts to support the Breslover Rosh HaShannah *kibutz* in Meron, and authoring the *Chayey Nefesh* (a treatise in response to the *Nefesh HaChaim* by the prominent disciple of the Vilna Gaon, Rabbi Chaim Volozhin), Reb Gedaliah was known for his ability to speak to the searching souls of many of today's youth. Yet, for all of this, he saw as his true mission in life the reestablishment of a chassidic community in Safed. He literally gave his life for this cause.

Rosenfeld, Reb Zvi Aryeh Benzion (1922-1978). A scion of a Breslov family, the Rosenfelds trace their lineage back to Reb Aharon, the Rav of Breslov and Reb Shmuel Yitzchak, the Rav of Tcherin, both of whom were among the most prominent followers of Rebbe Nachman. Born in Gydinia, Poland in 1922, Reb Zvi Aryeh was stricken with diphtheria when he was just six months old. His father, Reb Yisrael Abba, went to the Chofetz Chaim and asked the aged sage to alter the baby's name (customarily done for someone seriously ill). The name Benzion was added.

The family arrived in the United States in 1924. Growing up in the Brownsville section of Brooklyn, Reb Zvi Aryeh attended the Rabbi Chaim Berlin School and then Yeshivah Torah Vodaat High School. Afterwards he studied under the world renowned Rabbi Avraham Yafen, in the Navardik — Beis Yosef Yeshivah. At age twenty-three, after completing the entire Talmud for the second time along with his many other studies, Reb Zvi Aryeh was ordained as a rabbi.

Assuming responsibility for some of his father's charitable obligations, after the latter's passing in 1947, Reb Zvi Aryeh began corresponding with Reb Avraham Sternhartz in Jerusalem. Making his first of over fifty trips to the Holy Land in 1949, he met with Reb Avraham, who instilled in Reb Zvi Aryeh the burning need to spread Rebbe Nachman's teachings in America. This became his life's mission, and for thirty years Reb Zvi Aryeh was a pioneer in the *baal teshuvah* movement in the United States — all the while introducing more and more people to Rebbe Nachman's teachings. He encountered angry parents, threats to his life and family, and was even made to face charges for kidnapping (see *Rabbi Nachman's Stories* #12). Yet, he continued his work, bringing literally thousands of Jews in contact with Judaism and Rebbe Nachman. Included among his students were those who opened the way for pilgrimages to Uman and many who continue to be active in different aspects of the world Breslov scene today.

Forever giving lessons and lectures, Reb Zvi Aryeh loved to share his vast knowledge of the Talmud, Midrash, Zohar, Kabbalah and Rebbe Nachman's teachings in classes attended by Sefardim and Ashkenazim alike. He also excelled in worldly wisdom and was able to dispense sound advice in financial matters. Yet, materially he himself lived a very meager existence, with only a teacher's salary to support himself and his family.

Aside from the time he spent teaching in school and lecturing on Rebbe Nachman, Reb Zvi Aryeh devoted himself to collecting the funds to build the Breslov Yeshivah in Jerusalem. Exhorted by Reb Avraham Sternhartz and encouraged by Reb Eliyahu Chaim Rosen, he raised most of the construction costs. When the building was finished, he continued to raise funds to publish Rebbe Nachman's works in Hebrew. He also pioneered the translation of Rebbe Nachman's teachings into English. This began with *Rabbi Nachman's Wisdom,* which Rabbi Aryeh Kaplan translated at Reb Zvi Aryeh's behest. Actually, Reb Zvi Aryeh himself edited the book.

Reb Zvi Aryeh also raised and distributed funds for the needy Breslover families in Israel. He had an immense love for the Holy Land and wished to settle there himself. The one thing which always held him back was the new students that kept joining his classes each year. He once decided that should a whole year go by without a new student being attracted, he'd move to Jerusalem. Stricken with cancer at age 56, he finally moved to Jerusalem in the summer of 1978, thereby giving himself a few months to prepare for his passing.

Even when he became bed-ridden and extremely weak, his students would study the Talmud and Zohar at his bedside, with Reb Zvi Aryeh following the discourse and interjecting points from time to time. A father figure to his students, many of them came to Israel for a few days just to spend one last time with him. For as long as it was possible, he continued reciting the *Tikkun HaKlali*, often with the assistance of one his students. Reb Zvi Aryeh left a legacy which includes thousands of hours of taped classes and lectures, all of which give insight into Rebbe Nachman's teachings as they relate to all aspects of Torah.

Shapiro, Reb Shmuel (1913-1989). Born in Jerusalem, Reb Shmuel was one of the most outstanding students in the Etz Chaim Yeshivah under its world-renowned Rosh Yeshivah, Rabbi Isar Zalman Meltzer. Attracted to Breslov by Reb Shmuel Horowitz, he became a chassid in 1934. When learning of this, his Rosh Yeshivah said, "Whoever made him a Breslover will never leave Gehennom." To which Reb Shmuel Shapiro countered, "Correct. Because he'll never go in!"

Known as "the Tzaddik of Jerusalem," Reb Shmuel always kept his eyes lowered in public, never looking at any of the physical attractions of this world. He would spend all night in the fields in *hitbodedut* and then put in a full day's Torah study in some obscure synagogue, always shunning the public eye. In preparation for Rosh HaShannah he would spend the month of Elul in Meron, where Rabbi Shimon bar Yochai is buried. "Here I have everything I need. A synagogue, a *mikvah* and mountains for *hitbodedut*. It's Gan Eden on earth," he was heard to say. Together with Reb Moshe Burstein and other Breslover Chassidim, he was taken to Jordan as a civilian hostage during Israel's War of Independence.

His one great desire, one that seemed to elude perpetually him, was to visit Rebbe Nachman's gravesite in Uman. In 1970, he traveled to America to get a special (stateless) passport so that he could apply for a visa to Russia. Even with this so called "white passport," it took nearly three years, but he finally made it. Not satisfied with the one trip, he longed to spend Rosh Hashannah there. This was finally made possible by changes in Soviet policy and he visited Uman, on an Israeli passport, for Rosh HaShannah 5749 (1988). Shortly afterwards he passed away, having suffered from Parkinson's Disease for nearly thirteen years.

Tefilinsky, Reb Yaakov Gedaliah (1942-1971). A nephew to Reb Yaakov Meir Schechter, Reb Yaakov Gedaliah was born in Jerusalem. He studied in Yeshivat Mir and became an accredited scholar and scribe. Childless for ten years after his marriage, he made the pilgrimage with great self-sacrifice to Rebbe Nachman's gravesite in 1969 (long before *glasnost*). A year to the day after his pilgrimage, his only child was born! Reb Yaakov Gedaliah was a legend in his adherence to having *hitbodedut* in the fields. Always weak and sickly, he passed away a few months after his daughter's birth.

* * *

Burstein, Reb Moshe (b.1912). A leading figure in Breslov in Jerusalem, Reb Moshe was born in Poltosk, Poland and arrived in the Holy Land in 1935 with his wife and infant son. Moving to Jerusalem's Jewish Quarter, he founded the daily Breslov *minyan* there. During the War of Independence (1948), he was held as a civilian hostage by the Jordanians along with eight other Breslovers. After his release, he was resettled in the Katamon section of Jerusalem, where he bought, rebuilt and administered the Breslover Synagogue. Reb Moshe was one of Reb Avraham Sternhartz's closest disciples and was a *ba'al tefilah* in the Meron *kibutz* for Rosh HaShannah for many years. For fifty years he longed to be worthy of getting to Rebbe Nachman's gravesite. When this finally happened, in the spring of 1988, he recited the *Shehechiyanu* Blessing.

Burstein, Reb Nachman (b.1934). The eldest son of Reb Moshe Burstein, Reb Nachman's expertise in the traditional melodies of

Breslover Chassidim is unparalleled. At age thirty, he was appointed the prayer leader for Musaf in the Breslov *minyan* in Meron on Rosh HaShannah. An erudite scholar, he is a walking encyclopedia on Rebbe Nachman and his teachings and currently one of the leading Breslover Chassidim in Jerusalem.

Dorfman, Reb Michel (b.1911). Born near Kiev, Reb Michel became a Breslover Chassid in his early teens. He married the granddaughter of Reb Avraham Sternhartz. Escaping the Stalinist purges of the Ukraine, he settled in Moscow in the late 1930s where he survived the war, only to be exiled to Siberia for nearly seven years. After Stalin's death, he was given a reprieve and allowed to return to Moscow. Reb Michel was a key figure in maintaining the Breslov *kibutz* on Rosh HaShannah in Uman, which, even after Stalin, had to be done clandestinely as all religious gatherings remained prohibited.

It was Reb Michel's efforts and self-sacrifice that eventually led to the lifting of the "iron curtain" which prevented Breslover Chassidim from getting to Rebbe Nachman's gravesite. Even when visas were granted, the Russians only permitted tourists to be in Kiev and not Uman. Though he had a "record," having already spent time in Siberia, Reb Michel was still willing to place himself in great danger in order to travel with American tourists (who had no visas) to Uman so that he could show them the place where Rebbe Nachman was buried. Today, thanks to him and others who've emulated his self-sacrificing ways, the Russian authorities are permitting pilgrimages. Reb Michel was finally allowed to settle in Israel in 1970, and he is currently the Rosh Yeshivah of the Breslov Yeshivah in Jerusalem.

Gelbach, Reb Yitzchok (b.1916). Reb Yitzchok was born in Likev, Poland. At age twelve, he found a copy of *Hishtafkhut HaNefesh*, which introduced him to Breslover Chassidut. After meeting with Reb Yitzchok Breiter, he became a committed chassid. He studied in the famous yeshivot of Baranovitz and Kaminetz. With the outbreak of World War Two, Reb Yitzchok was exiled to a labor camp in Siberia. Given his freedom after the war, he immediately traveled to Uman where he visited Rebbe Nachman's gravesite. From Russia, Reb Yitzchok traveled to Germany, spent a few years in the Displaced Persons Camps and arrived in Jerusalem in 1949, where he now resides.

Kramer, Reb Moshe (b. 1937). Born in Jerusalem, Reb Moshe was drawn to Rebbe Nachman's teachings at a young age. He studied in Jerusalem's Mirrer Yeshivah and later became the son-in-law of Reb Gedaliah Koenig. As one of the leaders in Breslov today, Reb Moshe's clarity in the Rebbe's teachings has made him a popular source of information for those seeking to understand the more difficult passages of Rebbe Nachman's works.

Shechter, Reb Yaakov Meir (b. 1931). One of the foremost and fiery leaders on the Breslov scene today, Reb Yaakov Meir was born in the Old City of Jerusalem where he learned from the leading Breslover Chassidim of the past generation, particularly from Reb Avraham Sternhartz. His father was a prominent Breslover Chassid, Reb Dovid Shechter. After his family was expelled from the Old City in 1948, he lived in Katamon, later on moving to the Meah Shearim area, near the Breslov Yeshivah.

* * *

The Breslov Research Institute
extends grateful thanks to

Max & Racheal Assoulin

Meyer & Roxanne Assoulin

Eli Assoulin

Yitzchok Leib & China Leah Bell

Bob & Toby Dobin

Simcha & Chanah Druck

Gershon & Channah Ginsburg

Alvin & Elaine Gordon

Alex & Yehudit Gross

Shoshanna Kasheri

Stan & Sara Kopel

Yehudah & Chayah Levinson

David & Valerie Mizrahi

Shelly & Chani Rosenfeld

Mark & Mozelle Safdieh

Moshe & Esther Schorr

Yonatan & Devorah

whose support made this book possible